CORE

J2ME™ Technology & MIDP

John W. Muchow

Prentice Hall PTR, Upper Saddle River, NJ 07458
www.phptr.com

Sun Microsystems Press
A Prentice Hall Title

A CIP catalog record for this book can be obtained from the Library of Congress.

The publisher offers discounts on this book when ordered in bulk quantities.
For more information, contact Corporate Sales Department, Prentice Hall PTR,
One Lake Street, Upper Saddle River, NJ 07458. Phone 800-382-3419: FAX: 201-236-7141.
E-mail: corpsales@prenhall.com.

Editorial/Production Supervison: *Pine Tree Composition*
Acquisitions Editor: *Gregory G. Doench*
Editorial Assistant: *Brandt Kenna*
Cover Design Director: *Jerry Votta*
Cover Designer: *Nina Scuderi*
Art Director: *Gail Cocker-Bogusz*
Manufacturing Manager: *Alexis Heydt-Long*
Marketing Manager: *Debby vanDijk*
Project Coordinator: *Anne R. Garcia*

Sun Microsystems Press Publisher: *Michael Llwyd Alread*

10   9   8   7   6   5   4   3   2

ISBN 0-13-066911-3

Sun Microsystems Press
A Prentice Hall Title

This book is dedicated, from the heart,
to my Mom and Dad

Contents

PART I:

INTRODUCTION TO J2ME, CLDC, AND MIDP

v

PART II:

PROGRAMMING WITH MIDP

x   Contents

PART III

APPENDICES

Preface

It is estimated that in Japan alone over 20 million Java 2 Micro Edition (J2ME) enabled mobile phones were manufactured in 2001. The opportunity for those interested in writing for the J2ME platform speaks for itself. With its support for a broad range of devices and portability across platforms, acceptance among manufacturers and service providers has been astounding.

The focus of this book is on application development using the Mobile Information Device Profile (MIDP) and Connected, Limited Device Configuration (CLDC). Together, these application programming interfaces (API's) form a complete J2ME development toolkit for wireless devices including: mobile phones, pagers and personal organizers.

Who Is This Book For

As a developer at heart, I have often sought a book that covered "all I need to know" to get started with a technology that was of interest. Instead I found myself putting together pieces and parts based on information from various websites, newsgroups, how-to articles, and the like. There was never one definitive guide covering everything: where to find the software, how to install and configure my computer, and learning to write applications from the ground up. Most important of all, there always seemed to be gap between what information I could find and what appeared to be available as part of the specification describing the technology.

I hope this book is as close to one-stop shopping as you will find for learning and developing applications for J2ME and the Mobile Information Device Profile. It has what I feel are the essentials to get up and running, everything from downloading and installing the software to writing applications from simple to comprehensive. The entire programming interface is covered in a logical step-by-step manner, leaving no stone unturned. It also includes a quick reference guide for both MIDP and CLDC.

Although this book takes a step-by-step approach to teaching application development with MIDP, the assumption is made that the reader will have experience as a software developer. Further, as J2ME is a subset of Java 2 Standard Edition, a background in Java programming is essential to make the most of this book.

Focus of this Book

With many years of experience as a developer, and an extensive background in technical training, I've discovered that most people (myself included) learn best by example. With that in mind, this book provides an abundance of source code, with the intention of presenting solutions to real-world programming issues. With over 70 examples, you'll have an excellent base of code to build upon:

- Creating a "clipboard" to share data among components
- Using streams to read and write persistent storage
- Searching and sorting records in persistent storage
- Low-level event handling
- Primitive drawing operations (arcs, rectangles, text, etc.)
- Creating simple animations
- Scheduling timers

- Creating a client request and interpreting a server response using HTTP
- How and when to use HTTP request methods GET and POST
- Managing sessions with a Java Servlet through cookies and URL-rewriting
- Using a thread to download network data in the background
- Download and view files and images
- Many additional examples . . .

Contents

This book is divided into three sections:

Part I: Introduction to J2ME, CLDC, and MIDP

We begin with an overview of Java 2 Micro Edition. This includes information about the architecture of J2ME and how configurations and profiles make it possible for this micro version of Java to support devices with an exceptionally wide range of capabilities. Also included are step-by-step instructions for installing the required software and configuring your computer to develop J2ME applications (MIDlets).

Part II: Programming with MIDP

Here you will find the bulk of information about programming with the MID Profile. Presented in a tutorial fashion, we cover each aspect of the application programming interface. For each topic there is a brief introduction, information about the API, followed by one or more examples to bring home the concepts presented. Following is a list of the main topics:

- Basics of MIDlets and the Display
- Event Handling

- High-level User Interface
- Low-level User Interface
- Case Study: Building a Display Manager
- Persistent Storage with the Record Management System
- Case Study: Todo-List MIDlet
- Scheduling Timers and Tasks
- Network Communication with the Generic Connection Framework
- MIDP for the Palm OS

The case studies tie together concepts presented throughout the book. The first builds a simple, yet very useful class to facilitate managing objects displayed on a mobile device. You'll learn why such a class is needed, how to design and create the class, and will see the class used within a MIDlet that demonstrates how to animate a series of images.

The second case-study builds a todo-list application. At nearly 900 lines of code this comprehensive example covers many aspects of MIDlet development from interface and data design to the internal application logic. This application also makes extensive use of the persistent storage mechanism provided in MIDP.

Part II: Appendices

There are three appendices:

- Over the Air User Initiated Provisioning Recommended Practice
  This addendum to the MID Profile covers the recommended procedure for deploying MIDlets
- CLDC Quick Reference
  Connected, Limited Device Configuration API divided into the following sections: java.io, java.lang, java.util, javax.microedition.io
- MIDP Quick Reference
  Mobile Information Device Profile API

Conventions Used in This Book

The fields and methods for each API are listed in tables as shown:

Table P-I Form Class: javax.microedition.lcdui.Form	
Method	*Description*
Constructors	
Form (String title)	Create a form and add Item(s) in the array
...	
Methods	
int **append**(Image img)	Append an Image to a form
...	

To clarify the hierarchy of classes within MIDP, occasionally I'll show a list of classes along with the declaration of each class. For example:

```
Display         (public class Display)
Displayable     (public abstract class Displayable)
    Screen      (public abstract class Screen extends Displayable)
        TextBox (public class TextBox extends Screen)
        List    (public class List extends Screen implements Choice)
...
```

The courier font will be used when referencing Java source code.

For consistency throughout the code examples, I have chosen to name all MIDP objects starting with a two letters acronym, followed by a descriptive name for the use of the field/variable. For example, a TextBox soliciting input for a phone number may have the name tbPhoneNumber. Whenever possible I have followied the Java convention of using the first two letters of a series of words (such as in tb for the word TextBox). For those objects that consist of one word (e.g., Form) I have chosen a two letter acronym that seems most logical and easy to associate with the object (e.g., fm for Form).

Whenever you encounter one of the acronyms listed in the following table you will know the field/variable is associated with an MIDP object.

MIDP Naming conventions	
MIDP Object	*Acronym*
Alert	al
AlertType	at
Canvas	cv
Command	cm
ChoiceGroup	cg
DateField	df
Font	ft
Form	fm
Gauge	ga
Graphics	gr
Image	im
ImageItem	ii
List	ls
RecordStore	rs
StringItem	si
TestBox	tb
TextField	tf
Ticker	tk
Timer	tm
TimerTask	tt

Mobile Information Device Emulators

Sun Microsystems provides two reference implementations of MIDP. These software packages are available for developers to use as a testing ground, and also provide device manufacturers with a model, or starting point, for creating an implementation of MIDP for a device(s).

The implementations available from Sun are:

- MIDP and CLDC as standalone packages
  Applications are compiled and run from the command line

- J2ME Wireless Toolkit
  Applications are compiled and run within a minimal development environment

The actual look and feel of MIDP components may vary across implementations and/or devices. This has to do with the fact MIDP does not spell out how components are to look, rather, it specifies the functionality they must provide.

For instance, the figure below shows the same application running on three different emulators. Although each looks different, the functionality remains consistent.

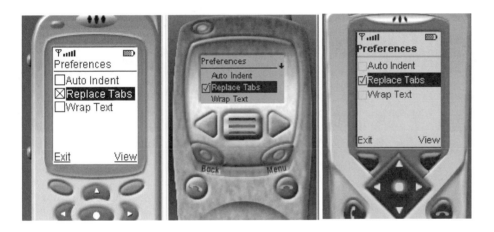

Throughout the book, all application screen-shots were created with one of the two Sun Microsystems reference implementations. If you download and install an implementation of MIDP from a device manufacturer, or a third-party source, examples may look different than shown in the book, however, the functionality should be equivalent.

CoreJ2ME.com Website

There is a companion website for this book: www.CoreJ2ME.com. Here you will find the latest source code for the examples in this book, important notes about changes to the MIDP and/or CLDC specification and how this effects the examples (if at all), how-to articles, links to the software, information about J2ME and MIDP training, and a developer resources section that includes links to tools, faqs, discussion areas, newsgroups and mailing lists, as well as other J2ME related websites.

Acknowledgments

Without the tireless efforts of Patty Donovan and her colleagues at Pine Tree Composition, this book would not be in your hands. A sincere thank you for responding to my continuous flood of email and managing all the last minutes changes. Patty, it was truly a pleasure to work with you.

My guess is that there were many people at Prentice Hall who played a part in this project. The few that I worked with directly include Jim Markham and Eileen Clark, my thanks to both of you. Jim, an additional thanks, your positive attitude was most enjoyable and your willingness to help unsurpassed. Greg Doench with Prentice Hall and Rachel Borden with Sun Microsystems Press, thanks for entertaining my proposal for this book. I remember an early conversation and my words "Oh, I think it'll be about 300 pages or so." If you double that and add one hundred, I was pretty close.

Thanks to the technical reviewers, Amy Bannister and Jerry Hoff for finding the time to review the material and provide feedback, suggestions and fixes.

Thank you to Marty Hall, author of *Core Servlets*. Unbeknown to you, your encouragement and enthusiasm early on were pivotal in my decision to write this book.

Now that it is complete, looking back I can honestly say the most enjoyable aspect was exploring the technology and creating the examples. Which leads me to give thanks to the efforts of those at Sun Microsystems and members of the Expert Group for JSR 30 (CLDC) and 37 (MIDP) for making all this a reality. An additional thanks to the development teams at Sun for creating the reference implementations of the software, in all its shapes and forms, including CLDC, MIDP and the J2ME Wireless Toolkit.

To Suze, a most sincere and heartfelt thank you for your patience, love, and support.

John W. Muchow
Excelsior, Minnesota

About the Author

John W. Muchow received a Master's Degree in Computer Science in 1988. Since that time he has worked as a software and systems engineer, technical trainer and train-the-trainer program coordinator. John currently works as an independent J2ME trainer and consultant, and is also founder of The Wireless Mind, Inc. a business devoted to training wireless developers, with a specific focus on J2ME and the Mobile Information Device Profile. He can be reached at John@CoreJ2ME.com or John@TheWirelessMind.com

THE BASICS OF J2ME

Topics in this Chapter

- Java Editions

- Why J2ME?

- Configurations

- Profiles

- Java Virtual Machines

- Big Picture View of the Architecture

- Compatibility between Java Editions

- Putting all the Pieces Together

Chapter 1

It all started with one version of Java—now known as Java 2 Standard Edition (J2SE)—and the tagline "Write Once, Run Anywhere ™." The idea was to develop a language in which you would write your code once, and then it would run on any platform supporting a Java Virtual Machine.

Since its launch in 1995, the landscape has changed significantly. Java has extended its reach far beyond desktop machines. Two years after the introduction of Java, a new edition was released, Java 2 Enterprise Edition, providing support for large-scale, enterprise-wide applications. The most recent addition to the family is the Micro Edition, targeting "information appliances," ranging from Internet-enabled TV set-top boxes to cellular phones.

Java Editions

Let's begin with a quick summary of the Java platforms currently available:

- **Standard Edition** (J2SE): Designed to run on desktop and workstations computers.

- **Enterprise Edition** (J2EE): With built-in support for Servlets, JSP, and XML, this edition is aimed at server-based applications.
- **Micro Edition** (J2ME): Designed for devices with limited memory, display and processing power.

Note

In December of 1998, Sun introduced the name "Java 2" (J2) to coincide with the release of Java 1.2. This new naming convention applies to all editions of Java, Standard Edition (J2SE), Enterprise Edition (J2EE), and Micro Edition (J2ME).

Figure 1–1 shows various Java editions.

Figure 1-1   The various Java editions

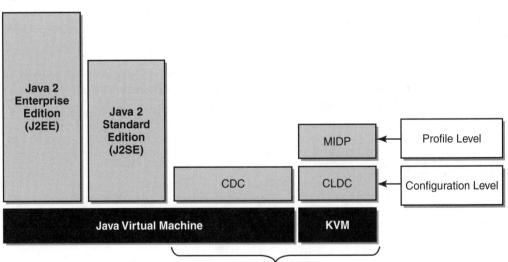

Why J2ME?

J2ME is aimed squarely at consumer devices with limited horsepower. Many such devices (e.g., a mobile phone or pager) have no option to download and install software beyond what was configured during the manufacturing process. With the introduction of J2ME, "micro" devices no longer need to be "static" in nature. Not unlike a web browser downloading Java applets, an implementation of J2ME on a device affords the option to browse, download and install Java applications and content.

Small consumer electronics have a way of changing our lives. Mobile phones let us communicate when away from our home or office. Personal digital assistants (PDAs) let us access email, browse the internet and run applications of all shapes and forms. With the introduction of Java for such devices, we now have access to the features inherent to the Java language and platform. That is, a programming language that is easy to master, a runtime environment that provides a secure and portable platform and access to dynamic content, not to mention an estimated developer community of over 2 million people.

Although it would be nice to have the entire J2SE Application Programming Interface (API) available on a micro device, it's not realistic. For example, a mobile phone with its limited display cannot provide all the functionality available in the Abstract Window Toolkit, the first graphical user interface released with Java. The "Micro Edition" was introduced to address the special needs of consumer devices that are outside the scope of J2SE and J2EE.

The capabilities of devices within the "Micro Edition" may vary greatly. An Internet Screenphone (a hardware device designed to provide access to email, news, online banking, etc.) may have a much larger display than a pager. However, even devices that seem similar in size may vary greatly in their capabilities. A cell phone and PDA are both limited in physical size, yet a typical cell phone may have a display with a total resolution of 12,288 pixels (96×128), whereas a PDA resolution may start at 20,000 pixels and go up from there.

One Java platform will most definitely not fit all. To better understand how J2ME will accommodate a broad range of consumer electronics and embedded devices, we need to introduce two new concepts, configurations and profiles.

Configurations

To support the broad range of products that fit within the scope of J2ME, Sun introduced the Configuration.

A ***Configuration*** defines a Java platform for a broad range of devices. A Configuration is closely tied to a Java Virtual Machine (JVM). In fact, a Configuration defines the Java language features and the core Java libraries of the JVM for that particular Configuration.

The dividing line as to what a Configuration applies is for the most part based on the memory, display, network connectivity (or limitations of) and processing power available on a device.

The Sun J2ME FAQ states the following: "The J2ME technology has two design centers—things that you hold in your hand and things you plug into a wall." This may be a good general definition, but that's exactly what it is, general. Don't let this be your sole guide in deciding which Configuration applies.

Following are typical characteristics of devices within the two currently defined Configurations:

Connected Device Configuration (CDC)

- 512 kilobytes (minimum) memory for running Java
- 256 kilobytes (minimum) for runtime memory allocation
- Network connectivity, possibly persistent and high bandwidth

Connected, Limited Device Configuration (CLDC)

- 128 kilobytes memory for running Java
- 32 kilobytes memory for runtime memory allocation
- Restricted user interface
- Low power, typically battery powered
- Network connectivity, typically wireless, with low bandwidth and intermittent access

Although this division seems pretty clear, this won't always be the case. Technology is continually advancing. Remember your first computer? What was "state-of-the-art" in 1985 (when I purchased my first personal computer) pales in comparison to what is available today.

The point is, as technology offers us more processing power, with increased memory and screen capabilities, the overlap between these categories will become larger. This is a nice segue to our next discussion, Profiles.

Profiles

It's all well and good that devices will fall within one Configuration or the other. For example, a typical cellular phone, PDA and pager will all fit the guidelines of the CLDC. However, what seems limiting to one device in a Configuration may be an abundance to another. Recall the analogy of the cellular phone screen size versus that of a PDA.

To address this broad range of capabilities, and to provide for more flexibility as technology changes, Sun introduced the concept of a Profile to the J2ME platform.

A *Profile* is an extension, if you will, to a Configuration. It provides the libraries for a developer to write applications for a particular type of device. For example, the Mobile Information Device Profile (MIDP) defines APIs for user interface components, input and event handling, persistent storage, networking and timers, taking into consideration the screen and memory limitations of mobile devices.

Beginning in Chapter 3, the remainder of this book will focus on MIDP specifically. This will include everything from the hardware and software requirements to complete coverage of all the APIs.

How are Configurations and Profiles Developed?

Excerpt from J2ME FAQ (*http://java.sun.com/j2me/faq.html*): Configurations and Profiles are defined by open industry working groups utilizing Sun's Java Community Process Program. In this way industries can decide for themselves what elements are necessary to provide a complete solution targeted at their industry. For more information on the Sun Community Process Program, see: *http://jcp.org*

Java Virtual Machines

As you well know, the engine behind any Java application (or applet, servlet, etc.) is the JVM.

Once you've compiled your Java source code into a class file(s), and optionally included them in a Java Archive (JAR) file, the JVM translates the class files (more accurately, the byte code in the class files) into machine code for the platform running the JVM. The JVM is also responsible for providing security, allocating and freeing memory and managing threads of execution. It's what makes your Java programs go, so to speak.

For CDC, the virtual machine has the same specification as J2SE. For CLDC, Sun has developed what is referred to as a reference implementation of a virtual machine, known as the K Virtual Machine, or simply KVM. This virtual machine was designed to handle the special considerations of resource-constrained devices. It's clear the KVM is not the "traditional" Java virtual machine:

- The virtual machine itself requires only 40 and 80 kilobytes of memory
- Only 20–40 kilobytes of dynamic memory (heap) are required
- Can run on 16-bit processors clocked at only 25 MHz

The KVM is Sun's implementation of a JVM that fits the guidelines of the CLDC. It is not necessarily the only JVM that is or will be available.

How are the KVM and CLDC Related?

From Sun's documentation: "CLDC is the *specification* for a 'class' of Java virtual machines that can run on the categories of devices targeted by CLDC and support the profiles." Essentially, the CLDC outlines requirements that must be met by the virtual machine. The KVM is what is known as a reference implementation—it is a virtual machine that meets the CLDC requirements.

Big Picture View of the Architecture

We've covered an assortment of information about J2ME. Let's put all this together into two separate scenarios. The first is a "generic" software architecture, if you will, of J2ME. The second is the architecture as it will apply to our interests as we progress through the book.

Generic Architecture

It begins with the host Operating System (OS) as the base (see Figure 1–2), followed by the virtual machine (VM). The VM will take one of two forms:

- For systems complying with the CDC, it will be the "traditional" virtual machine; that is, the same feature set as in the Java 2 Standard Edition.
- For systems complying with the CLDC, it will be the KVM or a virtual machine that meets the specifications as required by the CLDC.

CLDC or CDC core libraries are next in the heirarchy. Profiles are the topmost layer, and are designed to provide a toolkit for writing applications for a particular device family.

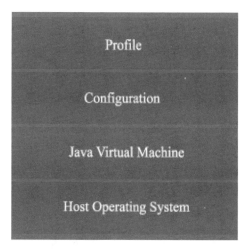

Profile

Configuration

Java Virtual Machine

Host Operating System

Figure 1-2 "Generic" J2ME architecture

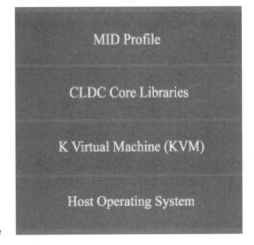

Figure 1-3 MID Profile architecture

MIDP Architecture

As before, the host OS is the base. The virtual machine will be the KVM. Remember, the KVM is Sun's implementation of a JVM meeting the CLDC specification—it may not be the only implementation available of a virtual machine for MIDP. CLDC core libraries are next, followed by MID Profile.

Compatibility between Java Editions

At the beginning of this section, I introduced Sun's Java tagline: "Write Once, Run Anywhere." Now that we've introduced Configurations, Profiles and a KVM, do you think this still applies? Well, the answer is, sort of.

Will J2SE applications run on J2ME?

J2ME is basically a slimmed down version of J2SE. Many components have been removed to keep the platform small and efficient. An obvious example is that of the Abstract Window Toolkit—many mobile devices do not have the screen capabilities to provide advanced user interface components such as overlapping windows and drop-down menus.

On the other hand, if you write J2SE code that adheres only to the classes that are available within the J2ME Configuration you are targeting, then your programs will run on both platforms. Keep in mind, such applications will most likely be very constrained, with little to no user interface, as J2ME and J2SE offer completely different APIs for handling the display.

Will J2ME applications run on J2SE?

The same rules apply here. If you limit the code to what is common on both platforms, the answer is yes. However, the majority of software you write for a J2ME device will require special interface and event handling code. Thus, you are greatly limited to what types of programs will be appropriate for both platforms.

Putting all the Pieces Together

Sun created the Java 2 Micro Edition to allow development of Java applications for devices that do not have the same processing power and memory found on a typical desktop platform. Products may include cellular phones, PDAs, pagers, entertainment and automotive navigation systems, to name just a few.

J2ME is divided into two broad categories, known as Configurations. CDC is a set of APIs to support "fixed" devices such as a television set-top box. CLDC is a set of APIs targeted at devices that have limited processing power, display and memory. The majority of these devices will also be mobile (e.g., cellular phones and pagers).

A Configuration is closely tied to a Java virtual machine. For CDC, the virtual machine is compatible with the virtual machine of the Java 2 Standard Edition. The KVM, a virtual machine that takes into consideration the limited resources available on devices that fit this configuration, was developed for the CLDC.

On top of Configurations are device Profiles. Here you will find the APIs for user interface design, networking support and persistent storage. The Mobile Device Information Profile and the associated libraries are the main focus of this book.

CONNECTED, LIMITED DEVICE CONFIGURATION (CLDC)

Topics in this Chapter

- Hardware Requirements

- Software Requirements

- The Java Virtual Machine Specification

- Handling Security

- Class File Verification

- J2SE Inherited Classes

- CLDC Specific Classes

- K Virtual Machine

Chapter 2

The goal of the CLDC is twofold. The first goal is to define a specification for a JVM and the second is to define a set of Java classes (libraries). Each goal has a common theme: to support a wide range of devices with limited memory, display capabilities and resources. This chapter will cover the CLDC from top to bottom. Here is the breakdown of topics we'll cover:

- Hardware and software: A look at the minimum requirements for the CLDC.
- JVM: The JVM as defined by the CLDC is a subset of the J2SE virtual machine. We will compare the differences in relation to the Java language, as well as the virtual machine itself.
- Security: Important to any discussion on Java, we will cover both low-level and application security.
- Class File Verification: To reduce the memory requirements and application start-up time, an additional class file pre-verification step has been added, which we'll introduce here.
- J2SE Inherited Libraries: A comprehensive list of all the classes that are inherited from J2SE.

- CLDC Specific Libraries: Introduction to the Generic Connection Framework—a set of classes and interfaces to facilitate access to remote storage and network systems.
- KVM: We will conclude this chapter with an overview of the KVM—Sun's reference implementation of a JVM designed to meet the CLDC specification.

CLDC and CLDC Next Generation

Sun's reference implementation of CLDC version 1.0 is based on the following Java Specification Request: *http://jcp.org/jsr/detail/30.jsp*

Features being considered for CLDC "Next Generation" may include support for floating point numbers, additional error handling capabilities, and a minimal security manager. See the Java Specification Request: *http://jcp.org/jsr/detail/139.jsp*

All Java Specification Requests for J2ME: *http://jcp.org/jsr/tech/ j2me.jsp*

For additional information about Sun's Java Community Process: *http://jcp.org*

Going Forward

The goal of this book is to cover programming for CLDC and Mobile Information Device Profile (MIDP). From here forward, we will target our discussions and examples to mobile devices. To keep with this theme, I will use the terms "mobile device" or, simply, "device" to refer to products that fall within the specifications set forth by both CLDC and MIDP.

Hardware Requirements

When defining requirements, it is very important to take into consideration the range of hardware (processors, memory, etc.) and software (operating systems and their capabilities) likely to be found on mobile devices. To keep the door open to as many devices as possible, few requirements were set.

With the exception of available memory, the CLDC does not have specific hardware requirements. The minimal memory requirements are as follows:

- 128 kilobytes of memory for running the JVM and the CLDC libraries (more on the libraries later in this chapter). Regardless of the implementation (ROM, Flash, etc.) this memory must preserve its contents, even when the device is powered off. This memory is often referred to as *nonvolatile memory*.
- 32 kilobytes of memory available during application runtime for allocation of objects. This memory is often referred to as *volatile memory* or "the heap."

Although it goes somewhat against the grain of why Java is such a powerful platform on a mobile device, there is no requirement that a manufacturer support dynamic downloading of applications and/or data. If this is the case (i.e., J2ME programs available on the device will be installed during the manufacturing process), then the amount of memory required may be significantly less.

Software Requirements

The software side is not much different—the CLDC has a minimal set of requirements. The host OS must be capable of running the JVM and managing Java applications on the device, including:

- Selecting and launching of applications
- The ability to remove Java applications from the device

The implementation of these features is not specified in the CLDC, and thus is device-dependent and left to the manufacturer.

The Java Virtual Machine Specification

The intention of the JVM is to be as compliant, as is reasonably possible, with the virtual machine of J2SE, given the memory and processing constraints of mobile devices. Instead of stepping through each requirement, let's see how the Java Language and JVM implemented for CLDC differ from that of J2SE.

Java Language Differences

There are three main areas that distinguish the Java Language for CLDC versus that defined in the Java Language Specification.[1]

Floating Point Math

Floating point math is inherently processor intensive. Given this, and the fact that the majority of devices will not have special hardware for handling float point numbers, the CLDC implementation of the Java language does not support floats. This support (or lack thereof) is carried throughout all Java code you write—no float variables, constants, arrays, arithmetic or return values from methods.

Finalization

Within a J2SE class, you can declare a method with the name `finalize()`. This method will be called before the garbage collector frees the object. Although the garbage collector will free memory used by an object, it is not aware of system resources that may have been acquired (file handles, sockets, etc.). The `finalize()` method is where you can place code to clean up allocated resources.

Unfortunately, the CLDC does not support the `finalize()` method. The specification is a bit sketchy on why, but we can make a safe assumption the overhead and/or processor requirements are too steep.

Error Handling

The JVM will support a limited set of error handling exceptions. The reason for the limitations are twofold:

- The exception handling in J2SE is quite comprehensive, and unfortunately, comes with a matching price—a significant demand on the system.

---

[1]*The Java Language Specification* by James Gosling, Bill Joy, and Guy L. Steele. Addison-Wesley, 1996, ISBN 0-201-63451-1.

- Often times, embedded systems will provide their own internal error handling. A simple solution for the most serious of errors (from a hardware point of view, most definitely not the convenience of the user) is to perform a reset of the device. In such a case, the error cannot be handed up to you as a developer—it's too late at this point.

The exception classes supported in the CLDC are listed later in this chapter in the section titled "J2SE Inherited Libraries."

Java Virtual Machine Differences

The Java virtual machine supporting CLDC differs from the Java Language Specification as follows:

Floating Point Math

As mentioned earlier, the implementation of the Java language for CLDC lacks support for floating point numbers. This carries over to the JVM as well.

Java Native Interface

To reduce the potential of corruption to system level information, and in keeping with reducing memory requirements, support for invoking native methods and APIs of other programming languages was eliminated. However, an implementation of the JVM may link native code directly into the virtual machine. The drawback is that an application that accesses the native code may not be portable to other JVMs.

Custom Class Loader

The CLDC requires the JVM to implement a class loader. There are tight controls on the loader—it cannot be replaced, overridden or modified. The loader itself is device-dependent (read: defined and implemented by the device manufacturer), including how classes are loaded and in what manner error conditions are handled.

Reflection

In J2SE, you can use Reflection classes to get information about the running VM. This may include information about the class files loaded, as well as their methods and fields. Unfortunately, Reflection is not available on a JVM supporting the CLDC.

Thread Groups

For this JVM implementation, threads are processed on an object-by-object basis. The JVM does not support the `ThreadGroup` class—thus, you cannot perform operations such as starting/stopping a group of threads through one method call.

To mimic this functionality, you could roll your own thread processing code; for example, storing a group of thread objects within a collection class (such as `Vector`) and providing methods to start/stop all objects within the collection.

Finalization

The Java Language in CLDC does not support finalization; accordingly, this JVM lacks support as well.

Weak References

J2SE allows what are known as weak references to objects. This means the garbage collector recognizes that an object is being referenced, yet the object is still a candidate for garbage collection. Now that you understand what a weak reference is, you can set that thought aside. This JVM does not support weak references.

Handling Security

Any device running a Java application needs protection from malicious code (intentional or otherwise) that may access system information or resources. Regardless of the JVM, this type of "low-level" security is implemented using class file verification.

What is different about the JVM running on CLDC is that the verification process is now two steps. We'll cover the specifics of class file verification and the required steps in the next section.

At the application level, programs written using J2SE can load a security manager. The manager doles out access, or not, through a series of method calls, checking for proper permissions.

Although this model is sufficient for J2SE, once again the requirements of the JVM to implement this level of security may prove to be beyond the capabilities of many mobile devices. As an alternative, the CLDC defines what is referred to as a "sandbox" model. The idea is that code will be run inside an environment that restricts access outside the scope of the "sandbox." The boundaries are defined by the APIs available through the Configuration and Profile(s)—access is not allowed outside these classes.

Class File Verification

Verifying the integrity of class files is not a trivial operation. Running on J2SE, the verifier code itself takes a minimum of 50 kilobytes, not to mention heap space requirements and processing time. To spread the work load on a mobile device, verification is now done in two steps:

1. **Pre-verification:** As part of the development process, or at a minimum, before a class file is loaded on a device, a software program is run to insert additional attributes into the class file. This information reduces the amount of time and memory necessary when the JVM carries out step 2 of verification. Class files will be approximately 5% larger after pre-verification.

Stack Maps

The attributes added to a class file are referred to as "stack maps," as in this information describes what variables and operands are part of the interpreter stack space.

---

2. **In-device verification:** Once a device loads a pre-verified class file, the in-device verifier runs through each instruction. There

are several checks done to validate the code. At any point, the verifier can report an error and reject the class file.

> ## Memory Savings
>
> The code to verify a class file (once it has been pre-verified) is in the range of 10 kilobytes, with less than 100 bytes of heap space required. This is a significant reduction over that of the "conventional" verifier available as part of J2SE.

J2SE Inherited Classes

In an ideal world, a mobile device would run the same JVM as J2SE and have access to the entire J2SE core libraries, all 1+ megabytes. That would be nice. Now, back to our world.

Near the beginning of this chapter, when describing the hardware requirements, we stated the CLDC implementation requires approximately 160 kilobytes of memory to run the JVM and core libraries (128k and 32k, respectively). We are a few bytes short of the J2SE footprint. Obviously, a few classes had to go. Following is a list of the classes that made the cut.

System Classes

java.lang.Class
java.lang.Object
java.lang.Runnable (interface)
java.lang.Runtime
java.lang.String
java.lang.StringBuffer
java.lang.System
java.lang.Thread
java.lang.Throwable

Data Type Classes

java.lang.Boolean
java.lang.Byte

java.lang.Character
java.lang.Integer
java.lang.Long
java.lang.Short

Collection Classes

java.util.Enumeration (interface)
java.util.Hashtable
java.util.Stack
java.util.Vector

Input/output Classes

java.io.ByteArrayInputStream
java.io.ByteArrayOutputStream
java.io.DataInput (interface)
java.io.DataInputStream
java.io.DataOutput (interface)
java.io.DataOutputStream
java.io.InputStream
java.io.InputStreamReader
java.io.OutputStream
java.io.OutputStreamWriter
java.io.PrintStream
java.io.Reader
java.io.Writer

Calendar and Time Classes

java.util.Calendar
java.util.Date
java.util.TimeZone

Utility Classes

java.lang.Math
java.util.Random

Exception Classes

java.io.EOFException
java.io.InterruptedIOException

java.io.IOException
java.io.UnsupportedEncodingException
java.io.UTFDataFormatException
java.lang.ArithmeticException
java.lang.ArrayIndexOutOfBoundsException
java.lang.ArrayStoreException
java.lang.ClassCastException
java.lang.ClassNotFoundException
java.lang.Exception
java.lang.IllegalAccessException
java.lang.IllegalArgumentException
java.lang.IllegalMonitorStateException
java.lang.IllegalThreadStateException
java.lang.IndexOutOfBoundsException
java.lang.InstantiationException
java.lang.InterruptedException
java.lang.NegativeArraySizeException
java.lang.NullPointerException
java.lang.NumberFormatException
java.lang.RuntimeException
java.lang.SecurityException
java.lang.StringIndexOutOfBoundsException
java.util.EmptyStackException
java.util.NoSuchElementException

Error Classes

java.lang.Error
java.lang.OutOfMemoryError
java.lang.VirtualMachineError

Internationalization

java.io.InputStreamReader
java.io.OutputStreamWriter

InputStreamReader and OutputStreamWriter can be used to convert (read/write) sequences of bytes to/from Unicode.

Property Support

There is a very limited set of properties you can query about the system. Below is a list of the properties available, and a sample method call for each:

- Get the host platform / device
  `System.getProperty("microedition.platform")`
- Get the default character encoding
  `System.getProperty("microedition.encoding")`
- Get the supported configuration name and version
  `System.getProperty("microedition.configuration")`
- Get the supported profile(s) names
  `System.getProperty("microedition.profiles")`

Accessing Runtime Information

All Java programs can access an object named `Runtime` (`java.lang.Runtime`). This class provides access to system information in a device-independent manner. For example, the following code will print the values of total and free memory to the console.

```
Runtime rtime= Runtime.getRuntime();
System.out.println("Total memory: " + rtime.total Memory());
System.out.println("Free memory: " + rtime.free Memory());
```

CLDC Specific Classes

Mobile devices may span the gamut as far as support (or lack thereof) for file systems and networking. The Generic Connection Framework (GCF) is a set of classes and interfaces designed to facilitate access to storage and network systems, without specifying hardware and software requirements.

Although the J2SE networking and I/O classes are comprehensive, weighing in at nearly 200 kilobytes, they are also much too large for many mobile devices. The GCF was designed to support many devices and protocols, both current and those yet to be developed.

The first concept to understand is that the GCF does **not** include implementations for any protocols, it simply lays the groundwork. The actual classes providing the implementation(s) are done at the Profile level. For example, any device manufacturer providing support for the MIDP is required to implement the HTTP protocol (using the class `HttpConnection`).

GCF provides one class, `Connector`, to open any type of connection. For example:

```
Connector.open("http://www.corej2me.com");
```

If the call is successful, a `Connection` type is returned. The object returned will implement one of the six interfaces defined by GCF. These are listed below:

```
javax.microedition.io.InputConnection
javax.microedition.io.OutputConnection
javax.microedition.io.StreamConnection
javax.microedition.io.ContentConnection
javax.microedition.io.StreamConnectionNotifier
javax.microedition.io.DatagramConnection
```

In Chapter 14 we will provide more detail about the GCF and the `HttpConnection` class.

K Virtual Machine

Let's take a few minutes to look inside Sun's implementation of a JVM that meets the CLDC specification.

The KVM was designed to be as small and efficient as possible, yet steadfast in the core competencies of the Java language. With memory typically a precious commodity on small resource constrained devices, the runtime footprint is only (approximately) 60 kilobytes. Which explains where the K in KVM originates, as in, the virtual machine will run in only a few tens of *kilobytes* of memory.

Sun's reference implementation of the KVM is written in C to facilitate portability. The majority of code comprising the KVM will not change regardless of the platform. Device dependent code is limited to memory management, handling of fatal errors, processing of events, code initialization and cleanup.

Since the KVM is simply a implementation of a virtual machine that meets the CLDC requirements, as we've outlined in this chapter, there is not a great deal of additional information to provide. If you would like to learn more about the specifics of the C code that comprise the KVM or would like to learn the details of how to port the software to another platform, you can find an abundance of information in the KVM Porting Guide, included as part of Sun's CLDC download.

When we get to Chapter 4, we'll download and install the CLDC, which will include Sun's reference implementation of the KVM.

MOBILE INFORMATION DEVICE PROFILE (MIDP)

Topics in this Chapter

- Hardware and Software Requirements

- MID Profile Architecture

- The MIDlet Suite

- Accessing JAR/JAD attributes from a MIDlet

At this point we need to take a closer look at the hardware and software requirements of a device that intends to implement the MIDP. You'll also learn about the architecture of applications running on a mobile device and you will become familiar with the MIDlet Suite as a means to package your programs.

Hardware and Software Requirements

There's no better way to state the hardware requirements than to simply list them out, one by one:

- The screen must support at least 96×54 pixels.
- There must be at least one type of user input available: one-handed keyboard (telephone keypad), two-handed keyboard (typical QWERTY keyboard) or a touch screen.
- 128 kilobytes non-volatile memory to run Mobile Information Device (MID) components.

- At least 8 kilobytes of non-volatile memory for applications to store persistent data, such as application settings and data.
- 32 kilobytes of volatile memory to run Java.
- Wireless network connectivity.

The native operating system running on a mobile device may vary as much as the devices themselves. Therefore, it is important to set minimal software requirements, leaving the door open to a wide range of devices that can implement the MID Profile. Here is the final tally of requirements as listed in the specification:

- The operating system running on the device must provide minimal scheduling, exception handling and processing of interrupts. There must also be sufficient capabilities to run a JVM.
- The software must support writing of bitmapped graphics to the display.
- Using any of the three input types described above, the software must accept input and pass the information to the JVM.
- To support persistent data, there must be capabilities to read and write to/from non-volatile memory. Remember, there is no requirement defined for a file system. Any application data that needs to persist when the device is shut off will need to be written to memory.

MIDP and MIDP Next Generation

Sun's reference implementation of MIDP version 1.0 is based on the following Java Specification Request: *http://jcp.org/jsr/detail/37.jsp*

Features being considered for MIDP "Next Generation" may include support for HTTPS, sockets and datagrams, extensions to the low-level interface, and an XML parser. See the Java Specification Request: *http://jcp.org/jsr/detail/118.jsp*

All Java Specification Requests for J2ME: *http://jcp.org/jsr/tech/j2me.jsp*

For additional information about Sun's Java Community Process: *http://jcp.org*

- There must be access to the networking features on the device (specifically, the ability to read and write information across a wireless network).

MID Profile Architecture

To visually portray the architecture of an MID we begin with the hardware, which is shown as the bottom-most level in Figure 3–1. One step up, running on the hardware, is the native operating system.

Moving to the upper right of Figure 3–1, you'll notice our first reference to an application running on an MID, the native application. Until the introduction of J2ME, these were typically the only types of programs available on a mobile device. A good example of a native program would be that of the configuration program that comes installed on the device, allowing you to set the type of ring, volume, date and time, and so forth.

The CLDC is installed on the native operating system and is the foundation for MIDP. Notice that MIDP applications have access to both the libraries of CLDC and MIDP.

OEM-specific (original equipment manufacturer) classes are provided by the manufacturer of the device. Functionality added may include options such as the ability to answer incoming calls or to look up entries in a phone

Figure 3–1 Mobile information device architecture

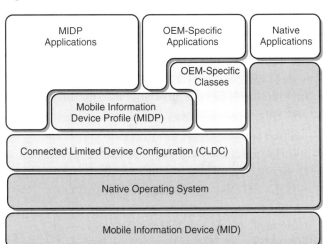

book. The downside is that these classes are specific to the device and as a result, you toss portability out the window.

OEM-specific applications may access MIDP APIs and/or OEM-specific classes. If the latter are used, once again, applications may not be portable to other devices.

The MIDlet Suite

A MIDlet is a Java application designed to be run on a mobile device. More specifically, a MIDlet has as its core Java classes the CLDC and MIDP. A MIDlet suite consists of one or more MIDlets packaged together using a Java Archive (JAR) file.

Before learning the finer points of packaging MIDlets, let's take a minute to learn how applications are managed on a mobile device.

Runtime Environment and Application Management

The Application Manager is the software on a mobile device that is responsible for installing, running and removing MIDlets. This software is device-dependent (i.e., designed and implemented by the manufacturer of the device).

When the application manager starts a MIDlet, it will make all the following available to the application:

- Access to the CLDC and the Java virtual machine: MIDlets can make use of any classes defined within the CLDC. If you recall from the previous chapter, the CLDC classes are a subset of J2SE and also include the GCF (an interface) for supporting input/output and network connectivity.
- Access to MIDP-defined classes: These libraries define and implement the user interface, persistent storage, network support using HTTP, timers and managing user interaction with the device.
- Access to JAR file: If the MIDlet was delivered using a JAR file, any classes or other resources (e.g., images) within the archive must be made available to the MIDlet. We will cover JAR files in the next section.

- Access to the Java Application Descriptor file (JAD): Along with a JAR file, a MIDlet may have access to a JAD file. If a JAD file is available, the contents must be available to the MIDlet. We will show how to access the contents of a JAD file as this chapter progresses.

Sharing Resources

Within a suite, MIDlets can share resources. As an example, it may be beneficial for the MIDlets to have access to a "common" area in persistent storage. One idea is to share the application preferences the user has configured. As the user goes from one MIDlet to another, these preferences are carried along with them, providing a consistent look and feel. We will present more information about MIDlets reading/writing to the same persistent storage area when we look at the Record Management System.

Java Archive File (JAR)

The delivery of a production-packaged application will generally consist of many files. In addition to Java classes, other files such as images and application data, known as resources, are quite common. You bundle all this information together into a single entity known as a JAR file.

Learning about JAR Files

Visit Sun's Java Tutorial online for more information about JAR files:
http://java.sun.com/docs/books/tutorial/jar/index.html

In addition to class and resource files, a JAR contains a file known as a manifest. This file describes the contents of the JAR. The manifest file has the name `manifest.mf` and is stored as part of the JAR file itself. Table 3.1 lists the system attributes that may be defined within the manifest file.

The manifest file does not require all attributes in Table 3.1 be defined. However, if the following six are not inside the manifest file, the application manager will refuse to load the JAR:

MIDlet-Name
MIDlet-Version
MIDlet-Vendor
MIDlet-<n> (one entry for each MIDlet in the JAR file)
MicroEdition-Profile
MicroEdition-Configuration

Table 3.1 Manifest Attributes

Attribute	Purpose	Required
MIDlet-Name	Name of the MIDlet suite.	Yes
MIDlet-Version	Version number of the MIDlet.	Yes
MIDlet-Vendor	Who developed the MIDlet.	Yes
MIDlet-<n>	Reference to a specific MIDlet inside a MIDlet suite. This attribute contains up to three pieces of information: 1. MIDlet name 2. Icon for this MIDlet (optional) 3. Class name the application manager will call to load this MIDlet	Yes
MicroEdition-Profile	What J2ME Profile is required by the MIDlet(s).	Yes
MicroEdition-Configuration	What J2ME Configuration is required by the MIDlet(s).	Yes
MIDlet-Icon	Icon used by the application manager. Shown alongside the MIDlet-Name on the device. This must be a PNG image file.	No
MIDlet-Description	Text describing the MIDlet.	No
MIDlet-Info-URL	URL that may have more information about the MIDlet and/or the vendor.	No

Here is an example of a simple manifest file:

```
MIDlet-Name: Todo List
MIDlet-Version: 1.0
MIDlet-Vendor: Core J2ME
MIDlet-1: TodoList, /images/Todo.png, Todo.TodoMIDlet
MicroEdition-Profile: MIDP-1.0
MicroEdition-Configuration: CLDC-1.0
```

Java Application Descriptor File (JAD)

In addition to a JAR file, a JAD file may be available as part of the MIDlet suite to provide information about the MIDlet(s) within the JAR. The rationale behind including a JAD file is as follows:

1. To provide information to the application manager about the contents of a JAR. With this information, decisions can be made as to whether or not a MIDlet(s) is suitable for running on the device.

2. Provide a means for parameters to be passed to a MIDlets(s) without having to make changes to the JAR file. An example of this will be shown shortly.

The application manager requires the JAD file have an extension of .jad.

Table 3.2 is a list of the system attributes that may be inside a JAD file. You can also define your own attributes as you see necessary for your application. Simply create names that do not start with "MIDlet-" and you are good to go. An example of a custom (user-defined) attribute will be shown in the next section.

As with the manifest file, there is a required set of attributes that must be defined in the JAD file:

```
MIDlet-Name
MIDlet-Version
MIDlet-Vendor
MIDlet-<n> for each MIDlet
MIDlet-Jar-URL
MIDlet-Jar-Size
```

Table 3.2 Java Application Descriptor (JAD) Attributes		
Attribute	*Purpose*	*Required*
MIDlet-Name	Name of the MIDlet suite.	Yes
MIDlet-Version	Version number of the MIDlet.	Yes
MIDlet-Vendor	Who developed the MIDlet.	Yes
MIDlet-<n>	See Table 3.1.	Yes°
MIDlet-Jar-URL	URL of the JAR file.	Yes
MIDlet-Jar-Size	The JAR file size in bytes.	Yes
MIDlet-Data-Size	The minimum number of bytes required for persistent data storage.	No
MIDlet-Description	Text describing the MIDlet.	No
MIDlet-Delete-Confirm°°	Message shown to a user to confirm a request to delete a MIDlet suite.	No
MIDlet-Install-Notify°°	URL to receive installation status report.	No

°See the Sidebar "Is MIDlet-<n> required in the JAD file?"
°°Attributes added as part of the addendum "Over the Air User Initiated Provisioning." See Appendix A.

MIDlet-Name, MIDlet-Version and MIDlet-Vendor must be identical to the attributes with the same name inside the manifest file (of the JAR). If not, the application manager will not load the JAR file. If any other attribute names are duplicated in both files, and the value of those attributes is not the same, those in the application descriptor file will take precedence.

Is MIDlet-<n> Required in the JAD File?

The MIDP specification version 1.0 does not show the MIDlet-n attribute as one that is required in the JAD file. However, without this entry, I was not able to preview MIDlets in the device emulator. Including this attribute in both files is not a problem, and actually, this may provide more clarity as to how these files work together. For completeness, all examples that include a JAD file will specify the MIDlet-n attribute.

A simple JAD file may look as follows:

MIDlet-Name: Todo List
MIDlet-Version: 1.0
MIDlet-Vendor: Core J2ME
MIDlet-Jar-URL: http://www.corej2me.com/TodoMIDlet.jar
MIDlet-Jar-Size: 17043
MIDlet-1: TodoList, /images/Todo.png, Todo.TodoMIDlet

Entering Attributes

The attributes in the manifest and JAD file can be in any order. All entries are "name:value" pairs, with a carriage return separating the entries. Any whitespace after "name:" is ignored.

Accessing JAR/JAD Attributes from a MIDlet

Attributes declared inside the manifest and JAD file are accessible to the MIDlet(s) inside the suite by calling the following method:

```
javax.microedition.midlet.MIDlet.getAppProperty(String name)
```

Examples 3.1, 3.2, and 3.3 are samples that print entries from both files.

Example 3.1: manifest.mf

```
MIDlet-Name: Show Properties MIDlet
MIDlet-Version: 1.0.1
MIDlet-Vendor: Core J2ME
MIDlet-1: ShowProps, , ShowProperties
MicroEdition-Profile: MIDP-1.0
MicroEdition-Configuration: CLDC-1.0
MIDlet-Description: A simple property list example
MIDlet-Data-Size: 1500
```

Example 3.2:   ShowProperties.jad

```
MIDlet-Name: Show Properties MIDlet
MIDlet-Version: 1.0.1
MIDlet-Vendor: Core J2ME
MIDlet-Jar-URL: ShowProperties.jar
MIDlet-Jar-Size: 1132
MIDlet-1: ShowProps, , ShowProperties
MIDlet-Description: A simple property list example
JadFile-Version: 1.5
MIDlet-Data-Size: 500
```

Figure 3–2 shows the output of the MIDlet. We will go into the details of how to compile the Java code, pre-verify the class files and preview MIDlets in the next chapter.

Example 3.3:   ShowProperties.java

```java
import javax.microedition.midlet.*;

public class ShowProperties extends MIDlet
{
  public void startApp() throws MIDletStateChangeException
  {
    System.out.println("Vendor: " +
          getAppProperty("MIDlet-Vendor"));
    System.out.println("Description: " +
          getAppProperty("MIDlet-Description"));
    System.out.println("JadFile Version: " +
          getAppProperty("JadFile-Version"));
    System.out.println("MIDlet-Data-Size: " +
          getAppProperty("MIDlet-Data-Size"));
  }

  public void pauseApp()
  { }

  public void destroyApp(boolean unconditional)
  { }

}
```

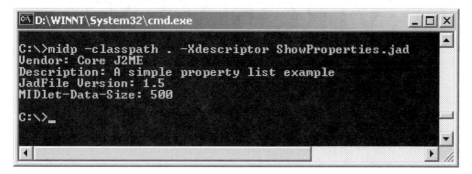

Figure 3–2   Attributes from the manifest and JAD files

To keep from cluttering the code with concepts that we have not yet covered, I've kept this example to the bare minimum. Don't be concerned with any code that looks unfamiliar. What is important are the following points:

- The file `manifest.mf` is stored as part of the JAR file, `ShowProperties.jar`.
- `ShowProperties.jar` is referenced from within the JAD file with this line:

  `MIDlet-Jar-URL: ShowProperties.jar`
- The attributes MIDlet-Name, MIDlet-Version and MIDlet-Vendor are in both the manifest file and the JAD file. All the values are required to be identical.
- The attribute **MIDlet-Description** optional.
- **JadFile-Version** is a user-defined attribute. We know this based on the fact that it does not appear in either Table 3.1 or Table 3.2. Because attributes inside a JAD file are accessible from within a MIDlet, you can add attributes to the JAD without having to change or rebuild the JAR. Put another way, you can easily change/add parameters to be passed to the MIDlet.
- The attribute **MIDlet-Data-Size** is in both the manifest and the JAD file. As pointed out earlier, when there are attributes in both files that are identical, entries in the JAD file will take precedence. For that reason, the output in Figure 3–2 shows MIDlet-Data-Size as 500, the value from the JAD file. Keep in mind that this does **not** apply to MIDlet-Name, MIDlet-Version and MIDlet-Vendor, which are required to be in both files and MUST be identical.

DEVELOPMENT ENVIRONMENT

Topics in this Chapter

- Download the Software

- Install the Software

- Command Line Development

- Packaging a MIDlet

- Running a MIDlet on an Emulator

- Download MIDlet onto a Mobile Device

- Project Management using Java Packages

- J2ME Wireless Toolkit

Chapter 4

Now that we have covered all the background information, there's one last step before learning how to write MIDlets. We need to create the J2ME development environment.

In this chapter you'll learn what software is required, where to download the software, and how to set up the development environment. You'll also become familiar with the command line tools to compile, pre-verify and run a MIDlet.

We'll wrap up this chapter with the J2ME Wireless Toolkit—a free software tool provided by Sun to simplify the J2ME development cycle. This tools offers a basic GUI for project management, previewing and packaging of J2ME programs.

Download the Software

Before going any further, we need to download the software. There are three required software packages.

1. Java Development Kit (JDK)—1.3 or greater:
   http://java.sun.com/products/jdk/1.3

2. Connected, Limited Device Configuration (CLDC):

    http://java.sun.com/products/cldc

3. Mobile Information Device Profile (MIDP):

    http://java.sun.com/products/midp/

Operating System and Software Version Numbers

I will be using Microsoft Windows as the operating system as I describe how to install and configure J2ME. If you are on a different platform that is supported by J2ME, little should change. Follow the installation instructions that accompany the software and update the system environment variable PATH and MIDP_HOME as indicated below. The installation instructions that follow were written using these software versions: JDK-1.3.1, CLDC-1.0.3, and MIDP-1.0.3

Install the Software

Here we will walk through the installation of each software component, beginning with the Java development kit.

Java Development Kit

We need to install the JDK to have access to the Java compiler and the application for creating Java Archive files (jar.exe).

Install

Install the JDK using the instructions that are supplied as part of the download. If you choose to install to a directory other than the default, make note of the path you select. You will need this as we move through the installation.

Update the PATH Environment Variable

I highly recommend you update the PATH environment variable to point to the directory where the java executable files are located. This allows you to run the Java compiler from any directory without specifying the full path each time.

For Windows 2000 or Windows NT:

- from the Control Panel choose System.
- Click Environment (or Advanced/Environment)
  Find the PATH (or Path) entry and at the end, add the location of the \bin directory in your JDK install path. Assuming you installed version 1.3.1 of the JDK, and selected the default installation path, you would add the following to the end of the path: C:\jdk1.3.1\bin

---

Separating Path Entries in Microsoft Windows

Windows uses a semi-colon (;) to separate entries in the path. If there is not a semi-colon at the end of the path, you will need to add one, before appending the JDK path.

For Windows 98 or Windows 95

Windows includes a program called the System Configuration Editor. This program is a quick and easy way to update configurations files including: win.ini, system.ini, config.sys, and autoexec.bat. To start the editor from within Windows:

- Click the Start button
- Select Run
- Enter sysedit in the dialog box and click OK

Find your way to the autoexec.bat dialog box. Assuming you installed version 1.3.1 of the JDK and selected the default installation path, enter the following:

If there **is not** an entry for PATH add this line:

```
PATH=C:\jdk1.3.1\bin
```

If there **is** an entry for PATH, find the end of the entry and add:

```
C:\jdk1.3.1\bin
```

CLDC

Install

Open the Zip file you downloaded and extract the files to your hard drive. I recommend you use the path `c:\j2me` (you may need to substitute a different drive letter depending on your disk space availability and system configuration).

If you extract to the path `c:\j2me`, you will now have a directory structure that looks as follows:

```
C:\j2me
  |
  j2me_cldc
```

Update the PATH Environment Variable

You will also need to update your PATH environment variable to point to the directory where the CLDC executable files are located (the KVM and pre-verifier). Follow the same steps as outlined above to add to the PATH:

```
C:\j2me\j2me_cldc\bin
```

MIDP

Install

Open the Zip file you downloaded and extract the files to your hard drive. Once again, I recommend you use the path `c:\j2me`. You will now have a directory structure that looks as follows:

```
C:\j2me
  |
  j2me_cldc
  midp1.0.3fcs
```

Update the PATH Environment Variable

You will need to update your PATH to reference the directory where the MIDP executable file is located (this is the emulator for testing your MIDlets). Follow the same steps as outlined above to add to the PATH:

```
C:\j2me\midp1.0.3fcs\bin
```

Update/Insert the CLASSPATH Environment Variable

CLASSPATH specifies where to search for classes that are not part of the Java (JDK) platform itself. In our case, we need to update CLASSPATH to have a reference to the MIDP classes. You will also need to have a reference to the current directory "." as part of the CLASSPATH. Follow the same steps as outlined above to add/create the CLASSPATH:

```
CLASSPATH=C:\j2me\midp1.0.3fcs\classes;.
```

Notice there is a "." at the end to represent the current working directory.

Create MIDP_HOME Environment Variable

This variable points to the location of the \lib directory of your MIDP installation. There are 2 configuration files located here:

```
-internal.config
-system.config
```

Follow the same step as outlined previously to add/create the MIDP_HOME environment variable:

```
MIDP_HOME=c:\j2me\midp1.0.3fcs
```

MIDP comes bundled with an emulator that mimics the look and feel of a cellular phone. The emulator can be configured to support color or various shades of black and white (grayscale). Table 4.1 shows the range of values available.

To change the color support for the emulator locate the file `internal.config`. This file is in the \lib directory of your MIDP_HOME. For example, the full path to the file may look as follows:

```
C:\j2me\midp1.0.3fcs\lib\internal.config
```

Table 4.1	Screen Depth Options	
Value	*Number of Colors*	*Color Type*
1	2	Black and white
2	4	Grayscale
4	16	Grayscale
8	256	Color

Inside this file, change the parameter `system.display.screen_depth` to one of the values in Table 4.1:

```
system.display.screen_depth: 8
```

Additional Emulators

In the last section of this chapter we will introduce Sun's J2ME Wireless Toolkit. This J2ME development tool comes packaged with an emulator that can mimic several mobile phones as well as hand-held devices, such as PDAs and pagers.

Installation Checklist

If you've been diligent in following along, your PATH variable (with the exception of entries that may have already been part of your PATH) should look similar to the following:

```
PATH=C:\jdk1.3.1\bin;C:\j2me\j2me_cldc\bin;C:\j2me\midp1.0.3fcs\bin;
```

The directory hierarchy will be as follows:

```
c:\jdk\1.3.1\bin
c:\j2me
  |
  j2me_cldc
  |
  midp1.0.3fcs
```

```
D:\WINNT\System32\cmd.exe                                          _ □ ×
C:\>preverify
Usage: preverify [options] classnames¦dirnames ...

where options include:
  -classpath       <directories separated by ';'>
                   Directories in which to look for classes
  -d <directory>   Directory in which output is written (default is ./output/)
  -cldc            Checks for existence of language features prohibited
                   by CLDC (native methods, floating point and finalizers)
  -nofinalize      No finalizers allowed
  -nonative        No native methods allowed
  -nofp            No floating point operations allowed
  @<filename>      Read command line arguments from a text file
                   Command line arguments must all be on a single line
                   Directory names must be enclosed in double quotes (")
```

Figure 4–1   Testing the pre-verifier

Test Your Installation

Here are a few steps to quickly verify the CLDC , MIDP and JDK were installed correctly:

1. Go to a command prompt.
2. To test the CLDC installation, type in "**preverify**" and press enter. You should see a screen that looks similar to the output shown in Figure 4–1.
3. You can verify the MIDP installation by checking for the mobile device emulator. Type in "**midp -version**" and press enter. You should see a window pop up that looks similar to that of Figure 4–2.

Figure 4–2   Testing the MIDP Emulator

```
D:\WINNT\System32\cmd.exe                 _ □ ×

C:\>midp -version
Profile Spec : MIDP-1.0
Profile Impl : 1.0.3 dist
Configuration: CLDC-1.0

C:\>
```

```
C:\WINNT\System32\cmd.exe                                          _□×

C:\>java -version
java version "1.3.1"
Java(TM) 2 Runtime Environment, Standard Edition (build 1.3.1-b24)
Java HotSpot(TM) Client VM (build 1.3.1-b24, mixed mode)

C:\>
```

Figure 4–3   Testing the Java Development Kit

4. As a final check, test the JDK installation by typing "**java –version**" and press enter. You should see the output shown in Figure 4–3.

Troubleshooting

If any of the programs fail to run, here are a few things to look for:

*   Make sure each program is installed correctly. Use Windows Explorer to find the program causing the problem. For example, l ocate the program midp.exe—for my installation this in the directory: `C:\j2me\midp1.0.3fcs\bin`. Double-click the program and it should start. If you cannot locate the file or it doesn't run, you may need to uninstall and then reinstall the application.

    If it does run, but fails when called from the command line, you know that something is not correct in your PATH setting. Remember, the PATH variable tells Windows where to locate executable files.

*   Make sure you have a reference to the current working directory ("`.`") as part of the CLASSPATH environment variable. For example:

    `CLASSPATH=C:\j2me\midp1.0.3fcs\classes;. ("." at the end)`

*   Verify the directory paths in the PATH environment variable are correct. Once again, using Windows Explorer, locate the directory of the executable as shown above and look in the '*Address*' inside Explorer (see Figure 4–4). This is the full directory path to the program. You can copy and paste this directory into the PATH variable.

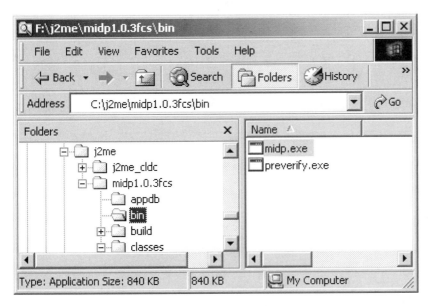

Figure 4–4 Verifying the PATH to the MIDP Emulator

Command Line Development

To learn the command live development process, it's easiest to walk through an example. Let's jump right in and write the code for a simple MIDlet that will display a textbox. You'll also see how to compile, pre-verify and run the resulting program.

Write the Java Code

To get started, create a new directory to hold your MIDlet projects. I prefer to use a directory name something along the lines of c:\midlets

Within this directory create a sub-directory called Welcome. With a text editor, open a new file with the name Welcome.java and enter the Java source code shown in Example 4.1. Save the file in the directory c:\midlets\Welcome (or whatever path you choose). The full path to the MIDlet source file should be something similar to:

```
c:\midlets\Welcome\Welcome.java
```

Example 4.1   Welcome.java

```java
import javax.microedition.midlet.*;
import javax.microedition.lcdui.*;

public class Welcome extends MIDlet implements CommandListener
{
  private Display display;   // Reference to Display object  private
  TextBox tbMain;            // Textbox to display a message
  private Command cmExit;    // Button to exit the MIDlet

  public Welcome()
  {
    display = Display.getDisplay(this);

    cmExit = new Command("Exit", Command.SCREEN, 1);

    tbMain = new TextBox("Welcome", "Core J2ME", 50, 0);
    tbMain.addCommand(cmExit);
    tbMain.setCommandListener(this);
  }

  // Called by application manager to start the MIDlet.
  public void startApp()
  {
    display.setCurrent(tbMain);
  }

  // A required method
  public void pauseApp()
  { }

  // A required method
  public void destroyApp(boolean unconditional)
  { }

  // Check to see if Exit command was selected
  public void commandAction(Command c, Displayable s)
  {
    if (c == cmExit)
    {
      destroyApp(false);
      notifyDestroyed();
    }
  }
}
```

Compile and Pre-verify

Here's how to compile the Java source code and pre-verify the resulting class file.

1. Compile the source code: Go to a command prompt. Change to the project directory where you saved the file. (e.g., `c:\midlets\Welcome`). Compile the program by entering:

   ```
   javac -bootclasspath c:\j2me\midp1.0.3fcs\classes Welcome.java
   ```

   The option `"-bootclasspath c:\j2me\midp1.0.3fcs\classes"` indicates where to locate the Java bootstrap (startup) class files. We must point to the MIDP classes; otherwise, the JDK classes will be used.

   The file `Welcome.class` will be created, by default, in the same directory as the Java source file.

2. Pre-verify the class file by entering the following from the command prompt:

   ```
   preverify -classpath c:\j2me\midp1.0.3fcs\classes;. -d . Welcome
   ```

   The option `"-classpath c:\j2me\midp1.0.3fcs\classes;."` specifies where the class files for pre-verification are located. This includes the MIDP classes that are needed as part of the verification process and your class file, `Welcome.class`, which is located in the current directory (specified by ".").

   The option "-d ." tells the pre-verifier where to put the verified class files. The "." specifies the current directory, the same location as the original class file.

Important Note

Using the above command line options, as written, will overwrite the original Java class file (from the Java compiler) with a new pre-verified class file (from the pre-verifier). You may want to separate the class files into two directories. One reason is, class files that are not pre-verified cannot be loaded by the application manager. I simply chose this option to keep the example simple. I will you show you how to maintain separate directories later in this chapter.

Figure 4–5　Welcome MIDlet

Run the MIDlet

We've taken the easy route through compiling and pre-verifying by keeping the command line options simple. Let's continue with the trend. Here's the quickest way to preview your MIDlet. While still at the command prompt, enter:

```
midp -classpath . Welcome
```

There it is—your first, albeit simple, MIDlet (see Figure 4–5).

Emulator Look and Feel

When running a MIDlet, the look and feel of the emulator is related to the MIDP implementation you have installed. Many of the screen-shots for the examples in this book were created with Sun Microsystems reference implementation of MIDP, version 1.0.

If you have installed a more current version, or are running an implementation provided by a device manufacturer or third-party, the emulator display may look different than what you see here. However, the base functionality of the MIDlet will not be affected.

The good news is, once you've developed a system for compiling, pre-verifying and previewing, not much changes. I like to put all the steps into a batch file (on Microsoft Windows OS). That way, I can run one program to perform all three steps. For example, here is a simple batch file that I used to create and test this MIDlet:

```
javac -bootclasspath c:\j2me\midp1.0.3fcs\classes Welcome.java
pause
preverify -classpath c:\j2me\midp1.0.3fcs\classes;. -d . Welcome
midp -classpath . Welcome
```

The **pause** command will wait for a keypress before executing the next command in the batch file. This way, if you have an error in your Java source file, you can press Control-C to exit the batch file, skipping pre-verification and running of the MIDlet.

Packaging a MIDlet

The previous example is all well and good if you simply want to write MIDlets and preview them in an emulator. I would venture a guess that is probably not your long-term goal. Let's look at how to package MIDlet(s) using JAR and JAD files.

Before we get into the details, let's make this discussion a little more interesting by creating a second MIDlet. This will give you an opportunity to see how the application manager handles multiple MIDlets within a suite.

MIDlet #2

The code for the second MIDlet is shown in Example 4.2. There are a few changes in the MIDlet; however, the output is quite similar. At this point, concentrate on the development process more than the code itself.

As with the first example, to keep the focus on how to compile and package your MIDlets, we'll save the code explanations for later in the book.

Create a directory to hold the new MIDlet: I used a directory called WelcomeBack, created as a subdirectory of c:\midlets. Type in the code shown in Example 4.2 and save it in a file called "WelcomeBack.java" in

Example 4.2 `WelcomeBack.java`

```java
import javax.microedition.midlet.*;
import javax.microedition.lcdui.*;

public class WelcomeBack extends MIDlet implements CommandListener
{
  private Display display;     // Reference to Display
  private List lsMain;         // List of items
  private Command cmExit;      // Button to exit the MIDlet

  public WelcomeBack()
  {
    display = Display.getDisplay(this);

    cmExit = new Command("Exit", Command.SCREEN, 1);

    lsMain = new List("Welcome Back", Choice.IMPLICIT);
    lsMain.append("Core J2ME", null);
    lsMain.addCommand(cmExit);
    lsMain.setCommandListener(this);
  }

  // Called by application manager to start the MIDlet.
  public void startApp()
  {
    display.setCurrent(lsMain);
  }

  // A required method
  public void pauseApp()
  { }

  // A required method
  public void destroyApp(boolean unconditional)
  { }

  // Check to see if Exit command was selected
  public void commandAction(Command c, Displayable s)
  {
    if (c == cmExit)
    {
      destroyApp(false);
      notifyDestroyed();
    }
  }
}
```

your new directory. Here are the steps to compile, pre-verify and run the MIDlet:

1. ```
   javac -bootclasspath c:\j2me\midp1.0.3fcs\classes
        WelcomeBack.java
   ```

2. ```
   preverify -classpath c:\j2me\midp1.0.3fcs\classes;. -d .
   WelcomeBack
   ```

3. ```
   midp -classpath . WelcomeBack
   ```

You can see the output in Figure 4–6.

The MIDlet Suite

Up to this point, we've been running our MIDlets, one at a time, from the command line. This works well for testing and debugging. However, it's time to put all the pieces together and create a MIDlet suite that contains our two MIDlets. Here's the basic process:

1. Package class files and any resources (images, application data, etc.) into a JAR file.
2. Create a JAD file that describes the contents of the MIDlets within the JAR.
3. Run the MIDlet suite by loading the JAD file on an emulator

Figure 4–6 WelcomeBack MIDlet
   ```

or download the JAR and JAD files onto a device that supports J2ME and the MID Profile.

Here are the steps to create a MIDlet suite for the two examples you just wrote.

Create the JAR File

1. Create a new directory to hold the class files from both examples: I used a directory with the name WelcomeJar, which I created as a subdirectory of c:\midlets.

2. Copy both class files (Welcome.class and WelcomeBack.class) into the directory.

3. Create a new file called manifest.txt and enter/save the text in Example 4.3.

Example 4.3 manifest.txt

```
MIDlet-Name: Welcome Examples
MIDlet-Version: 1.0
MIDlet-Vendor: Core J2ME Technology
MIDlet-1: Exampe1,/spin.png, Welcome
MIDlet-2: Example2, /spin.png, WelcomeBack
MicroEdition-Profile: MIDP-1.0
MicroEdition-Configuration: CLDC-1.0
```

---

4. Create a JAR file by running the following command:

```
jar cvfm Welcome.jar manifest.txt
    Welcome.class WelcomeBack.class
```

This will create the file Welcome.jar that contains the contents of manifest.txt and both class files. I realize this may be redundant, but it warrants being repeated: When stored in the JAR, the manifest file will have the name manifest.mf. The above reference to manifest.txt tells the jar program to create manifest.mf using the contents of the file manifest.txt.

Create the JAD File

Create a new file called `Welcome.jad` and enter/save the text in Example 4.4.

Example 4.4   `Welcome.jad`

```
MIDlet-Name: Welcome Examples
MIDlet-Version: 1.0
MIDlet-Vendor: Core J2ME Technology
MIDlet-Description: Two simple MIDlet examples
MIDlet-Jar-URL: Welcome.jar
MIDlet-Jar-Size: 1915
MIDlet-1: Exampe1,/spin.png, Welcome
MIDlet-2: Example2, /spin.png, WelcomeBack
```

Notice the reference to both the MIDlets:

```
MIDlet-1: Example1,/spin.png,Welcome
MIDlet-2: Example2,/spin.png,WelcomeBack
```

Each line contains the name of the MIDlet that will be displayed on the device; an (optional) image file to associate with each MIDlet, and the class file to load to start the MIDlet (Welcome and WelcomeBack).

Running a MIDlet on an Emulator

We can tie all this together by loading our MIDlet suite from a local file system or over the Internet.

From the File System

Here is the command line syntax to load the JAD file:

```
midp -classpath . -Xdescriptor Welcome.jad
```

Figure 4-7 Two MIDlets in a suite presented on device

In Figure 4–7 notice how application manager has extracted the MIDlet names and the images from the JAR\JAD file and shown them on the device display. Figures 4–8 and 4–9 show the MIDlets, Example1 and Example 2, respectively.

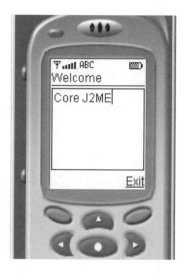

Figure 4-8 MIDlet "Example 1"

Figure 4–9   MIDlet "Example 2"

From a Webserver

If you want to use the emulator to run a MIDlet(s) that is stored on a web-server, you can reference the jad file by changing the url. For example, if I uploaded the MIDlet suite to the website http://www.corej2me.com, in the directory ch4/, I could reference the JAD file as follows:

```
midp -transient http://www.corej2me.com/ch4/Welcome.jad
```

The "-transient" option notifies the emulator that you want to run a description and JAR file located at a specified URL.

Download MIDlet onto a Mobile Device

The specifications for MIDP and CLDC do not define the process of downloading and installing MIDlets (deployment) onto a mobile device. However, there is an addendum to the MID Profile, "Over the Air User Initiated

Provisioning Recommended Practice,"[1] which, as its name implies, outlines the recommended practice to deploy MIDlets.

The document is not a how-to or requirements specification. Each device manufacturer will design and implement their own solution. In addition to downloading MIDlets "over the air" (OTA), a manufacturer may also opt to support installation through a cable connection to a computer, such as a serial or usb port.

If you would like to learn more about deploying MIDlets, Appendix A takes a look inside the OTA recommended practice. Also, visit the various device manufacturers websites to learn about their OTA support.

MIDlet Suite JAD and JAR

A JAD file is not required to be part of a MIDlet suite. The JAD file simply provides a means for an applicaton manager to know what is contained in the JAR file. With this information, the application manager can make decisions about what to download, or not. For example, if the value of the attribute `MIDlet-Jar-Size` specifies a JAR that is too large for the device, the application manager can gracefully refuse to load the MIDlet suite. This would obviously be preferred over simply trying to load each and every MIDlet until a failure occurs.

Project Management Using Java Packages

A Java package is a collection of classes and interfaces. Packages are helpful when your code grows beyond a few simple files. Examples of packages in J2ME include `javax.microedition.rms` for managing persistent storage and `javax.microedition.lcdui`, which provides user interface components such as forms and textboxes.

As we move forward, it's essential that you understand how Java uses packages to help keep your code organized. Also, it's a good time to introduce

---

[1]OTA—http://java.sun.com/products/midp/OTAProvisioning-1.0.pdf.

a better means of keeping track of class files; that is, knowing which class files are produced by the Java compiler and which are the output of the pre-verifier.

Following, we'll create a new directory hierarchy for our classes and will introduce a package statement into the Java code.

Create the Directory Structure

1. Make a directory for the new project—I used the name `Welcome Package`, which I created as a subdirectory of `c:\midlets`.
2. Within this directory, create three new sub-directories:
   - `jclasses`
   - `pclasses`
   - `resources`

   As mentioned previously, it is a good idea to place class files created by the Java compiler in a separate location from those that are created during pre-verification—that's what we've done here. Here's how my system looks:

   ```
   C:\midlets
          |
          WelcomePackage        => Java source code,
                                    manifest.txt and jad file
                |
                jclasses      => Output from the Java compiler
                pclasses      => Output from pre-verifier
                resources  => Resource files (images, etc)
   ```

Update the Files

1. Copy the Java source files (`Welcome.java` and `WelcomeBack.java`) into the `WelcomePackage` directory and add the package statement shown in Examples 4.5 and 4.6 to the top of each file. If you download the source code for this chapter, there will be an image file that you can copy into the `resources` directory.
2. Update `manifest.txt` and the JAD file to reference the new location of the images and the class files.

Example 4.5 `Welcome.java`

```
package corej2me;

import javax.microedition.midlet.*;
import javax.microedition.lcdui.*;

public class Welcome extends MIDlet implements CommandListener
{
  ...
}
```

Example 4.6 `WelcomeBack.java`

```
package corej2me;

import javax.microedition.midlet.*;
import javax.microedition.lcdui.*;

public class WelcomeBack extends MIDlet implements CommandListener
{
  ...
}
```

Example 4.7 `manifest.txt`

```
MIDlet-Name: Welcome Examples
MIDlet-Version: 1.0
MIDlet-Vendor: Core J2ME Technology
MIDlet-1: Example1,/resources/spin.png, corej2me.Welcome
MIDlet-2: Example2,/resources/spin.png, corej2me.WelcomeBack
MicroEdition-Profile: MIDP-1.0
MicroEdition-Configuration: CLDC-1.0
```

Example 4.8 `Welcome.jad`

```
MIDlet-Name: Welcome Examples
MIDlet-Version: 1.0
MIDlet-Vendor: Core J2ME Technology
MIDlet-Description: Two MIDlets in a suite
MIDlet-Jar-URL: Welcome.jar
MIDlet-Jar-Size: 2918
MIDlet-1: Example1,/resources/spin.png, corej2me.Welcome
MIDlet-2: Example2,/resources/spin.png, corej2me.WelcomeBack
```

Note the changes to the MIDlet-1 and MIDlet-2. The class files are now referenced using the package name—`corej2me.Welcome` and `corej2me.WelcomeBack`.

If you choose to leave out the images, simply remove the reference as shown below. Any whitespace between the commas will be ignored.

```
MIDlet-1: Example1, ,corej2me.Welcome
MIDlet-2: Example2, ,corej2me.WelcomeBack
```

Compile and Pre-verify

1. Compile the source:

   ```
   javac -bootclasspath c:\j2me\midp1.0.3fcs\classes -d jclasses
     *.java
   ```

   "-d" option tells the compiler to write the classes files into the directory that we created, jclasses.

2. Pre-verify the Java class files:

   ```
   preverify -classpath c:\j2me\midp1.0.3fcs\classes; -d pclasses
     jclasses
   ```

   "-d" option tells the pre-verifier to store the verified classes in the directory `pclasses`. The last entry on the line ("`jclasses`") tells the pre-verifier where to look for classes to verify.

Create the JAR

1. Run the jar executable to create the archive file:

   ```
   jar cvfm Welcome.jar manifest.txt -C pclasses . resources
   ```

   This creates a JAR file called `Welcome.jar`, using the file `manifest.txt` as the contents of the manifest file (a file called `manifest.mf` will be stored in the JAR).

   "`-C pclasses .`" tells the jar program to change to the `pclasses` directory and archive all (".") the files. "`resources`" informs the jar program to add all the files located in the directory named `resources`

   At this point, you will have two files:

   - `Welcome.jad`: Application descriptor file
   - `Welcome.jar`: Java archive containing the MIDlets, manifest and the image files

Run the MIDlets

To view your new MIDlets, once again you have two options:

1. From the File System:

```
midp -classpath pclasses -Xdescriptor  Welcome.jad
```

2. From a Webserver:

   Upload the JAR and JAD files to a webserver and change the URL to point to the new location. For example:

```
midp -transient http://www.corej2me.com/ch4/Welcome.jad
```

What Have We Gained

By going through this exercise we've created a system, if you will, for managing our projects. We now know by looking at the project hierarchy that we can quickly determine what the contents of each directory are; that is, the whereabouts of the source code, Java classes files, pre-verified class files and resources (see Figure 4–10).

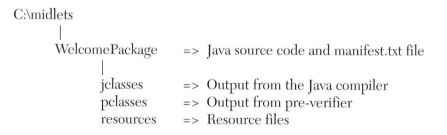

```
C:\midlets
     |
       WelcomePackage        => Java source code and manifest.txt file
          |
            jclasses          => Output from the Java compiler
            pclasses          => Output from pre-verifier
            resources         => Resource files
```

As a further refinement, you may also find it helpful to further break down the `resources` directory; for example, adding subdirectories to organize your image files.

One last note: Refer once again to Figure 4–10 and notice the directory `corej2me` below `jclasses` and `pclasses`. These directories were created by the Java compiler and the pre-verifier, respectively. Because we added the statement 'package corej2me' to our source files, each program created the directory matching the package name and placed its output in that directory.

Java compiler class files are written to:

```
c:\midlets\WelcomePackage\jclasses\corej2me
```

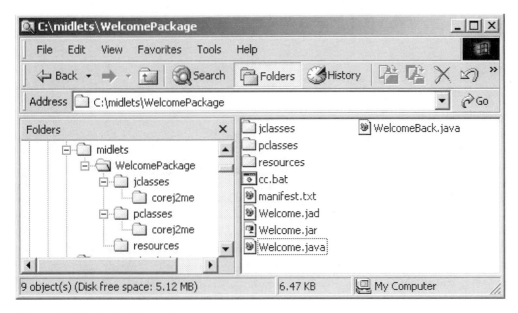

Figure 4–10   Project hierarchy

The pre-verified classes file are written to:

```
c:\midlets\WelcomePackage\pclasses\corej2me
```

J2ME Wireless Toolkit

Although it's not particularly difficult to compile, pre-verify and package your MIDlets, you may want a little help as your projects grow in size and complexity. Sun created the J2ME Wireless Toolkit (from here forward, Toolkit) in an effort to help manage J2ME projects.

The project hierarchy that we just created, with the different directories for source, class files and resources, can be managed by the Toolkit. As we will see, it also includes a GUI interface for making changes to the manifest file and the Java Application Descriptor file.

In this section, we'll download and install the Toolkit, create a project, specify the manifest and JAD attributes, and compile and run a MIDlet. We'll conclude this chapter by looking at the directory structure created and managed by the Toolkit.

Download

Following is the web address where you can download the latest version of the J2ME Wireless Toolkit.[2]

http://java.sun.com/products/j2mewtoolkit/

JDK Version Requirement

The Wireless Toolkit requires version 1.3 or higher of the JDK. You can determine which version you have installed by entering "java –version" at a command prompt. If you need to upgrade your JDK software, you can download version 1.3 at *http://java.sun.com/products/jdk/1.3.*

Installation

Run the application that you downloaded to begin the installation. To follow along with the examples covered here, I recommend you use the default paths when installing the Toolkit.

What is Forte?

Forte is a comprehensive development environment that comes in various flavors. You can download versions for C, C++ and Java, among others. The Java version of Forte is available in the Community Edition, which is free, or the Internet Edition. Both include a source code editor, compiler, debugger and tools to create and deploy your applications. The Internet Edition adds support for JSP and Servlets, XML, CORBA, RMI, JDBC and complete version control capabilities.

---

[2]The information presented here pertains to the Wireless Toolkit, Release 1.0.3.

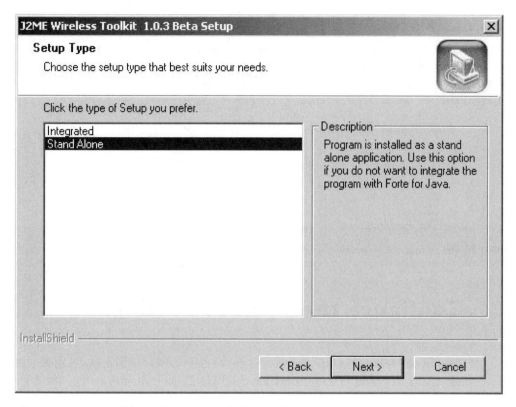

Figure 4-11   Install the Toolkit as a stand alone application

At one point in the installation, you will be prompted as to whether to install the Toolkit as a stand alone application or as an integrated tool with Forte. Choose stand alone. Forte is a complete GUI development environment available from Sun. Our discussion will apply to using the Toolkit as a stand alone program (see Figure 4–11).

Create a New Project

Once the installation is complete, launch the Toolkit. You should see a screen similar to that shown in Figure 4–12.

Click on New Project and a dialog box will appear as in Figure 4–13. Enter the Project Name and MIDlet Class Name as shown.

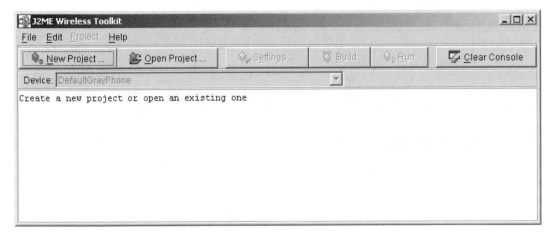

Figure 4-12   The main project window of the Toolkit

Configure the Project Settings

Once you select Create Project, a new dialog box will appear that will allow you to specify the settings for the JAD and the manifest file (see Figure 4–14).

The first tab, labeled *Required,* is a combination of all the attributes that must be defined between the JAR and manifest file. In the previous chapter

Figure 4-13   Creating a new project

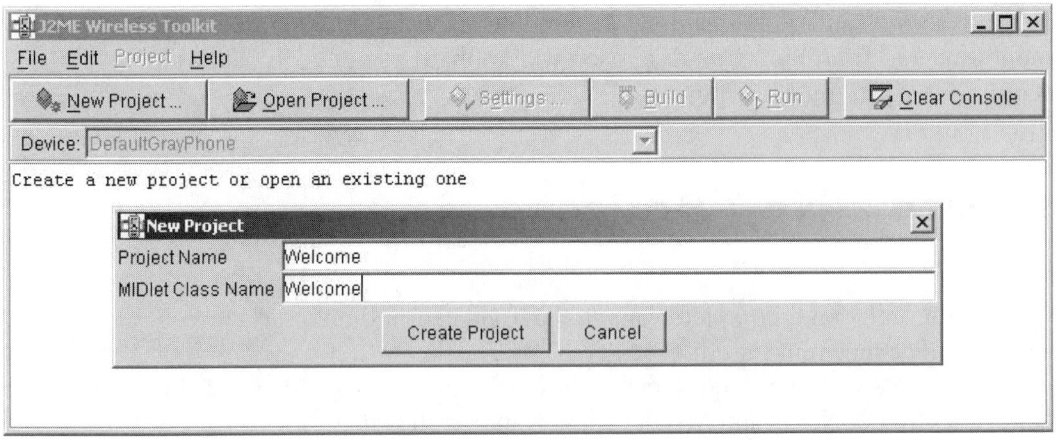

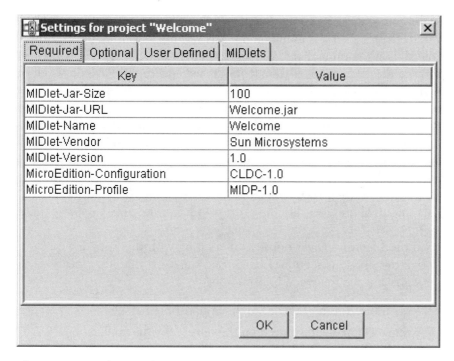

Figure 4–14   Choosing the project options

we learned that the manifest and JAD files must contain the following
entries:

Manifest

MIDlet-Name
MIDlet-Version
MIDlet-Vendor
MIDlet-<n> for each MIDlet in the JAR file
MicroEdition-Profile
MicroEdition-Configuration

JAD

MIDlet-Name
MIDlet-Version
MIDlet-Vendor
MIDlet-<n> for each MIDlet
MIDlet-Jar-URL
MIDlet-Jar-Size

The only entry that is not found on the *Required* tab is MIDlet-<n>. This is a required attribute, yet it is found on the *MIDlets* tab, which we'll visit shortly.

While still on the same dialog box, click on the tab labeled *Optional*. Here you will see the remainder of the attributes we covered in Chapter 3, all of which are optional (see Figure 4–15).

Click on the tab *User Defined* to add your own attributes. For example, in Figure 4–16 I have added an attribute Jadfile-Version and assigned it the value 2.0. When you build the project, which we'll do in a minute, this user-defined attribute (as with all other user-defined attributes) will be inserted into the JAD file.

Finally, click on the *MIDlets* tab. Here is where you add and modify the MIDlet-<n> attributes. Modify the entries to have the same values as those shown in Figure 4–17.

Notice the *Icon* and *Class* entries. In keeping with the same logic of our example in the previous section, I have used the same directory locations. A MIDlet entry has the following information:

- Key: Identifies the MIDlet to the application manager.
- Name: The name displayed on the device (by the application manager).

Figure 4–15 Optional attributes

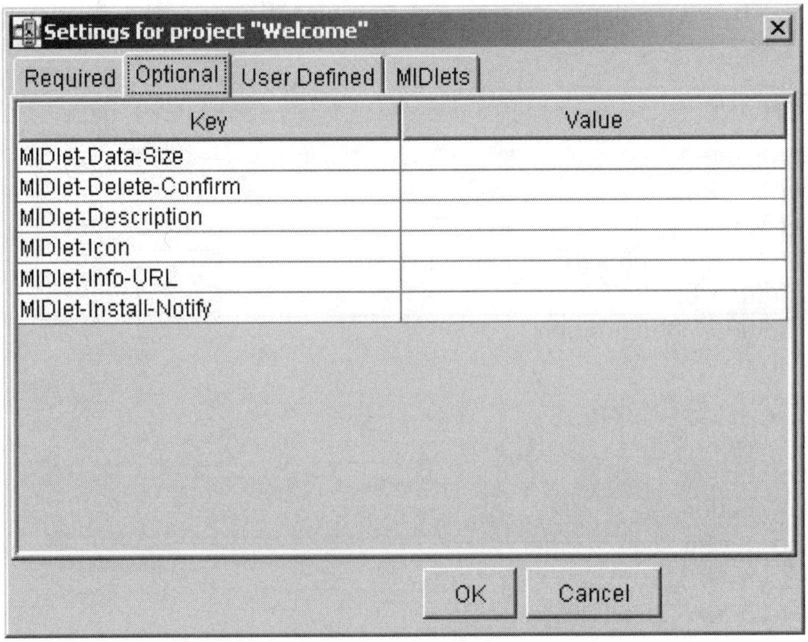

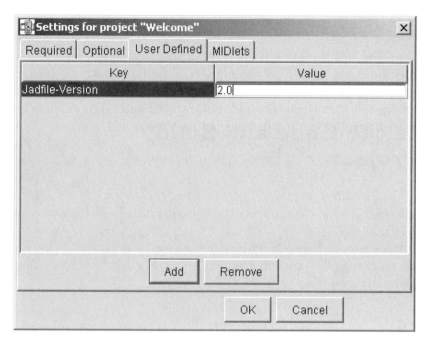

Figure 4–16   User-defined attributes

Figure 4–17   Configure specific MIDlet attributes

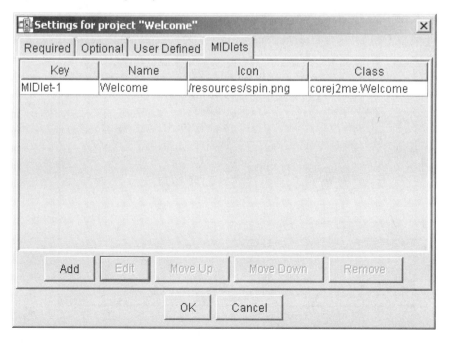

- Icon: Optional icon to be displayed next to the name (by the application manager).
- Class: The class loaded by the application manager when the MIDlet is selected.

Write the Code and Build the Project

Let's take a quick look at the directory structure that the Toolkit has created for us (see Figure 4–18).

Although not identical, this directory structure has a similar look to the hierarchy we created in the previous section, Project Management Using Java Packages (see Figure 4–10).

Figure 4–18   Wireless Toolkit project hierarchy

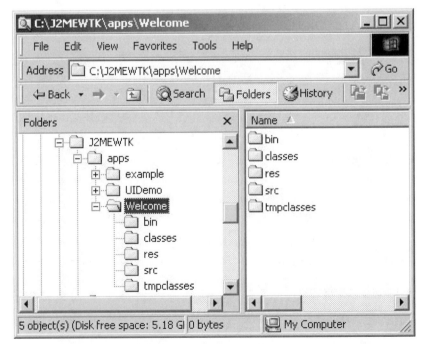

\bin   => manifest, JAD and JAR files
\classes   => class files generated by the Java compiler
\res   => any resource files (images, data, etc)
\src   => Java source code
\tmpclasses => pre-verified class files

We need to make one additional directory in the current project structure. In our last example, we stored the MIDlet image files in a directory named `resources`. Go ahead and add this directory below the `\res` directory. The project should now look as in Figure 4–19.

Find the source file named Welcome.java that you created in the directory `/WelcomePackage`. Copy this file to the `\src` directory. Also, copy the image file spin.png to the `\res\resources` directory.

Figure 4–19   Project hierarchy with new subdirectory "resources"

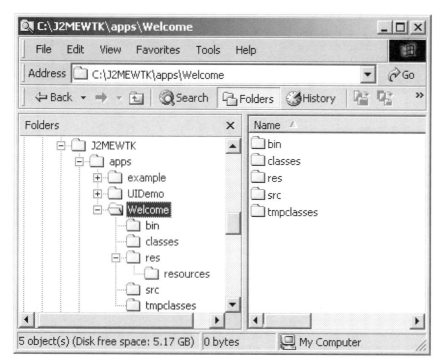

Now, wander your way back to the Toolkit and choose the *Build* option. This will compile the source code; pre-verify the classes; and create the manifest, JAR and JAD files.

Using Java Packages

Take a moment and page back to Example 4.5. This is where we added a package name to the `welcome.java` file. If you take one last look at the project structure (see Figure 4–20), you will see that the Toolkit creates the necessary subdirectories for this package; that is:

```
\classes\corej2me    => class files generated by the Java compiler
\tmpclasses\corej2me => pre-verified class files
```

Figure 4–20 Package directory names have been inserted by the Toolkit

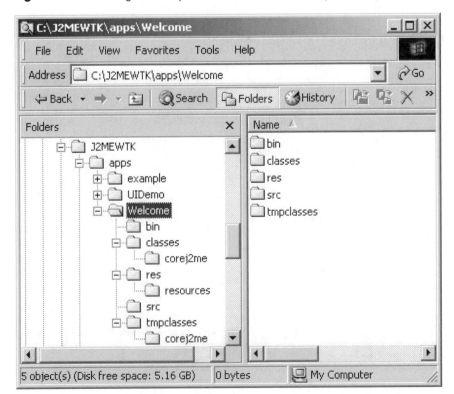

Locating the JAR and JAD Files

If you look inside the directory \bin you will see the manifest, JAD and JAR files the Toolkit created for you. Here are the contents of the manifest and JAD files:

Example 4.9 `manifest.mf`

```
MIDlet-1: Welcome, /resources/spin.png, corej2me.Welcome
MIDlet-Name: Welcome
MIDlet-Vendor: Sun Microsystems
MIDlet-Version: 1.0
MicroEdition-Configuration: CLDC-1.0
MicroEdition-Profile: MIDP-1.0
```

Example 4.10 `welcome.jad`

```
Jadfile-Version: 2.0
MIDlet-1: Welcome, /resources/spin.png, corej2me.Welcome
MIDlet-Jar-Size: 2050
MIDlet-Jar-URL: Welcome.jar
MIDlet-Name: Welcome
MIDlet-Vendor: Sun Microsystems
MIDlet-Version: 1.0
```

A couple points of clarification about these files:

- Notice the entries that were on the "Required" tab of the settings dialog and how they are written to the correct file.
  - **Both files:** MIDlet-Name, MIDlet-Version, MIDlet-Vendor
  - **Manifest file:** MicroEdition-Profile, MicroEdition-Configuration
  - **JAD file:** MIDlet-Jar-Size, MIDlet-Jar-URL
- The user-defined attribute JadFile-Version is written to the JAD file.
- The MIDlet-1 attribute is written to both files.

Configuring the Emulator

When running MIDlets that access the Internet, you may need to go through a proxy server. If so, the Toolkit allows you to configure the server name and port number. To configure the emulator, select *Preferences* from the Edit menu (see Figure 4–21).

Are you curious about what's going on inside your MIDlet? You can peer inside by specifying trace options.

- Trace garbage collection: Each time the garbage collector is run you will see information about how many objects are on the heap, the size of the largest free object and the amount of memory allocated to all existing objects.
- Trace class loading: Each class name will be displayed as it is loaded.

Figure 4–21   Configuring the Emulator preferences

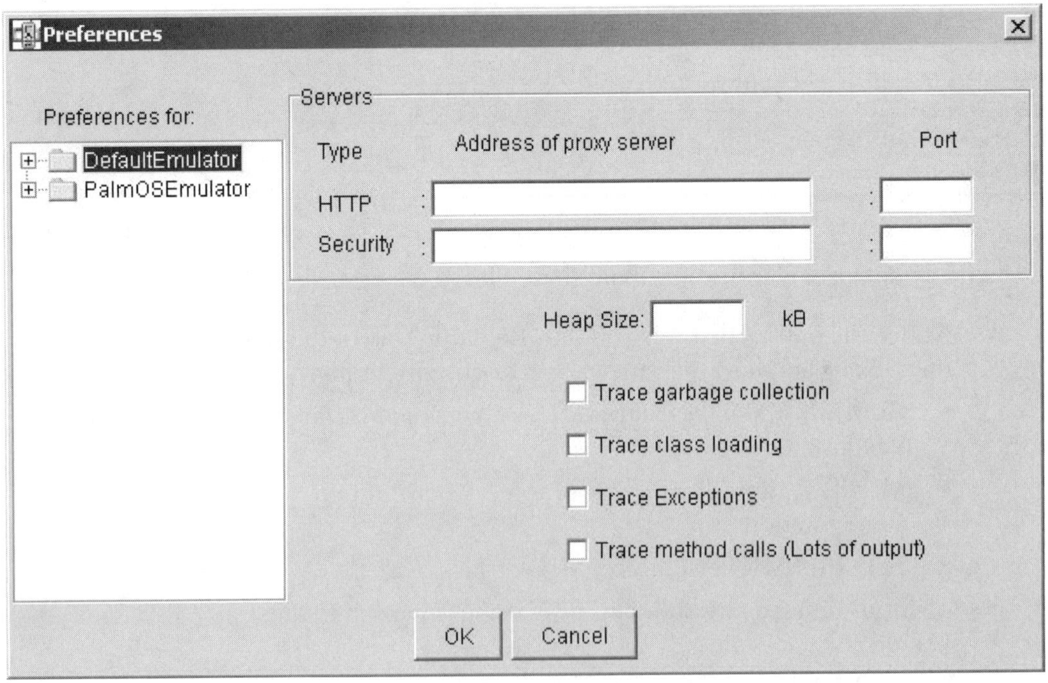

- Trace method calls: All objects and their associated method calls are logged. Be forewarned, this requires a great deal of system overhead, and accordingly, generates a lot of output.
- Display exceptions: All caught and uncaught exceptions are displayed.

Toolkit Summary

The Wireless toolkit can be very helpful for providing project management and minimal debugging (tracing) support. In addition, changes to the manifest and JAD files can be done through an intuitive GUI interface. It may be more a matter of personal preference as to whether the command line or Toolkit approach is better.

As far as "integrated development environments" (programs that offer source code editing, line-by-line debugging, "wizards" to speed application development, team development features, etc.) we briefly mentioned Forte, which can be used as an IDE along with the Wireless Toolkit. Several other IDEs that directly target development using MIDP and CLDC are available from third-party vendors. No doubt, as time passes and the technology progresses, so will the availability and sophistication of the development tools.

BASICS OF MIDLETS AND THE DISPLAY

Topics in this Chapter

- MIDlet

- MIDletStateChangeException

- Display

- Displayable

W ith the framework in place for the compiling, pre-verifying and running of MIDlets, let's start the journey to learn the Mobile Information Device Profile API. This chapter will introduce our first four classes, `MIDlet`, `MIDletStateException`, `Display` and `Displayable`.

MIDlet

A MIDlet is an application that is built upon the `MIDlet` class. The application manager communicates with a MIDlet through methods in this class. This communication is a two-way street. As an example, just as the application manager can pause a MIDlet (e.g., to allow a user to answer an incoming phone call), a MIDlet can make a request to be paused (and later restarted).

MIDlet Lifecycle

A MIDlet goes through several phases as part of its lifecycle and is always considered to be in one of three states:

- Paused: A MIDlet is placed in the paused state after the constructor has been called, but prior to being started by the application manager. Once the MIDlet has been started, it may alternate between the Paused and Active states any number of times during its lifecycle.
- Active: The MIDlet is running.
- Destroyed: The MIDlet has released any resources it acquired, and has been shut down by the application manager.

We'll see more about state transitions in an example shown later.

Creating a MIDlet

We create a MIDlet by extending the MIDlet class. This class is abstract and includes three abstract methods, startApp(), destroyApp(), and pauseApp(). We'll talk about abstract classes and methods shortly.

Following is the shell of a MIDlet. It includes all the methods required by the MIDlet class.

```
public class Shell extends MIDlet
{
  // This method (constructor) is NOT required
  public Shell()
  {
  }

  // Called by application manager to start the MIDlet
  public void startApp()
  {
  }

  // Called by application manager before pausing the MIDlet
  public void pauseApp()
  {
  }

  // Called by application manager to prior to shutdown
  public void destroyApp(boolean unconditional)
  {
  }
}
```

MIDlet API

Table 5.1 MIDlet Class: javax.microedition.midlet.MIDlet	
Method	*Description*
Communication from application manager to MIDlet	
abstract void **destroyApp** (boolean unconditional)	MIDlet is about to be shut down
abstract void **pauseApp**()	MIDlet is about to be placed into paused state
abstract void **startApp**()	MIDlet has been placed into active state
Communication from MIDlet to application manager	
final void **notifyDestroyed**()	MIDlet is requesting to be shut down
final void **notifyPaused**()	MIDlet is requesting to be paused
final void **resumeRequest**()	MIDlet is requesting to become active (after being paused)
Attribute request from MIDlet to application manager	
final String **getAppProperty** (String key)	Get attributes from JAR and/or JAD files

Communication from Application Manager

When a MIDlet is about to be placed into the active state, the application manager will call `startApp()`. This method may be called many times throughout the lifecycle of a MIDlet. Therefore, it's important to think carefully about what you place inside this method. For example, code that needs to persist across the lifetime of the MIDlet should be allocated once, inside the constructor, not here, where it maybe run multiple times.

In many cases this method does little more than request a `Displayable` object (we'll cover more on this shortly) be made visible:

```
public void startApp()
{
  // Make the main form visible
  display.setCurrent(fmMain);
}
```

pauseApp() is a notification that the MIDlet is about to be placed into the paused state. The intention is that the MIDlet will free as many resources as possible.

destroyApp() signals the MIDlet that it is about to be shut down. Any resources that are still in use by the MIDlet need to be released at this time. This method can also be called by the MIDlet itself to begin shutdown; for example, when a user requests to exit the application. See notify-Destroyed() later.

Communication to Application Manager

When a MIDlet needs to shut itself down, (e.g., if a user opted to exit the MIDlet), the method notifyDestroyed() can be called to signal the application manager of the request.

A typical sequence may go as follows:

- User requests to exit
- Call destroyApp() to clean up any resources
- Call notifyDestroyed() to tell application manager it is safe to shut down the MIDlet

It is important to note that before calling notifyDestroyed(), the MIDlet is responsible for releasing any resources.

If a MIDlet would like to be placed into the paused state, notify-Paused() will send the request to the application manager.

Once paused, resumeRequest() tells the application manager that the MIDlet is ready to be active once again.

Query MIDlet Attributes

getAppProperty() can request the application manager to query for various attributes from the JAD file (Table 3.2) and the manifest file (stored in the JAR) (Table 3.1) as well as any user-defined attributes.

The following code is a partial listing of how you might call this method.

```
System.out.println("Vendor: " +
                  getAppProperty("MIDlet-Vendor"));
System.out.println("Description: " +
                  getAppProperty("MIDlet-Description"));
System.out.println("MIDlet-Data-Size: " +
                  getAppProperty("MIDlet-Data-Size"));
```

Access to these attributes is one way in which a MIDlet suite can pass parameters to your MIDlet. See Chapter 3, Example 3.3, which shows how to query attributes and print the results to the console.

Example: Following State Transitions

We can watch a MIDlet go through several state transitions by printing messages inside the methods that are called whenever a state change takes place (see Example 5.1).

Example 5.1   `StateTransitions.java`

```java
import javax.microedition.midlet.*;

public class StateTransitions extends MIDlet
{
  public StateTransitions()
  {
    System.out.println("Inside constructor()");
  }

  // A required method
  // Called by application manager to start the MIDlet
  public void startApp()
  {
    System.out.println("Inside startApp()");
  }

  // A required method
  // Called by application manager before pausing the MIDlet
  public void pauseApp()
  {
    System.out.println("Inside pauseApp()");
  }

  // A required method
  // Called by application manager to prior to shutdown
  public void destroyApp(boolean unconditional)
  {
    System.out.println("Inside destroyApp()");
  }
}
```

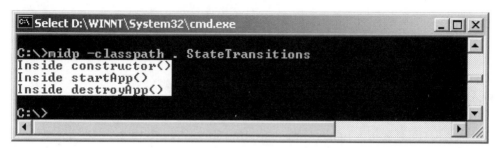

Figure 5–1   Displaying state transitions of a MIDlet

This MIDlet does little more than show a brief message as it changes state (see Figure 5–1). Notice the messages as the MIDlet constructor is called, followed by `startApp()`, and ending with `destroyApp()` once the MIDlet is about to be shut down.

One clarification is in order. A moment ago I mentioned that a MIDlet is placed in the Paused state after the constructor is called. However, from the output of this program, you'll notice the Paused method is never invoked. So why is this? You can think of it this way: The program must be placed into some state when it is loaded into memory. This will always be the Paused state. Since this is done internally by the application manager, it is not necessary to call `pauseApp()`. Rest assured, all future requests by the application manager to pause the MIDlet will go through `pauseApp()`.

Here is one more point of interest. Earlier I mentioned that `startApp()`, `pauseApp()` and `destroyApp()` are all abstract methods inside the class `MIDlet`. When we declare a MIDlet using "extends"

```
public class TestMIDlet extends MIDlet
```

and do not specify the class as abstract, we agree to implement all abstract methods, even if the body of the methods contains no code. Our agreement is based on the definition of an abstract class/method in the Java language. See the Sidebar "Inside Abstract Classes and Methods" for more information.

MIDletStateChangeException

During the course of a MIDlet's lifecycle, if an error occurs when changing states, this exception is thrown. Two methods within the `MIDlet` class can also throw `MIDletStateChangeException`: `destroyApp()` and `startApp()`.

Quick Review: Inside Abstract Classes and Methods

Using the keyword *abstract* in a method declaration (`public abstract void pauseApp()`) indicates that the method has no implementation inside the class in which the method is declared. Rather, it is up to a subclass to provide the method body. The only exception is, if a subclass is declared as an abstract class, then the body of an abstract method can be deferred even further, to a subclass of that class. Once you define a method as abstract, the class itself must be declared abstract.

So why use an abstract class? The short answer is, the ability to encapsulate what we consider common functionality for all subclasses. For example, the MIDlet class is declared as abstract:

```
public abstract class MIDlet {
    ...
    protected abstract void startApp()
                throws MIDletStateChangeException;
    protected abstract void pauseApp();
    protected abstract void destroyApp(boolean
                unconditional) throws
        MIDletStateChangeException;
}
```

With this definition, we know that any subclass of a MIDlet will provide an implementation of these three methods. The only exception is that, if a subclass is declared as abstract, then these methods may be deferred to a subclass further down the hierarchy.

So as an application developer, when would you throw such an exception? Here's a possible scenario: When a user requests to exit a MIDlet, in most cases, the application manager will immediately try to shut down the MIDlet. However, what if a MIDlet is receiving data over a network connection? It would be much preferred to finish receiving the data before being shut down.

We can throw this exception, in essence, requesting the application manager to let us continue. Example 5.2 shows how to throw and catch this exception.

Table 5.2	MIDletStateChangeException Class: javax.microedition. midlet.MIDletStateChangeException

Constructor	Description
MIDletStateChangeException()	Create exception object with no text
MIDletStateChangeException(String s)	Create exception object with text

MIDletStateChangeException API

There are two constructors for creating this exception, one with and one without a text message. (see Table 5.2).

Example: Throwing an Exception

Let's look at example where we will both throw and catch this exception. The MIDlet below will display a Form with a simple message and a Command (button) labeled "Exit."

Command versus Button

A Command is an object that holds information about an action, such as a user requesting to exit a MIDlet. Figure 5–2 shows a Command with the label "Exit" that is mapped to the button directly below the label. As we'll see in the Chapter 6 when we discuss event processing, Commands are not always shown on the display next to a button. However, as it applies to this chapter, whenever we use the term Command, it is sufficient to think of it as a button on a device.

As stated earlier, when a user requests to exit a MIDlet, the application manager will attempt to immediately stop the MIDlet. This example throws and catches the MIDletStateChangeException. Doing so will give our MIDlet another chance to wrap up any ongoing activity, such as completing a download of data. Our example will go like this: The first time the user presses the Exit button, we will call:

```
destroyApp(false);
```

By passing in `false`, we are informing the method that this is **not** an unconditional exit. `destroyApp()` will throw a `MIDletStateChange-Exception`, requesting that we not be shutdown. We will catch this exception inside `commandAction()` and set a flag indicating that the next time the Exit button is pressed we will be ready to exit. The MIDlet will then continue running or, using our analogy, continue downloading data until the user once again requests to exit.

Example 5.2 `TestException.java`

```java
import javax.microedition.midlet.*;
import javax.microedition.lcdui.*;

public class TestException extends MIDlet implements CommandListener
{
  private Display display      // Reference to Display
                               //    object
  private Form fmMain;         // A form
  private Command cmExit;      // A button to exit the MIDlet
  private boolean safeToExit = false;  // Is it safe to exit?

  // MIDlet constructor
  public TestException()
  {
    display = Display.getDisplay(this);

    cmExit = new Command("Exit", Command.SCREEN, 1);
    fmMain = new Form("Test Exception");
    fmMain.addCommand(cmExit);
    fmMain.setCommandListener(this);
  }

  // Called by application manager to start the MIDlet.
  public void startApp()
  {
    display.setCurrent(fmMain);
  }

  // We are about to be placed in the Paused state
  public void pauseApp()
  {
  }
```

(continued)

Example 5.2 *(Continued)*

```
// We are about to enter the Destroyed state
public void destroyApp(boolean unconditional) throws
  MIDletStateChangeException
{
  System.out.println("Inside destroyApp()");

  // If we do not need to unconditionally exit
  if (unconditional == false)
  {
    System.out.println("Requesting not to be shutdown");
    throw new MIDletStateChangeException("Please don't
      shut me down.");
  }
}

// Check to see if the Exit command was selected
public void commandAction(Command c, Displayable s)
{
  if (c == cmExit)
  {
    try
    {
      // Are we ready to exit yet?
      if (safeToExit == false)
        destroyApp(false);
      else
      {
        destroyApp(true);
        notifyDestroyed();
      }
    }
    catch (MIDletStateChangeException excep)
    {
      safeToExit = true;    // Next time, let's exit
      System.out.println(excep.getMessage());
      System.out.println("Resuming the Active state");
    }
  }
}
}
```

Don't worry if feel you've missed the boat when looking at the code and reading the description that follows. We have yet to cover all the classes. However, we'll give you enough information to get you through this example.

This MIDlet has a `Form` and a `Command` (button) that will make up the user interface. To access these objects, we need to add an import statement:

```
import javax.microedition.lcdui.*;
```

Our class declaration has also been modified with an "implements" clause:

```
public class TestException extends MIDlet implements CommandListener
```

Because we will add a `Command` to the device display, we need some way to interact with that `Command`. `CommandListener` is just part of the interaction. We'll get to the rest in a moment.

```
private Form fmMain;          // A form
private Command cmExit;       // A button to exit the MIDlet
private boolean safeToExit = false;   // Is it safe to exit
```

`fmMain` and `cmExit` declare objects that will appear on the display of the device. `safeToExit` is a flag indicating whether or not we are willing to shut down the MIDlet.

The MIDlet constructor, `TestException()`, gets a reference to the display and also creates a new `Command` (our Exit button) and a new `Form`:

```
fmMain.addCommand(cmExit);
fmMain.setCommandListener(this);
```

The first line above adds (associates) the "Exit" `Command` to the `Form`. The second line creates a listener to facilitate event handling. When an event occurs (such as a user pressing the "Exit" button), the method `commandAction()` is called.

```
public void commandAction(Command c, Displayable s)
{
  if (c == cmExit)
  {
    try
    {
      // Are we ready to exit yet?
      if (safeToExit == false)
        destroyApp(false);
      else
      {
        destroyApp(true);
        notifyDestroyed();
      }
    }
    catch (MIDletStateChangeException excep)
    {
```

```
            safeToExit = true;    // Next time, let's exit
            System.out.println(excep.getMessage());
            System.out.println("Resuming the Active state");
        }
    }
}
```

The first check inside this method is to see if the event that was captured is from the "Exit" Command. If yes, we check the `safeToExit` variable to see if it set to `false`. If so, we call `destroyApp(false)`.

Inside `destroyApp()` will throw an exception if the value passed in is `false`. This exception is then caught inside in the `commandAction()` method. We will set the `safeToExit` variable to `true`, and the MIDlet will continue running.

The next time the Exit Command is requested, `safeToExit` will be `true` and we'll call `destroyApp(true)`. Passing in `true` signals that this is an unconditional exit; that is, the MIDlet will be shut down upon exiting `destoyApp()`, no questions asked.

Figure 5–2 shows the messages written to the console after selecting Exit Command once. The second time the Exit Command is requested, the MIDlet will be shut down.

Figure 5–2   Throwing and catching MIDletStateChangeException

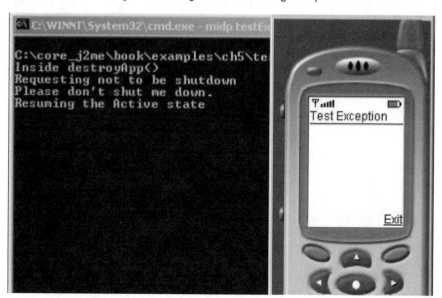

Display

Each MIDlet has a reference to **one** Display object. This object can retrieve information about the current display (e.g., the range of colors supported) and includes methods for requesting that objects (Forms, TextBoxes, etc.) be displayed. The Display object is best thought of as the manager of the display controlling what is shown on the device and when.

Although there is only one Display object per MIDlet, there may be many objects within a MIDlet that may be displayable—Forms, TextBoxes, ChoiceGroups, and so forth. We'll cover this idea when we discuss the Displayable object in the next section.

Creating a Display Object

A Display object is made available to a MIDlet through a call to a static method declared inside the Display class. This reference is often held for the lifetime of the MIDlet in a variable, as shown here.

```
public class DisplayStats extends MIDlet
{
  private Display display; // Reference to Display object

  // MIDlet constructor
  public DisplayStats()
  {
    display = Display.getDisplay(this);
      ...
  }
...
}
```

Display API

The methods for getting and setting the current Displayable will make more sense near the end of this chapter when we introduce the Displayable class. Here's the general idea: displayable components are those that have a visual appearance on a device (a Form, TextBox, Canvas, etc.). Each is a subclass of Displayable. The methods getCurrent() and setCurrent() are used to move between various displayable components.

Table 5.3	Display Class: javax.microedition.lcdui.Display

Method	*Description*
static Display **getDisplay**(MIDlet m)	Get Display object for this MIDlet
Displayable **getCurrent**()	Get current Displayable object
void **setCurrent**(Alert alert, Displayable nextDisplayable)	Show an Alert followed by the specified Displayable object
void **setCurrent**(Displayable nextDisplayable)	Show a new Displayable object
boolean **isColor**()	Does the device support color?
int **numColors**()	How many colors (or shades of gray) are available?
void **callSerially**(Runnable r)	Request a runnable object be called after repainting

Example: Getting Device Information

Example 5.3 uses two methods inside the `Display` class to report information about color support on a device.

Although we have yet to introduce the `Alert` class, I've opted to show an example of the method `setCurrent(Alert, Displayable)` from Table 5.3. Don't worry about the specifics of the `Alert` at this point. You can look ahead to Chapter 8 if you are curious about any of the parameters passed to the `Alert` object. In a sentence, an `Alert` is a dialog box that displays a text message along with an (optional) image. The output for this example is shown in Figure 5–3.

Example 5.3	`DisplayStats.java`

```
import javax.microedition.midlet.*;
import javax.microedition.lcdui.*;

public class DisplayStats extends MIDlet implements CommandListener
{
   private Display display;      // Reference to Display object
   private Form fmMain;          // A form
   private Alert alTest;         // An Alert
   private Command cmExit;       // A button to exit the MIDlet
```

Example 5.3 *(Continued)*

```
// MIDlet constructor
public DisplayStats()
{
  display = Display.getDisplay(this);

  cmExit = new Command("Exit",Command.SCREEN,1);
  fmMain = new Form("Welcome");
  fmMain.addCommand(cmExit);
  fmMain.setCommandListener(this);

  System.out.println("Display " + (display.isColor() ?
        "does" : "does not") + " support Color");
  System.out.println("Number of colors: " + display.numColors());
}

// Called by application manager to start the MIDlet.
public void startApp()
{
  alTest = new Alert("Alert","This alert screen
            will be followed by the main form",null,null);
  alTest.setTimeout(Alert.FOREVER);
  display.setCurrent(alTest,fmMain);
}

// We are about to be placed in the Paused state
public void pauseApp()
{
}

// We are about to enter the Destroyed state
public void destroyApp(boolean unconditional)
{
}

// Check to see if the Exit command was selected
public void commandAction(Command c,Displayable s)
{
  if (c == cmExit)
  {
    destroyApp(true);
    notifyDestroyed();
  }
}
}
```

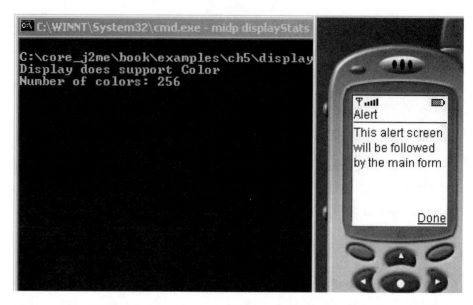

Figure 5–3   An Alert dialog and writing to the console the number of colors supported on the device

Even if you don't understand each line, the majority of the code should look familiar to that of the previous example. I have added a declaration for the `Alert` near the top of the file. Also, the following code creates the new `Alert` object and sets the timeout value to FOREVER, meaning this `Alert` will be on the display until the user selects the "Done" Command. Such a display is often referred to as modal.

```
alTest = new Alert("Alert","This alert screen will be
        followed by the main form",null,null);
alTest.setTimeout(Alert.FOREVER);
```

With one call, we notify the application manager to display the `Alert` we just defined, and once dismissed, display our main `Form`, `fmMain`:

```
display.setCurrent(alTest, fmMain);
```

Displayable

As mentioned in the previous section, there is only one `Display` object per MIDlet. However, a `Display` can show any number of `Displayable` objects. As the name implies, a `Displayable` object can be viewed on a device. The MIDP includes two subclasses of `Displayable`: `Screen` and `Canvas`. Here are a few class definitions to help clarify:

```
abstract public class Displayable
public abstract class Canvas extends Displayable
public abstract class Screen extends Displayable
```

Objects that subclass `Screen` (`Textbox`, `List`, `Form` and `Alert`) are all high-level user interface components, as their implementation and presentation on the device are handled for you. The `Canvas` object is used for custom graphics and low-level event handling, such as when writing games, and requires a little more finesse on your part to update the display.

Creating Displayable Object

We don't create `Displayable` objects directly; instead, we reference subclasses of `Displayable`. For example, as you saw earlier, `Screen` and `Canvas` extend the `Displayable` class. Thus, we can extend either of these classes, which in turn gives us access to the `Displayable` methods.

Here are three general ways which this is done:

1. Extend the Canvas class directly:

    ```
    public class GameScreen extends Canvas
    {
        draw images, shapes, text …
    }
    ```

2. Use subclasses of `Screen`:

    MIDP includes several components that are subclasses of Screen: these include `TextBox`, `List`, `Form` and `Alert`. Using these classes you don't need to subclass `Screen` directly. For example, here are a few lines to create a `Form` and `TextBox`.

    ```
    private Form fmMain;
    private TextBox tbMessage;
    ...
    fmMain = new Form("Test Exception");
    tbMessage = new TextBox("Title", "Contents", 25, TextField.ANY);
    ```

3. Extend `Form`, `TextBox`, `List` or `Alert`:

    Often times it makes the most sense to extend these classes to encapsulate functionality. For example, in Chapter 12 we will create a `To Do list` MIDlet with several different "screens" the user will see, each a subclass of `Form`:

```
// Get user preferences
public class FormPrefs extends Form implements CommandListener

// Add a new todo item
public class FormAdd extends Form implements CommandListener
```

Extending the `Form` class and implementing the `Command-Listener` interface allows each of the aforementioned forms to manage its own events, resulting in a much more consist and manageable application.

Displayable API

Through the API we can add and remove `Commands` and `listeners`. Given that we've touched upon neither, here's the two-minute elevator pitch.

`Commands` are available to provide a means for user interaction. As we saw in Example 5.2, a `Command` was added to a `Form` to provide a way for a user to exit the MIDlet.

```
cmExit = new Command("Exit",Command.SCREEN,1);  // Create command
fmMain = new Form("Test Exception");            // Create form
fmMain.addCommand(cmExit);         // Add command to form
fmMain.setCommandListener(this);   // Listen for events
```

Table 5.4   Displayable Class: javax.microedition.lcdui.Displayable

Method	*Description*
void **addCommand**(Command cmd)	Add Command to Displayable object
void **removeCommand**(Command cmd)	Remove Command from Displayable object
void **setCommandListener**(CommandListener l)	Add CommandListener to Displayable object
boolean **isShown**()	Is the Displayable object visible on the screen?

Listeners are used in conjunction with a Command to "listen" for events. Once an event occurs, the listener will call the method commandAction(). Within this method, we can determine which Command initiated the event and proceed accordingly. We will cover the details of Commands Chapter 6.

```
public void commandAction(Command c, Displayable s)
{
  if (c == cmExit)
  {
    destroyApp(true);
    notifyDestroyed();
  }
}
```

EVENT HANDLING

Topics in this Chapter

- The Big Picture

- Command Objects

- Item Objects

- Command and CommandListener

- Item and ItemStateListener

Chapter 6

Event processing is essential to most every MIDlet. It's hard to imagine an application where there is no user interaction whatsoever, even if this interaction is as simple as requesting to start or stop a MIDlet. Learning the classes that facilitate event processing is the goal of this chapter. We'll discuss only those events that apply to high-level user interface components. Low-level event handling (including key codes, game actions, and pointer events) will be addressed in Chapter 9 when we introduce the `Canvas` class.

The Big Picture

To greatly oversimplify, event handling is nothing more than recognizing when an event occurs and taking an action based on that event. For example, recognizing that a help button has been pressed and displaying a help message. To break this down to the lowest level, there are three key steps to successfully managing an event.

1. The hardware (the physical device itself) must recognize that something has occurred: a button has been pressed, a button

has been released, an adapter has been plugged in, an adapter has been removed. You get the picture.

2. The software on the device (the application manager) needs to be notified of the event.

3. This is the point where we come into the picture as a MIDlet developer. A message from the application manager will be sent to the MIDlet. This message will contain information about the event so we can make decisions as to how to proceed (e.g., the event may be a request to show a help message on the display).

Before a MIDlet can recognize a message from the application manager about an event, it must set up what we refer to as a "listener." There are two "listener" interfaces available in the MID Profile: `CommandListener` and `ItemStateListener`.

When you want to process events, you will need a class that implements one or both of these interfaces. As part of the class that implements the interface(s), you will write the method(s) `commandAction()` and/or `itemStateChanged()`. This is where you place the code to decipher what event occurred and how you would like to handle the event.

Quick Review: What is an Interface?

In Java, an interface is a class that defines a set of methods, and optionally, one or more constant declarations. An interface does not include the implementation of any of the methods in the class. When a class implements an interface, the class must contain all the methods defined in the interface. For example, when you create a MIDlet that implements the `CommandListener` interface, your class must have a method called `commandAction()` (which happens to be the only method defined in the `CommandListener` interface).

Before we talk any further about listeners, we need to introduce two new objects: `Command` and `Item`.

Command Objects

A Command is an object that holds information about an event. The simplest way to think of a Command is as a "button," something that you press or select. Figure 6–1 shows a Command with the label "Exit." This Command is associated with the button directly below it on the device.

This idea, that a Command is a button, is a good starting point. However, because of limited screen space and the differences in availability of buttons on a device, it's not always that simple. We will explore this further as we delve into this chapter.

Soft-Buttons and Keys

To keep the terminology consistent, I use the word "key(s)" when referencing the numbers/letters on a cellular phone or the alphanumeric/symbols on a pager. A button(s) will refer to all other options on the device, such as a power on/off button, menu button, or help button. The latter are often referred to as soft-buttons.

Processing events requires a little legwork up front. Here are the steps:

1. Create a Command object to hold information about an event.
2. Add the Command to a Form, Textbox, List or Canvas.
3. Add a "listener" to the above Form, Textbox, and so forth.

Upon detection of an event the "listener" will be called (sent a message). The end result is a call to the method commandAction(). Within this method you can determine what Command initiated the action and process the event accordingly.

Here are a few lines of code to allocate a Form add a Command to the Form and create a "listener" to detect events.

```
private Form fmMain;        // A Form
private Command cmExit;     // A Command to exit the MIDlet
    . . .
```

```
fmMain = new Form("Core J2ME");          // Form object
cmExit = new Command("Exit", Command.EXIT, 1); // Command object
...
fmMain.addCommand(cmExit);               // Add Command to Form
fmMain.setCommandListener(this);         // Listen for Form events


...

public void commandAction(Command c, Displayable s)
{
  if (c == cmExit)
  {
     destroyApp(true);
     notifyDestroyed();
  }
}
```

Item Objects

A second type of event handling is done through an `Item`. An `Item` is any component that can be added to a `Form`. `ChoiceGroup`, `DateField`, `Gauge` and `TextField` are all subclasses of `Item` and each can process events. `Items` are accessible only as part of a `Form`, whereas `Commands` are available on `Forms`, as well as a `Textbox`, `List`, or `Canvas`.

Once you add an `Item` to a `Form`, as with `Commands`, you must add a listener. Once there is a change to an `Item` (e.g., a `Gauge` has been incremented or a `DateField` has been changed), the listener object will be notified (sent a message). Think of this message as a call to the method `itemStateChanged()`. This method can decipher what `Item` was modified and process the change as necessary.

Note

StringItem and *ImageItem* are also subclasses of *Item*. However, once allocated, these objects are static and thus do not receive/acknowledge events.

Shown next is a small piece of code to create a `Form`, append a `Date Field`, and create a "listener" for event handling.

```
private Form fmMain;                   // A Form
private DateField dfToday;             // A DateField
...
fmMain = new Form("Core J2ME");        // Form object
dfToday = new DateField("Today:", DateField.DATE); // DateField
...
fmMain.append(dfToday);                // Add DateField to Form

fmMain.setItemStateListener(this);     // Listen for events
...

public void itemStateChanged(Item item)
{
  // If the datefield initiated this event...
  if (item == dfToday)
    ...
}
```

Note

We will discuss `Textbox, List, Form, Canvas, Alert, Choice Group, DateField, Gauge, ImageItem, StringItem` *and* `TextField` *in upcoming chapters.*

Command and CommandListener

When creating a new `Command` object to hold event information, there are three parameters: the label, type and priority. Using the following `Command` declaration, let's look at each parameter in detail.

```
cmHelp = new Command("Help", Command.HELP, 1);
              |           |        |
            label       type   priority
```

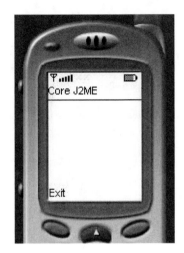

Figure 6-1   A Command mapped to
a "generic" soft-button

1. **Label:** This specifies the text that you would like to associate
   with the Command. The label may be shown directly on the
   screen or displayed inside a menu.

   Figures 6–1 shows a Command with the label "Exit." The
   Command is mapped to the soft-button shown directly below
   the label.

   Figure 6–2 shows two Commands, with the labels "Upload"
   and "Download" placed inside a menu.

Figure 6-2   Commands available in a
menu

Figure 6-3 This device has a soft-button specifically intended to display help

2. **Type:** If at all possible, we'd like to directly map Commands to relevant soft-buttons on a device. For example, if a device has a soft-button labeled "Help" it would be very intuitive for the user if there was a Command mapped to that soft-button to display a help message (see Figure 6–3).

   We specify our intent to map a Command to a specific soft-button using this parameter. For example, with the line of code shown above, we are specifying the intent of this Command to display help information.

Note

Specifying the type of Command *(e.g.,* Command.HELP*) does not perform any action when the user initiates the event. That is, no help information will be displayed simply because we created a* Command *with that intent. Regardless of the type you specify, you are still responsible for writing the code to carry out the action.*

The available types for this parameter are shown in Table 6.1.

Table 6.1	Command Types: javax.microedition.lcdui.Command
Value	*Description*
BACK	A request to move to the previous screen.
CANCEL	A request to cancel an operation. For example, when showing a screen to prompt for a web address, you may have both OK and CANCEL as options on the screen.
EXIT	A request to exit the MIDlet.
HELP	A request to display help information.
ITEM	A request to map the Command to an "item" on the screen. For example, when using a List component, you can mimic the functionality of a context-sensitive menu by mapping Commands to the various entries in the List.
OK	Specify positive acknowledgement from a user. For example, after downloading data, you may present a screen that says "Download Complete" with a Command of this type and a label "OK."
SCREEN	For Commands in which it is unlikely there will be a specific key mapping available. For example, you might have Commands to initiate uploading and downloading of data. The labels "Upload" and "Download" will not have direct key mapping on a device.
STOP	A request to stop an operation. For example, if downloading data, this option may be available so a user can end the download without having to wait for the operation to complete.

3. **Priority:** In relation to other Commands you define, this value represents where this Command falls in the line of priority. The higher the number, the lower the priority. These values may be helpful for the application manager when arranging items that appear in a menu or for ordering of soft-buttons on the display.

   As with the type, the priority is only a request from you as a developer. The actual key mapping and priority assigned will be decided and handled by the device.

Command and CommandListener API

Table 6.2 Command Class: javax.microedition.lcdui.Command	
Method	*Description*
Constructor	
Command (String label, int commandType, int priority)	Create a new Command
Methods	
int **getCommandType**()	Get type assigned to Command
String **getLabel**()	Get label assigned to Command
int **getPriority**()	Get priority assigned to Command

Table 6.3 CommandListener Interface: javax.microedition.lcdui. CommandListener	
Method	*Description*
void **commandAction** (Command c, Displayable d)	Called when the Command "c" on the Displayable "d" initiates an event

Example: Accessing Commands through Button or Menu

Previously it was mentioned that the easiest way to think of a Command is as a button on a device. Example 6.1 illustrates that it is not always quite that simple.

Example 6.1 `AccessingCommands.java`

```java
import javax.microedition.midlet.*;
import javax.microedition.lcdui.*;

public class AccessingCommands extends MIDlet implements CommandListener
{
```

(continued)

Example 6.1   *(Continued)*

```
private Display display;    // Reference to Display
private Form fmMain;        // A Form
private Command cmExit;     // A Command to exit the MIDlet

public AccessingCommands()
{
  display = Display.getDisplay(this);

  cmExit = new Command("Exit", Command.EXIT, 1);

  fmMain = new Form("Core J2ME");
  fmMain.addCommand(cmExit);
  fmMain.setCommandListener(this);
}

// Called by application manager to start the MIDlet.
public void startApp()
{
  display.setCurrent(fmMain);
}

public void pauseApp()
{ }

public void destroyApp(boolean unconditional)
{ }

// Check to see if our Exit command was selected
public void commandAction(Command c, Displayable s)
{
  if (c == cmExit)
  {
    destroyApp(false);
    notifyDestroyed();
  }
}
}
```

Inside the constructor we create Command and Form objects, add the Command to the Form and set a "listener."

```
cmExit = new Command("Exit", Command.EXIT, 1);
fmMain = new Form("Core J2ME");
```

```
fmMain.addCommand(cmExit);
fmMain.setCommandListener(this);
```

When the user interacts with the Form, such as pressing a button, the method commandAction() is called. We know from our previous discussion that this event started at the hardware level, worked its way through the application manager and finally arrived here.

```
public void commandAction(Command c, Displayable s)
{
   if (c == cmExit)
   {
     destroyApp(false);
     notifyDestroyed();
   }
}
```

We check to see if the Command that was selected by the user (the value passed in as parameter "c") was the Exit Command. If so, we call destroy-App() to clean up any resources we acquired and follow this with a call to notifyDestroyed() to tell the application manager it is safe to shut down this MIDlet.

There should be no surprises in the output shown in Figure 6–4. The Form displays the title "Core J2ME" and the Command "Exit" is above a soft-button on the device. Pressing the button exits the MIDlet.

Now, let's take a look at the same MIDlet when run inside a wireless hand-held emulator (see Figure 6–5).

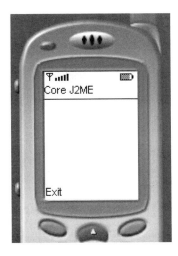

Figure 6–4 Accessing the Exit Command with a soft-button

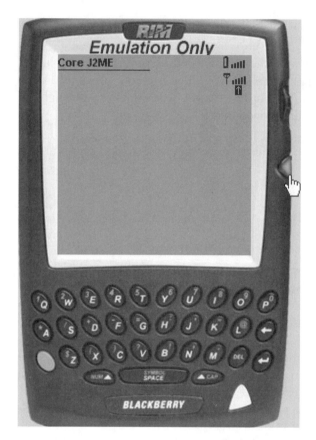

Figure 6–5 Exit Command not available through a soft-button (*Blackberry wireless handle screen-shots courtesy Research in Motion Limited.*)

What happed to the "Exit" Command? To exit the MIDlet, you need to enable the menu by selecting the button on the middle right. Once the menu appears, select the active menu item with the button on the upper right (see Figure 6–6).

As we mentioned back in Chapter 3, one of the objectives of MIDP is to support a wide range of devices with differences not only in processing power and memory, but also in size and hardware configuration. This MIDlet is a good example as it will run on two different devices with two different interfaces. Although the end result is the same, the handheld device placed the Exit Command on a menu, whereas the cellular phone mapped the same Command to a soft-button.

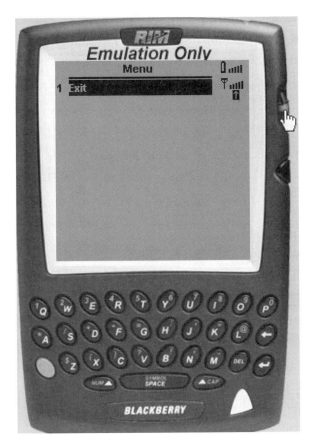

Figure 6–6 Exit Command must be accessed using a menu (*Blackberry wireless handle screen-shots courtesy Research in Motion Limited.*)

To complete that thought, the actual implementation of the Command is not defined by the API, only the characteristics and functionality. Put another way, how a Command is presented on the display, and whether it is mapped to a key or placed in a menu, is up to the device manufacturer.

Example: Mapping Command to Buttons

In the previous example, the handheld device placed our exit Command in a menu. Let's take a look at Example 6.2, where a device maps a Command to a specific soft-button.

Version 1.0.3 of Sun's J2ME Wireless Toolkit (see Chapter 4) supports six emulators:

Table 6.4   Wireless Toolkit Emulators

Keyword	*Description*
DefaultColorPhone	256 colors, 96 × 128 pixels, ITU[1] keyboard
DefaultGrayPhone	256 shades of black and white, 96 × 128 pixels, ITU[1] keyboard
MinimumPhone	Black and white, 96 × 54 pixels, ITU[1] keyboard
Motorola_i85s	Motorola i85s
RIM-Blackberry-957	RIM Blackberry wireless handheld
PalmOS_Device	Handheld devices running Palm OS version 3.5 or higher[2]

[1]ITU is the "classic" phone keypad: numbers 0-9, * and #.
[2]Palm OS Emulator (POSE) and ROM image are required. http://www.palmos.com/dev/tech/tools/emulator/

To preview your MIDlet, run the following from the command line in the directory that contains the JAD file:

```
c:\j2mewtk\bin\emulator -Xdescriptor:your.jad
       -Xdevice:emulator -classpath .
```

Replace **emulator** with one of the keywords from Table 6.4, and change **your.jad** to the name of the Java application descriptor file that references your MIDlet. You may need to change the path to the J2ME Wireless Toolkit, depending on your installation. The classpath may also need to be changed (from ".") to the location of the preverified class files.

One final clarification: The aforementioned emulators require you to preview using a JAD file. Thus, you will need to create a JAR file that holds your MIDlet classes and also include a reference to the JAR inside the JAD file. See Chapter 4 for more information about how to create these files.

Example 6.2 `MappingCommands.java`

```java
import javax.microedition.midlet.*;
import javax.microedition.lcdui.*;

public class MappingCommands extends MIDlet implements
    CommandListener
{
  private Display display;       // Reference to Display
  private Form fmMain;           // The main Form
  private TextBox tbHelp;        // Textbox to display a help message
  private Command cmExit;        // Exit the MIDlet
  private Command cmHelp;        // Ask for Help
  private Command cmBack ;       // Go "back" to main form

  public MappingCommands()
  {
    display = Display.getDisplay(this);

    cmHelp = new Command("Help", Command.HELP, 1);
    cmBack = new Command("Back", Command.BACK, 1);
    cmExit = new Command("Exit", Command.EXIT, 1);

    // Create the Form, add Commands, listen for events
    fmMain = new Form("Core J2ME");
    fmMain.addCommand(cmExit);
    fmMain.addCommand(cmHelp);
    fmMain.setCommandListener(this);

    // Create the help Textbox with a maximum of 25 characters
    tbHelp = new TextBox("Help", "Help text here...", 25, 0);
    tbHelp.addCommand(cmBack);
    tbHelp.setCommandListener(this);

  }

  // Called by application manager to start the MIDlet.
  public void startApp()
  {
    display.setCurrent(fmMain);
  }
```

(continued)

Example 6.2   (Continued)

```
public void pauseApp()
{ }

public void destroyApp(boolean unconditional)
{ }

// Process events
public void commandAction(Command c, Displayable s)
{
  if (c == cmExit)
  {
    destroyApp(false);
    notifyDestroyed();
  }
  else if (c == cmHelp)
    display.setCurrent(tbHelp);
  else if (c == cmBack)
    display.setCurrent(fmMain);
}
}
```

There are several additional components added to this MIDlet:

```
TextBox tbHelp;   // Textbox to display a help message
Command cmHelp;   // Ask for Help
Command cmBack ;  // Go "back" to main Form (from Help)
```

Let's see how the "traditional" cellular device displays the MIDlet. In Figure 6–7, the screen shot on the left is the main Form, with the Exit and Help Commands. When you press the Help button, the Textbox appears as shown by the screen shot on the right.

You can follow the logic of this MIDlet by looking at the commandAction() method:

```
public void commandAction(Command c, Displayable s)
{
  if (c == cmExit)
  {
    destroyApp(false);
    notifyDestroyed();
  }
```

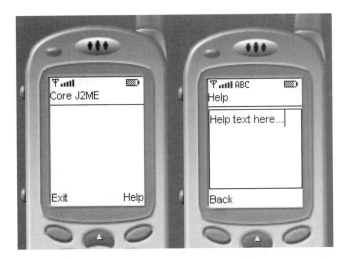

Figure 6–7 Commands Exit and Back mapped to soft buttons

```
else if (c == cmHelp)
  display.setCurrent(tbHelp);
else if (c == cmBack)
  display.setCurrent(fmMain);
}
```

Depending on what button was pressed, we either change the current display to show the help `TextBox`, or we exit the MIDlet. Now, let's see how a different mobile device, with limited screen size, handles the same MIDlet (see Figure 6–8).

Figure 6–8 Back command mapped to a soft button

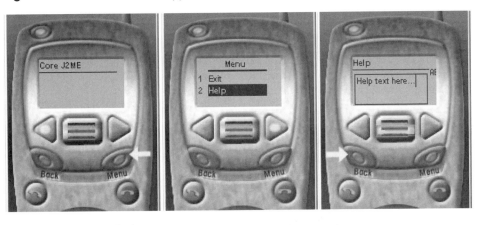

Given the screen limitations of this device, there are no commands shown directly on the display. On the left-most screen shot in Figure 6–8 notice there is soft-button to engage the menu. Once visible you'll find the commands we've defined. The right-most screen shot shows the help text. Notice how the device has performed a direct mapping of the "Back" Command to the soft-button with the same name. We don't need to go through a menu to invoke this Command.

```
cmBack = new Command("Back", Command.BACK, 1);
```

When we specified our intention with the above declaration, the application manager was able to map the "Back" Command to the appropriate button on the device.

Example: Too Many Commands. Now What?

In our first example, we saw that the handheld device added the Exit Command to a menu. The reason was that there was no button that directly correlated to Exit. If we add more Commands without button mappings, the handheld will add these to the menu as well.

If you were to venture a guess, how do you think our cellular device will handle more Commands than can fit on the display? Let's look at Example 6.3 and see.

Example 6.3   `TooManyCommands.java`

```java
import javax.microedition.midlet.*;
import javax.microedition.lcdui.*;

public class TooManyCommands extends MIDlet implements CommandListener
{
   private Display display;      // Reference to Display
   private Form fmMain;          // The main Form
   private TextBox tbAction;     // Textbox upload/download
   private Command cmExit;       // Exit the MIDlet
   private Command cmBack ;      // Go "back" to main form
   private Command cmUload;      // "upload" data
   private Command cmDload;      // "download" data

   // The constructor
   public TooManyCommands()
   {
     display = Display.getDisplay(this);
```

Example 6.3   *(Continued)*

```java
    cmExit = new Command("Exit", Command.EXIT, 1);
    cmBack = new Command("Back", Command.BACK, 1);
    cmUload = new Command("Upload", Command.SCREEN, 2);
    cmDload = new Command("Download", Command.SCREEN, 3);

    // Create the Form, add Commands, listen for events
    fmMain = new Form("Core J2ME");
    fmMain.addCommand(cmExit);
    fmMain.addCommand(cmUload);
    fmMain.addCommand(cmDload);
    fmMain.setCommandListener(this);

    // Create a Textbox, add Command, listen for events
    tbAction = new TextBox("Process Data",
                    "Upload/download data ", 25, 0);
    tbAction.addCommand(cmBack);
    tbAction.setCommandListener(this);
  }

  // Called by application manager to start the MIDlet.
  public void startApp()
  {
    display.setCurrent(fmMain);
  }

  public void pauseApp()
  { }

  public void destroyApp(boolean unconditional)
  { }

  // Process events
  public void commandAction(Command c, Displayable s)
  {
    if (c == cmExit)
    {
      destroyApp(false);
      notifyDestroyed();
    }
    else if (c == cmUload || c == cmDload)
      display.setCurrent(tbAction);
    else if (c == cmBack)
     display.setCurrent(fmMain);
  }
}
```

I have added two new Commands, cmUload and cmDload. Notice the priorities assigned:

```
cmUload = new Command("Upload", Command.SCREEN, 2);
cmDload = new Command("Download", Command.SCREEN, 3);
```

By assigning "Upload" a higher priority than "Download" we are stating our preference regarding the relative importance of each Command. You'll see the end result of this request in Figure 6–9, where "Upload" appears before "Download."

Let's imagine these Commands invoke sending and receiving of data over a network. The new TextBox, tbAction, will act as our upload/download screen, which is set as the current Displayable inside command Action().

```
public void commandAction(Command c, Displayable s)
{
  if (c == cmExit)
  {
    destroyApp(false);
    notifyDestroyed();
  }
  else if (c == cmUload || c == cmDload)
    display.setCurrent(tbAction);
  else if (c == cmBack)
    display.setCurrent(fmMain);
}
```

I have also added a Command to go back from the TextBox to the main Form. Figure 6–9 shows the display as it looks on a cellular device.

Figure 6–9 Commands mapped to both soft-buttons and a menu

As with the handheld, the device has created a menu to hold the "Upload" and "Download" Commands. The "Exit" Command has been mapped to a soft-button.

You can see there is a great deal of flexibility as to how a device can present Commands on the display. As a developer you specify your intention of the Commands when defining them –Command.BACK, Command.HELP, and so forth. However, there are no guarantees how they will be displayed/ processed on any one device. You have to agree, this can make for some interesting design considerations when trying to create user interfaces that look and feel consistent across a range of devices.

Setting **Command** Priorities

For another look at setting priorities, page ahead to Figure 8–7 and the corresponding code in Example 8.3. Priorities are used within this example to arrange the order of options in a menu.

Item and ItemStateListener

An Item is any component that can be added to a Form. The MIDP library includes the following Items: ChoiceGroup, DateField, Gauge, ImageItem, StringItem and TextField.

With the exception of StringItem and ImageItem, each of the aforementioned Items can detect user interaction. When you add an Item to a Form, you create a "listener" to capture user events (for any/all Items on the Form). Once a change has been detected, the method itemStateChanged() will be called. Inside this method you can determine which Item was changed and how you want to proceed.

The specification does not require itemStateChanged() to be called on each and every change. However, it does set forth some rules:

- If an Item has changed, itemStateChanged() must be called for the changed Item before it will acknowledge changes in a subsequent Item.
- If a MIDlet makes a change to an Item (as compared to user interaction), itemStateChanged() will not be called. For

example, if you write code inside your MIDlet to change the value of a `DateField`, this will not generate an event.

- If the device running the MIDlet can recognize when a user has moved from one `Item` to another (changed focus), `itemStateChanged()` must be called when leaving one `Item` and before getting to the next.

Creating an Item

`Item` is an abstract class, thus, we do not create instances of the `Item` class. Rather, we create objects that have subclassed `Item`. These include: `ChoiceGroup`, `DateField`, `TextField`, `Gauge`, `ImageItem` and `StringItem`.

Here we create a `DateField`, add it to a `Form` and set a listener so the `Displayable` object (the `Form`) can detect events. If you recall from Chapter 5, we add listeners to `Displayable` objects (a `Canvas`, or subclasses of `Screen`, which include `Form`, `List`, `TextBox` and `Alert`).

```
private DateField dfDate;  // Display the date

// Create the date and populate with current date
dfDate = new DateField("Date is:", DateField.DATE);
dfDate.setDate(new java.util.Date());

fmMain = new Form("Core J2ME");
fmMain.append(dfDate);

// Capture Command events (cmExit)
fmMain.setCommandListener(this);
```

ItemState and ItemStateListener API

Table 6.5 Item Class: javax.microedition.lcdui.Item	
Method	*Description*
String **getLabel**()	Get the label assigned to the Item
void **setLabel**(String label)	Set label for the Item

Table 6.6	ItemStateListener Interface: javax.microedition.lcdui. ItemStateListener	
Method	*Description*
void **itemStateChanged**(Item item)	Called when "item" has been changed

Example: Capturing Events on an Item Object

In our final example for this chapter, Example 6.4, we will create a Date-Field and add a listener to the main Form to capture events. Once you select the DateField on the device, you can change the month, day and year. When you exit the DateField display, itemStateChanged() will be called. To reassure ourselves that we actually enter this method, we will change the label on the DateField, which will be reflected on the display.

Example 6.4   CaptureItemEvents.java

```java
import javax.microedition.midlet.*;
import javax.microedition.lcdui.*;

public class CaptureItemEvents extends MIDlet implements
    ItemStateListener, CommandListener
{
  private Display display;      // Reference to Display object
  private Form fmMain;          // The main Form
  private Command cmExit;       // A Command to exit the MIDlet
  private DateField dfDate;     // Display the date

  public CaptureItemEvents()
  {
    display = Display.getDisplay(this);

    // Create the date and populate with current date
    dfDate = new DateField("Date is:", DateField.DATE);
    dfDate.setDate(new java.util.Date());

    cmExit = new Command("Exit", Command.EXIT, 1);
```

(continued)

Example 6.4   (Continued)

```
    // Create the Form, add Command and DateField
    // listen for events from Command and DateField
    fmMain = new Form("Core J2ME");
    fmMain.addCommand(cmExit);
    fmMain.append(dfDate);

    // Capture Command events
    fmMain.setCommandListener(this);

    // Capture Item events
    fmMain.setItemStateListener(this);
  }

  // Called by application manager to start the MIDlet.
  public void startApp()
  {
    display.setCurrent(fmMain);
  }

  public void pauseApp()
  { }

  public void destroyApp(boolean unconditional)
  { }

  public void commandAction(Command c, Displayable s)
  {
    if (c == cmExit)
    {
      destroyApp(false);
      notifyDestroyed();
    }
  }

  public void itemStateChanged(Item item)
  {
    dfDate.setLabel("New Date: ");
  }
}
```

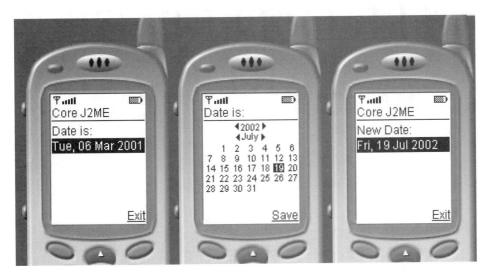

Figure 6-10 Capturing events with ItemStateListener

From left to right on Figure 6–10, the first screen shot shows the `Form` and the `DateField`. Once you choose to edit the date, you will see the screen shot in the middle, where you can interactively make changes. Upon selecting "Save," the method `itemStateChanged()` is called. Within this method, we change the label on the `DateField`. The result of this change is reflected in the rightmost screen shot.

Note

itemStateChanged() is not inevitably called for every change on an *Item*. For example, when the `DateField` component is shown on the display, changing the day will not initiate an event. For Sun's MIDP implementation of `DateField`, the method `itemStateChanged()` will be called when the user exits the `DateField`. The decision regarding when an event is acknowledged is determined by the device implementation.

HIGH-LEVEL USER INTERFACE: PART I

Topics in this Chapter

- Screen
- Form
- Item
- DateField
- Gauge
- StringItem
- TextField
- Choice and ChoiceGroup
- Image and ImageItem

Chapter 7

Now that we've examined how events are managed within a MIDlet, we need to focus on how to create the user interface. In Chapter 5 we introduced the `Display` and `Displayable` classes. If you recall, there is one `Display` object and any number of `Displayable` objects in a given MIDlet. The `Screen` is one of two `Displayable` objects defined as part of the core API, the other being `Canvas`.

This chapter will focus on the first of four components that are derived from the `Screen` class, the `Form`. It will also cover all the predefined components that may be added to a `Form`, including `DateField`, `Gauge`, `StringItem`, `TextField`, `ChoiceGroup` and `ImageItem`.

When we get to the next chapter, you'll learn about the remaining subclasses of `Screen`: `List`, `Textbox`, `Alert` and `Ticker`.

Note

> As we work through our examples, keep in mind that the MIDP defines the requirements for a set of classes. It is a toolkit for writing applications for various mobile devices. It does not specify how to implement the libraries.
>
> So what does that mean? The functionality across implementations will be the same, yet the presentation may be different. As an example, a `TextField` will always have a consistent set of methods for entering and modifying text, but the look and feel may vary from device to device.
>
> All the examples in this book will use the MIDP provided by Sun. If you run these examples with another vendor's implementation, keep in mind that the appearance of components may be different.

Screen

The `Screen` class itself is not something that you can see. Rather, `Screen` is a parent class for components that have an actual look and feel on the display. To further clarify, let's look at an illustration of the user interface hierarchy, starting with the `Displayable` class.

Figure 7–1   Displayable class hierarchy

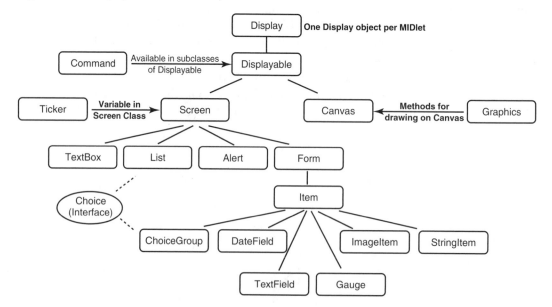

To further clarify the hierarchy shown in Figure 7–1, the class definitions follow:

Display	(public class Display)
Displayable	(public abstract class Displayable)
Screen	(public abstract class Screen extends Displayable)
TextBox	(public class TextBox extends Screen)
List	(public class List extends Screen implements Choice)
Alert	(public class Alert extends Screen)
Form	(public class Form extends Screen)
Item	(public abstract class Item)
ChoiceGroup	(public class ChoiceGroup extends Item implements Choice)
DateField	(public class DateField extends Item)
TextField	(public class TextField extends Item)
Gauge	(public class Gauge extends Item)
ImageItem	(public class ImageItem extends Item)
StringItem	(public class StringItem extends Item)
Canvas	(public abstract class Canvas extends Displayable)
Command	(public class Command)
Ticker	(public class Ticker)
Graphics	(public class Graphics)
Choice	(public interface Choice)

The MIDP includes two classes that are direct descendents of the Displayable class: Screen and Canvas. The Screen (and its subclasses) are for high-level user interface components; the Canvas is for custom graphics and event handling.

If we break this down further, you can see that Form, List, TextBox and Alert are all subclasses of the Screen class. Ticker (a scrolling ticker tape) is not a subclasss; rather, it is a field (variable) defined inside the Screen class. Thus, a Ticker can be part of any Screen.

If you look carefully you'll notice that Item is *not* a subclass of Form. However, it is illustrated as such in Figure 7–1 to make the point that sub-classes of Item are displayed on a Form.

Let's look at the methods available in the Screen class.

Screen API

Table 7.1	Screen Class: javax.microedition.lcdui.Screen
Method	*Description*
String **getTitle**()	Get title associated with the Screen
void **setTitle**(String s)	Set title for the Screen
Ticker **getTicker**()	Get Ticker associated with the Screen
void **setTicker**(Ticker ticker)	Set Ticker for the Screen

Form

If you come from a desktop computing platform, the limitations of the display on a mobile device may take some getting used to. Overlapping windows, toolbars and cascading menus are nowhere to be found.

All is not lost, however. A Form gives you the option to show multiple components on the display. The implementation will provide scrolling, as needed, to accommodate the components. Think of a Form as a container that can hold any number of components, where each is a subclass of Item (see Figure 7–1).

A Form has methods to append, insert, replace and delete components. When you append a component to a Form, the append method returns a numeric index indicating where the component was placed, with an index value starting at 0. Several other methods use this index as an input parameter; thus, you may find it helpful to keep a copy of this index in a variable. Other methods are available to determine the number of components on a Form and request the index (position) of a specific component.

Form API

Table 7.2	Form Class: javax.microedition.lcdui.Form
Method	*Description*
Constructors	
Form (String title)	Create a form
Form (String title, Item[] items)	Create a form and add Item(s) in the array
	(continued)

Method	Description
Table 7.2 *(Continued)*	
Method	*Description*
Methods	
int **append**(Image img)	Append an Image
int **append**(Item item)	Append an Item
int **append**(String str)	Append a String
void **delete**(int itemNum)	Delete an Item
void **insert**(int itemNum, Item item)	Insert an Item prior to the Item specified
Item **get**(int itemNum)	Get an Item
void **set**(int itemNum, Item item)	Set (replace) an Item
void **setItemStateListener**(ItemStateListener iListener)	Add a listener
int **size**()	Get the number of Items on a form

Item

An Item is a component that can be added to a Form. ChoiceGroup, DateField, Gauge, ImageItem, StringItem and TextField are all subclasses of Item.

Working along with an Item is the class ItemStateListener. When you want to process events on an Item, you register a "listener" that will be sent a message when an event occurs. The recipient of this message is the method itemStateChanged(). Within this method, you can determine which Item changed and decide what action you would like to take.

The following code appends a DateField to a Form and creates a listener for processing events.

```
private Form fmMain;                              // A Form
private DateField dfToday;                        // A DateField
...
fmMain = new Form("Core J2ME");                   // Form object
dfToday = new DateField("Today:", DateField.DATE); // DateField
...
fmMain.append(dfToday);        // Add Item (DateField) to Form
fmMain.setItemStateListener(this);    // Listen for Form events
```

```
...

public void itemStateChanged(Item item)
{
  if (item == dfToday)
    ...
}
```

ITEM API

Table 7.3	Item Class: javax.microedition.lcdui.Item

Method	Description
String **getLabel**()	Get the label assigned to the Item
void **setLabel**(String label)	Set label for the Item

Example: Juggling Items on a Form

There are some special considerations that are important to understand when inserting, appending and replacing Items on a Form. Example 7.1 will walk through these operations and point out the pitfalls, hopefully saving you a little time in the long run.

Example 7.1	FormJuggle.java

```
import javax.microedition.midlet.*;
import javax.microedition.lcdui.*;

public class FormJuggle extends MIDlet implements CommandListener
{
  private Display display;        // Reference to display object
  private Form fmMain;            // The main form
  private Command cmInsert;       // Command to insert items
  private DateField dfDate;       // Display date
  private TextField tfSize;       // Product size
  private TextField tfQuantity;// Product quantity
  private int dateIndex;         // Index of dfDate
```

(continued)

Example 7.1   (*Continued*)

```java
public FormJuggle ()
{
  display = Display.getDisplay(this);

  // Create the date and populate with current date
  dfDate = new DateField("", DateField.DATE);
  dfDate.setDate(new java.util.Date());

  // Define two textfields and two commands
  tfSize = new TextField("Size", "Large", 5, TextField.ANY);
  tfQuantity = new TextField("Quantity:", "3", 2,
     TextField.NUMERIC);
  cmInsert = new Command("Insert", Command.SCREEN, 1);

  // Create the form, add insert command
  fmMain = new Form("Form Stuff");
  fmMain.addCommand(cmInsert);

  // Append date to form & save index value where it was inserted
  dateIndex = fmMain.append(dfDate);

  // Capture events
  fmMain.setCommandListener(this);
}

// Called by application manager to start the MIDlet.
public void startApp()
{
  display.setCurrent(fmMain);
}

public void pauseApp()
{ }

public void destroyApp(boolean unconditional)
{ }

public void commandAction(Command c, Displayable s)
{
  if (c == cmInsert)
  {
    // One item on form, insert textfield prior to datefield
    if (fmMain.size() == 1)
```

(*continued*)

Example 7.1   (Continued)

```
    {
      fmMain.insert(dateIndex, tfQuantity);
      dateIndex += 1;    // Date index has changed, update it
    }
    // If two items and last item is datefield, replace it
    else if (fmMain.size() == 2 && fmMain.get(1) == dfDate)
      fmMain.set(dateIndex, tfSize);
  }
 }
}
```

There are three Items we will add to the Form: a DateField and two TextFields. At this point don't worry about the specifics of these components.

1. dfDate: show the current date
2. tfSize: show the product size
3. tfQuantity: show the product quantity

The constructor—FormJuggle()—allocates all the items and appends dfDate to the form. tfSize and tfQuantity are not placed on the form at this time.

There is one line that we need to clarify:

```
        dateIndex = fmMain.append(dfDate);
```

We need to save the index of where this item is inserted. Later, we will use this index to specify where to insert a new item.

There is also a Command on the form labeled "Insert." The method commandAction() will be called when this Command is invoked. This method is where we need to focus our attention. Here is the code we are interested in:

```
        if (c == cmInsert)
        {
          // One item on form, insert textfield prior to datefield
          if (fmMain.size() == 1)
          {
            fmMain.insert(dateIndex, tfQuantity);
            dateIndex += 1;    // Date index has changed, update it
          }
          // If two items and last item is datefield, replace it
```

```
    else if (fmMain.size() == 2 && fmMain.get(1) == dfDate)
       fmMain.set(dateIndex, tfSize);
}
```

If there is just one item on the form (dfDate), then we will insert tfQuantity. Notice the insert method takes two parameters. The first is index of where to place the new item, the second is the item to insert.

Now, before we move on, think about what just happened. When you insert an item, it is placed prior to the index you specify. In our example, dateIndex has a value of 0 because it was the only item currently on the form. The value for dateIndex is no longer accurate, as the new item is now at index 0. To correct this, we increment dateIndex by 1 so any future reference will access the correct item.

After the first time through commandAction(), our form has two items with the indices 0 and 1:

fmMain
    tfQuantity   Index = 0
    dfDate   Index = 1

If the "Insert" button is pressed a second time, commandAction() will drop into this block of code:

```
    else if (fmMain.size() == 2 && fmMain.get(1) == dfDate)
       fmMain.set(dateIndex, tfSize);
```

If there are two items on the form, and the item at index 1 equals dfDate, then we will set (replace) that item with tfSize. Here is the resulting form:

fmMain
    tfQuantity   Index = 0
    tfSize   Index = 1

Can you see why we need this check:

```
    fmMain.get(1) == dfDate
```

Without it, should we come into commandAction() a third time

```
    fmMain.set(dateIndex, tfSize);
```

will try to replace what is at dateIndex (which has value of 1), with tfSize. Well, tfSize is already at index 1 (see Figure 7–2). The point to be made is that it's important to understand the indexing of components and how inserting and deleting affects the index values. Figure 7–2 shows various screen shots of this MIDlet.

Figure 7-2   From the left, the initial screen. The center is the display after pressing "Insert" once. The rightmost, after pressing "Insert" a second time.

The remaining sections of this chapter will cover each of the Item components that are available as part of the MIDP.

DateField

Using the DateField component, you manipulate a Date object (as defined in java.util.Date) using the keys and/or soft buttons on a mobile device. The look and feel, as provided in Sun's MIDP implementation, is shown in Figure 7–3.

Figure 7-3   An easy-to-use interface for updating the date and time

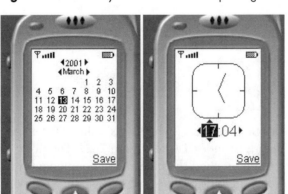

Table 7.4	DateField Modes: javax.microedition.lcdui.DateField	
Value	**Description**
DATE	Allow the user to edit only the date
TIME	Allow the user to edit only the time
DATE_TIME	Allow the user to edit both the date and time

When creating a DateField object you specify whether the user can edit the date, the time, or both—see the mode constants declared in the Table 7.4.

DateField API

Table 7.5	DateField Class: javax.microedition.lcdui.DateField	
Method	**Description**
Constructors	
DateField(String label, int mode)	Create DateField
DateField(String label, int mode, TimeZone timeZone)	Create DateField with specified TimeZone information
Methods	
Date **getDate**()	Get current value
void **setDate**(Date date)	Set new date/time value
int **getInputMode**()	Get the current input mode
void **setInputMode**(int mode)	Set new input mode

Example: Creating an Alarm Clock

Let's create a simple alarm clock MIDlet (see Example 7.2). This application will allow the user to specify a date and time, and will sound an alarm and display a message when the appointed time has arrived.

To make this example a little more realistic, I've included two components that we have yet to introduce: the Timer and Alert. With a Timer you can schedule tasks to occur at some future time (in our case, a task to display a message). The message will be contained as part of an `Alert` component. An `Alert` is similar to a pop-up window or dialog box. Once again, don't worry about the details of these components, as we'll cover them as we progress through the book.

Example 7.2   Snooze.java

```java
import java.util.*;
import javax.microedition.midlet.*;
import javax.microedition.lcdui.*;
import java.util.Timer;
import java.util.TimerTask;

public class Snooze extends MIDlet implements
        ItemStateListener, CommandListener
{
  private Display display;     // Reference to display object
  private Form fmMain;         // The main form
  private Command cmSnooze;    // Start the timer
  private Command cmReset;     // Reset to current date/time
  private Command cmExit;      // Exit the MIDlet
  private DateField dfSnoozeTime  // How long to snooze
  private int dateIndex;       // Index of DateField on Form
  private Date currentTime;    // Current time
  private Timer tmSnooze;      // The timer
  private SnoozeTimer ttSnooze;    // Called by the timer
  private boolean dateOK = false; // Was user input valid?

  public Snooze()
  {
    display = Display.getDisplay(this);

    // The main form
    fmMain = new Form("When to sound the alarm:");

    // Save today's date
    currentTime = new Date();

    // DateField with todays date as a default
    dfSnoozeTime = new DateField("", DateField.DATE_TIME);
    dfSnoozeTime.setDate(currentTime);
```

(continued)

Example 7.2   (*Continued*)

```
  // All the commands/buttons
  cmSnooze = new Command("Snooze", Command.SCREEN, 1);
  cmReset = new Command("Reset", Command.SCREEN, 1);
  cmExit = new Command("Exit", Command.EXIT, 1);

  // Add to form and listen for events
  dateIndex = fmMain.append(dfSnoozeTime);
  fmMain.addCommand(cmSnooze);
  fmMain.addCommand(cmReset);
  fmMain.addCommand(cmExit);
  fmMain.setCommandListener(this);
  fmMain.setItemStateListener(this);
}

public void startApp ()
{
  display.setCurrent(fmMain);
}

public void pauseApp()
{ }

public void destroyApp(boolean unconditional)
{ }

public void itemStateChanged(Item item)
{
  if (item == dfSnoozeTime)
  {
    // If the user selected date and/or time that is
    // earlier than today, set a flag. We are using
    // getTime() method of Date  class, which returns
    // milliseconds since January 1, 1970
    if (dfSnoozeTime.getDate().getTime() <
              currentTime.getTime())
      dateOK = false;
    else
      dateOK = true;
  }
}
```

(*continued*)

Example 7.2 *(Continued)*

```
public void commandAction(Command c, Displayable s)
{
  if (c == cmSnooze)
  {
    if (dateOK == false)
    {
      Alert al = new Alert("Unable to set alarm",
          "Please choose another date & time.", null, null);
      al.setTimeout(Alert.FOREVER);
      al.setType(AlertType.ERROR);
      display.setCurrent(al);
    }
    else
    {
      // Create a new timer
      tmSnooze = new Timer();
      ttSnooze = new SnoozeTimer();

      // Amount of time to delay
      long amount = dfSnoozeTime.getDate().getTime() -
          currentTime.getTime();
      tmSnooze.schedule(ttSnooze,amount);

      // Remove the commands
      fmMain.removeCommand(cmSnooze);
      fmMain.removeCommand(cmReset);

      // Remove the DateField
      fmMain.delete(dateIndex);

      // Change the Form message
      fmMain.setTitle("Snoozing...");
    }
  }
  else if (c == cmReset)
  {
    // Reset to the current date/time
    dfSnoozeTime.setDate(currentTime = new Date());
  }
  else if (c == cmExit)
  {
    destroyApp(false);
    notifyDestroyed();
  }
}
```

(continued)

Example 7.2 (*Continued*)

```
/*----------------------------------
 * New class - Handle the timer task
 *----------------------------------*/
 private class SnoozeTimer extends TimerTask
 {
   public final void run()
   {
     Alert al = new Alert("Time to wake up!");
     al.setTimeout(Alert.FOREVER);
     al.setType(AlertType.ALARM);
     AlertType.ERROR.playSound(display);
     display.setCurrent(al);

     // Cancel this timer task
     cancel();
   }
 }
}
```

The images shown in Figure 7–4 from the left are the MIDlet main screen, the interface to change the time, and a menu option to either reset the current date/time or start the timer.

Figure 7–4 Set an alarm by specifying the time and choosing the Snooze option to start the timer

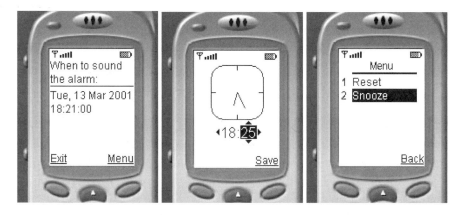

Before we move on, let me ask you this: Why is there is a menu on the display if we never defined any type of menu in the code? The short answer is, the implementation can decide how it wants to present Command objects on the display. To accommodate the limited screen size, the implementation has chosen to place the commands inside a menu. If you need a refresher, head back to Chapter 6 where we introduced event handling.

The DateField component is initialized with the current date and time as returned by the system running the MIDlet.

```
currentTime = new Date();

dfSnoozeTime = new DateField("", DateField.DATE_TIME);
dfSnoozeTime.setDate(currentTime);
...
fmMain.setItemStateListener(this);
```

When you create a new component passing in DateField.DATE_TIME, the user will have the option to change both the date and the time.

The last line above sets up a listener that recognizes events for the DateField component—actually, for any component that is a subclass of Item—that is, contained on fmMain. Once an event is recognized, the method itemStateChanged() will be called.

Before setting the alarm, we need to be sure the alarm time is greater than the current date and time. We do this by comparing the time selected by the user, with the current time we have stored in the variable currentTime.

```
if (dfSnoozeTime.getDate().getTime() <
                          currentTime.getTime())
   dateOK = false;
 else
   dateOK = true;
```

To get the time from the dfSnoozeTime component requires two steps:

1.   Get a reference to a Date object using the method:

   dfSnoozeTime.getDate()

2.   Get the time from the Date object by calling the method:

   dfSnoozeTime.getDate().getTime()

What's interesting about this check is that the method getTime() returns the number of milliseconds since the beginning of time (the beginning of time as far as the computer is concerned—January 1, 1970). With this one call, we cover all our bases and there is no need to compare the year, month, day and time separately.

Once the snooze option (from the menu) has been selected we will be directed to the method commandAction(). First, we must check to see if the date and time selected is valid. We do this by checking the variable dateOK that we set earlier in itemStateChanged(). If not, we will create an Alert to notify the user to enter a different date and time. If everything looks good, we will schedule a timer and determine how long to snooze:

```
// Create a new timer
tmSnooze = new Timer();
ttSnooze = new SnoozeTimer();

// Amount of time to delay
long amount = dfSnoozeTime.getDate().getTime() -
              currentTime.getTime();
tmSnooze.schedule(ttSnooze,amount);
```

Once again, we use the getTime() method to determine how long until the alarm should sound. The amount of time is the difference between the user selected time and the current time (in milliseconds). We will cover all the specifics of the Timer class in Chapter 13.

At the appointed time, the run() method inside the class Snooze-Timer is called. We create a new Alert, set it as the current screen and cancel the timer.

```
public final void run()
{
  Alert al = new Alert("Time to wake up!");
  al.setTimeout(Alert.FOREVER);
  al.setType(AlertType.ALARM);
  AlertType.ERROR.playSound(display);
  display.setCurrent(al);

  // Cancel this timer task
  cancel();
}
```

From the left, Figure 7–5 shows the display when the MIDlet is "snoozing," the Alert screen once the run() method is called, and the Alert shown if the user selects an invalid date and time.

Figure 7–5 The main screen, alarm message, alert dialog

One last point, if you compare the left-most screen shot in Figures 7–4 and 7–5, you'll notice both the DateField and the menu are removed from the display in Figure 7–5. Take a look in commandAction(); after creating the timer you will see the code to remove the commands cmSnooze and cmReset (which effectively removes the menu), delete the DateField component and change the message on the Form to "Snoozing."

Note

Once again, MIDP defines the requirements for a set of classes. It does not specify how to implement the profile. For example, the look and feel of the DateField *component may be completely different from one implementation to the next; however, the functionality provided must always match with the requirements as outlined in the specification.*

Gauge

If you've spent any amount of time on a computer, you've become accustomed to seeing progress meters in many shapes and forms. Familiar examples include a percentage indicator that is displayed when downloading a file

Figure 7–6 Interactive Gauge

or a progress meter shown when installing software. Should you need to provide a similar interface on a mobile device, the Gauge component may be the ticket.

A Gauge has two means of being updated. The first is referred to as interactive mode, where the user makes the changes. The second, for lack of a better term, is a non-interactive mode. It is up to you as the developer to change the values (see Figures 7–6 and 7–7).

Figure 7–7 Non-interactive Gauge

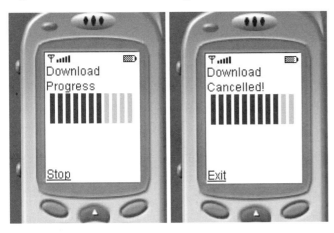

Gauge API

Table 7.6 Gauge Class: javax.microedition.lcdui.Gauge	
Method	*Description*
Constructor	
Gauge(String label, boolean interactive, int maxValue, int initialValue)	Create a new gauge
Methods	
int **getValue**()	Get current value of gauge
void **setValue**(int value)	Set new value for gauge
int **getMaxValue**()	Get maximum allowed gauge value
void **setMaxValue**(int maxValue)	Set maximum allowed gauge value
boolean **isInteractive**()	Is this an interactive gauge?

Example: Interactive Gauge

Following is a MIDlet (Example 7.3) with an interactive Gauge where the user can adjust what will appear to be the sound/volume of the application.

Example 7.3   InteractiveGauge.java

```
import javax.microedition.midlet.*;
import javax.microedition.lcdui.*;

public class InteractiveGauge extends MIDlet implements CommandListener
{
  private Display display;      // Reference to display object
  private Form fmMain;          // The main form
  private Command cmExit;       // Exit the form
  private Gauge gaVolume;       // Volume adjustment

  public InteractiveGauge ()
  {
    display = Display.getDisplay(this);
```

(continued)

Example 7.3 *(Continued)*

```
    // Create the gauge and exit command
    gaVolume = new Gauge("Sound Level", true, 30, 4);
    cmExit = new Command("Exit", Command.EXIT, 1);

    // Create form, add commands, listen for events
    fmMain = new Form("");
    fmMain.addCommand(cmExit);
    fmMain.append(gaVolume);
    fmMain.setCommandListener(this);
  }

  // Called by application manager to start the MIDlet.
  public void startApp()
  {
    display.setCurrent(fmMain);
  }

  public void pauseApp()
  { }

  public void destroyApp(boolean unconditional)
  { }

  public void commandAction(Command c, Displayable s)
  {
    if (c == cmExit)
    {
      destroyApp(false);
      notifyDestroyed();
    }
  }
}
```

In the constructor method we have added a call to create a new Gauge component:

```
    gaVolume = new Gauge("Sound Level", true, 30, 4);
```

We've specified true, to indicate we want an interactive gauge. The maximum value has been set to 30 and we have a starting value of 4. You can see the output in Figure 7–6.

Example: Non-interactive Gauge

Example 7.4 shows how to change the value of a gauge using methods inside the Gauge class. We'll use a Timer to provide our MIDlet with periodic "interruptions," if you will, where we increment the gauge.

Example 7.4   NonInteractiveGauge.java

```java
import javax.microedition.midlet.*;
import javax.microedition.lcdui.*;
import java.util.Timer;
import java.util.TimerTask;

public class NonInteractiveGauge extends MIDlet implements CommandListener
{
    private Display display;            // Reference to display object
    private Form fmMain;                // The main form
    private Command cmExit;             // Exit the form
    private Command cmStop;             // Stop the download
    private Gauge gaProgress;           // Progress indicator
    private Timer tm;                   // The Timer
    private DownloadTimer tt;           // The task to run

    public NonInteractiveGauge ()
    {
        display = Display.getDisplay(this);

        // Create the gauge, exit and stop command
        gaProgress = new Gauge("Download Progress", false, 20, 1);
        cmExit = new Command("Exit", Command.EXIT, 1);
        cmStop = new Command("Stop", Command.STOP, 1);

        // Create form, add commands, listen for events
        fmMain = new Form("");
        fmMain.append(gaProgress);
        fmMain.addCommand(cmStop);
        fmMain.setCommandListener(this);
    }

    // Called by application manager to start the MIDlet.
    public void startApp()
```

(continued)

Example 7.4 *(Continued)*

```
{
  display.setCurrent(fmMain);

  // Create a timer that fires off every 1000 milliseconds
  tm = new Timer();
  tt = new DownloadTimer();
  tm.scheduleAtFixedRate(tt, 0, 1000);
}

public void pauseApp()
{ }

public void destroyApp(boolean unconditional)
{ }

public void commandAction(Command c, Displayable s)
{
  if (c == cmExit)
  {
    destroyApp(false);
    notifyDestroyed();
  }
  else if (c == cmStop)
  {
    tm.cancel();
    fmMain.removeCommand(cmStop);
    fmMain.addCommand(cmExit);
    gaProgress.setLabel("Download Cancelled!");
  }
}

/*----------------------------------
 * New class - Handle the timer task
 *----------------------------------*/
private class DownloadTimer extends TimerTask
{
  public final void run()
  {
    // Is current value of gauge less than the max?
    if (gaProgress.getValue() < gaProgress.getMaxValue())
      gaProgress.setValue(gaProgress.getValue() + 1);
    else
```

(continued)

Example 7.4   (Continued)

```
      {
          // Remove stop command and replace with Exit
          fmMain.removeCommand(cmStop);
          fmMain.addCommand(cmExit);

          // Change the gauge label
          gaProgress.setLabel("Download Complete!");

          // Stop the timer
          cancel();
      }
    }
  }
}
```

If you look inside the constructor, when compared to Example 7.3, you'll notice we've changed the second parameter to `false`, thus requesting a non-interactive gauge:

```
gaProgress = new Gauge("Download Progress", false, 20, 1);
```

The next area of interest is inside `startApp()` where we create the timer. We've chosen a timer that fires off at a fixed rate. Every 1000 milliseconds the run method inside `DownloadTimer()` is called:

```
// Create a timer that fires off every 1000 milliseconds
tm = new Timer();
tt = new DownloadTimer();
tm.scheduleAtFixedRate(tt, 0, 1000);
```

Head down to the code that is called by the timer, `DownloadTimer()`. Our first check is to see if we've reached the maximum value of our gauge. If not, increment the current value of the gauge by one. If we've reached the maximum, remove the Stop button and replace it with an Exit button, change the label on the gauge to tell the user the download is complete and cancel the timer:

```
        if (gaProgress.getValue() < gaProgress.getMaxValue())
           gaProgress.setValue(gaProgress.getValue() + 1);
        else
        {
           // Remove stop command and replace with Exit
           fmMain.removeCommand(cmStop);
           fmMain.addCommand(cmExit);
```

```
    // Change the gauge label
    gaProgress.setLabel("Download Complete!");

    // Stop the timer
    cancel();
}
```

The download gauge is shown in Figure 7–7. The screen shot on the right shows the updated label on the gauge if the user cancels the download.

As with all high-level interface components, the implementation decides how the gauge will look on the screen. Take one last glance at Figures 7–6 and 7–7 and you'll notice this implementation shows two different styles of gauges—a progressive scale and a bar scale—depending on whether or not the gauge is interactive.

StringItem

A `StringItem` displays a static label and text message. A user cannot edit either the label or the text, and as a result, a `StringItem` does not recognize events.

As a developer, once you create a `StringItem`, you can get/set the text message with methods inside the `StringItem` class. If you would like to get/set the label, you can do so using methods inherited from the `Item` class.

StringItem API

Table 7.7 StringItem Class: javax.microedition.lcdui.StringItem	
Method	*Description*
Constructor	
StringItem(String label, String text)	Create a new StringItem
Methods	
String **getText**()	Get current value of the text
void **setText**(String text)	Set new value of the text

Example: Changing the Label and Message Text

The MIDlet that follows (Example 7.5) shows how to change both the label and the text message.

Example 7.5   ChangeLabelText.java

```java
import javax.microedition.midlet.*;
import javax.microedition.lcdui.*;

public class ChangeLabelText extends MIDlet implements CommandListener
{
  private Display display;      // Reference to Display object
  private Form fmMain;          // The main form
  private StringItem siUser;    // The message
  private Command cmNext;       // Next label and message
  private Command cmExit;       // Command to exit the MIDlet

  public ChangeLabelText ()
  {
    display = Display.getDisplay(this);

    // Create text message and commands
    siUser = new StringItem("UserId: ", "johnm");
    cmNext = new Command("Next", Command.SCREEN, 1);
    cmExit = new Command("Exit", Command.EXIT, 1);

    // Create Form, Commands & StringItem, listen for events
    fmMain = new Form("Preferences");
    fmMain.addCommand(cmExit);
    fmMain.addCommand(cmNext);
    fmMain.append(siUser);
    fmMain.setCommandListener(this);
  }

  // Called by application manager to start the MIDlet.
  public void startApp()
  {
    display.setCurrent(fmMain);
  }

  public void pauseApp()
  { }
```

(continued)

Example 7.5 (Continued)

```java
public void destroyApp(boolean unconditional)
{ }

public void commandAction(Command c, Displayable s)
{
  if (c == cmNext)
  {
    // This method is inherited from the Item class
    siUser.setLabel("Account #: ");

    // Change the text
    siUser.setText("731");

    // Remove the Next command
    fmMain.removeCommand(cmNext);
  }
  else if (c == cmExit)
  {
    destroyApp(false);
    notifyDestroyed();
  }
}
}
```

In the constructor we define a StringItem containing a label and a text message. We also add the Command cmNext which will invoke a call to commandAction(), where we change the label and the text. Figure 7–8 shows the output of this example.

Figure 7–8 Changing the label and the text

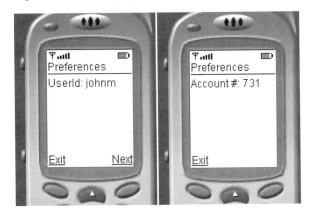

Example: Alternative to StringItem

There is one more option for showing a text message—you can append a `String` directly on a `Form`. Using this option, you have no label as you do when using `StringItem` and updating the text requires a little more work, as we'll see.

If you refer back to the `Form` class, there is a method `append(String str)`, which we will use in our next example to insert a text message on the display:

```
msgIndex = fmMain.append("UserId: johnm");
```

To display the same information as the previous example ("UserId: johnm"), we combine what was previously a separate label and text into one string.

As you walk through the following code (Example 7.6) notice that we save the index of where this string is inserted (into the variable `msgIndex`.) We'll need this index at a later time to retrieve the string.

Example 7.6   StringItemAlternative.java

```
import javax.microedition.midlet.*;
import javax.microedition.lcdui.*;

public class StringItemAlternative extends MIDlet implements
CommandListener
{
  private Display display;  // Reference to Display object
  private Form fmMain;      // The main form
  private Command cmNext;   // Next label and message
  private Command cmExit;   // Command to exit the MIDlet
  private int msgIndex;     // Index of message text on form
  private int count = 0;    // How many times through our loop

  public StringItemAlternative ()
  {
    display = Display.getDisplay(this);

    // Create commands
    cmNext = new Command("Next", Command.SCREEN, 1);
    cmExit = new Command("Exit", Command.EXIT, 1);
```

(continued)

Example 7.6   (Continued)

```
// Create Form, add Command & message, listen for events
fmMain = new Form("Preferences");
fmMain.addCommand(cmExit);
fmMain.addCommand(cmNext);

// Save the index location of this item
msgIndex = fmMain.append("UserId: johnm");

fmMain.setCommandListener(this);
}

// Called by application manager to start the MIDlet.
public void startApp()
{
  display.setCurrent(fmMain);
}

public void pauseApp()
{ }

public void destroyApp(boolean unconditional)
{ }

public void commandAction(Command c, Displayable s)
{
  if (c == cmNext)
  {
    if (count++ == 0)
    {
      //-------------------------------
      // Option # 1
      // First time through this method
      //-------------------------------
      StringItem tmpItem = (StringItem)
              fmMain.get(msgIndex);

      System.out.println("tmpItem.getLabel(): " +
          tmpItem.getLabel());
      System.out.println("tmpItem.getText(): " +
          tmpItem.getText());

      //inherited from Item class
      tmpItem.setLabel("Account #: ");
```

(continued)

Example 7.6   (Continued)

```
            tmpItem.setText("731");
      }
      else
      {
          //--------------------------------
          // Option # 2
          // Second time through this method
          //--------------------------------
          fmMain.set(msgIndex,
              new StringItem("Password: ", "superPants"));

          // Remove the Update command
          fmMain.removeCommand(cmNext);
      }
   }
   else if (c == cmExit)
   {
      destroyApp(false);
      notifyDestroyed();
   }
  }
}
```

Let's look at two ways in which we can change the text message. Both are shown in the method `commandAction()`.

Option I

Get the index of the `String` we previously inserted using `fmMain.get(msgIndex)`. The return value from this call is an `Item`, so we must cast it to a `StringItem` in order to access the class methods.

```
StringItem tmpItem = (StringItem) fmMain.get(msgIndex);
```

I've inserted two `prinltncalls` to take a closer look at the label and the text of `tmpItem` (see Figure 7–9). Notice `getLabel()` returned null and `getText()` returned the original text message we appended to the form.

So, here's what we can surmise, our call:

```
fmMain.append("UserId: johnm");
```

Figure 7-9 StringItem label and text

was essentially translated into:

```
fmMain.append(new StringItem(null, "UserId: johnm"));
```

The last two lines of this code block set the label (which was previously null) and the text message to new values. See Figure 7–10 (center screen shot).

```
tmpItem.setLabel("Account #: ");
tmpItem.setText("731");
```

Option 2

With one line of code, we can replace the original text with a new `Item`. Using the `set()` method of the `Form`, we replace the `Item` located at `msgIndex`:

```
fmMain.set(msgIndex,
      new StringItem("Password: ", "superPants"));
```

Because this is a new `StringItem` we are inserting, we have the option to break this into a label and a message (as above), or simply concatenate both into one string and pass this as the text message:

```
fmMain.set(msgIndex,
      new StringItem(null, "Password: superPants"));
```

The choice as to which you use depends, more than anything, on whether or not you will need to access the individual elements ("password" and "superPants") of the string. If so, save yourself a little work and call `StringItem` with two parameters, one for the label and one for the text.

The output of this option is shown in Figure 7–10 (right-most screen shot).

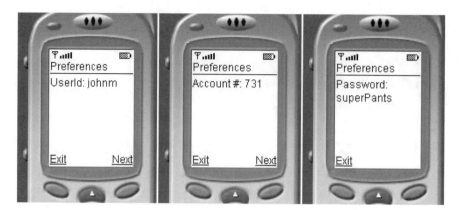

Figure 7–10   Alternatives to display and edit static text

TextField

Start with the picture in your mind of a single-line text-entry box. A common example would be a name or email address field that you might see on any standard online form. Now, add support for multiple lines of text and the option to filter the user input, such as only allowing numbers. At this point, you have a TextField component. If you are familiar with HTML form development, a TextField is similar to both a combination of a text input and text area, with a few twists.

When you create a TextField you can specify an input constraint. A constraint provides restrictions on the data that a user may enter. For example, you may have a TextField that prompts for an email address—the code behind the TextField can help by limiting the characters it accepts to only those that are valid as part of an email address. There are four constraints to support the following specific types of input: email addresses, URLs, numeric values and phone numbers. There is an additional constraint that does no filtering at all, essentially passing all characters through to the TextField. Table 7.8 lists the available constraints.

In addition to constraints, when you create a TextField you specify how many characters you anticipate you will need. As you might guess, there are no guarantees your requested size will be allocated; however, there is a method provided that will return the number of characters the TextField will support once created. Before calling a method that may extend the

Table 7.8	TextField Constraints: javax.microedition.lcdui.TextField
Value	*Description*
CONSTRAINT_MASK	Use this mask when you need to determine the current value of the constraint. See the section entitled "A Look Inside Constraint Values" for more information.
ANY	Allow any character input.
EMAILADDR	Allow only characters that are valid within an email address.
NUMERIC	Allow only numbers. This includes both positive and negative numbers. You do not have an option to request only positive or only negative values.
PASSWORD	Masks all character input to provide privacy when entering data. This constraint can be combined with other constraints to provide masking. See the section entitled "Using the Password Modifier" for more information.
PHONENUMBER	Allow only characters that are valid as part of a phone number. This may be device and/or local specific.
URL	Allow only characters that are valid within a URL.

length of the `TextField`, save yourself some debugging time by checking the size before inserting data.

One last thought to keep in mind: The number of characters allocated for a `TextField` is not necessarily the same as the number of characters that will appear on the display. The implementation will add support for scrolling if the screen cannot display the text in its entirety.

TextField API

Table 7.9	TextField Class: javax.microedition.lcdui.TextField
Method	*Description*
Constructor	
TextField(String label, String text, int maxSize, int constraints)	Create a new TextField

(continued)

Table 7.9 (Continued)	
Methods	
void **delete**(int offset, int length)	Delete characters at a specified offset
void **insert**(String src, int position)	Insert String at a specified offset
void **insert**(char[] data, int offset, int length, int position)	Insert specified characters from array into TextField at a specified offset
void **setChars**(char[] data, int offset, int length)	Set (replace) characters with data from array
void **setString**(String text)	Set (replace) TextField contents from String
int **getChars**(char[] data)	Get contents of TextField into an array
String **getString**()	Get contents of TextField into a String
int **getConstraints**()	Get constraints defined for TextField
void **setConstraints**(int constraints)	Set constraints for TextField
int **getMaxSize**()	Get max number of characters in TextField
int **setMaxSize**(int maxSize)	Set max number of characters in TextField
int **getCaretPosition**()	Get current caret (cursor) position
int **size**()	Number of characters currently in TextField

Example: Processing Text Input with a Character Array

Area codes seem to be in a continual state of change (not unlike the price of a postage stamp). The codes where I live have changed three times in as many years. Let's write a simple application (Example 7.7) to simulate verification of area codes.

First, we'll prompt the user for a phone number. Next, we'll perform a simple lookup for the area code in a table. If the user's area code is found, we'll assume there is a new area code for the phone number entered, and we will update the TextField with the new code. The program has few bells and whistles; however, it does show how to insert and delete characters from a TextField, along with code to search and access a multi-dimensional array.

Example 7.7   VerifyAreaCode.java

```java
import javax.microedition.midlet.*;
import javax.microedition.lcdui.*;

public class VerifyAreaCode extends MIDlet implements CommandListener
{
  private Display display;        // Reference to Display object
  private Form fmMain;            // The main form
  private Command cmTest;         // Next label and message
  private Command cmExit;         // Command to exit the MIDlet
  private TextField tfPhone;      // Phone number
  private String areaCodeTable [][] = {
                  {"512", "912"},  // Old area code, new area code
                  {"717", "917"}};

  public VerifyAreaCode ()
  {
    display = Display.getDisplay(this);

    // Create commands
    cmTest = new Command("Test", Command.SCREEN, 1);
    cmExit = new Command("Exit", Command.EXIT, 1);

    // Textfield for phone number
    tfPhone = new TextField("Phone:", "", 10,
                            TextField.PHONENUMBER);

    // Create Form, add Commands & textfield, listen for events
    fmMain = new Form("Area Codes");
    fmMain.addCommand(cmExit);
    fmMain.addCommand(cmTest);
    fmMain.append(tfPhone);
    fmMain.setCommandListener(this);
  }

  // Called by application manager to start the MIDlet.
  public void startApp()
  {
    display.setCurrent(fmMain);
  }
```

(continued)

Example 7.7 *(Continued)*

```
public void pauseApp()
{ }

public void destroyApp(boolean unconditional)
{ }

public void commandAction(Command c, Displayable s)
{
  if (c == cmTest)
  {
    if (tfPhone.size() == 10)
    {
      char buffer[] = new char[10];

      // Get phone number into byte array
      tfPhone.getChars(buffer);

      // Call method to check the area code table.
      // Create a new StringItem to display,
      // passing in 'null' as the StringItem
      StringItem tmp = new StringItem(null, ("The area code " +
              (areaCodeLookup(buffer) ? "has" : "has not") +
              " been updated."));

      // Place at the end of the form
      if (fmMain.size() == 1)  // Only tfPhone on form
        fmMain.append(tmp);
      else                     // Replace previous StringItem
        fmMain.set(1, tmp);
    }
  }
  else if (c == cmExit)
  {
    destroyApp(false);
    notifyDestroyed();
  }
}

/*----------------------------------------------------
 * Compare the area code the user entered with the
 * area code table. If a match is found, replace
 * the user's code with the new code from the table
 *----------------------------------------------------*/
```

(continued)

Example 7.7   *(Continued)*

```
private boolean areaCodeLookup(char [] buffer)
{
  // Get the area code (only) from the users entry
  String str = new String(buffer, 0, 3);

  for (int x = 0; x < areaCodeTable.length; x++)
  {
    // If we find a match in the table
    if (str.equals(areaCodeTable[x][0]))
    {
      // Delete the area code
      tfPhone.delete(0, 3);

      // Insert the new area code
      tfPhone.insert(areaCodeTable[x][1].toCharArray(),0,3,0);
      return true;
    }
  }
  return false;
}
}
```

The interesting code begins inside commandAction(), starting with the call to getChars() to place the phone number into a byte array.

```
tfPhone.getChars(buffer);
StringItem tmp = new StringItem(null, ("The area code " +
        (areaCodeLookup(buffer) ? "has" : "has not") +
                        " been updated."));
```

If you look carefully at the line that allocates a new StringItem, you will see a reference to the method areaCodeLookup(). Let's jump into that method.

First, we need to extract the area code and store it inside a String.

```
// Get the area code (only) from the users entry
String str = new String(buffer, 0, 3);
```

Now, loop through the area code table looking for a match between the area code the user entered and those in the table. If a match is found, using the delete() method of the TextField, remove three characters, starting at position zero:

```
tfPhone.delete(0, 3);
```

At this point we have a phone number with no area code. The next line will insert three characters into tfPhone, at the beginning, using characters from the area code table. Pay close attention to the values of the offsets in both the tfPhone and the area code table. It is also worth mentioning that we must convert the desired String from the area code table into a character array, as this is the data type expected by the insert() method.

```
tfPhone.insert(areaCodeTable[x][1].toCharArray(), 0, 3, 0);
```

Figures 7–11 and 7–12 show the output. From the left the figure demonstrates entering the phone number, the number before pressing the Test key and the updated phone number with new area code.

Using the Password Modifier

If at any point you need to mask characters on the screen, (e.g., when entering a password), you can apply the PASSWORD modifier to a constraint. Currently, this is the only modifier available.

Figure 7–11   From left: Form containing an empty TextField; the TextField data entry screen

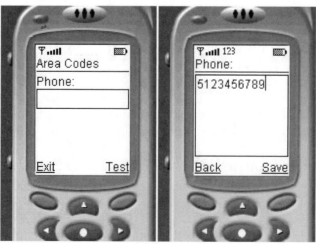

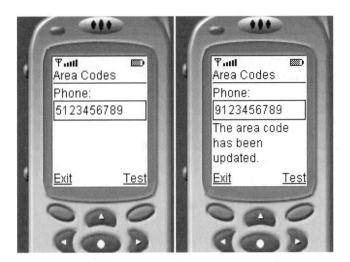

Figure 7-12 From left: Form and TextField with updated contents; the TextField after validating the area code

Here is a simple `TextField` declaration that will accept any character and will mask the input as each character is entered.

```
tfPwd = new TextField("Password:", "", 10,
              TextField.ANY | TextField.PASSWORD);
```

Figure 7–13 shows the how the password modifier looks on the display.

Figure 7-13 Password modifer; characters are masked as they are entered

Mask Character

Unfortunately, you cannot choose the character you would like displayed for masking. The good news is, it's a safe assumption that most devices will choose the "*" character, which most users recognize as a means of hiding data input.

A Look Inside Constraint Values

To help you maintain your sanity as you write code using constraints, let's look a little deeper at the values assigned to each constraint. Begin by skimming over Table 7.10.

Table 7.10   Constraints Values

Constraint	Decimal/Hex Value	Binary Value
ANY	0	00000000 00000000 00000000
EMAILADDR	1	00000000 00000000 00000001
NUMERIC	2	00000000 00000000 00000010
PHONENUMBER	3	00000000 00000000 00000011
URL	4	00000000 00000000 00000100
PASSWORD (modifier)	0x10000	00000001 00000000 00000000
CONSTRAINT_MASK	0xFFFF	00000000 **11111111 11111111**

Whether intentional or not in the design of the specification, you cannot combine constraints (PASSWORD is a special case, as I'll point out). I realize this is not realistic. However, for the sake of argument, let's combine EMAILADDR and NUMERIC. If you were to combine these as part of a TextField declaration, it would look similar to the following:

```
TextField tfEmail = new TextField("Email:", "", 10,
                TextField.EMAILADDR | TextField.NUMERIC);
```

Here is how we combine the fields using a logical OR operation:

```
TextField.EMAILADDR     00000000 00000000 00000001
TextField.NUMERIC       00000000 00000000 00000010
                        -----------------------------
   logical OR           00000000 00000000 00000011
```

Unfortunately, if you look in the Table 7.10 you'll see that 00000011 is the value for PHONENUMBER! Most definitely, this is not what we had in mind.

Now, let's combine, PASSWORD with EMAILADDR and see what we get

```
TextField.EMAILADDR     00000000 00000000 00000001
TextField.PASSWORD      00000001 00000000 00000000
                        -----------------------------
   logical OR           00000001 00000000 00000001
```

A reasonable assumption would be that the first (right-most) 16 bits are reserved for constraints. Because PASSWORD is outside the range of these values, we don't have a collision with another constraint.

Note

PASSWORD *is a modifier that is to be used along with other constraints. With the exception of* PASSWORD, *you cannot combine constraints!*

To drag this through the mud just a little further, let's see how the constraint mask works. This mask was created to work in conjunction with the method getConstraints(). As we'll show below, the reason for the mask is to remove the PASSWORD modifier. When you need to know the value of the constraint for a TextField, you call this method and perform a logical *AND* operation as follows:

```
TextField.getConstraints() & TextField.CONSTRAINT_MASK
```

This will return an integer that represents the current constraint setting. For example, here is a declaration specifying the constraint ANY along with the modifier PASSWORD:

```
TextField tfPwd = new TextField("Password:", "", 10,
                TextField.ANY | TextField.PASSWORD);
```

Before we move on, lets look at the results of combining the constraint along with the modifier (which will reveal what is passed to the constructor above):

```
TextField.ANY          00000000 00000000 00000000
TextField.PASSWORD     00000001 00000000 00000000
                       -------------------------
       constraint value   00000001 00000000 00000000
```

If at some point we would like to know the constraint setting for `tfPwd`, we can call the method `getConstraints()`. Here is what the method will return:

```
tfPwd.getConstraints()    00000001 00000000 00000000
```

In decimal that is 65536, which is a value nowhere to be found in the Table 7.10. To get the value we are looking for, we need to mask off the modifier:

```
tfPwd.getConstraints() & TextField.CONSTRAINT_MASK
```

which looks as follows:

```
       tfPwd.getConstraints()    00000001 00000000 00000000
TextField.CONSTRAINT_MASK     00000000 11111111 11111111
                              ----------------------------
       logical AND            00000000 00000000 00000000
```

Ah, that's better. We can now look up the value of 0 (zero) in the table and see that this `TextField` is using the `ANY` constraint.

If you would like to check for the `PASSWORD` modifier specifically, you could insert something along the lines of:

```
if ((tfPwd.getConstraints() & TextField.PASSWORD) != 0)
    System.out.println("Password modifier applied");
```

No doubt constraints can be quite helpful for filtering input. However, before you jump in, make sure you understand what functionality they provide, and equally important, their limitations.

Validating User Input

Although `TextField` supports input constraints, it is by no means a foolproof way to validate user input. For example, using the `NUMERIC` constraint will most definitely limit the input to numbers (that's the good news). The bad news is, there is no constraint to specify only positive or only negative values. If your application requires one or the other, you will need to add code to check for this once you get the value from the `TextField`.

Choice and ChoiceGroup

Before we can learn about the `ChoiceGroup`, we need to introduce the `Choice` interface. If you recall from Chapter 6, an interface is a class that defines a set of methods. It is up to the classes that "implement" the interface to provide the body of each method.

The `Choice` interface defines methods that all have to do with manipulating various types of predefined selections. There are two classes provided in the MIDP that implement the `Choice` interface:

```
public class ChoiceGroup extends Item implements Choice {
...
}

public class List extends Screen implements Choice {
...
}
```

A `ChoiceGroup` comes in two types: multiple and exclusive (think checkboxes and radio groups, respectively; see Table 7.12). Screen shots of both `ChoiceGroups` using Sun's reference implementation of MIDP are shown in Figure 7–14.

When we get to Chapter 8, we cover the specifics of the `List` component.

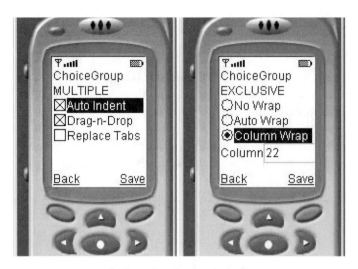

Figure 7-14 Multiple and exclusive ChoiceGroups

ChoiceGroup API

Table 7.11 ChoiceGroup Class: javax.microedition.lcdui.ChoiceGroup	
Method	*Description*
Constructor	
ChoiceGroup(String label, int choiceType)	Create a ChoiceGroup with no elements
ChoiceGroup(String label, int choiceType, String[] stringElements, Image imageElements)	Create a ChoiceGroup and populate with data from the arrays
Methods	
int **append**(String stringPart, Image imagePart)	Add element to end
void **delete**(int elementNum)	Delete element
void **insert**(int elementNum, String stringElement, Image imageElement)	Insert element
void **set**(int elementNum, String stringPart, Image imagePart)	Set (replace) element
String **getString**(int elementNum)	Get text (String) associated with element
Image **getImage**(int elementNum)	Get Image associated with element

(continued)

Table 7.11	(Continued)
int **getSelectedIndex**()	Get the index of the selected element
void **setSelectedIndex**(int elementNum, boolean selected)	MULTIPLE Choice Group-set element to specified boolean value
	EXCLUSIVE Choice Group-set element to true
	IMPLICIT-invalid type for Choice Group
int **getSelectedFlags**(boolean[] selectedArray_return)	Store selection status in an array
void **setSelectedFlags**(boolean[] selectedArray)	Set selection status from an array
boolean **isSelected**(int elementNum)	Is the element currently selected?
int **size**()	Number of elements

The `ChoiceGroup` component implements the `Choice` interface. There are three pre-defined choice types, two of which are available with `ChoiceGroup` (see Table 7.12).

Event Handling for ChoiceGroup

There are two ways in which to detect the status of selections within a ChoiceGroup.

1. `ItemStateListener`

   When a user changes a value in a `ChoiceGroup`, if the `Form` containing the `ChoiceGroup` has registered an `ItemState-Listener`, the method `itemStateChanged()` will be

Table 7.12	ChoiceTypes: javax.microedition.lcdui.Choice
Value	*Description*
EXCLUSIVE	Only one selection available at any time
MULTIPLE	Zero or more selections available at any time
IMPLICIT	Not available for ChoiceGroup (see List component in Chapter 8)

called. Inside this method you can inquire as to which Choice-Group element(s) are selected using either getSelected Flags() or getSelectedIndex().

Should it be helpful as part of your application logic, this functionality allows you to track what actions a user is performing on a ChoiceGroup. This may be helpful when a choice selected affects other information on the display.

For example, in Figure 7–14 notice the "Column Wrap" option. Below this is a TextField component that allows for a user to specify the column in which to generate a text wrap. With this type of event handling, you could add or remove the Text-Field based on whether or not "Column Wrap" is selected.

2. CommandListener

If there is a CommandListener registered with the Form that contains the ChoiceGroup, you can add a Command(s) to signal your program to query the selection status. This signal will arrive as a call to the method commandAction().

For example, in Figure 7–14 if a user selected the "Save" command you could make note of the preferences selected and write them to persistent storage for later recall.

Example: Exclusive Choice

Examples 7.8 and 7.9 will each construct a ChoiceGroup using the append() method. When we learn about the Image class in the next section, you'll see how to create a ChoiceGroup using an array of String and Image objects.

Our first example will be that of an exclusive choice, where only one option can be selected at any time. It is required by the device implementation to always have one item selected. If you don't specify which item to select when creating the list, the implementation will decide, most likely selecting the first element.

If you look inside the constructor you'll see the how to declare an exclusive ChoiceGroup:

```
cgEmail = new ChoiceGroup("Email Options", Choice.EXCLUSIVE);
```

A few lines down, we append entries into the ChoiceGroup. We are also making note of the index of the "reply" entry:

```
replyIndex = cgEmail.append("Reply", null);
```

Example 7.8   ExclusiveChoiceGroup.java

```java
import javax.microedition.midlet.*;
import javax.microedition.lcdui.*;

public class ExclusiveChoiceGroup extends MIDlet implements CommandListener
{
  private Display display;        // Reference to display object
  private Form fmMain;            // The main form
  private Command cmExit;         // A Command to exit the MIDlet
  private Command cmView;         // View the choice selected
  private ChoiceGroup cgEmail;    // Choice group
  private int replyIndex;         // Index of "reply" in choice group
  private int choiceGroupIndex;   // Index of choice group on form

  public ExclusiveChoiceGroup ()
  {
    display = Display.getDisplay(this);

    // Create an exclusive (radio) choice group
    cgEmail = new ChoiceGroup("Email Options", Choice.EXCLUSIVE);

    // Append options, with no associated images
    cgEmail.append("Read", null);
    replyIndex = cgEmail.append("Reply", null);
    cgEmail.append("Forward", null);
    cgEmail.append("Delete", null);

    // Set "reply" as the default/selected option
    cgEmail.setSelectedIndex(replyIndex, true);

    cmExit = new Command("Exit", Command.EXIT, 1);
    cmView = new Command("View", Command.SCREEN,2);

    // Create Form, add components, listen for events
    fmMain = new Form("");
    choiceGroupIndex = fmMain.append(cgEmail);
    fmMain.addCommand(cmExit);
    fmMain.addCommand(cmView);
    fmMain.setCommandListener(this);
  }

  // Called by application manager to start the MIDlet.
  public void startApp()
  {
```

(continued)

Example 7.8   *(Continued)*

```
   display.setCurrent(fmMain);
 }

 public void pauseApp()
 { }

 public void destroyApp(boolean unconditional)
 { }

 public void commandAction(Command c, Displayable s)
 {
   if (c == cmView)
   {
     // Build a string showing which option was selected
     StringItem siMessage = new StringItem("You selected: ",
             cgEmail.getString(cgEmail.getSelectedIndex()));
     fmMain.append(siMessage);

     // Delete the choice group & view button
     fmMain.delete(choiceGroupIndex);
     fmMain.removeCommand(cmView);
   }
   else if (c == cmExit)
   {
     destroyApp(false);
     notifyDestroyed();
   }
 }
}
```

We'll use this index to pre-select an entry in the `ChoiceGroup`. Keep in mind, if you do not specify which entry to show as selected, the device implementation will decide for you.

```
   cgEmail.setSelectedIndex(replyIndex, true);
```

Once the user has selected an entry and pressed the "View" command, we display a message showing which entry they chose. Inside `command-Action()` we will create a new `StringItem` to display the message:

```
StringItem siMessage = new StringItem("You selected: ",
    cgEmail.getString(cgEmail.getSelectedIndex()));
```

The label for the `StringItem` is "You selected". The text message is created by nesting two `ChoiceGroup` method calls inside `StringItem`

- `cgEmail.getSelectedIndex()` returns the integer value of the currently selected entry. This value is passed as a parameter to the next method.
- `cgEmail.getString()` returns a `String` object of the item selected.

The end result of these two calls is a text string that shows which option was chosen. Before leaving `commandAction()` we'll remove the `ChoiceGroup` and "View" `Command` from the display. Here is the output for this example:

Figure 7-15   On the left, "Reply" is the default selection. In the middle, choose "Delete" and press the "View" command. The result is shown on the right.

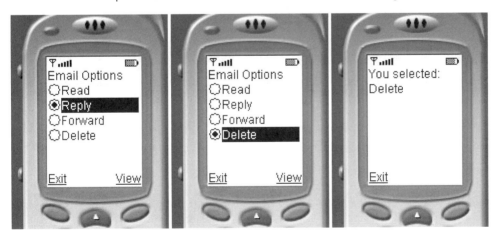

Example: Multiple Choice

Often times, having a single selection is not sufficient. For example, when a user is setting preferences, you may like to present a list of features, and the user simply places a checkmark by each feature they would like to enable.

You can very easily transform a ChoiceGroup into a multi-selection list, as we'll see in the next example. We'll also include the following:

- A "select all" feature. The result is the same as if the user clicked each option individually to enable it.
- An option to print to the console the selection status of each item in the ChoiceGroup.

Example 7.9   MultipleChoiceGroup.java

```java
import javax.microedition.midlet.*;
import javax.microedition.lcdui.*;

public class MultipleChoiceGroup extends MIDlet implements
                    ItemStateListener, CommandListener
{
  private Display display;            // Reference to display object
  private Form fmMain;                // The main form
  private Command cmExit;             // A Command to exit the MIDlet
  private Command cmView;             // View the choice selected
  private int selectAllIndex;         // Index of the "Select All" option
  private ChoiceGroup cgPrefs;        // Choice Group of preferences

  private int choiceGroupIndex;       // Index of choice group on form

  public MultipleChoiceGroup ()
  {
    display = Display.getDisplay(this);

    // Create a multiple choice group
    cgPrefs = new ChoiceGroup("Preferences", Choice.MULTIPLE);

    // Append options, with no associated images
    cgPrefs.append("Auto Indent", null);
    cgPrefs.append("Replace Tabs", null);
    cgPrefs.append("Wrap Text", null);
    selectAllIndex = cgPrefs.append("Select All", null);

    cmExit = new Command("Exit", Command.EXIT, 1);
    cmView = new Command("View", Command.SCREEN,2);
```

(continued)

Example 7.9   *(Continued)*

```
  // Create Form, add components, listen for events
  fmMain = new Form("");
  choiceGroupIndex = fmMain.append(cgPrefs);
  fmMain.addCommand(cmExit);
  fmMain.addCommand(cmView);
  fmMain.setCommandListener(this);
  fmMain.setItemStateListener(this);
}

public void startApp()
{
  display.setCurrent(fmMain);
}

public void pauseApp()
{ }

public void destroyApp(boolean unconditional)
{ }

public void commandAction(Command c, Displayable s)
{
  if (c == cmView)
  {
    boolean selected[] = new boolean[cgPrefs.size()];

    // Fill array indicating whether each element is checked
    cgPrefs.getSelectedFlags(selected);

    for (int i = 0; i < cgPrefs.size(); i++)
      System.out.println(cgPrefs.getString(i) +
              (selected[i] ? ": selected" : ": not selected"));

  }
  else if (c == cmExit)
  {
    destroyApp(false);
    notifyDestroyed();
  }
}

public void itemStateChanged(Item item)
{
```

(continued)

Example 7.9   (*Continued*)

```
if (item == cgPrefs)
{
  // Is "Select all" option checked ?
  if (cgPrefs.isSelected(selectAllIndex))
  {
    // Set all checkboxes to true
    for (int i = 0; i < cgPrefs.size() - 1; i++)
      cgPrefs.setSelectedIndex(i, true);

    // Remove the check by "Select All"
    cgPrefs.setSelectedIndex(selectAllIndex, false);
  }
}
}
}
```

Figure 7–16   Multiple ChoiceGroup. On the left, one element selected; on the right, the result of choosing "Select All."

Changing a `ChoiceGroup` from exclusive (single-choice/radio group) to multiple is nearly effortless. Merely change the "type" parameter sent to the `ChoiceGroup` constructor:

```
cgPrefs = new ChoiceGroup("Preferences", Choice.MULTIPLE);
```

Our "select all" feature will be carried out when the user selects the last element in the `ChoiceGroup` (see Figure 7–16). To identify this element, we need to save the index of where this element was inserted in the `ChoiceGroup`:

```
selectAllIndex = cgPrefs.append("Select All", null);
```

As we learned earlier, once we've added an `ItemStateListener` to a `Form`, any time a change is made to an `Item` (`DateField`, `Gauge`, `ChoiceGroup` and `TextField`) the method `itemStateChanged()` will be called. Here's how we create the "listener":

```
fmMain.setItemStateListener(this);
```

Note

When using `ItemStateListener`, the device implementation will decide when to call the method `itemStateChanged()`. It is not required that this method be called on every change.

Sun's implementation of MIDP (version 1.0) does call `itemState Changed()` each time you select/unselect a `ChoiceGroup` element. However, for a `DateField`, `itemStateChanged()` is only called once you leave the `DateField` edit screen.

Inside `itemStateChanged()` we check to see if `selectAllIndex` has been chosen by the user, and if so, we will loop through the entire `ChoiceGroup` setting the selected status to `true` (selected) for each other element.

To keep the display interface consistent, I've also chosen to reset the "select all" element to `false` when leaving `itemStateChanged()`. If you think about this for a moment, it makes sense. If I were to leave it checked, and a user were to "unselect" a different element(s) in the `ChoiceGroup`, you would have to click the "select all" option twice (once to turn it off, another to turn it back on) to reset all elements to `true` (selected) again.

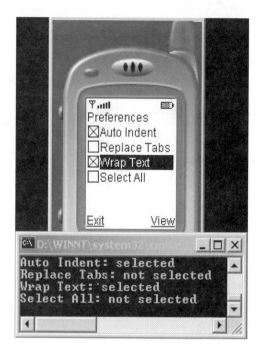

Figure 7–17   Clicking the View command. The console shows the selection status of each element in the Choice Group.

```
if (cgPrefs.isSelected(selectAllIndex))
{
  // Set all checkboxes to true
  for (int i = 0; i < cgPrefs.size() - 1; i++)
    cgPrefs.setSelectedIndex(i, true);

  // Remove the check by "Select All"
  cgPrefs.setSelectedIndex(selectAllIndex, false);
}
```

Image and ImageItem

The `ImageItem` class allows you to specify how you would like an image displayed on a Form—for example, centered horizontally, to the left or to the right (see Figures 7–18 and 7–19). However, your preference is not cast in stone. It is still up to the device implementation to decide where the image will actually appear. When you consider the range of devices that may implement the MID Profile, this flexibility, from an implementation point of view, makes sense.

Before going any further with ImageItem, we need to introduce the Image class. An image on a mobile device can come in two flavors:

- Immutable: As the name implies, once you create this type of image, it cannot be changed. In most cases, you will create an immutable image from a resource, such as a file, or content stored in a data structure, such as a byte array. You can also convert a mutable image to immutable.

  Immutable images can be placed on a Form (Figure 7–22), shown alongside each element of a ChoiceGroup or List (Figure 7–21), or displayed as part of an Alert component (Figure 8–16).

- Mutable: These image objects provide the ultimate in flexibility. When you create this type of image, you are doing nothing more than setting aside a chunk of memory that you will draw into, at some point, to create the image. An immutable image becomes visible when you specifically request it to be drawn to the display (e.g., using the paint() method as part of the Canvas class). We will learn more about mutable images in Chapter 9.

Table 7.13 lists the methods for managing an Image. Table 7.15 lists the methods of the ImageItem class.

Image API

Table 7.13 Image Class: javax.microedition.lcdui.Image	
Method	*Description*
Create an Image[1]	
static Image **createImage**(String name)	Create immutable image from resource
static Image **createImage**(Image source)	Create immutable image from existing Image
static Image **createImage**(byte[] imageData, int imageOffset, int imageLength)	Create immutable image from array data
static Image **createImage**(int width, int height)	Create mutable image

(continued)

Table 7.13	(Continued)

Methods

Graphics **getGraphics**()	Get reference to Graphics object for *mutable* image
int **getHeight**()	Get the height of Image
int **getWidth**()	Get the width of Image
boolean **isMutable**()	Determine if image is mutable

[1]Constructor is not used to create an Image.

Specifying Image Layout

If you would like to specify a preference as far as how an `Image` will be displayed (left, right, center, etc.), this is done through the `ImageItem` class. See Table 7.14 for a list of the various layouts available. The following code creates an image and appends it to a form requesting that the image be centered in the display.

```
// Create an image
Image im = Image.createImage("/someimage.png");

// Append to a form with the specified layout
fmMain.append(new ImageItem(null, im,
                ImageItem.LAYOUT_CENTER, null));
```

Table 7.14	ImageItem Layouts: javax.microedition.lcdui.Image

Value	*Description*
LAYOUT_DEFAULT	Use the default layout of the device implementation.
LAYOUT_LEFT	The image should appear on the left.
LAYOUT_RIGHT	The image should appear on the right.
LAYOUT_CENTER	Center the image horizontally.
LAYOUT_NEWLINE_BEFORE	Insert a newline before the image is drawn. This assures that previous text/images will appear above the image (not sharing the same horizontal space).
LAYOUT_NEWLINE_AFTER	Insert a newline after the image is drawn. Subsequent text/images will appear below the image.

ImageItem API

Method	Description
Constructor	
ImageItem(String label, Image img, int layout, String altText)	Create an ImageItem
Methods	
Image **getImage**()	Get Image associated with ImageItem
void **setImage**(Image img)	Set Image to be associated with ImageItem
int **getLayout**()	Get the current layout directives
void **setLayout**(int layout)	Set new layout directive
String **getAltText**()	Get alternate text to display if image cannot be shown on the device
void **setAltText**(String text)	Set alternate text to display if image cannot be shown on the device

Table 7.15 ImageItem Class: javax.microedition.lcdui.ImageItem

A Look Inside Layout Directives

Take a moment to review the layout directives in Table 7.16.

Table 7.16 Layout Directives

Directive	Decimal/ Hex Value	Binary Value
LAYOUT_DEFAULT	0	00000000 00000000
LAYOUT_LEFT	1	00000000 00000001
LAYOUT_RIGHT	2	00000000 00000010
LAYOUT_CENTER	3	00000000 00000011
LAYOUT_NEWLINE_BEFORE	0x100	00000001 00000000
LAYOUT_NEWLINE_AFTER	0x200	00000010 00000000

It may not be obvious at first glance; however, it's important to understand that the first four directives were not intended to be combined (with each other). Although a bit contrived, here is an example combining LAYOUT_RIGHT with LAYOUT_CENTER:

```
ImageItem.LAYOUT_RIGHT         00000000 00000010
ImageItem.LAYOUT_CENTER        00000000 00000011
                               ------------------
logical OR                     00000000 00000011
```

You've gained nothing by combining these directives. In fact, you are left with a directive equaling one of the original values, LAYOUT_CENTER.

On the other hand, the last two directives are specifically intended to be used along with other directives. For example:

```
ImageItem.LAYOUT_CENTER           00000000 00000011
ImageItem.LAYOUT_NEWLINE_BEFORE   00000001 00000000
                                  ------------------
logical OR                        00000001 00000011
```

Notice that the result is a unique value. That's a good thing. With this unique value the MIDP implementation can mask off the upper or lower eight bits and determine what directives were used to create the current value. For instance:

```
Result from above         00000001 00000011
Mask off upper 8 bits     11111111 00000000
                          ------------------
logical AND               00000001 00000000
```

The result tells us the original request was a directive combined with LAYOUT_NEWLINE_BEFORE. Masking the other side:

```
Result from above         00000001 00000011
Mask off lower 8 bits     00000000 11111111
                          ------------------
logical AND               00000000 00000011
```

Referring back to Table 7.16, we now know the entire directive that was originally requested—LAYOUT_CENTER combined with LAYOUT_NEW-LINE_BEFORE.

This is important for two reasons. First, the MIDP implementation on a device needs to be able to correctly determine what directives you requested. Second, when you call the method ImageItem.getLayout(), you will be returned an integer value that is a combination of the directives currently assigned to the object. You will need to pull apart the integer value, by masking off bits, to determine what directives were applied when creating the ImageItem.

We can take this one step further:

```
ImageItem.LAYOUT_CENTER           00000000 00000011
ImageItem.LAYOUT_NEWLINE_BEFORE   00000001 00000000
ImageItem.LAYOUT_NEWLINE_AFTER    00000010 00000000
                                  ------------------
   logical OR                     00000011 00000011
```

Once again, we still have a unique value. The implementation can determine (by masking off bits) that we have requested a newline before drawing the image, as well as a newline after drawing the image.

Example: Immutable Image from a File

Example 7.10 shows how to create an Image from a file resource (a PNG file stored in a JAR file) and uses ImageItem to demonstrate several placement directives.

Example 7.10   ImmutableImageFromFile.java

```java
import javax.microedition.midlet.*;
import javax.microedition.lcdui.*;

public class ImmutableImageFromFile extends MIDlet  implements CommandListener
{
  private Display display;      // Reference to Display object
  private Form fmMain;          // The main form
  private Command cmExit;       // Command to exit the MIDlet

  public ImmutableImageFromFile()
  {
    display = Display.getDisplay(this);

    cmExit = new Command("Exit", Command.EXIT, 1);
    fmMain = new Form("");
    fmMain.addCommand(cmExit);
    fmMain.setCommandListener(this);
```

(continued)

Example 7.10   (Continued)

```
try
{
  // Read the appropriate image based on color support
  Image im = Image.createImage((display.isColor()) ?
              "/image_color.png":"/image_bw.png");

  // Code Block A
  fmMain.append("A1");
  fmMain.append(new ImageItem(null, im,
              ImageItem.LAYOUT_NEWLINE_BEFORE|
              ImageItem.LAYOUT_CENTER|
              ImageItem.LAYOUT_NEWLINE_AFTER, null));
  fmMain.append("A2");

  // Code Block B
  // fmMain.append("B1");
  // fmMain.append(new ImageItem(null, im,
  //             ImageItem.LAYOUT_NEWLINE_BEFORE |
  //             ImageItem.LAYOUT_LEFT|
  //             ImageItem.LAYOUT_NEWLINE_AFTER, null));
  // fmMain.append("B2");

  // Code Block C
  // fmMain.append("C1");
  // fmMain.append(new ImageItem(null, im,
  //             ImageItem.LAYOUT_NEWLINE_BEFORE |
  //             ImageItem.LAYOUT_RIGHT|
  //             ImageItem.LAYOUT_NEWLINE_AFTER, null));
  // fmMain.append("C2");

  // Code Block D
  // fmMain.append("D1");
  // fmMain.append(im);
  // fmMain.append("D2");
  //
  //
  //

  // View the layout directives
  //    System.out.println("Layout Directives:" +
  //    ((ImageItem)fmMain.get(1)).getLayout());
```

(continued)

Example 7.10 *(Continued)*

```
      display.setCurrent(fmMain);
    }
    catch (java.io.IOException e)
    {
      System.err.println("Unable to locate or read .png file");
    }
  }

  public void startApp()
  {
    display.setCurrent(fmMain);
  }

  public void pauseApp()
  {
  }

  public void destroyApp(boolean unconditional)
  {
  }

  public void commandAction(Command c, Displayable s)
  {
    if (c == cmExit)
    {
      destroyApp(false);
      notifyDestroyed();
    }
  }
}
```

I have created four code blocks inside the constructor method, the first three defining a unique combination of directives the last, no directive. To see the output of each block, you will need to run the MIDlet four times, once for each block of code. As it is shown in Example 7.9, Code Block A will be compiled and run; all the remaining blocks are commented out.

Before we look at the output, let's see how to read an image from a resource.

```
// Read the appropriate image based on color support
    Image im = Image.createImage((display.isColor()) ?
              "/image_color.png":"/image_bw.png");
```

```
fmMain.append("A1");
fmMain.append(new ImageItem(null, im,
             ImageItem.LAYOUT_NEWLINE_BEFORE|
             ImageItem.LAYOUT_CENTER|
             ImageItem.LAYOUT_NEWLINE_AFTER, null));
fmMain.append("A2");
```

I have two PNG image files that I created: image_color.png and image_bw.png. We create an `Image` object using the appropriate file, based on the color support of the device. Next, we append a text string, followed by the image (with various layout directives), followed by another text string. The reason for the text strings will be apparent as you run each code block. You'll see how the directives affect the image placement.

Figures 7–18 and 7–19 show how the display changes based on the layout directives specified.

Example: Reading and Displaying a File

Although reading the contents of a file has little to do with image processing, there is some thought behind why this topic is placed here.

Figure 7–18 Image layout: Code Block A and B.
Left screenshot: LAYOUT_NEWLINE_BEFORE | LAYOUT_CENTER | LAYOUT_NEWLINE_AFTER.
Right screenshot: LAYOUT_NEWLINE_BEFORE | LAYOUT_LEFT | LAYOUT_NEWLINE_AFTER

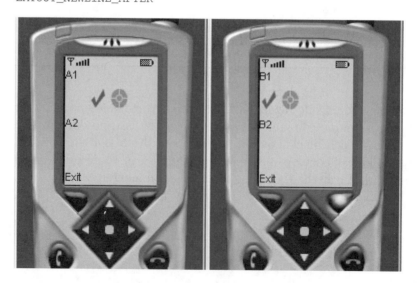

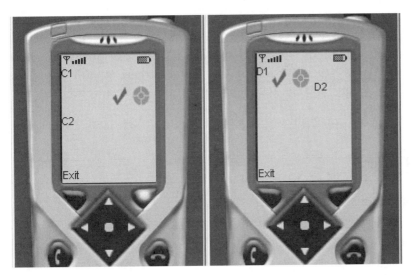

Figure 7-19 Image layout using Code Block C and D.
Left screenshot: LAYOUT_NEWLINE_BEFORE | LAYOUT_RIGHT |
LAYOUT_NEWLINE_AFTER.
Right screenshot: No Directives

In the previous example we created an Image object from a file. An obvious question at the time would have been, how does a MIDlet locate the file? The answer lies with the class loader. The loader knows how to search and access resources inside the MIDlet Suite. It stands to reason if the loader can find resources, our MIDlets should be able to as well. And yes, this is true. To show how this is accomplished, the next example will read and display the contents of a file resource.

For our example, let's assume we want to store help information in a text file. The benefit over this approach, versus hard-coding the text in the application, is that if the help text ever changes, we simply need to update the MIDlet Suite (JAR file) with the new help file.

Up to this point, I've still avoided the question, how do we access a resource? We can obtain a reference to the input stream of a resource with following code:

```
InputStream is = getClass().getResourceAsStream("help.txt");
```

Although accessing the resource is quite simple, explaining how this works is not as straightforward. During execution of your MIDlet, for each object loaded, there is runtime information stored. One reason this is necessary is for the JVM to identify the methods associated with an object. You can access this same runtime information using the Java.lang.Object.

getClass(). The end result of this call is an object of the class Class (no, that's not a typo, there is a class called Class).

One of the methods available inside Class is getResource AsStream(). This method returns an input stream to the resource requested. From here, you can read the contents of the stream and process it however you see fit.

Let's look at Example 7.11.

Example 7.11   ReadDisplayFile.java

```java
import javax.microedition.midlet.*;
import javax.microedition.lcdui.*;
import java.io.*;

public class ReadDisplayFile extends MIDlet implements CommandListener
{
  private Display display;    // Reference to Display object
  private Form fmMain;        // Main form
  private Command cmHelp;     // Command to show a help file
  private Command cmExit;     // Command to exit the MIDlet
  private Alert alHelp;       // Alert to display help file text

  public ReadDisplayFile ()
  {
    display = Display.getDisplay(this);

    cmHelp = new Command("Help", Command.SCREEN, 1);
    cmExit = new Command("Exit", Command.EXIT, 1);

    fmMain = new Form("Read File");
    fmMain.addCommand(cmExit);
    fmMain.addCommand(cmHelp);
    fmMain.setCommandListener(this);
  }

  public void startApp()
  {
    display.setCurrent(fmMain);
  }

  public void pauseApp()
  { }
```

(continued)

Example 7.11 *(Continued)*

```
public void destroyApp(boolean unconditional)
{ }

public void commandAction(Command c, Displayable s)
{
  if (c == cmHelp)
  {
    String str;
    // Access the resource and read its contents
    if ((str = readHelpText()) != null)
    {
      // Create an Alert to display the help text
      alHelp = new Alert("Help", str, null, null);
      alHelp.setTimeout(Alert.FOREVER);

      // Display the alert followed by the main form
      display.setCurrent(alHelp, fmMain);
    }
  }
  else if (c == cmExit)
  {
    destroyApp(false);
    notifyDestroyed();
  }
}

private String readHelpText()
{
  InputStream is = getClass().getResourceAsStream("help.txt");
  try
  {
    StringBuffer sb = new StringBuffer();
    int chr, i = 0;
    // Read until the end of the stream
    while ((chr = is.read()) != -1)
        sb.append((char) chr);

    return sb.toString();
  }
  catch (Exception e)
  {
    System.out.println("Unable to create stream");
```

(continued)

Example 7.11   (Continued)

```
    }
    return null;
  }
}
```

There are two sections of code worth pointing out. The method read-HelpText() is home to the code for opening an input stream and reading the help file into a StringBuffer. Inside commandAction() is the call to readHelpText(), which also displays a modal Alert dialog with the help information. The output for the MIDlet is shown in Figure 7–20.

Whether you are reading a text file as we've done here, or have a need to access any other resource in a MIDlet suite, the steps for acquiring and reading from a stream will vary little.

Example: Array of Images with ChoiceGroup

In the previous section we discussed the ChoiceGroup component. Now that we are familiar with the Image object, we can now show an additional example of how to create a ChoiceGroup using an array of Image objects and String objects (Example 7.12). Let's take a look:

Figure 7–20   Displaying the contents of a file stored in a MIDlet suite

Example 7.12   ChoiceGroupWithImages.java

```java
import javax.microedition.midlet.*;
import javax.microedition.lcdui.*;

public class ChoiceGroupWithImages extends MIDlet implements CommandListener
{
  private Display display        // Reference to display object
  private Form fmMain;           // Main form
  private Command cmExit;        // Command to exit the MIDlet
  private Command cmView;        // View the choice selected
  private ChoiceGroup cgPrefs;   // Choice Group of preferences

  public ChoiceGroupWithImages ()
  {
    display = Display.getDisplay(this);

    try
    {
      // Create array of image objects
      Image images[] = {Image.createImage("/up.png"),
                        Image.createImage("/down.png"),
                        Image.createImage("/help.png") };

      // Create array of corresponding string objects
      String options[] = {"Upload", "Download", "Help"};

      // Create a choice group using arrays
      cgPrefs = new ChoiceGroup("Select Option:",
                    Choice.EXCLUSIVE, options, images);

    }
    catch (java.io.IOException e)
    {
      System.err.println("Unable to locate or read .png file");
    }

    cmExit = new Command("Exit", Command.EXIT, 1);
    cmView = new Command("View", Command.SCREEN,2);

    // Create Form, add components, listen for events
    fmMain = new Form("");
    fmMain.append(cgPrefs);
    fmMain.addCommand(cmExit);
    fmMain.addCommand(cmView);
    fmMain.setCommandListener(this);
  }

  public void startApp()
  {
    display.setCurrent(fmMain);
  }
```

(continued)

Example 7.12   (Continued)

```
public void pauseApp()
{ }

public void destroyApp(boolean unconditional)
{ }

public void commandAction(Command c, Displayable s)
{
  if (c == cmView)
  {
    boolean selected[] = new boolean[cgPrefs.size()];

    // Fill array indicating whether each element is checked
    cgPrefs.getSelectedFlags(selected);

    // Print to console the status of each element
    for (int i = 0; i < cgPrefs.size(); i++)
      System.out.println(cgPrefs.getString(i) +
          (selected[i] ? ": selected" : ": not selected"));
  }
  else if (c == cmExit)
  {
    destroyApp(false);
    notifyDestroyed();
  }
}
}
```

Inside the constructor class, we create an array of Image objects and a corresponding array of String objects; we also allocate a ChoiceGroup passing in these same arrays.

```
Image images[] = {Image.createImage("/up.png"),
                  Image.createImage("/down.png"),
                  Image.createImage("/help.png") };

// Create array of corresponding string objects
String options[] = {"Upload", "Download", "Help"};

// Create a choice group using arrays
cgPrefs = new ChoiceGroup("Select Option:",
                Choice.EXCLUSIVE, options, images);
```

The interface will also include a "View" command to see the current status of each selection in the ChoiceGroup (see Figure 7–21).

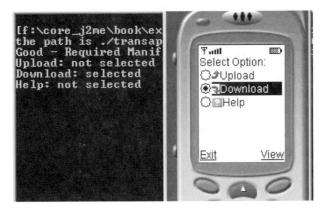

Figure 7–21 ChoiceGroup component using an array of Image objects. The console output is displayed when selecting the View command.

Example: Mutable Image and Graphics Object

A mutable image is a no-frills `Image` object. Until you draw into the image, using methods in the `Graphics` class, it is nothing more than an off-screen area in memory. You create a mutable image by specifying the desired width and height of the image.

We'll conclude this chapter by creating a mutable image, drawing text into the image, converting the mutable image to immutable and placing the resulting image onto a `Form` (Example 7.13). The reason for running through these hoops is that a `Form` (as well as an `Alert`, `Choice` and `ImageItem`) only accepts immutable images. Therefore, if you create a mutable image during application runtime and you plan to use the image on a `Form`, `Alert`, `Choice` or `ImageItem`, you will need to follow a similar set of steps.

Example 7.13   MutableImage.java

```
import javax.microedition.midlet.*;
import javax.microedition.lcdui.*;

public class MutableImage extends MIDlet implements CommandListener
{
    private Display display;        // Reference to display object
    private Form fmMain;            // Main form
    private Command cmExit;         // Command to exit the MIDlet
    private static final String message = "Core J2ME";
```

(continued)

Example 7.13   MutableImage.java

```
public MutableImage()
{
  display = Display.getDisplay(this);

  // Create a mutable image and get graphics object for image
  Image tmpImg = Image.createImage(80, 20);
  Graphics graphics = tmpImg.getGraphics();

  // Specify a font face, style and size
  Font font = Font.getFont(Font.FACE_SYSTEM,
             Font.STYLE_ITALIC, Font.SIZE_MEDIUM);
  graphics.setFont(font);

  // Center the text in the image
  graphics.drawString(message,
    (tmpImg.getWidth() / 2) - (font.stringWidth(message) / 2), 0,
    Graphics.TOP | Graphics.LEFT);

  // Draw a rectangle around the image
  graphics.drawRect(0,0,
      tmpImg.getWidth() - 1, tmpImg.getHeight() - 1);

  cmExit = new Command("Exit", Command.EXIT, 1);
  fmMain = new Form("");
  fmMain.addCommand(cmExit);
  fmMain.setCommandListener(this);

  // Convert the image to immutable and add to the form
  fmMain.append(Image.createImage(tmpImg));
  display.setCurrent(fmMain);
}

public void startApp()
{
  display.setCurrent(fmMain);
}

public void pauseApp()
{
}

public void destroyApp(boolean unconditional)
{
}

public void commandAction(Command c, Displayable s)
{
  if (c == cmExit)
```

(continued)

Example 7.13   (Continued)

```
    {
      destroyApp(false);
      notifyDestroyed();
    }
  }
}
```

Figure 7–22 shows the end result—a mutable image converted to immutable and placed on a `Form`.

We create a mutable image by calling the `createImage()` method that requires two integer values: the width and height. Before we can draw or write into the image, we need to obtain a reference to a `Graphics` object.

```
Image tmpImg = Image.createImage(80, 20);
Graphics graphics = tmpImg.getGraphics();
```

We now have a means to draw directly into the image. To make this a little more interesting, we specify a font, center the text message inside the image and draw a rectangle around the image to show the boundaries (bounding-box). We wrap all this up by converting the mutable image to immutable and appending to the form.

```
// Convert the image to immutable and add to the form
fmMain.append(Image.createImage(tmpImg));
display.setCurrent(fmMain);
```

We'll cover the specifics of fonts and graphics in Chapter 9.

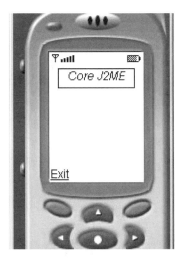

Figure 7–22 A mutabe image with centered text, converted to immutable and appended to a Form

HIGH-LEVEL
USER INTERFACE:
PART II

Topics in this Chapter

- List

- TextBox

- Alert and AlertType

- Ticker

Chapter 8

We started Chapter 7 by introducing the `Screen` and the `Form` classes. Then we dug deeper, looking at all the components that were subclasses of `Item`, each of which can be added to a `Form`. Let's revisit the hierarchy diagram shown earlier.

All the user interface components we covered up to this point, with the exception of `Form`, were subclasses of `Item`. We are now about to introduce `List`, `TextBox`, `Alert` and `Ticker`. Each of these is on the same "level," if you will, as the `Form`. It's probably better to say that each extends the `Screen` class, as does the `Form`. The one exception is the `Ticker` class. `Ticker` not a subclass of `Screen`. To be more precise, it is a variable defined in the `Screen` class. The actual declarations are as follows:

```
public abstract class Screen extends Displayable  {
...
private Ticker ticker = null;
...
}
```

Thus, a `Ticker` can be associated with any (and actually with multiple) `Screen` object(s). There will be more on the `Ticker` class near the end of this chapter.

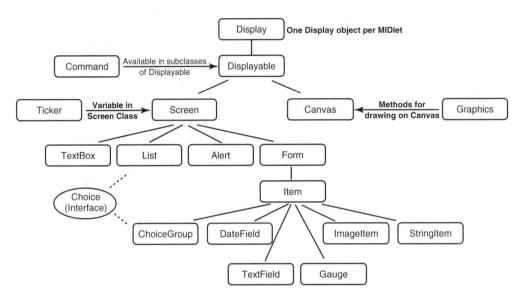

Figure 8-1   Displayable class hierarchy

Repeated from Chapter 7, here are the class definitions for the hierarchy shown in Figure 8–1:

Display	(public class Display)
Displayable	(public abstract class Displayable)
Screen	(public abstract class Screen extends Displayable)
TextBox	(public class TextBox extends Screen)
List	(public class List extends Screen implements Choice)
Alert	(public class Alert extends Screen)
Form	(public class Form extends Screen)
Item	(public abstract class Item)
ChoiceGroup	(public class ChoiceGroup extends Item implements Choice)
DateField	(public class DateField extends Item)
TextField	(public class TextField extends Item)
Gauge	(public class Gauge extends Item)
ImageItem	(public class ImageItem extends Item)
StringItem	(public class StringItem extends Item)
Canvas	(public abstract class Canvas extends Displayable)
Command	(public class Command)
Ticker	(public class Tickler)
Graphics	(public class Graphics)
Choice	(public interface Choice)

One significant difference between the components presented in this chapter and those covered thus far is how they are presented on the display. A Form can hold any number of Items. And along with that, a Form will handle any scrolling necessary to accommodate multiple components.

For example, a Form prompting a user for bank account information may contain several TextFields pertaining to an account number, email address and password. Each of these may be visible on the display at the same time. The Form will provide scrolling if necessary.

In contrast, a List, TextBox and Alert each operate independently. Once a TextBox is set as the active display, it is the only component visible. The same applies to an Alert and List. In essence, a Form is like a container for other visual components, whereas List, TextBox and Alert are standalone.

Bear in mind that whether we are referring to a Form, List or TextBox or Alert, each can accommodate Command objects as well. So when I state that TextBox is the only component on the display, this does not consider any Command objects that may be present.

List

A List contains a series of choices presented in one of three formats. Two of these are shown in Figure 8–2: multiple and exclusive.

Figure 8-2 Multiple and Exclusive Lists

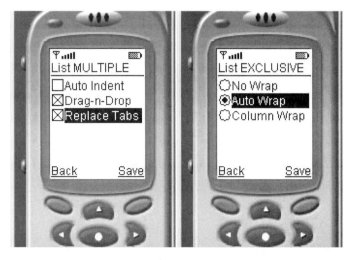

Figure 8–3   Implicit List

The third type is the implicit list (see Figure 8–3). Notice the simplicity of the list and the lack of radio buttons and checkboxes. I've also removed the "Save" command from the display. In a moment, you'll understand why such a command is no longer necessary.

Event Handling for List

In Chapter 6 we discussed event handling. However, given the differences in dealing with user interaction of a List versus ChoiceGroup, this topic deserves some additional attention.

If you page back to Figure 7–14 and compare this to Figure 8–2, you'll notice just how similar the List and ChoiceGroup appear to be. The appearance is where the resemblance ends. Event handling for each is quite different. Let's quickly recap the event handling options for a ChoiceGroup:

1. Specify an ItemStateListener for the Form containing the ChoiceGroup. When a user changes a selection, the method itemStateChanged() is called.

2. Add a Command(s) to the Form containing the ChoiceGroup; for example, a "Save"or "Exit" Command. When a Command is issued by the user, the method commandAction() will be called.

Event Changes to a `ChoiceGroup` (or any Item)

The specification does not require `itemStateChanged()` to be invoked each time a change is detected. Look back to Chapter 6 in the section `Item` and `ItemStateListener` for the rules set forth regarding when events/changes must be acknowledged.

Following are the event handling options for a `List`:

1. Exclusive and multiple lists: No event is triggered when a user changes a `List` element. To determine the status of the various elements, you will need a break in the action. Typically, this will be when a user selects a `Command` (as explained earlier for a `ChoiceGroup`).

   For example, you may have a multiple-selection list on the screen with various application preferences, as shown in Figure 8–2. When a user chooses to "Save," you could write the preferences to persistent storage.

2. Implicit list: Upon selection of an element in the `List`, an event is immediately generated. As with exclusive and multiple, the method `commandAction()` will be called. Given what we know from pervious run-ins with this method, it is only invoked if a `CommandListener` is registered. Following is a partial example to register a listener for an implicit `List`:

   ```
   lsmain = new List("Email Options", Choice.IMPLICIT);
   lsmain.setCommandListener(this);
   ```

   The classic example of an implicit `List` is that of a menu. When presented with a series of options in a menu (see Figure 8–3), once you make a selection the action is implicitly carried out. Put another way, once you choose an option from a menu, the menu goes away and you are whisked off to the code that carries out the action.

   To put that description into a picture, visualize a pull-down menu inside a word processor. If you click on the Edit menu, you'll typically see options such as cut, copy, paste, search and replace. Once you've moved the mouse over your choice and clicked, the menu disappears and the action is carried out.

As a final clarification, unlike the ChoiceGroup, a List does not have the option of registering an ItemState-Listener.

Comparison of ChoiceGroup versus List

ChoiceGroup and List are so closely related that without a little nudge you may have a hard time differentiating between a List and a ChoiceGroup. Here are a few thoughts to help clarify:

Similarities

- Both implement the Choice interface. This interface defines a common set of methods: adding, deleting and getting elements, to name just a few.
- Both can show explicit choices (radio buttons) or multiple choices (check boxes).

Appearance Difference

- A ChoiceGroup appears as part of a Form. That is, there may be other components on the display. To be specific, there may be other objects of the Item class on the Form. Keep in mind that due to the limited display size, a user may need to scroll up and down to see all the components.
- A List occupies the display as a single entity. No other components will be visible at the same time. Once again, you may need to scroll up and down to see all the elements in the list, but the list is the sole component active on the display.
- One point to drill home: Whether we are referring to a Form (with a ChoiceGroup) or a List, both can accommodate Command objects. So when we say that a list is the only entity on the display, this does not take into consideration any commands that may be available. See Figure 8–4, which shows a list and two commands: "Exit" and "Add."

Implementation Differences

- ChoiceGroup can have the following types:

  MULTIPLE: Any number of elements can be selected
  (Checkbox)

  EXCLUSIVE: One element is selected at any given time
  (Radio Group)

- List can have the following types:

  MULTIPLE: Any number of elements can be selected
  (Checkbox)

  EXCLUSIVE: One element is selected at any given time
  (Radio Group)

  IMPLICIT: Selection of an element generates an event
  (Menu)

- Event processing for a ChoiceGroup can use either an
  ItemStateListener to detect changes, which will result in
  a call to the method itemStateChanged(), or you can have
  a Command object on a Form trigger a call to the method
  commandAction().

- A List is not a subclass of Item: Therefore, there is no listener available to detect changes to individual elements. Events
  for an implicit list are generated as soon as a selection is made.
  With a list you also have the option to use a Command object to
  initiate an event. Whether an implicit list or a command(s) trigger an event, the method commandAction() is called.

List API

Table 8.1 List Class: javax.microedition.lcdui.List	
Method	*Description*
Constructor	
List(String title, int listType)	Create a new List with no elements
List(String title, int listType, String[] stringElements, Image[] imageElements)	Create a new List and populate with data from the arrays

(continued)

Table 8.1	(Continued)

Method	Description
int **append**(String stringPart, Image imagePart)	Add element to end
void **delete**(int elementNum)	Delete an element at specified index
void **insert**(int elementNum, String stringPart, Image imagePart)	Insert element at specified index
void **set**(int elementNum, String stringPart, Image imagePart)	Set (replace) element at specified index
String **getString**(int elementNum)	Get text of element at specified index
Image **getImage**(int elementNum)	Get Image of element at specified index
int **getSelectedIndex**()	Get index of selected element
void **setSelectedIndex**(int elementNum, boolean selected)	MULTIPLE LIST—set element to specified boolean value EXCLUSIVE LIST—set element to true IMPLICIT LIST—set element to true
int **getSelectedFlags**(boolean[] selectedArray_return)	Store selection status in an array
void **setSelectedFlags**(boolean[] selectedArray)	Set selection status from an array
boolean **isSelected**(int elementNum)	Determine if element is selected
int **size**()	Number of elements in List

The `List` component implements the `Choice` interface. There are three pre-defined choice types, of which each is defined in Table 8.2.

Table 8.2	ChoiceTypes: javax.microedition.lcdui.Choice

Value	Description
EXCLUSIVE	Only one selection available at any time
MULTIPLE	Zero or more selections available at any time
IMPLICIT	Selection of an element generates an event

Example: Implicit List

Let's look at Example 8.1, which creates an implicit list using an array of
Image objects and an array of String objects.

Example 8.1   ImplicitList.java

```java
import javax.microedition.midlet.*;
import javax.microedition.lcdui.*;

public class ImplicitList extends MIDlet implements CommandListener
{
   private Display display;        // Reference to Display object
   private List lsDocument;        // Main list
   private Command cmExit;         // Command to exit
   private Command cmAdd;          // Command to add an element

   public implicitList()
   {
      display = Display.getDisplay(this);

      // Create the Commands
      cmExit = new Command("Exit", Command.EXIT, 1);
      cmAdd = new Command("Add", Command.SCREEN, 1);

      try
      {
         // Create array of image objects
         Image images[] = {Image.createImage("/ff.png"),
                       Image.createImage("/rr.png"),
                       Image.createImage("/new.png")};

         // Create array of corresponding string objects
         String options[] = {" Next", " Previous", " New"};

         // Create list using arrays, add commands, listen for events
         lsDocument = new List("Document Option:",
                             List.IMPLICIT, options, images);
         lsDocument.addCommand(cmExit);
         lsDocument.addCommand(cmAdd);
         lsDocument.setCommandListener(this);
```

(continued)

Example 8.1   (Continued)

```java
    }
    catch (java.io.IOException e)
    {
      System.err.println("Unable to locate or read .png file");
    }
}

public void startApp()
{
  display.setCurrent(lsDocument);
}

public void pauseApp()
{
}

public void destroyApp(boolean unconditional)
{
}

public void commandAction(Command c, Displayable s)
{
  // If an implicit list generated the event
  if (c == List.SELECT_COMMAND)
  {
    switch (lsDocument.getSelectedIndex())
    {
      case 0:
        System.out.println("Next");
        break;

      case 1:
        System.out.println("Previous");
        break;

      case 2:
        System.out.println("New");
        break;
      default:
        System.out.println("New Element");
    }
  }
  else if (c == cmAdd)
```

(continued)

Example 8.1 *(Continued)*

```
  {
    try
    {
      // Add a new element. Using size() as the insertion point,
      // the element will appended to the list.
      lsDocument.insert(lsDocument.size(), " Delete ",
                        Image.createImage("/delete.png"));
    }
    catch (java.io.IOException e)
    {
      System.err.println("Unable to locate or read .png file");
    }
  }
  else if (c == cmExit)
  {
    destroyApp(false);
    notifyDestroyed();
  }
}
}
}
```

Figure 8–4 shows the initial display when starting the MIDlet. Notice the images and corresponding text that were created using the arrays of images and strings, respectively. The screen shot on the left in Figure 8–5 shows the display when selecting the "Add" command for the first time. The right screen shot is the result of selecting "Add" a second time.

Figure 8–4 Implicit List created with an array of Strings and an array of Images

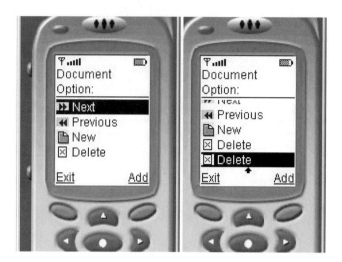

Figure 8-5   Inserting new elements into a List

Here is the the code for adding a new element in to the list:

```
lsDocument.insert(lsDocument.size(), " Delete ",
                  Image.createImage("/delete.png"));
```

If you don't give this a moment's thought, something interesting about the `insert()` method will slip right by. Consider the index where we are requesting to insert the element:

```
lsDocument.size()
```

The result of this call is the value 3, which is correct: It is the number of elements in our list. We are requesting the insert to take place at this same position. However, indexing of elements in a list begins with 0. The second element is at index 1, and so forth. Is it starting to sink in?

lstDocument: Before inserting a new element

Value	"Next"	"Previous"	"New"
Index	0	1	2

The specification states the following for the insert method:

"Inserts an element into the `Choice` just prior to the element specified"

Using this definition, we are requesting to insert an element just prior to element 3, but there is no element at that position, so index 3 does not exist! The designers of the specification had an option at this point. They could have chosen to treat this as an error condition and thrown an exception, or to add default functionality to capture this case. They decided upon the latter, which is where the interesting "side-effect" comes in. If you insert an element and specify the current length of the list, the element will be appended.

Inserting Elements into the Middle of a List

When inserting into a `List`, take a moment to make certain you understand how the list will change. Remember, elements are inserted into a list prior to the element specified.

If a list has 3 elements as shown below and an element ("Z") is inserted by specifying an insert index of 2, the new element will be inserted prior to element 2, as shown below. The element inserted will have the index 2, and the element previously at position 2 will now have an index of 3.

```
somelist.insert(2, "Z", null);
```

Before Insertion:

Elements	A	B	C
Index	0	1	2

After Insertion:

Elements	A	B	Z	C
Index	0	1	2	3

Before leaving this example take a minute to look over the code in `commandAction()`. Notice the check to see if the `Command` that initiated the event was an implicit `List`. Also, look at the switch statement that uses `lsDocument.getSelectedIndex()` to determine which element was selected and print a message to the console.

```
public void commandAction(Command c, Displayable s)
    {
        if (c == List.SELECT_COMMAND)
        {
            switch (lsDocument.getSelectedIndex())
            {
```

```
        case 0:
          System.out.println("Next");
          break;
        ...
      }
      ...
    }
}
```

Example: Multiple Choice List

Changing our List from implicit to multiple choice is a piece of cake. All
that changes is the declaration of the List.

Implicit:

```
lsDocument = new List("Document Option:",
                  List.IMPLICIT, options, images);
```

Multiple Choice:

```
lsDocument = new List("Document Option:",
                  List.MULTIPLE, options, images);
```

The last List example will create a multiple choice list and fill an array
(of boolean values) with the selection status of each entry. The MIDlet and
console output (shown when the "View" option is selected) are shown in
Figure 8–6.

Figure 8–6   Multiple Choice List

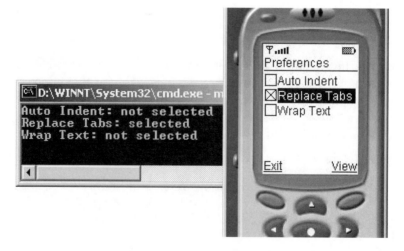

Example 8.2   MultipleChoiceList.java

```java
/*----------------------------------------------------
 * MultipleChoiceList.java
 *
 * Create multiple choice list and save selection
 * status of each element in an array.
 *--------------------------------------------------*/

import javax.microedition.midlet.*;
import javax.microedition.lcdui.*;

public class MultipleChoiceList extends MIDlet implements CommandListener
{
  private Display display;        // Reference to display object
  private Command cmExit;         // A Command to exit the MIDlet
  private Command cmView;         // View the choice selected
  private List lsPrefs;           // Choice Group of preferences

  public MultipleChoiceList()
  {
    display = Display.getDisplay(this);

    // Create a multiple choice list
    lsPrefs = new List("Preferences", List.MULTIPLE);

    // Append options, with no associated images
    lsPrefs.append("Auto Indent", null);
    lsPrefs.append("Replace Tabs", null);
    lsPrefs.append("Wrap Text", null);

    cmExit = new Command("Exit", Command.EXIT, 1);
    cmView = new Command("View", Command.SCREEN, 2);

    // Add commands, listen for events
    lsPrefs.addCommand(cmExit);
    lsPrefs.addCommand(cmView);
    lsPrefs.setCommandListener(this);
  }

  public void startApp()
  {
    display.setCurrent(lsPrefs);
  }
```

(continued)

Example 8.2   *(Continued)*

```
public void pauseApp()
{ }

public void destroyApp(boolean unconditional)
{ }

public void commandAction(Command c, Displayable s)
{
  if (c == cmView)
  {
    boolean selected[] = new boolean[lsPrefs.size()];

    // Fill array indicating whether each element is checked
    lsPrefs.getSelectedFlags(selected);

    for (int i = 0; i < lsPrefs.size(); i++)
      System.out.println(lsPrefs.getString(i) +
            (selected[i] ? ": selected" : ": not selected"));

  }
  else if (c == cmExit)
  {
    destroyApp(false);
    notifyDestroyed();
  }
}
}
```

TextBox

A TextBox is a multi-line text entry screen. When a user is entering text, you can filter the input to allow only certain characters (e.g., only numbers).

Does this component sound similar to another component we've seen previously? Just as a List and ChoiceGroup are closely related, so are a TextBox and TextField. So closely tied are the two that they share the same set of constraints for restricting the user input. The constraints are defined in the TextField class, and are shown in Table 8.4.

When you create a TextBox you specify how many characters you would like the TextBox to hold. The actual size returned may be different than what you requested. Therefore, a method is provided that will return the maximum number of characters: getMaxSize().

Comparison of TextBox versus TextField

The difference between a TextBox and TextField come down to a few key points:

Similarities

- Both share the input constraints as specified in the TextField class.
- Both have a maximum capacity that may be different than what can be displayed on the device at any one time. Scrolling will be provided by the implementation as necessary.

Appearance Difference

- A TextField is a subclass of Item, and therefore appears as part of a Form. There may be other components on the Form at the same time.
- When on the display, a TextBox is the only component visible.

  Note: A Form (with a TextField) or a TextBox may not be the sole components on the display: both can also accommodate Command objects (see Figure 8–7).

Implementation Differences

- When you want to process events on a TextField, you can use an ItemStateListener to detect changes that will result in a call to the method itemStateChanged() or you can have a Command object on the Form trigger a call to the method commandAction().
- TextBox events are handled exclusively through Command objects. Because a TextBox is not a subclass of Item, there is no ItemStateListener available.

TextBox API

Table 8.3 TextBox Class: javax.microedition.lcdui.TextBox	
Method	*Description*
Constructors	
TextBox (String title, String text, int maxSize, int constraints)	Create a new TextField
Methods	
void **delete**(int offset, int length)	Delete characters
void **insert**(String src, int position)	Insert characters from a String
void **insert**(char[] data, int offset, int length, int position)	Insert characters from an array into specified 'position'
void **setChars**(char[] data, int offset, int length)	Replace TextBox contents with data from an array
int **getChars**(char[] data)	Place TextBox contents into an array
String **getString**()	Place TextBox contents into a String
void **setString**(String text)	Set (replace) TextBox contents from a String
int **getConstraints**()	Get the constraints defined
void **setConstraints**(int constraints)	Set the constraints
int **getMaxSize**()	Get total characters that can be stored
int **setMaxSize**(int maxSize)	Set total characters that can be stored
int **getCaretPosition**()	Get current input position
int **size**()	Number of characters currently in TextBox

Example: Add Copy and Paste to TextBox

There are no copy and paste operations available as part of the base functionality of a TextBox. Let's write some additional code to add this support.

This next MIDlet will have a menu with three options: Mark, Copy and Paste. "Mark" will make note of the current offset (caret position) in the TextBox. "Copy" will place characters into the clipboard (a character array)

Table 8.4	TextField Constraints: javax.microedition.lcdui.TextField
Value	*Description*
CONSTRAINT_MASK	Use this mask when you need to determine the current value of the constraint. See the section "A Look Inside Constraint Values" in Chapter 7 for more information.
ANY	Allow any character input.
EMAILADDR	Allow only characters that are valid within an email address.
NUMERIC	Allow only numbers. This includes both positive and negative numbers. You do not have an option to request only positive or only negative values.
PASSWORD	Masks all character input to provide privacy when entering data. This constraint can be combined with other constraints to provide masking. See the section "Using the Password Modifier" in Chapter 7 for more information.
PHONENUMBER	Allow only characters that are valid as part of a phone number. This may be device and/or local specific.
URL	Allow only characters that are valid within a URL.

Figure 8-7 Setting the starting point to copy text to the clipboard

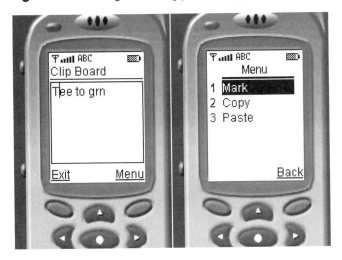

Figure 8–8   Move to the ending point and copy the text "ee" to the clipboard

from the mark previously set to the current position. When "Paste" is selected, the clipboard contents will be inserted into the TextBox.

Figures 8–7 through 8–9 show the copy and paste in action.

The source code for this MIDlet is shown in Example 8.3.

Figure 8–9   Move to the insertion point and paste the text "ee" into the TextBox

Example 8.3   SimpleClipBoard.java

```java
import javax.microedition.midlet.*;
import javax.microedition.lcdui.*;

public class SimpleClipBoard extends MIDlet implements CommandListener
{
  private Display display;            // Reference to Display object
  private TextBox tbClip;             // Main textbox
  private Command cmExit;             // Command to exit
  private Command cmStartMark;        // Command to start marking a block
  private Command cmCopy;             // Command to copy to clipboard
  private Command cmPaste;            // Command to paste into textbox
  private int beginOffset = 0;        // The start index of copy
  private char[] clipBoard = null;    // The clipboard
  private int clipBoardChars = 0;     // Number of chars in clipboard

  public SimpleClipBoard()
  {
    display = Display.getDisplay(this);

    // Create the Commands. Notice the priorities assigned
    cmExit = new Command("Exit", Command.EXIT, 1);
    cmStartMark = new Command("Mark", Command.SCREEN, 2);
    cmCopy = new Command("Copy", Command.SCREEN, 3);
    cmPaste = new Command("Paste", Command.SCREEN, 4);

    tbClip = new TextBox("Clip Board", "AaBbcc",
                         8, TextField.ANY);
    tbClip.addCommand(cmExit);
    tbClip.addCommand(cmStartMark);
    tbClip.addCommand(cmCopy);
    tbClip.addCommand(cmPaste);
    tbClip.setCommandListener(this);

    // Allocate a clipboard big enough to hold the entire textbox
    clipBoard = new char[tbClip.getMaxSize()];
  }

  public void startApp()
  {
    display.setCurrent(tbClip);
  }

  public void pauseApp()
  {
  }
```

(continued)

Example 8.3 *(Continued)*

```java
public void destroyApp(boolean unconditional)
{
}

public void commandAction(Command c, Displayable s)
{
  if (c == cmStartMark)
  {
    beginOffset = tbClip.getCaretPosition();
  }
  else if (c == cmCopy &&
          (tbClip.getCaretPosition() > beginOffset))
  {
    // Allocate an array to hold the current textbox contents
    char[] chr = new char[tbClip.size()];

    // Get the current textbox contents
    tbClip.getChars(chr);

    // The count of characters in the clipboard
    clipBoardChars = tbClip.getCaretPosition() - beginOffset;

    // Copy the text into the clipboard
    // arraycopy(source, sourceindex, dest, destindex, count)
    System.arraycopy(chr, beginOffset,
                    clipBoard, 0, clipBoardChars);
  }
  else if (c == cmPaste)
  {
    // Make sure the paste will not overrun the textbox length.
    if ((tbClip.size() + clipBoardChars) <=
        tbClip.getMaxSize())
      tbClip.insert(clipBoard, 0, clipBoardChars,
                    tbClip.getCaretPosition());
  }
  else if (c == cmExit)
  {
    destroyApp(false);
    notifyDestroyed();
  }
}
}
```

Implementing the clipboard is quite simple. There are three variables we need: one to store the starting position of the copy, another to store the actual text and one to tell us how many characters are in the clipboard.

```
private int beginOffset = 0;   // The start index of copy
private char[] clipBoard = null; // The clipboard
private int clipBoardChars = 0;  // Number of chars in clipboard
```

Once a request is made to "mark" the current position, we simply get the caret position and store it.

```
beginOffset = tbClip.getCaretPosition();
```

When we need to copy to the clipboard we get the current characters in the TextBox, determine how many of those same characters we need based on the starting offset and current position and copy the result into the clipboard buffer.

```
char[] chr = new char[tbClip.size()];

// Get the current textbox contents
tbClip.getChars(chr);

// The count of characters in the clipboard
clipBoardChars = tbClip.getCaretPosition() - beginOffset;

// Copy the text into the clipboard
// arraycopy(source, sourceindex, dest, destindex, count)
System.arraycopy(chr, beginOffset, clipBoard, 0, clipBoardhars);
```

Pasting requires a check to be sure that we don't attempt to write off the end of the TextBox. If everything looks good, copy from the clipboard into the TextBox using insert().

```
// Make sure the paste will not overrun the textbox length.
if ((tbClip.size() + clipBoardChars) <= tbClip.getMaxSize())
   tbClip.insert(clipBoard, 0, clipBoardChars,
               tbClip.getCaretPosition());
```

Regarding the order of items as they appear in the menu (see Figure 8–7), we are stating our preference with the following code:

```
cmStartMark = new Command("Mark", Command.SCREEN, 2);
cmCopy = new Command("Copy", Command.SCREEN, 3);
cmPaste = new Command("Paste", Command.SCREEN, 4);
```

By sequentially increasing the priorities (a higher number has a lower priority), the implementation can decide how to order elements in the menu.

Figure 8–10   Sharing a clipboard across multiple TextBox components

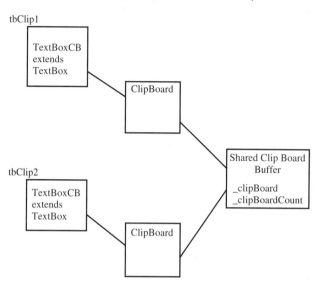

Example: Sharing a Clipboard across TextBoxes

We've seen with the MIDlet in Example 8.3 that adding support for copy and paste is a walk in the park. However, we need a more realistic example to show how you might actually implement such a concept.

Let's improve our application design by encapsulating the variables that deal with the clipboard into a new class, appropriately named ClipBoard. We'll also extend the TextBox class to support our new clipboard. The new class will be called TextBoxCB. As part of this extension, each TextBoxCB object will manage its own event processing. That is, each will have its own set of Commands to mark, copy, cut and paste.

Look at Figure 8–10 for a diagram of the big picture.

tbClip1 and tbClip2 will be instances of our new TextBoxCB class. Within each will be a reference to a ClipBoard object (one object for each TextBoxCB). To make this example more intriguing, I've created just one character array to store text copied to a clipboard. This allows us to share the clipboard contents between any number of TextBoxCB objects.

You'll notice in Figure 8–10 the reference to the shared clipboard buffer. This is done by simply declaring the character array that holds the clipboard contents as a static variable. Thus, there is only one instance of _clipBoard, regardless of how many clipBoard objects we create. It's as simple as the following:

```
public class ClipBoard
{
  ...
  private static char[] _clipBoard = new char[1000];
  private static int _clipBoardCount = 0;
  ...
}
```

Figures 8–11, 8–12, 8–13, 8–14, and 8–15 walk through the MIDlet, cutting text from one TextBox and pasting into another.

Figure 8-11 The main display: a List component showing two selections

Figure 8-12 On left, inside TextBox1, move the cursor to the beginning of the text to cut; on right, select the "Mark" option to begin marking the text block

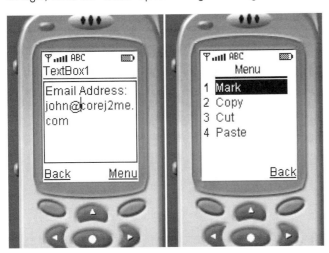

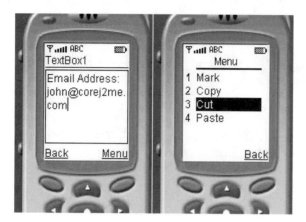

Figure 8–13   On left, move to the end of the text; on right, select "Cut" to place the text into the clipboard

Figure 8–14   The text has been cut and placed into the clipboard

Figure 8–15   On left, inside TextBox2, move the cursor to the end of the text; on right, the result after choosing "Paste" from the Menu.

Example 8.4 shows the source code to implement this MIDlet.

Example 8.4   ClipBoard.java

```java
/*---------------------------------------------------
 * ClipBoard.java
 *
 * Core clipboard code -  mark, copy, cut and paste
 *-------------------------------------------------*/
import javax.microedition.midlet.*;
import javax.microedition.lcdui.*;

public class ClipBoard
{
  //--------------------------------------------------
  // Allocate clipboard. Note, both clipboard & count
  // of characters are shared across all instances
  //--------------------------------------------------
  private static char[] _clipBoard = new char[1000];
  private static int _clipBoardCount = 0;

  private int beginOffset = 0;   // The start index of copy
  private TextBox tb = null;     // textbox for this instance

  /*--------------------------------------------------
   * Hold reference to textbox that created clipboard
   *------------------------------------------------*/
  public ClipBoard(TextBox textbox)
  {
    tb = textbox;
  }

  /*--------------------------------------------------
   * Set starting point of copy
   *------------------------------------------------*/
  public void startMark()
  {
    beginOffset = tb.getCaretPosition();
  }

  /*--------------------------------------------------
   * Copy text into the clipboard
   *------------------------------------------------*/
```

(continued)

Example 8.4   *(Continued)*

```
public void copy()
{
  copy2clipboard();
}


/*---------------------------------------------------
 * Copy text into the clipboard. If successful copy,
 * delete text from the textbox.
 *--------------------------------------------------*/
public void cut()
{
  if (copy2clipboard())
    tb.delete(beginOffset,
              tb.getCaretPosition() - beginOffset);
}


/*---------------------------------------------------
 * Do the actual copy into the clipboard
 *--------------------------------------------------*/
private boolean copy2clipboard()
{
  // Can only mark (copy/cut) going forward
  if (tb.getCaretPosition() > beginOffset)
  {
    // Allocate an array to hold the current textbox contents
    char[] chr = new char[tb.size()];

    // Get the current textbox contents
    tb.getChars(chr);

    // The count of characters in the clipboard
    _clipBoardCount = tb.getCaretPosition() - beginOffset;

    // Copy the text into the clipboard
    // arraycopy(source, sourceindex, dest, destindex, count)
    System.arraycopy(chr, beginOffset,
                     _clipBoard, 0, _clipBoardCount);
    return true;
  }
  else
    return false;
}
```

(continued)

Example 8.4   (*Continued*)

```
/*-------------------------------------------------
 * Paste text from clipboard into the textbox
 *-----------------------------------------------*/
public void paste()
{
  // Make sure the paste will not overrun the textbox length
  if ((tb.size() + _clipBoardCount) <= tb.getMaxSize())
    tb.insert(_clipBoard, 0,
              _clipBoardCount, tb.getCaretPosition());
}
}
```

Example 8.4 shows the code for the `ClipBoard` class. Here is where the work is done for mark, copy, cut and paste. Each `TextBoxCB` will allocate an instance of this class. If you look at the following code, you'll see how each textbox shares the same clipboard contents.

```
private static char[] _clipBoard = new char[1000];
private static int _clipBoardCount = 0;

private int beginOffset = 0;  // The start index of copy
private TextBox tb = null;    // textbox for this instance
```

The two static declarations result in only one instance of `_clipBoard` and `_clipBoardCount`, regardless of how many instances of this class are created. On the flip side, each instance has its own reference to the beginning offset of a marked block of text and a reference to the `TextBox` associated with this clipboard.

With this design, each clipboard and the associated `TextBox` can mark, copy and cut text, yet the actual contents in the clipboard are shared across all `TextBox` instances.

Example 8.5   TextBoxCB.java

```
/*-------------------------------------------------
 * TextBoxCB.java
 *
 * A textbox that includes a clipboard. This class
 * encapsulates all the commands necessary to show
 * a menu for mark, copy, cut and paste.
 *-----------------------------------------------*/
```

(*continued*)

Example 8.5   (Continued)

```java
import javax.microedition.midlet.*;
import javax.microedition.lcdui.*;

public class TextBoxCB extends TextBox implements CommandListener
{
    private ClipBoard clipboard;      // The clipboard class
    private Command cmBack;           // Command to go back
    private Command cmStartMark;      // Command to start marking a block
    private Command cmCopy;           // Command to copy to clipboard
    private Command cmCut;            // Command to cut to clipboard
    private Command cmPaste;          // Command to paste into textbox
    private SharedClipBoard midlet;   // The midlet

    public TextBoxCB(String title, String text, int maxSize,
                    int constraints, SharedClipBoard midlet)
    {
        // Call the TextBox constructor
        super(title, text, maxSize, constraints);

        // Save reference to MIDlet so we can access its methods
        this.midlet = midlet;

        // Create the Commands. Notice the priorities assigned
        cmBack = new Command("Back", Command.BACK, 1);
        cmStartMark = new Command("Mark", Command.SCREEN, 2);
        cmCopy = new Command("Copy", Command.SCREEN, 3);
        cmCut = new Command("Cut",  Command.SCREEN, 4);
        cmPaste = new Command("Paste", Command.SCREEN, 5);

        this.addCommand(cmBack);
        this.addCommand(cmStartMark);
        this.addCommand(cmCopy);
        this.addCommand(cmCut);
        this.addCommand(cmPaste);
        this.setCommandListener(this);

        // Create a clipboard
        clipboard = new ClipBoard(this);
    }
```

(continued)

| Example 8.5   (Continued) |

```
public void commandAction(Command c, Displayable s)
{
  if (c == cmStartMark)
  {
    // Start to mark a block of text
    clipboard.startMark();
  }
  else if (c == cmCopy)
  {
    // Copy text to clipboard
    clipboard.copy();
  }
  else if (c == cmCut)
  {
    // Cut text to clipboard
    clipboard.cut();
  }
  else if (c == cmPaste)
  {
    // Paste from clipboard to textbox
    clipboard.paste();
  }
  else if (c == cmBack)
  {
    // Return to the list component
    midlet.showList();
  }
}
}
```

One of the first orders of business is to declare this class as extending a TextBox.

```
public class TextBoxCB extends TextBox implements CommandListener
```

Inside the constructor we call the super class of the TextBox and also save a reference to the MIDlet itself.

```
// Call the TextBox constructor
super(title, text, maxSize, constraints);

// Save reference to MIDlet so we can access its methods
this.midlet =  midlet;
```

With the reference to `midlet`, we can call `midlet.showList()` to return to the `List` component (see Figure 8–11) that called the `TextBox`. This action will occur when a user selects the "Back" `Command` as shown in Figure 8–14.

You'll see that we've declared a series of commands for marking, copying, cutting and pasting text. With this approach, all event handling is done within the `TextBox`. This is a cleaner approach than adding additional event processing outside this class.

Finally, inside `commandAction()` there is minimal code. It acts as more of a central dispatcher routing the MIDlet to the appropriate code based on the user selections.

Example 8.6 is the main MIDlet, if you will. It ties together the previous two examples into one comprehensive application. The main interface is a `List` component with two entries.

```
lsMain = new List("ClipBoard Testing", List.IMPLICIT);
lsMain.append("TextBox1", null);
lsMain.append("TextBox2", null);
```

Example 8.6   SharedClipBoard.java

```
/*-------------------------------------------------
 * SharedClipBoard.java
 *
 * A List component that can show one of two
 * textboxes. Each textbox shares a common clipboard
 *-------------------------------------------------*/
import javax.microedition.midlet.*;
import javax.microedition.lcdui.*;

public class SharedClipBoard extends MIDlet
                             implements CommandListener
{
  private Display display;      // Reference to Display object
  private List lsMain;          // Main list
  private TextBoxCB tbClip1;    // Textbox with clipboard
  private TextBoxCB tbClip2;    // Textbox with clipboard
  private Command cmExit;       // Command to exit

  public SharedClipBoard()
  {
    display = Display.getDisplay(this);
```

(continued)

Example 8.6 *(Continued)*

```
   // Create list
   lsMain = new List("ClipBoard Testing", List.IMPLICIT);
   lsMain.append("TextBox1", null);
   lsMain.append("TextBox2", null);

   // Create the exit command, add to list
   cmExit = new Command("Exit", Command.EXIT, 1);
   lsMain.addCommand(cmExit);
   lsMain.setCommandListener(this);

   // Allocate textboxes
   tbClip1 = new TextBoxCB("TextBox1",
                           "Email Address:  john@corej2me.com",
                           50, TextField.ANY, this);
   tbClip2 = new TextBoxCB("TextBox2",
                           "Web Address:  www.",
                           50, TextField.ANY, this);
}

public void startApp()
{
  showList();
}

public void pauseApp()
{
}

public void destroyApp(boolean unconditional)
{
}

public void showList()
{
  // Display the list component
  display.setCurrent(lsMain);
}

public void commandAction(Command c, Displayable s)
{
  // If an implicit list generated the event
  if (c == List.SELECT_COMMAND)
  {
```

(continued)

Example 8.6   (Continued)

```
    switch (lsMain.getSelectedIndex())
    {
      case 0:
        // Display textbox 1
        display.setCurrent(tbClip1);
        break;

      case 1:
        // Display textbox 2
        display.setCurrent(tbClip2);
        break;
    }
  }
  else if (c == cmExit)
  {
    destroyApp(false);
    notifyDestroyed();
  }
 }
}
```

This is followed by allocation of two `TextBoxCB` objects.

```
// Allocate textboxes
tbClip1 = new TextBoxCB("TextBox1",
                "Email Address:  john@corej2me.com", 50,
                TextField.ANY, this);
tbClip2 = new TextBoxCB("TextBox2",
                "Web Address:  www.", 50,
                TextField.ANY, this);
```

Because we opted to place the majority of the event processing code (mark, copy, cut and paste) into the `TextBoxCB` class, the code inside commandAction() is kept to a minimum. It essentially displays the appropriate `TextBox` based on the user selection.

```
switch (lsMain.getSelectedIndex())
      {
        case 0:
          display.setCurrent(tbClip1);
          break;
        case 1:
          display.setCurrent(tbClip2);
          break;
      }
```

Alert and AlertType

An `Alert` is a very simple dialog box that will support text and an `Image` (both are optional). The most common use of an `Alert` is to show a warning or error message. Figure 8–16 shows an `Alert`. Notice the three visual attributes you can control: title, image and text.

There are a few limitations to an `Alert` that you need to be aware of. First, `Command` objects (buttons) are not allowed on an `Alert`. User interaction is entirely managed by the implementation. In addition, no input can be solicited from a user. For example, you cannot add a `TextField` or `TextBox` to prompt for information.

There are two types of `Alerts`:

1. Modal: The `Alert` is on the display until a user dismisses it (see Table 8.5).
2. Timed: The `Alert` is on the display for a specific number of milliseconds.

Each device will have a default type for all alerts. You can determine the default by calling the method `getDefaultTimeout()`. A return value equivalent to `Alert.FOREVER` indicates modal; any other value indicates the time in milliseconds that an alert will be shown.

Figure 8-16 Alert dialog with a title, Image and text

Table 8.5 Alert Type: javax.microedition.lcdui.Alert	
Value	*Description*
FOREVER	Specifies the Alert is visible until acknowledged by the user (also known as modal).

If you need to display an `Alert` type other than the default, call the method `setTimeout()`. The following creates a modal alert:

```
Alert  al;
al = new Alert("Error", "Error Message ", null, null);
al.setTimeout(Alert.FOREVER);
```

After you've created an `Alert` and set the attributes, there are two methods in the `Display` class to show the `Alert`.

1. `Display.setCurrent(Alert, Displayable)`

```
fmMain = new Form("Welcome");
alTest = new Alert("Alert", "Message Here ", null,
                  null);
alTest.setTimeout(Alert.FOREVER);
...
display.setCurrent(alTest, fmMain);
```

This will display a modal alert. Once the alert has been acknowledged by the user, the alert will be removed from the display and the form, `fmMain`, will be displayed. The same logic applies if you change this to a timed alert. Once the alert has been displayed for the requested time, the alert will be replaced on the display by the form `fmMain`.

2. `Display.setCurrent(Alert)`

```
alTest = new Alert("Alert", "Message Here ", null,
                  null);
alTest.setTimeout(Alert.FOREVER);
...
display.setCurrent(alTest);
```

Presenting an `Alert` in this fashion assumes there is a `Displayable` object visible (a `TextBox`, `List`, `Form` or `Canvas`) when making this call. The reason is that, once the `Alert` has been dismissed (either acknowledged by the user or reached its requested display time), the previous `Displayable` will be shown.

Alert API

Table 8.6 Alert: javax.microedition.lcdui.Alert	
Method	*Description*
Constructors	
Alert(String title)	Create a new Alert
Alert(String title, String alertText, Image alertImage, AlertType, alertType)	Create a new Alert with an Image and an associated sound (AlertType)
Methods	
Image **getImage**()	Get Image associated with Alert
void **setImage**(Image img)	Associate an Image with Alert
String **getString**()	Get text associated with Alert
void **setString**(String str)	Set text for Alert
int **getDefaultTimeout**()	Get default time Alert is displayed
int **getTimeout**()	Get actual time Alert will be displayed
void **setTimeout**(int time)	Set amount of time to display Alert
AlertType **getType**()	Get the AlertType
void **setType**(AlertType type)	Set the AlertType

Using Commands and Listeners with Alerts

`Alert` is a subclass of `Screen`, which is a subclass of `Displayable`. Even though the following methods are declared as public inside the `Displayable` class, they cannot be used with an `Alert`. Calling these methods will throw the exception `IllegalStateException`:

```
addCommand(Command)
removeCommand(Command)
setCommandListener(CommandListener)
```

Sound Support

In addition to the visual attributes, you can associate a sound with an `Alert`. This is done using the `AlertType` class.

There are five pre-defined sounds that are tied to various conditions: alarm, confirmation, error, info and warning (see Table 8.7). The idea is this: When you want to present an `Alert` and associated sound for general information, you would request the "info" sound. An `Alert` for an error condition would request the "error" sound, and so forth.

You can play a sound in one of two ways:

1. If the `Alert` has an associated `AlertType`, the sound will be played when the `Alert` is displayed. You can associate a sound by either specifying the `AlertType` as the last parameter to the constructor or using the method `setType()`. An example of each is shown here:

    Option #1:
    ```
    Alert  al;
    al = new Alert("Alert", "Message ", null,
          AlertType.WARNING);
    ```

    Option #2:
    ```
    Alert  al;
    al = new Alert("Alert", "Message ", null, null);
    ...
    al.setType(AlertType.WARNING);
    ```

2. You can play a sound directly, without creating an `Alert` dialog box.
    ```
    AlertType.INFO.playSound(myDisplay);
    ```

This may be helpful when you would like to signify something has taken place without changing what's on the display. For example, if a user requested to download data in the background, a simple confirmation sound when the download completed would be helpful.

The `AlertType` is provided as an audible means to notify a user. Ideally, the sound would match the condition. For example, an error condition may trigger a louder and longer sound than that of a simple confirmation signifying a successful download. Bear in mind that a device may actually ignore requests to play a sound. Furthermore, if sounds are available, each is not guaranteed to be unique.

AlertType API

Table 8.7 AlertType Types: javax.microedition.lcdui.AlertType	
Value	*Description*
ALARM	Indicates arrival of a previous request to be notified
CONFIRMATION	Indicates completion of an event or action
ERROR	Indicates an error has occurred
INFO	Indicates general, non-critical information
WARNING	Indicates potential problem or situation

Table 8.8 AlertType Method: javax.microedition.lcdui.AlertType	
Method	*Description*
boolean **playSound**(Display display)	Play a sound on the device

Example: Playing Sounds

Example 8.7 will not show an actual Alert; rather, it will play the various sounds available through the AlertType class. The MIDlet is shown in Figure 8–17.

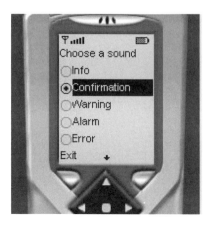

Figure 8-17   Play the various sounds

Example 8.7   SoundAlert.java

```java
import javax.microedition.midlet.*;
import javax.microedition.lcdui.*;

public class SoundAlert extends MIDlet implements
                        ItemStateListener, CommandListener
{
  private Display display;      // Reference to display object
  private Form fmMain;          // Main form
  private Command cmExit;       // Command to exit the MIDlet
  private ChoiceGroup cgSound;  // Choice group

  public SoundAlert()
  {
    display = Display.getDisplay(this);

    // Create an exclusive (radio) choice group
    cgSound = new ChoiceGroup("Choose a sound", Choice.EXCLUSIVE);

    // Append options, with no associated images
    cgSound.append("Info", null);
    cgSound.append("Confirmation", null);
    cgSound.append("Warning", null);
    cgSound.append("Alarm", null);
    cgSound.append("Error", null);

    cmExit = new Command("Exit", Command.EXIT, 1);

    // Create Form, add components, listen for events
    fmMain = new Form("");
    fmMain.append(cgSound);
    fmMain.addCommand(cmExit);
    fmMain.setCommandListener(this);
    fmMain.setItemStateListener(this);
  }

  public void startApp()
  {
    display.setCurrent(fmMain);
  }

  public void pauseApp()
  { }
```

(continued)

Example 8.7 *(Continued)*

```java
public void destroyApp(boolean unconditional)
{ }

public void commandAction(Command c, Displayable s)
{
  if (c == cmExit)
{
    destroyApp(false);
    notifyDestroyed();
  }
}

public void itemStateChanged(Item item)
{
  switch (cgSound.getSelectedIndex())
  {
    case 0:
      AlertType.INFO.playSound(display);
      break;

    case 1:
      AlertType.CONFIRMATION.playSound(display);
      break;

    case 2:
      AlertType.WARNING.playSound(display);
      break;

    case 3:
      AlertType.ALARM.playSound(display);
      break;

    case 4:
      AlertType.ERROR.playSound(display);
      break;
  }
}
}
```

This MIDlet uses an exclusive `ChoiceGroup` (radio buttons) and registers an `ItemStateListener` for the `Form` that contains the `Choice-Group`. Bring to mind how this listener works. When a change is detected on an `Item` (`ChoiceGroup` is a subclass of `Item`), the method `item-StateChanged()` is called. Inside this method, we determine which entry in the choice was selected and play the appropriate sound:

```
public void itemStateChanged(Item item)
{
  switch (cgSound.getSelectedIndex())
  {
  case 0:
    AlertType.INFO.playSound(display);
    break;
    ...
  }
}
```

Playing Sounds

Although you can request a sound to be played, the implementation has the option to ignore the request altogether or to play the same sound for all/some of the `AlertTypes`.

Example: Modal Alert with Image

Let's look at a MIDlet (Example 8.8) that shows a modal `Alert` containing both a text message and an image.

Example 8.8   ModalAlert.java

```
import javax.microedition.midlet.*;
import javax.microedition.lcdui.*;

public class ModalAlert extends MIDlet implements CommandListener
{
```

(continued)

Example 8.8   *(Continued)*

```
private Display display;    // Reference to Display object
private Form fmMain;        // Main form
private Alert alTest;       // Alert to show text and image
private Command cmExit;     // Command to exit the MIDlet

public ModalAlert()
{
  display = Display.getDisplay(this);

  cmExit = new Command("Exit", Command.SCREEN, 1);
  fmMain = new Form("Welcome");
  fmMain.append("Text string inside the Form");
  fmMain.addCommand(cmExit);
  fmMain.setCommandListener(this);
}

public void startApp()
{
  showAlert();
}

public void pauseApp()
{
}

public void destroyApp(boolean unconditional)
{
}

public void showAlert()
{
  try
  {
    // Create an image
    Image im = Image.createImage("/coffee.png");

    // Create Alert, add text and image, associate a sound
    alTest = new Alert("New Alert", "Time for more Java",
                       im, AlertType.INFO);

    // Set Alert to type Modal
    alTest.setTimeout(Alert.FOREVER);
```

(continued)

Example 8.8   (Continued)

```
    }
    catch(Exception e)
    {
      System.out.println("Unable to read png image.");
    }

    // Display the Alert. Once dismissed, display the form
    display.setCurrent(alTest, fmMain);
  }

  public void commandAction(Command c, Displayable s)
  {
    if (c == cmExit)
    {
      destroyApp(true);
      notifyDestroyed();
    }
  }
}
```

The bulk of the new code is inside showAlert(). Here we create an image, add the image and a text message to a new Alert, and set the timeout value to Alert.FOREVER, resulting in a modal Alert.

```
Image im = Image.createImage("/coffee.png");

// Create Alert, add text and image, associate a sound
alTest = new Alert("New Alert", "Time for more Java",
                    im, AlertType.INFO);

// Set Alert to type Modal
alTest.setTimeout(Alert.FOREVER);
```

The last line before exiting the method shows the Alert on the display. Notice the reference to fmMain.

```
display.setCurrent(alTest, fmMain);
```

Once an alert has been acknowledged by the user, the Alert is removed from the display and a previously defined Displayable object will be shown. For this example the Displayable is fmMain, which we specified using the aforementioned line.

The method setCurrent() is overloaded, meaning there is another method with the same name with different calling parameters. Instead of

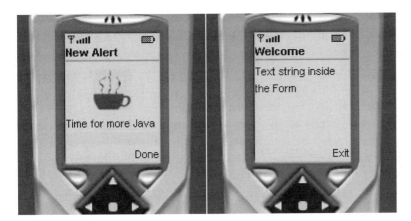

Figure 8–18 Alert with image and text; on the right, the Displayable object (Form) that is shown when the alerted is dismissed

passing in an `Alert` and a `Displayable` (as above), you can simply call with a `Displayable` object:

    Display.setCurrent(alTest);

Although this call will succeed (an `Alert` is a subclass of `Screen`, which is a subclass of `Displayable`), we need to think this through. Once the `Alert` is acknowledged the MIDlet will attempt to show the previous `Displayable`. In our example, if you follow the logic closely you'll see that we have not shown any `Displayable` objects before calling `showAlert()`. The constructor was called, followed by `startApp()`, followed by `showAlert()`. The allocation of our `Form` (a `Displayable`) inside the constructor is not sufficient to appease the application manager. We must have actually shown a `Displayable` on the device. If not, a `NullPointerException` will be thrown.

Figure 8–18 shows the alert on the left and the form that appears once the alert is dismissed.

Ticker

Just as most C programmers wrote "Hello world" as their first program, Java has its own rite of passage—the scrolling text applet. The idea of sliding text across the display lives on. MIDP includes a scrolling text component known as the `Ticker`.

At this point we have covered all the components that extend the `Screen` class, making this an ideal time to introduce this class. A `Ticker` can be "attached" to any `Screen`, including an `Alert`. In fact, the same `Ticker` can be shared among `Screens`, giving the illusion that the `Ticker` is attached to the device display, not the individual screens that make up the application. This is a nice effect, as we'll see in an example.

Whether the text scrolls at the top or bottom and the speed at which scrolling occurs is decided by the implementation. However, you can be assured that the scrolling is continuous—as the trailing end of the text rolls off the screen, the beginning of the text will appear again.

Ticker API

Table 8.9 Ticker Class: javax.microedition.lcdui.Ticker	
Method	*Description*
Constructor	
Ticker(String str)	Create a new Ticker with the specified ticker text
Methods	
String **getString**()	Get the text associated with the Ticker
void **setString**(String str)	Set the text to associate with the Ticker

Example: One Ticker, Two Components

In Example 8.9, we create a `Ticker` that is tied to both a `List` and an `Alert`. As you move between the two, the `Ticker` won't miss a beat.

Example 8.9 SharedTicker.java

```
import javax.microedition.midlet.*;
import javax.microedition.lcdui.*;

public class SharedTicker extends MIDlet implements CommandListener
{
```

(continued)

Example 8.9   *(Continued)*

```
private Display display;      // Reference to Display object
private List lsProducts;      // Main productlist
private Alert alHelp;         // Alert to show text and image
private Ticker tkSale;        // Ticker of what's on sale
private Command cmExit;       // Command to exit the MIDlet

public SharedTicker()
{
  display = Display.getDisplay(this);

  cmExit = new Command("Exit", Command.SCREEN, 1);

  tkSale = new Ticker("Current Sale: Torchiere
                       Lamp only $29.00");

  lsProducts = new List("Products", Choice.IMPLICIT);
  lsProducts.append("Floor Lamp", null);
  lsProducts.append("Chandelier", null);
  lsProducts.append("Help", null);
  lsProducts.addCommand(cmExit);
  lsProducts.setCommandListener(this);
  lsProducts.setTicker(tkSale);
}

public void startApp()
{
  display.setCurrent(lsProducts);
}

public void pauseApp()
{
}

public void destroyApp(boolean unconditional)
{
}

public void showAlert()
{
  try
  {
    // Create an image
    Image im = Image.createImage("/help.png");
```

(continued)

Example 8.9   *(Continued)*

```java
      // Create Alert, add text and image, no sound
      alHelp = new Alert("Help Information",
                          "Over 300 unique lighting products!",
                          im, null);
      alHelp.setTimeout(Alert.FOREVER);
      alHelp.setTicker(tkSale);
    }
    catch(Exception e)
    {
      System.out.println("Unable to read png image.");
    }

    // Display the Alert. Once dismissed, return to product list
    display.setCurrent(alHelp, lsProducts);

  }

  public void commandAction(Command c, Displayable s)
  {

    if (c == List.SELECT_COMMAND)
    {
      switch (lsProducts.getSelectedIndex())
      {
        case 0:
          System.out.println("Floor Lamp selected");
          break;

        case 1:
          System.out.println("Chandelier selected");
          break;

        case 2:
          showAlert();
          break;
      }
    }
    else if (c == cmExit)
    {
      destroyApp(true);
      notifyDestroyed();
    }
  }
}
```

Figure 8–19 A List component with a Ticker

Attaching a `Ticker` to multiple components is as simple as calling the method `setTicker()`, passing a reference to the same `Ticker` object. Here are the lines to set the `Ticker` for our `List` and `Alert`:

```
lsProducts.setTicker(tkSale);
...
alHelp.setTicker(tkSale);
```

Figure 8–19 displays the `List` along with the `Ticker` running at the top.

If you select the "Help" option from the `List`, an `Alert` will be shown (see Figure 8–20). Notice the ticker is still running and displaying the same text as on the previous screen.

Figure 8–20 An Alert with the same Ticker as shown in Figure 8–19

LOW-LEVEL USER INTERFACE

Topics in this Chapter

- Canvas
- Graphics

Chapter 9

Ignorance is bliss. Up to this point we've never given a second thought as to how a `Form`, `TextBox` or any other visual component appears on the display. We simply made a request to allocate and display a component, and left it at that. If the need never arose to move beyond "high-level" components we'd be set.

Then again, there is a whole new world on the other side. If we take the initiative to learn how to draw onto the display, the possibilities are nearly[1] endless. Those interested in writing custom components and games will make extensive use of the classes presented in this chapter.

Two key classes make up the low-level API, `Canvas` and `Graphics`.

- The **Canvas** forms the backdrop. Not unlike an artists' canvas, it has a specific height and width and is drawn onto to create

---

[1]There are limits to the drawing operations. MIDP supports only a subset of the capabilities available in J2SE.

what the end user will see. Whatever is drawn becomes visible on the display. The canvas class also provides methods for low-level event handling.

- We draw onto a canvas with a **Graphics** object (often referred to as a graphics context). This class has methods for drawing lines, arcs, rectangles and text. This class also includes methods to specify color as well as font preferences.

The exploration into creating a custom interface begins with the Canvas.

Canvas

Let's start out at the outermost level and work our way in. From the big picture, a Canvas is a subclass of Displayable, as is the Screen class you learned about in Chapter 7. Figure 9–1 revisits the user interface hierarchy.

One last time, here are the class definitions for the hierarchy shown in Figure 9–1:

Figure 9–1 Displayable class hierarchy

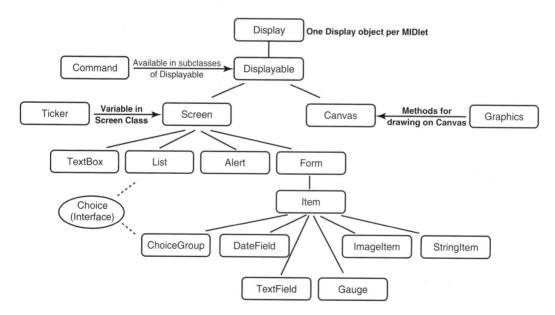

Display	(public class Display)
Displayable	(public abstract class Displayable)
Screen	(public abstract class Screen extends Displayable)
TextBox	(public class TextBox extends Screen)
List	(public class List extends Screen implements Choice)
Alert	(public class Alert extends Screen)
Form	(public class Form extends Screen)
Item	(public abstract class Item)
ChoiceGroup	(public class ChoiceGroup extends Item implements Choice)
DateField	(public class DateField extends Item)
TextField	(public class TextField extends Item)
Gauge	(public class Gauge extends Item)
ImageItem	(public class ImageItem extends Item)
StringItem	(public class StringItem extends Item)
Canvas	(public abstract class Canvas extends Displayable)
Command	(public class Command)
Ticker	(public class Ticker)
Graphics	(public class Graphics)
Choice	(public interface Choice)

To backtrack for just a moment, you learned in Chapter 5 that there is only one `Display` object per MIDlet; however, there can be any number of `Displayable` objects. For example, a MIDlet can bounce between displaying a `Form`, followed by a `TextBox`, followed by a `List`, returning back to the `Form`. What is displayed and when is completely at our whim as the developer. We can now throw a `Canvas` into the mix, alternating between this `Displayable` and any other.

Creating the Canvas

You won't directly request to display an instance of the `Canvas` class. Rather, you create a subclass of `Canvas`, and ask that this object be set as the current `Displayable`.

For example:

```
class AnimationCanvas extends Canvas
                      implements CommandListener
{
  private Command cmExit;              // Exit midlet
  ...
  cmExit = new Command("Exit", Command.EXIT, 1);
```

```
addCommand(cmExit);
setCommandListener(this);
...
protected void paint(Graphics g)
{
...
}
}

AnimationCanvas canvas = new AnimationCanvas(this);
display.setCurrent(canvas);
```

Notice the last two lines. A new `AnimationCanvas` object is created and set as the current `Displayable`.

Only moments ago it was stated that when using a `Canvas`, it is the developer's responsibility to draw onto the `Canvas` with a `Graphics` object. If we create and immediately request to display the `Canvas`, when and where does the drawing take place? Hold that thought: After learning about the coordinate system we'll explore this further in the section "Painting on the Canvas."

Coordinate System

The origin for drawing begins in the upper left corner of the display, location 0,0 (see Figure 9–2). x values increase heading to the right, y values increase heading down.

There are a few caveats worth mentioning. When working with a `Graphics` object we have the option to translate the origin as the `Graphics` object knows it. Second, when drawing text, an additional concept

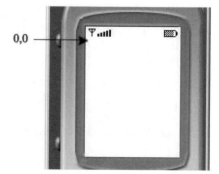

Figure 9–2 Coordinate system

0,0

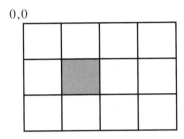

Figure 9–3   Pixel drawn when starting a line

known as an anchor point is tossed in. I will talk to each of these as we work through this chapter.

When drawing a line or shape (arc, rectangle, etc.), the thickness (known as the pen) is always 1 pixel wide. For example, if you request to start a line at 1,1, visualize a square pixel with a starting point at 1,1 and ending at 2,2 (always moving down and to the right). Even before moving the pen, a pixel has been filled! See Figure 9–3.

With that in mind, continue that same line ending at 3,1. How many pixels will be "filled" for the entire line segment 1,1 to 3,1? (If you guessed 2, try again.)

If you picture the starting and ending point individually—that is, a square pixel is filled at each coordinate location (once again, always filling down and to the right)—it's a little easier for this to sink in and it should be clear why three pixels are drawn for the aforementioned line (1,1 to 3,1) (see Figure 9–4).

How does this affect drawing of shapes? If we request to draw a rectangle starting at 1,1 and ending at 3,3, which image in Figure 9–5 accurately depicts the result?

0,0

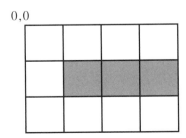

Figure 9–4   Pixels drawn for line segment 1,1 to 3,1

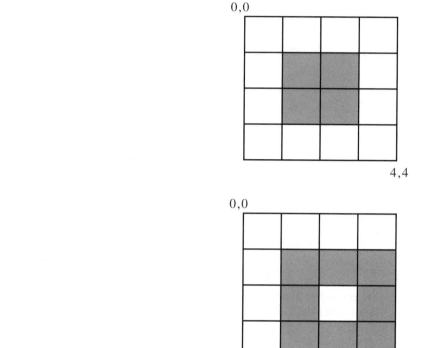

Figure 9-5 Drawing a rectangle from 1,1 to 3,3

If you are unsure, let me tell you this: The same drawing paradigm applies to shapes as well as lines. Namely, a pixel is filled at each coordinate location.

In requesting a rectangle to be drawn with dimensions 1,1 to 3,3 the pen will need to move to each coordinate boundary: $1,1 \rightarrow 3,1 \rightarrow 3,3$ back to 1,1.[2] If you follow the path of the pen, it will become obvious why the lower image in Figure 9–5 is the resulting rectangle. Here's the sequence:

1. Drop the pen at 1,1, which fills the pixel 1,1 to 2,2.
2. Move the pen to the rightmost coordinate: 3,1. This fills the pixel at 2,1 to 3,2 and the pixel at 3,1 to 4,2.
3. Move the pen down to coordinate 3,3. This fills the pixel at 3,3 to 4,4.

---

[2]The implementation may opt for a different order; however, the idea is the same.

4. Move the pen to the leftmost coordinate: 1,3. This fills the pixel at 2,3 to 3,4 and the pixel at 1,3 to 2, 4.

5. Move the pen to the starting coordinate: 1,1. This fills the pixel at1,2 to 2, 3.

Knowing what we do about the pen and its pixel width, what is the outcome of drawing a line from 0,0 to 0,0? Is there anything drawn at all? If you are not sure, read the sidebar "Drawing with a Pen."

Drawing with a Pen

The idea of the pen always filling the pixel down and to the right of the specified coordinate is not much different then drawing on paper. If you hold a pen over a piece of paper and bring the tip in contact with the writing surface, a "dot" will appear. The size of this dot, for our purpose, is one pixel in width and height. If you move the pen on the paper, regardless of the direction, each movement will fill another pixel.

Keep this in mind, regardless of the shape drawn:

- The pixel at the starting coordinate is filled, down and to the right.

- Each additional coordinate that makes up the shape has a pixel filled, down and to the right.

Canvas Width and Height

Table 9.1 shows the two methods to query a `Canvas` for its width and height. These values will always be the same for any one device.[3] If a call to `getWidth()` returns 200, every `Canvas` created on that particular device will have a width of 200.

---

[3]If a device supports upgrading of hardware and/or software, this may not always be true. The size of a canvas may change if the device itself changes.

Table 9.1 Canvas Coordinate Methods: javax.microedition.lcdui.Canvas	
Method	*Description*
int **getWidth**()	Get the canvas width
int **getHeight** ()	Get the canvas height

Painting on the Canvas

At the beginning of this chapter I mentioned that when using a Canvas, we are responsible for drawing. Shortly thereafter I proceeded to show something similar to the following

```
AnimationCanvas canvas = new AnimationCanvas(this);
display.setCurrent(canvas);
```

This declares a Canvas and requests it to be set as the current displayable. This is the same path we took when requesting to display other components such as Form or TextBox. So at what point do we draw onto the Canvas?

Here's how it works. As explained earlier, Canvas is a subclass of Displayable. All displayable objects are made visible through:

```
javax.microedition.lcdui.display.setCurrent(Displayable);
```

What differs between a Canvas and the other Displayable objects (Form, TextBox, List and Alert) is where the drawing of the component takes place and who is responsible for the drawing.

Shown on page 251 are the class definitions and several lines of pseudo code for Displayable, Canvas, Screen and the components Form, TextBox, List and Alert.

The Displayable class defines paint() as an abstract method. Following the rules defined by the Java language, both subclasses, Canvas and Screen, implement the paint() method. Here's the primary difference: the paint() method inside Canvas is abstract, meaning there is no method body. It is up to a subclass to implement this method.

Contrast this with the Screen, where the paint() method draws the title and Ticker (features common to all screens). Before leaving paint() the method paintContent() is called. Notice this method is declared as abstract, thus all subclasses (Form, TextBox, List and Alert) must implement this method.

```
abstract public class Displayable
        abstract void paint(Graphics g);

public abstract class Canvas extends Displayable
        protected abstract void paint(Graphics g);

public abstract class Screen extends Displayable
{
        abstract void paintContent(Graphics g);

        paint(Graphics g)
        {
                // Draw optional title
                // Draw optional Ticker
                ...
                paintContent(g);
        }
}

public class Form extends Screen
{
        void paintContent(Graphics g)
        {...}
}

public class TextBox extends Screen
{
        void paintContent(Graphics g)
        {...}
}

public class List extends Screen implements Choice
{
        void paintContent(Graphics g)
        {...}
}

public class Alert extends Screen
{
        void paintContent(Graphics g)
        {...}
}
```

Inside Form, TextBox, List and Alert paintContent() "knows" how to draw the component. For example, paintContent() inside List will draw a list on the device, the same method inside TextBox will draw a textbox, and so forth.

It boils down to this: Form, TextBox, List and Alert are drawn through the paint() method in the Screen class in concert with paint-Content() inside each individual component. Canvas has declared paint() as abstract. Therefore, whenever we subclass Canvas, we are responsible for implementing this method.

Once again, here is a block of code that creates a new canvas:

```
class AnimationCanvas extends Canvas
                      implements CommandListener
{
  private Command cmExit;            // Exit midlet
  ...
  cmExit = new Command("Exit", Command.EXIT, 1);
  addCommand(cmExit);
  setCommandListener(this);
  ...
  protected void paint(Graphics g)
  {
  ...
  }
}
```

Painting of Components

When working with a subclass of Displayable (Canvas and Screen) the component is made visible on the display through a call to

`javax.microedtion.lcdui.display.setCurrent(Displayable);`

The difference lies with "who" provides the code for the paint() method. When using a Canvas, you override the paint() method and write the code. For subclasses of Screen (Form, List, TextBox and Alert) the methods paint() and paintContents() comprise the code to draw each respective component.

The `paint()` method is always passed a reference to a `Graphics` object, which is used to draw onto the `Canvas`. For example, to write text and draw a rectangle onto a `Canvas`, the paint method may look something like this:

```
protected void paint(Graphics g)
{
  g.drawString("Hello", 0, 0,
                   Graphics.TOP | Graphics.LEFT);
  g.drawRect(5, 5, 10, 10);
  ...
}
```

We'll cover all methods of the `Graphics` class later in this chapter. For now, focus you attention on the methods in Table 9.2.

Table 9.2   Canvas Paint Methods: javax.microedition.lcdui.Canvas

Method	*Description*
abstract void **paint**(Graphics g)	Draw onto the canvas using the Graphics object specified
final void **repaint**()	Request the canvas to be painted
final void **repaint**(int x, int y, int width, int height)	Request a specified region of canvas to be painted
final void **serviceRepaints**()	Immediately process any pending paint requests
boolean is **DoubleBuffered**()	Does implementation provide double buffering?

`paint()` deserves top billing. This method serves as the workhorse for drawing to the display. You invoke the methods in the `Graphics` object (which is passed in as a parameter) to draw lines, arcs, rectangles and text.

`repaint()` is called to request the (entire) display to be updated. In Example 9–3, later in this chapter, we will track when a user clicks a mouse button down. As they hold down the mouse button and move it around the display, we want to visually trace each step. We do this by calling `repaint()` after each movement, drawing a line segment from the last position to the current position.

The version of `repaint()` that accepts four parameters specifies a specific region on the display to repaint. We will visit this again when discussing clipping within the graphics section.

`serviceRepaints()` will force any pending paint requests to be immediately issued. Use this with caution, as this call will block until all paint requests have been serviced.

Calling `paint()`

The `paint()` method is never to be called directly. The results of doing so are unpredictable. If you need to have the display updated, make your request known through a call to `repaint()`.

Communication with Application Manager

When the application manager is about to make a `Canvas` visible on the display, it will call the method `showNotify()`. When the `Canvas` has been removed from the display, the method `hideNotify()` is called.

Table 9.3   Application Manager Communication: javax.microedition.lcdui.Canvas

Method	*Description*
void **showNotify**()	Application manager is about to show the canvas on the display
void **hideNotify**()	Application manager has removed the canvas from the display

Here is the code for each method taken directly from the `Canvas` class.

```
protected void showNotify()
{ }

protected void hideNotify()
{ }
```

Clearly, calls to these methods from the application manager are pointless without a little effort on your part. For example, inside `showNotify()` may be an ideal time to initialize variables, start a thread, and so forth. `hideNotify()` may be home to code to reset variables, stop a thread, and so forth. These methods provide an opportunity to take part in the transition as a `Canvas` moves from inactive to active, and back again, throughout the lifecycle of the MIDlet.

In Chapter 10 we will write a simple animation example. `show-Notify()` will read an image from a file, set the preferred drawing coordinates and start a `Thread`. `hideNotify()` will reset a variable, effectively stopping the animation.

Event Handling

There are two general means of interaction between a user and the `Canvas`, `Commands` and low-level events. `Commands`, which we've seen before, will be touched upon ever so briefly. The low-level interface, consisting of key codes, game actions and pointer events, will be the prime focus of this section.

Commands

As a refresher, look back to Figure 9–1. `Canvas` is inherited from `Displayable`. There are four methods available through this inheritance:

- `addCommand(Command)`
- `isShown()`
- `removeCommand(Command)`
- `setCommandListener(CommandListener)`

This should tell you something about the `Canvas`. Specifically, it can process `Command` objects just as we did with a `Form`, `List` and `TextBox` (`Commands` cannot be added to an `Alert`). The code for creating a `Command`, adding to a `Canvas` and registering a listener are identical to the same steps we've done numerous times before:

```
class TestCanvas extends Canvas implements CommandListener
{
  private Command cmExit;            // Exit midlet
  ...
  cmExit = new Command("Exit", Command.EXIT, 1);
  addCommand(cmExit);
  setCommandListener(this);
  ...

  public void commandAction(Command c, Displayable d)
  {
```

```
        if (c == cmExit)
          ...
     }
   }
```

Key Codes

Key codes are numeric values that map directly to specific keys on a mobile device. The key codes that are guaranteed to be available on any MIDP are listed in Table 9.4. These codes correspond to the ITU-T keypad (0–9, *, #) the standard telephone keypad. Each key code has a static declaration similar to the following:

```
public static final int KEY_NUM0 = 48;
public static final int KEY_NUM1 = 49;
   ...
```

Table 9.4   Key Codes: javax.microedition.lcdui.Canvas

Name	Constant Value
KEY_NUM0	48
KEY_NUM1	49
KEY_NUM2	50
KEY_NUM3	51
KEY_NUM4	52
KEY_NUM5	53
KEY_NUM6	54
KEY_NUM7	55
KEY_NUM8	56
KEY_NUM9	57
KEY_STAR	42
KEY_POUND	35

For example, when "1" is pressed on the keypad, the key code returned is 49 (KEY_NUM1). The methods available for managing key codes are shown in Table 9.5.

Table 9.5 Key Code Methods: javax.microedition.lcdui.Canvas	
Method	*Description*
void **keyPressed**(int keyCode)	Invoked when a key is pressed
void **keyReleased**(int keyCode)	Invoked when a key is released
void **keyRepeated**(int keyCode)	Invoked when a key is repeated[1]
boolean **hasRepeatEvents**()	Does the implementation support repeated keys?
String **getKeyName**(int keyCode)	The text string representing the key code

[1]May not be supported on all devices.

keyPressed(), keyReleased() and keyRepeated() are simply place holders, each method body is empty. For example, keyPressed() looks as follows:

```
protected void keyPressed(int keyCode) {
}
```

The obvious implication is that you must override these methods and provide the code for processing key events. Each of these methods has the key code that triggered the event passed in as a parameter. You decide how to proceed based on the key code:

```
protected void keyPressed(int keyCode)
{
  if (keyCode == KEY_NUM1)
     ...
  else if (keyCode == KEY_NUM2)
     ...
}
```

Key Codes and Portability

To write portable applications you must stick to using the key codes defined in Table 9.4. Although other key codes may be generated by a device, there are no guarantees that such codes will be available from one device to another.

Example: Viewing Key Code Names

getKeyName() will return the text (String) representation for a key code (e.g., "*" for the key code KEY_STAR). In Example 9.1, a Canvas is created that detects events from Commands and key codes. When an event is generated through a key code, keyPressed() will be called, where the text for the code is printed to the Canvas.

Example 9.1   KeyCodes.java

```
/*--------------------------------------------------
 * KeyCodes.java
 *
 * Canvas for processing key code and commands
 *--------------------------------------------------*/
import javax.microedition.midlet.*;
import javax.microedition.lcdui.*;

public class KeyCodes extends MIDlet
{
  private Display   display;       // The display
  private KeyCodeCanvas canvas;    // Canvas

  public KeyCodes()
  {
    display = Display.getDisplay(this);
    canvas  = new KeyCodeCanvas(this);
  }

  protected void startApp()
  {
    display.setCurrent(canvas);
  }

  protected void pauseApp()
  { }

  protected void destroyApp( boolean unconditional )
  { }
```

(continued)

Example 9.1 (*Continued*)

```java
  public void exitMIDlet()
  {
    destroyApp(true);
    notifyDestroyed();
  }
}

/*----------------------------------------------------
 * Class KeyCodeCanvas
 *
 * Key codes and commands for event handling
 *--------------------------------------------------*/
class KeyCodeCanvas extends Canvas implements CommandListener
{
  private Command cmExit;            // Exit midlet
  private String keyText = null;     // Key code text
  private KeyCodes midlet;

  /*------------------------------------------------
   * Constructor
   *----------------------------------------------*/
  public KeyCodeCanvas(KeyCodes midlet)
  {
    this.midlet = midlet;

    // Create exit command & listen for events
    cmExit = new Command("Exit", Command.EXIT, 1);
    addCommand(cmExit);
    setCommandListener(this);
  }

  /*------------------------------------------------
   * Paint the text representing the key code
   *----------------------------------------------*/
  protected void paint(Graphics g)
  {
    // Clear the background (to white)
    g.setColor(255, 255, 255);
    g.fillRect(0, 0, getWidth(),getWidth());

    // Set color and draw text
    if (keyText != null)
    {
```

(*continued*)

Example 9.1   *(Continued)*

```
    // Draw with black pen
    g.setColor(0, 0, 0);
    // Center the text
    g.drawString(keyText, getWidth()/2, getWidth()/2,
                 Graphics.TOP | Graphics.HCENTER);
  }
}


/*--------------------------------------------------
 * Command event handling
 *--------------------------------------------------*/
public void commandAction(Command c, Displayable d)
{
  if (c == cmExit)
    midlet.exitMIDlet();
}


/*--------------------------------------------------
 * Key code event handling
 *--------------------------------------------------*/
protected void keyPressed(int keyCode)
{
  keyText = getKeyName(keyCode);
  repaint();
}
}
```

Notice there are two methods for managing events: `commandAction()` and `keyPressed()`. The first method works as it always has, receiving a `Command` object that generated the event and the `Displayable` object on which the event was received. The only check is to see if there was a request to exit the MIDlet.

```
public void commandAction(Command c, Displayable d)
{
  if (c == cmExit)
    midlet.exitMIDlet();
}
```

`keyPressed()` is called when a key code generates an event. The code is converted into a `String` and a request is made to repaint the `Canvas` (where `keyText` is displayed).

```
protected void keyPressed(int keyCode)
  {
    keyText = getKeyName(keyCode);
    repaint();
  }
```

This is our first run-in with the `paint()` method. Notice the `Graphics` object that is passed in. This object is used to render directly onto the `Canvas`, which is analogous to drawing onto the display. Within `paint()` we clear the display and write the text string that represents the key code pressed. For the time being, don't concern yourself with the methods of the `Graphics` class. If you get the gist of what is going on inside `paint()`, you're good to go.

```
protected void paint(Graphics g)
  {
    // Clear the background (to white)
    g.setColor(255, 255, 255);
    g.fillRect(0, 0, getWidth(),getWidth());

    // Set color and draw text
    if (keyText != null)
    {
      // Draw with black pen
      g.setColor(0, 0, 0);
      // Center the text
      g.drawString(keyText, getWidth()/2, getWidth()/2,
                  Graphics.TOP | Graphics.LEFT);
    }
  }
```

Figure 9–6 shows the output of `keyCodes.java` when pressing the * and 7 keys on the keypad.

Game Actions

MIDP defines a set of constants, referred to as game actions, to facilitate event handling for game related events (see Table 9.6). Each game action is defined as a static integer:

```
public static final int UP=1;
public static final int DOWN=6;
...
```

You are assured that each game action will be assigned a key code by the implementation. For example, on the device shown in Figure 9–7 the game

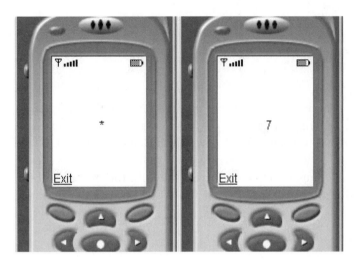

Figure 9–6   Printing key codes on a canvas

actions UP, RIGHT, LEFT, DOWN and FIRE may be mapped to the directional keys just below the display. Should a device not have such keys available, these same game actions may be mapped to the keypad using 2, 6, 4, 8 and 5, respectively.

With this design you don't need to concern yourself that one device may map "up" to a directional arrow and another may map the same action to the 2 key on the keypad.

Table 9.6 Game Actions: javax.microedition.lcdui.Canvas		
Name	*Description*	*Constant Value*
UP	Move up	1
DOWN	Move down	6
LEFT	Move left	2
RIGHT	Move right	5
FIRE	Fire	8
GAME_A	Custom	9
GAME_B	Custom	10
GAME_C	Custom	11
GAME_D	Custom	12

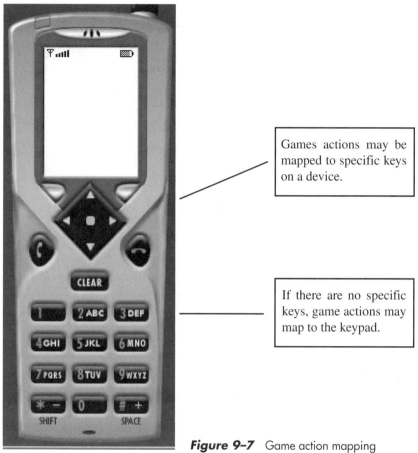

Games actions may be mapped to specific keys on a device.

If there are no specific keys, game actions may map to the keypad.

Figure 9-7 Game action mapping

The methods for working with game actions are listed in Table 9–7.

Table 9.7 Game Action Methods: javax.microedition.lcdui.Canvas	
Method	*Description*
int **getKeyCode**(int gameAction)	Determine key code for a game action
int **getGameAction**(int keyCode)	Get the game action, if any, for the key code
String **getKeyName**(int keyCode)	Get name for a key code[1]

[1]Can display the text associated with a game action if first converted to a key code. See description that follows.

getKeyCode() will always return a valid key code for any game action. For example, you may have initialization code that stores key codes for each action:

```
int keyFire  = getKeyCode(FIRE);
int keyRight = getKeyCode(RIGHT);
...
```

getGameAction() goes the opposite direction, returning a game action for a specified key code.

```
protected void keyRepeated(int keyCode)
{
  switch (getGameAction(keyCode))
  {
    case Canvas.FIRE:
    ...
  }
}
```

getKeyName() returns the name associated with a key code (e.g., "#" for KEY_POUND). Read that carefully—it does not return the name for a game action. However, this method will return the appropriate text if you convert a game action to a key code as follows:

```
getKeyName(getKeyCode(FIRE));
getKeyName(getKeyCode(RIGHT));
```

A second option is to let the conversion be done for you. For example, if a game action (such as a directional arrow) is pressed to initiate an event, keyPressed() will hand over the appropriate key code. From here you can get the associated text:

```
// Game action initiated the event...
  protected void keyPressed(int keyCode)
  {
    keyText = getKeyName(keyCode);
    ...
  }
```

Multiple Game Actions per Key Code

A key code can be mapped to, at most, one game action. For example, the key code KEY_NUM2 may be mapped to the game action Canvas.UP. However, the same key code cannot also be mapped to the game action Canvas.DOWN. Obviously, if this were true, you would have no way to decide which action to carry out. Do you move up or down when the event is fired?

However, we can flip the tables—a game action may be mapped to more than one key code. For example, the game action Canvas.UP may be mapped to a directional arrow (ideally one that points up) as well as an additional soft-key. Pressing either will invoke the same response, a request to carry out the "up action."

Detecting Game Actions

All low-level event handling on a Canvas is done through key codes (Commands, which are also available on a canvas, use the listener event model). Said another way, keyPressed(), keyReleased() and keyRepeated() are passed a key code when an event is triggered. Following are two options for working with game actions and their equivalent key codes:

Option #1

- During initialization, use getKeyCode() to request and store key codes for each game action.
- Inside keyPressed(), keyReleased() and keyRepreated(), branch based on the key code

Here is how this might look:

```
// During initialization
keyFire =  getKeyCode(FIRE);
keyRight = getKeyCode(RIGHT);
keyLeft = getKeyCode(LEFT);
...
// At runtime
protected void keyPressed(int keyCode)
{
   if (keyCode == keyFire)
      shootWeapon();
   else if (keyCode == keyRight)
        moveRight();
      ...
}
```

Option #2

- Inside `keyPressed()`, `keyReleased()` and `keyRepreated()`, convert the incoming key code into the corresponding game action
- Branch based on the game action

```
protected void keyPressed(int keyCode)
{
  switch (getGameAction(keyCode))
  {
     case Canvas.FIRE:
       shootWeapon();
       break;
     case Canvas.RIGHT:
       moveRight();
       break;
   ...
  }
}
```

Don't read anything into the use of if–then–else versus the switch statement. This is completely arbitrary. The end result for both options is the same—a means to decipher which game action initiated an event. How you detect and process game actions is a matter of preference and application logic.

Game Actions and Portability

Whether key codes for game actions are stored at initialization time or converted into a game action at runtime, we are in essence asking the implementation "so what key code is used for up, down, left, etc.". Once we know the action that fired the event, it's a simple matter to branch appropriately using an if–then–else or switch statement.

With this design you don't need to concern yourself with differences such as one device mapping the "up" action to a directional arrow and another mapping the same action to the 2 key on the keypad.

This design also provides for code that is portable. If you are diligent in using only the key codes shown in Table 9.4 and game actions Table 9.6, your event handling stands a good chance of running across a range of devices.

Example: Viewing Game Action Names

Example 9.2 prints the text associated with a game action. As with the previous example, `keyPressed()` will trap events and convert the incoming key codes into a text string. The `paint()` method will print the text onto the display (see Figure 9–8).

Example 9.2   GameActions.java

```
/*---------------------------------------------------
* GameActions.java
*
* Canvas for processing game actions
*---------------------------------------------------*/
import javax.microedition.midlet.*;
import javax.microedition.lcdui.*;

public class GameActions extends MIDlet
{
  private Display  display;          // The display
  private GameActionCanvas canvas;   // Canvas

  public GameActions()
  {
    display = Display.getDisplay(this);
    canvas  = new GameActionCanvas(this);
  }

  protected void startApp()
  {
    display.setCurrent(canvas);
  }

  protected void pauseApp()
  { }

  protected void destroyApp(boolean unconditional)
  { }

  public void exitMIDlet()
  {
```

(continued)

Example 9.2 *(Continued)*

```
      destroyApp(true);
      notifyDestroyed();
    }
}

/*---------------------------------------------------
 * GameActionCanvas.java
 *
 * Game action event handling
 *---------------------------------------------------*/
class GameActionCanvas extends Canvas implements CommandListener
{
  private Command cmExit;            // Exit midlet
  private String keyText = null;     // Key code text
  private GameActions midlet;

  /*-------------------------------------------------
   * Constructor
   *-------------------------------------------------*/
  public GameActionCanvas(GameActions midlet)
  {
    this.midlet = midlet;

    // Create exit command & listen for events
    cmExit = new Command("Exit", Command.EXIT, 1);
    addCommand(cmExit);
    setCommandListener(this);
  }

  /*-------------------------------------------------
   * Paint the text representing the key code
   *-------------------------------------------------*/
  protected void paint(Graphics g)
  {
    // Clear the background (to white)
    g.setColor(255, 255, 255);
    g.fillRect(0, 0, getWidth(), getHeight());

    // Set color and draw text
    if (keyText != null)
    {
      // Draw with black pen
```

(continued)

Example 9.2   *(Continued)*

```
      g.setColor(0, 0, 0);
      // Center the text
      g.drawString(keyText, getWidth()/2, getHeight()/2,
                  Graphics.TOP | Graphics.HCENTER);
   }
}

/*--------------------------------------------------
 * Command event handling
 *------------------------------------------------*/
public void commandAction(Command c, Displayable d)
{
   if (c == cmExit)
     midlet.exitMIDlet();
}

/*--------------------------------------------------
 * Game action event handling
 * A game action will be converted into a key code
 * and handed off to this method
 *------------------------------------------------*/
protected void keyPressed(int keyCode)
{
   switch (getGameAction(keyCode))
   {
     // Place logic of each action inside the case
     case FIRE:
     case UP:
     case DOWN:
     case LEFT:
     case RIGHT:
     case GAME_A:
     case GAME_B:
     case GAME_C:
     case GAME_D:
     default:
        // Print the text of the game action
        keyText = getKeyName(keyCode);
   }
   repaint();
   }
}
```

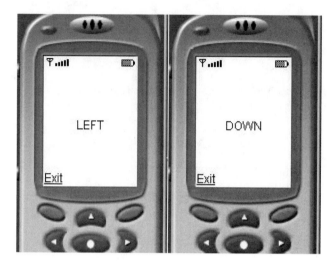

Figure 9–8   Printing game actions on a canvas

There is one line of code worth mentioning. Inside keyPressed() there is a call to getKeyName(). This method requires a key code, not a game action. Fortunately, if a game action initiated the event, it is converted to a key code prior to invoking keyPressed(). All that's remaining is to store the text representation of the key code into keyText. The paint() method will complete the cycle by displaying the text on the canvas.

```
protected void keyPressed(int keyCode)
{
    switch (getGameAction(keyCode))
    {
        ...
        // Print the text of the game action
        keyText = getKeyName(keyCode);
    ...
}
```

Pointer Events

The MID Profile includes a set of methods to interact with pointer devices such as a mouse or touch screen.

Table 9.8 Pointer Methods: javax.microedition.lcdui.Canvas	
Method	*Description*
boolean **hasPointerEvents**()	Does the platform support a pointer
boolean **hasPointerMotionEvents**()	Does the platform detect pointer motion ("click/point and drag")
void **pointerDragged**(int x, int y)	Invoked when pointer dragged
void **pointerPressed**(int x, int y)	Invoked when pointer pressed
void **pointerReleased**(int x, int y)	Invoked when pointer released

The interaction with a pointer follows the same philosophy as with key codes. The methods `pointerPressed()`, `pointerReleased()` and `pointerDragged()` are invoked when a pointer is pressed, released or dragged. Each method is merely a placeholder and must be overridden if you choose to support pointer events. For example, you may choose to track the current x and y location as a pointer is moved about on the canvas.

```
protected void pointerPressed(int x, int y)
{
  // Start location point where pointer pressed
  startx = x;
  starty = y;
}

protected void pointerDragged(int x, int y)
{
  // Current location of pointer
  currentx = x;
  currenty = y;
}

protected void pointerReleased (int x, int y)
{
  // End location point where pointer released
  endx = x;
  endy = y;
}
```

Figure 9–9   Tracking pointer events on a Canvas

Example: Following Pointer Events

Sun's implementation of MIDP version 1.0 (as installed in Chapter 4) supports pointer events.[4] Each click, drag and release of the mouse on a Canvas generates an event.

Example 9.3 is a pleasant diversion, an alternative to doodling with pen and paper. We'll track the pointer as it moves about on a Canvas. When the mouse button is clicked and held down, a line will be drawn tracing each movement. Letting up the mouse button stops the drawing. My first doodle was a self-portrait (see Figure 9–9).

---

[4] If using the wireless toolkit change the following entry in the "device" properties file: touch_screen=true. The property files are located in: x:/J2MEWTK/wtklib/devices

Example 9.3   Doodle.java

```java
/*---------------------------------------------------
 * Doodle.java
 *
 * Use pointer events to draw onto the Canvas
 *---------------------------------------------*/
import javax.microedition.midlet.*;
import javax.microedition.lcdui.*;

public class Doodle extends MIDlet
{
  private Display    display;      // The display
  private DoodleCanvas canvas;     // Canvas

  public Doodle()
  {
    display = Display.getDisplay(this);
    canvas  = new DoodleCanvas(this);
  }

  protected void startApp()
  {
    display.setCurrent(canvas);
  }

  protected void pauseApp()
  { }

  protected void destroyApp(boolean unconditional)
  { }

  public void exitMIDlet()
  {
    destroyApp(true);
    notifyDestroyed();
  }
}


/*---------------------------------------------------
 * Class DoodleCanvas
 *
 * Pointer event handling
 *---------------------------------------------*/
```

(continued)

Example 9.3   (Continued)

```
class DoodleCanvas extends Canvas implements CommandListener
{
  private Command cmExit;      // Exit midlet
  private Command cmClear;     // Clear display
  private int startx = 0,      // Where pointer was clicked
             starty = 0,
             currentx = 0,     // Current location
             currenty = 0;
  private Doodle midlet;
  private boolean clearDisplay = false;

  /*----------------------------------------------------
   * Constructor
   *--------------------------------------------------*/
  public DoodleCanvas(Doodle midlet)
  {
    this.midlet = midlet;

    // Create exit command & listen for events
    cmExit = new Command("Exit", Command.EXIT, 1);
    cmClear = new Command("Clear", Command.SCREEN, 1);
    addCommand(cmExit);
    addCommand(cmClear);
    setCommandListener(this);
  }

  /*----------------------------------------------------
   * Paint the text representing the key code
   *--------------------------------------------------*/
  protected void paint(Graphics g)
  {
    // Clear the background (to white)
    if (clearDisplay)
    {
      g.setColor(255, 255, 255);
      g.fillRect(0, 0, getWidth(), getHeight());

      clearDisplay = false;
      startx = currentx = starty = currenty = 0;

      return;
    }
```

(continued)

Example 9.3 (*Continued*)

```java
    // Draw with black pen
    g.setColor(0, 0, 0);

    // Draw line
    g.drawLine(startx, starty, currentx, currenty);

    // New starting point is the current position
    startx = currentx;
    starty = currenty;
  }

  /*-----------------------------------------------
   * Command event handling
   *---------------------------------------------*/
  public void commandAction(Command c, Displayable d)
  {
    if (c == cmExit)
      midlet.exitMIDlet();
    else if (c == cmClear)
    {
      clearDisplay = true;
      repaint();
    }
  }

  /*-----------------------------------------------
   * Pointer pressed
   *---------------------------------------------*/
  protected void pointerPressed(int x, int y)
  {
    startx = x;
    starty = y;
  }

  /*-----------------------------------------------
   * Pointer moved
   *---------------------------------------------*/
  protected void pointerDragged(int x, int y)
  {
    currentx = x;
    currenty = y;
    repaint();
  }
}
```

When the user clicks the mouse button (or touches the screen with a pointing device such as a stylus), the method `pointerPressed()` is called. The starting x and y location are noted.

```
protected void pointerPressed(int x, int y)
{
  startx = x;
  starty = y;
}
```

Each movement of the pointer (while the mouse button is down or the stylus is still on the display) is reported to:

```
protected void pointerDragged(int x, int y)
{
  currentx = x;
  currenty = y;
  repaint();
}
```

The current x and y locations are saved and a request is made to re-paint the display. This request will result in a call to `paint()`, where a line is drawn from the starting point to the current position.

```
// Draw line
g.drawLine(startx, starty, currentx, currenty);

// New starting point is the current position
startx = currentx;
starty = currenty;
```

The current x and y positions will become the starting point for the next line segment. Therefore, before leaving `paint()`, `startx` and `starty` are set to the current values of x and y.

To start a new doodle, select the "Clear" Command on the device (see Figure 9–9). Command events are always routed to `commandAction()`

```
public void commandAction(Command c, Displayable d)
{
  if (c == cmExit)
    midlet.exitMIDlet();
  else if (c == cmClear)
  {
    clearDisplay = true;
    repaint();
  }
}
```

If cmClear triggered the event, the flag clearDisplay is set. Back in paint() a check is made for this flag, when true the display is cleared by drawing a rectangle the size of the Canvas with a white background. The position markers are also reset at this time.

```
// Clear the background (to white)
if (clearDisplay)
{
  g.setColor(255, 255, 255);
  g.fillRect(0, 0, getWidth(), getHeight());

  clearDisplay = false;
  startx = currentx = starty = currenty = 0;

  return;
}
```

Graphics

A Graphic object (a.k.a. graphic context) is the instrument for drawing onto a Canvas. With over 30 methods, there is an abundance of operations from drawing of shapes and text to specifying fonts and colors.

For consistency, code examples in this section will use the variable g to refer to an instance of a Graphics object. Whenever you see a reference to g, assume it has been properly allocated/acquired and always refers to a valid Graphics object, for instance:

```
g.setColor(r, g, b);
g.drawLine(startx, starty, endx, endy);
```

This is a nice segue to the first topic.

Obtaining a Graphics Object

A Graphics object is the ticket to drawing onto a Canvas. There are two means to acquire a reference to this object. We witnessed the first when writing the paint() method inside the Canvas class. Here's a refresher:

```
class AnimationCanvas extends Canvas
                      implements CommandListener
{
  private Command cmExit;              // Exit midlet
```

```
...
cmExit = new Command("Exit", Command.EXIT, 1);
addCommand(cmExit);
setCommandListener(this);
...
protected void paint(Graphics g)
{
...
}
}
```

The second means to obtain a `Graphics` object is through a mutable `Image`. Let's digress for just a minute and review the image types presented in Chapter 7.

Immutable: Once created, these images cannot be altered. Immutable images are most often created from a resource, such as a file. The most common use of an immutable image is to display an image as part of another component. In Example 7.11 we created a `ChoiceGroup` with images that appear alongside each selection (see Figure 9–10). A `Form`, `List` and `Alert` can also be home to immutable images.

Mutable: These images are created by requesting a block of memory, specifying the height and width of the desired image. The image is empty until drawn into. Here's how to allocate a mutable image:

```
// Create mutable image and get graphics object for image
Image tmpImg = Image.createImage(80, 20);
Graphics g = tmpImg.getGraphics();
```

Figure 9–10   Immutable images inside a ChoiceGroup

Look what we just uncovered. There's our second reference to a
`Graphics` object, through a mutable image. Which also answers the question, how do you draw into a mutable image?

Before moving on, let's go over the fundamental difference between
the lifetime of a `Graphics` objects acquired inside `paint()` versus a
`Graphics` object acquired through an Image.

1. **Through `paint()` method**   The `Graphics` reference is
valid only inside paint(). Once leaving (even if you save a reference to the variable), the object cannot be used to draw onto
the `Canvas`.

2. **Through an `image`**   The `Graphics` reference is valid as
long as the `Image` and the variable that references the
`Graphics` object are in scope. For example, depending on
where the following declaration is made, `image` and `g` may be
available for the lifetime of the MIDlet.

```
Image image = Image.createImage(40, 40);
Graphics g = image.getGraphics();
```

24 bits are allocated for color support; 8 bits to each of the colors: red, green,
and blue. If a device does not support all possible colors in the range, it will
map color requests to the closest possible match available. This includes mapping a color request to an appropriate shade of gray for non-color devices.

Table 9.9   Color Support: javax.microedition.lcdui.Graphics

Method	Description
void **setColor**(int RGB)	Set color by combining each color component (Red, Green, Blue) into one integer value
void **setColor**(int red, int green, int blue)	Set color specifying each color component (Red, Green, Blue) separately
int **getColor**()	Get current color as one integer value
int **getBlueComponent**()	Get the blue component of the current color
int **getGreenComponent**()	Get the green component of the current color
int **getRedComponent**()	Get the red component of the current color
void **setGrayScale**(int value)	Set the grayscale
int **getGrayScale**()	Get current grayscale

Setting Colors

When setting the color, we have two choices: combine the three color components into one integer value or specify each color as a separate integer. When combining colors, blue occupies the lower eight bits, followed by green, ending with red. For example, let's randomly select a value for each color:

	Decimal	Hexadecimal	Binary
Red	0	0x0	0000 0000
Green	126	0x7E	0111 1110
Blue	255	0xFF	1111 1111

When combining each separate color into one integer, we need to shift a few bits around. Specifically, red needs to move up 16 bits, green up 8 bits, with blue occupying the lower 8 bits.

```
// Assume 'g' is a valid Graphics object
int red = 0,
    green = 126,
    blue = 255;
g.setColor((red << 16) | (green << 8) | blue);
```

The end result is an integer value with the binary representation:

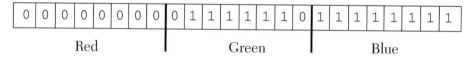

| 0 | 0 | 0 | 0 | 0 | 0 | 0 | 0 | 0 | 1 | 1 | 1 | 1 | 1 | 1 | 0 | 1 | 1 | 1 | 1 | 1 | 1 | 1 | 1 |

         Red   Green   Blue

The second option is to specify the colors separately:

```
g.setColor(red, green, blue);
```

Determining Color Support

You can check for color support on a mobile device through the method `javax.microedition.lcdui.Display.isColor()`. `true` is returned if the device supports color; otherwise `false` is returned.

There is an additional method— `javax.microedition.lcdui.Display.numColors()`—that returns the number of colors (or shades of gray) available.

Getting Colors

To get the current color configuration the options are the reverse of setting the colors: the current color selection can be returned as one integer value or a separate integer for each color.

For separate color values use getRedComponent(), getGreenComponent() and getBlueComponent(). When requesting the color be returned as one integer value, you can get the value assigned to each color (red, green and blue) by masking off the appropriate bits.

```
int colors, red, green, blue;
colors = g.getColor();

// Return the highest 8 bits
red = colors & 0xFF0000

// Return middle eight bits
green = colors & 0xFF00;

// Return lowest 8 bits
blue = colors & 0xFF
```

Using Grayscale

setGrayScale(int) allows selection of a shade of gray in the range of 0 to 255. As with a color device, if the value is outside the supported range, an appropriate match will be selected.

Background and Foreground Colors

MIDP does not support the concept of separate background and foreground colors. This should be apparent by looking at the methods for setting colors—setColor(int) and setColor(int, int, int). No distinction is made between the background and foreground.

Instead, fill operations are used to color the background. For example, to change the background to blue and draw a text string in white, we can follow these steps:

```
// Assume 'g' is a valid Graphics object
// Fill display with blue background
```

```
g.setColor(0, 0, 255);
g.fillRect(0, 0, getWidth(), getHeight());

// Set color to white and draw text
g.setColor(255,255,255);
g.drawString("Testing", 5, 5,
             Graphics.TOP | Graphics.LEFT);
```

We'll visit all the fill operations as we move through the remainder of this chapter.

Stroke Style

When drawing lines, arcs and rectangles we can choose between a solid or dashed stroke style. If you don't specify a preference, the default is solid. Figure 9–11 shows a line drawn in each stroke style.

Table 9.10 Stroke Methods: javax.microedition.lcdui.Graphics	
Method	*Description*
int **getStrokeStyle**()	Get the current stroke style
void **setStrokeStyle**(int style)	Set the stroke style (available styles are shown in Table 9.11)

Figure 9–11 SOLID and DOTTED stroke styles

Setting the preferred stroke is as easy as:

```
g.setStrokeStyle(Graphics.DOTTED);
```

or

```
g.setStrokeStyle(Graphics.SOLID);
```

Once the stroke style is set, every line, arc and rectangle drawn with the associated `Graphics` that will use that stroke style. There are a few important notes regarding the dotted stroke style:

- A dotted line is drawn by skipping pixels in drawing path
- Which pixels are skipped is determined by the implementation
- End points (of lines and arcs) and corners (of rectangles) are not guaranteed to be drawn

Table 9.11   Stroke Styles: javax.microedition.lcdui.Graphics

Property	Description
SOLID	Draw solid lines
DOTTED	Draw dotted lines

Drawing Lines

Let's start with the most basic drawing operation, a line. Each line has a starting `point`, (x1 y1) and ending (x2 y2) point (see Table 9.12). Regardless of the stroke style, the thickness of a line is always one pixel wide.

Back in Example 9.3, `doodle.java`, we used this method to draw line segments as a mouse was moved about on a `Canvas`. The starting location of the line and the current location of the mouse were specified as the parameters to `drawLine()`.

```
// Draw with black pen
g.setColor(0, 0, 0);

// Draw line
g.drawLine(startx, starty, currentx, currenty);
```

Table 9.12 Line Drawing: javax.microedition.lcdui.Graphics	
Method	*Description*
void **drawLine**(int x1, int y1, int x2, int y2)	Draw line specifying starting and ending points

Drawing Arcs

There are two methods to draw arcs: one to create an "outline" of an arc and the second to fill an arc (see Table 9.13).

Table 9.13 Arc Methods: javax.microedition.lcdui.Graphics	
Property	*Description*
void **drawArc**(int x, int y, int width, int height, int startAngle, int arcAngle)	Draw an arc inside a bounding box specified by x,y and width,height.
void **fillArc**(int x, int y, int width, int height, int startAngle, int arcAngle)	Fill an arc inside a bounding box specified by x,y and width,height.

Drawing an arc begins by specifying the bounding box (i.e., the outside dimensions of an "imaginary" box that will contain the arc). The startAngle is the location to start the arc, where 0 is found at 3 o'clock. Positive values go counter-clockwise. Therefore, if you choose a startAngle of 90 the arc would begin at 12 o'clock.

The arcAngle is how many degrees to rotate from the startAngle. A startAngle of 0 and arcAngle of 180 would begin at 3 o'clock and rotate counter-clockwise to 9 o'clock. A startAngle of 90 with an arcAngle of 180 would begin at 12 o'clock and rotate counter-clockwise to 6 o'clock.

Example: Modifying startAngle and arcAngle

Example 9.4 draws an arc inside a bounding box defined by 5,5 to 75, 75. The startAngle is 0 (3 o'clock) and the arcAngle is 225. Here is the request to create the arc:

```
g.drawArc(5, 5, 75, 75, 0, 225);
```

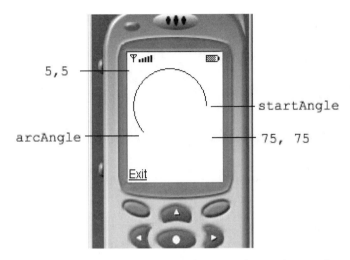

Figure 9-12 Drawing an arc with startAngle 0 and arcAngle 225

Figure 9–12 shows the resulting arc.

Example 9.4   Arcs.java

```
/*-------------------------------------------------------
 * Arcs.java
 *
 * Draw arc on a canvas
 *-----------------------------------------------------*/
import javax.microedition.midlet.*;
import javax.microedition.lcdui.*;

public class Arcs extends MIDlet
{
  private Display  display;     // The display
  private ArcsCanvas canvas;    // Canvas

  public Arcs()
  {
    display = Display.getDisplay(this);
    canvas  = new ArcsCanvas(this);
  }
```

(continued)

Example 9.4   (Continued)

```java
protected void startApp()
{
  display.setCurrent(canvas);
}

protected void pauseApp()
{ }

protected void destroyApp(boolean unconditional)
{ }

public void exitMIDlet()
{
  destroyApp(true);
  notifyDestroyed();
}
}

/*-------------------------------------------------
 * Class ArcsCanvas
 *
 * Draw Arcs
 *-----------------------------------------------*/
class ArcsCanvas extends Canvas implements CommandListener
{
  private Command cmExit;   // Exit midlet
  private Arcs midlet;

  public ArcsCanvas(Arcs midlet)
  {
    this.midlet = midlet;

    // Create exit command & listen for events
    cmExit = new Command("Exit", Command.EXIT, 1);
    addCommand(cmExit);
    setCommandListener(this);
  }

  /*-------------------------------------------------
   * Draw an arc
   *-----------------------------------------------*/
  protected void paint(Graphics g)
```

(continued)

Example 9.4   *(Continued)*

```
{
    // Start at 3 o'clock and rotate 225
    g.drawArc(5, 5, 75, 75, 0, 225);

    // Start at 12 o'clock and rotate 225
//    g.drawArc(5, 5, 75, 75, 90, 225);

    // Change the size of the bounding box
    // Start at 12 o'clock and rotate 225
//    g.drawArc(25, 35, 30, 50, 90, 225);

}

public void commandAction(Command c, Displayable d)
{
    if (c == cmExit)
        midlet.exitMIDlet();
}
}
```

Inside paint() are three calls to drawArc(). The result of the first call is shown in Figure 9–12:

```
g.drawArc(5, 5, 75, 75, 0, 225);
```

Notice in Figure 9–13 (on the left) how the arc changes when the startAngle is modified. The arcAngle is still 225; however, the starting position is now 90 (12 o'clock):

```
g.drawArc(5, 5, 75, 75, 90, 225);
```

Finally, the arc on the right in Figure 9–13 is the result of a change to the bounding box:

```
g.drawArc(25, 35, 30, 50, 90, 225);
```

Filling of arcs follows exactly the same principal: specify a bounding box and start angle and rotation of the arc. Lets change the original arc (Figure 9–12) from:

```
g.drawArc(5, 5, 75, 75, 0, 225);
```

to a filled arc:

```
g.fillArc(5, 5, 75, 75, 0, 225);
```

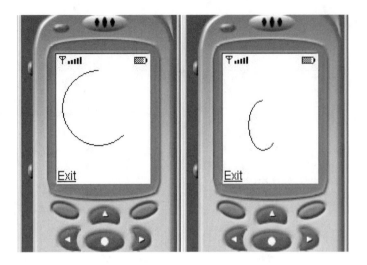

Figure 9–13   Leftmost arc is the same arc as Figure 9-12, with a startAngle of 90; Arc on the right has a modified bounding box.

The result is shown in Figure 9–14.

Make a few changes of your own to get a feel for drawing arcs and filled arcs. Specifically, try specifying a negative `arcAngle`, an option we didn't experiment with in the earlier examples.

Figure 9–14   Filled arc

Drawing Rectangles

Rectangles can have either square or rounded corners and can be drawn as an outline or filled (see Table 9.14).

Table 9.14 Rectangle Methods: javax.microedition.lcdui.Graphics	
Property	*Description*
void **drawRect**(int x, int y, int width, int height)	Draw a rectangle

void **drawRoundRect**(int x, int y,
        int width, int height,
        int arcWidth, int arcHeight)
	Draw a rounded rectangle

void **fillRect**(int x, int y, int width, int height)	Fill a rectangle

void **fillRoundRect**(int x, int y,
        int width, int height,
        int arcWidth, int arcHeight)
	Fill a rounded rectangle

The parameters for a non-rounded rectangle should be unmistakable. Specify the starting x and y location as well as the width and height. When creating a rectangle with rounded corners we also specify the horizontal diameter (`arcWidth`) and the vertical diameter (`arcHeight`) of the arc drawn at each corner.

Example: Four Rectangle Types

Example 9.5 creates a rectangle for each of the four types.

Example 9.5   Rectangles.java

```
/*------------------------------------------------
 * Rectangles.java
 *
 * Draw Rectangle on a canvas
 *------------------------------------------------*/
```

(continued)

Example 9.5   (Continued)

```
import javax.microedition.midlet.*;
import javax.microedition.lcdui.*;

public class Rectangles extends MIDlet
{
  private Display  display;        // The display
  private RectangleCanvas canvas; // Canvas

  public Rectangles()
  {
    display = Display.getDisplay(this);
    canvas  = new RectangleCanvas(this);
  }

  protected void startApp()
  {
    display.setCurrent(canvas);
  }

  protected void pauseApp()
  { }

  protected void destroyApp(boolean unconditional)
  { }

  public void exitMIDlet()
  {
    destroyApp(true);
    notifyDestroyed();
  }
}

/*-----------------------------------------------------
 * Class RectangleCanvas
 *
 * Draw arcs
 *---------------------------------------------------*/
class RectangleCanvas extends Canvas implements CommandListener
{
  private Command cmExit;  // Exit midlet
  private Rectangles midlet;
```

(continued)

Example 9.5 *(Continued)*

```
   public RectangleCanvas(Rectangles midlet)
   {
      this.midlet = midlet;

      // Create exit command & listen for events
      cmExit = new Command("Exit", Command.EXIT, 1);
      addCommand(cmExit);
      setCommandListener(this);
   }

   /*-------------------------------------------------
    * Draw an arc
    *-----------------------------------------------*/
   protected void paint(Graphics g)
   {
      g.drawRect(1, 1, 25, 25);
      g.drawRoundRect(28, 28, 45, 45, 15, 45);

//      g.fillRect(1, 1, 25, 25);
//      g.fillRoundRect(28, 28, 45, 45, 15, 45);

   }

   public void commandAction(Command c, Displayable d)
   {
      if (c == cmExit)
         midlet.exitMIDlet();
   }
}
```

Figure 9–15 shows the following two rectangles, the latter with rounded corners.

```
         g.drawRect(1, 1, 25, 25);
         g.drawRoundRect(28, 28, 45, 45, 15, 45);
```

To draw a filled rectangle, change the method call, leaving all the parameters unchanged. The results are shown in Figure 9–16.

```
      g.fillRect(1, 1, 25, 25);
      g.fillRoundRect(28, 28, 45, 45, 15, 45);
```

Figure 9–15 Rectangles with and without rounded corners

Figure 9–16 Filled rectangles with and without rounded corners

Rounded Rectangles

The horizontal and vertical diameter (`arcWidth` and `arcHeight`) specified when creating a rounded rectangle define the "sharpness of the arc," if you will, in each direction. The larger the value the more gradual the arc.

For example, when setting the horizontal diameter to 15 and the vertical diameter to 45, the arc in the vertical direction is more gradual than that in the horizontal direction. See Figure 9–17

```
g.drawRoundRect(28, 28, 45, 45, 15, 45)
```

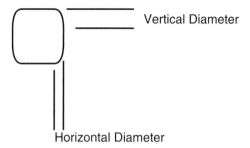

Figure 9–17 Determining the "sharpness" of corners on a rounded rectangle

Drawing Text

Anytime we draw text we must take into consideration the font style currently assigned to the Graphics context. Before going any further, this is an opportune time to learn about fonts.

Fonts

Font support within MIDP has been slimmed down significantly compared with J2SE. The most glaring omission is the lack of a FontMetrics class. Metrics define characteristics of a Font that deal with measurements such as the height of a character or the size of the gap between one character and the next. MIDP does provide various metric information, as we'll see, just not to the extent you may be accustomed too.

A new Font is requested through the static method Font.getFont().

```
Font font = Font.getFont(Font.FACE_SYSTEM,
                         Font.STYLE_PLAIN,
                         Font.SIZE_MEDIUM);
```

The idea behind using a static method is in an effort to conserve resources, specifically, limiting garbage collection. When requesting a Font keep in mind that the implementation may not be able to accommodate your request. If this is the case, the nearest match will be returned.

Table 9.15   Font: javax.microedition.lcdui.Font

Method	Description
static Font **getFont**(int face, int style, int size)	Request a new Font
static Font **getDefaultFont**()	Request the system Font

There are three attributes associated with a Font: the face, style and size. Table 9.16 shows the constants that are defined for each attribute. One attribute deserves special attention—the style. Unlike the face and size, you can combine style attributes using a logical OR (|) operator. Here is a request for the system (default) face, which has both a bold and italic style and is medium in size.

```
Font font = Font.getFont(Font.FACE_SYSTEM,
                Font.STYLE_BOLD | Font.STYLE_ITALIC,
                Font.SIZE_MEDIUM);
```

There are seven methods for querying a fonts attributes, and each is listed in Table 9.17. One method worth mentioning is getStyle(), which returns an integer that may be any combination of the style attributes

Table 9.16   Font Attributes: javax.microedition.lcdui.Font

Attribute	Description	Constant Value
FACE_SYSTEM	System characters	0
FACE_MONOSPACE	Monospace characters	32
FACE_PROPORTIONAL	Proportional characters	64
STYLE_PLAIN	Plain characters	0
STYLE_BOLD	Bold characters	1
STYLE_ITALIC	Italicized characters	2
STYLE_UNDERLINED	Underlined characters	4
SIZE_SMALL	Small characters	8
SIZE_MEDIUM	Medium characters	0
SIZE_LARGE	Large characters	16

(STYLE_PLAIN, STYLE_BOLD,   STLYE_ITALIC, STYLE_UNDER-
LINED). Let's walk through an example using the following font:

```
Font font = Font.getFont(
    Font.FACE_SYSTEM,
    Font.STYLE_BOLD | Font.STYLE_ITALIC | Font.STYLE_UNDERLINED,
    Font.SIZE_MEDIUM);

int style = font.getStyle();
```

The variable `style` will have the value 7. Here's why.

	Binary	Decimal
Font.STLYE_BOLD	00000001	1
Font.STYLE_ITALIC	00000010	2
Font.STLYE_UNDERLINED	00000100	4
Logical OR	00000111	7

If you would like to test for various style attributes you may write something as follows:

```
if (style == (Font.STYLE_BOLD | Font.STYLE_ITALIC))
    ...
```

We get the same end result using the methods `isPlain()`, `isBold()`,
`isItalic()` and `isUnderlined()`, such as:

```
if (font.isBold() && font.isItalic())
    ...
```

So why bother with the extra effort involved with `getStyle()`? Think
back to how fonts are allocated. If you remember, there are no guarantees
that your request will be granted. If the system does not support such a font,
the closest match will be returned.

With that in mind, let's assume that we prompt a user for their preferred
font attributes, with the intention of saving these attributes in the Record
Store. We could store the user preferences as three integer values:

```
int face = font.getFace();
int style = font.getStyle();
int size = font.getSize();
```

`getStyle()` neatly packages all the preferred style attributes (bold,
italic and underlined) into one variable, `style`. Without this method we
would need to query for each style attribute (`isBold()`, `isItalic()`
and `isUnderlined()`) and either store a reference to each one or go

through the hoops to create one variable that will represent a combination of each.

To complete this example, let's assume that each time the MIDlet is started we read user-preferences from the Record Store and update the system accordingly. To set the Font to the user-preferred setting, we could read the attributes previously written and with one call set the preferred Font:

```
int face, style, size;

// A custom method to read font attributes from rms
getFontAttributes();

// Request the user preferred font
Font font = Font.getFont(face, style, size);
```

Table 9.17   Attributes Methods: javax.microedition.lcdui.Font

Method	Description
int **getFace**()	Get the current face
int **getStyle**()	Get the combination of style attributes as one integer (logically or'ed)
int **getSize**()	Get the current size
boolean **isPlain**()	Is the plain (style) attribute set
boolean **isBold**()	Is the bold (style) attribute set
boolean **isItalic**()	Is the italic (style) attribute set
boolean **isUnderlined**()	Is the underlined (style) attribute set

Metrics describe information regarding various measurements of a Font. Before going any further we need to understand the terminology used when working with metrics (see Figure 9–18).

The ascent is the distance from the baseline to the top of the majority of characters. The descent is the distance from the baseline down to the bottom of the majority of characters (some may extend below this). Leading is the gap between the descent of one line and the ascent of the next. The font height is defined as the ascent + leading + descent, which makes up the distance between baselines.

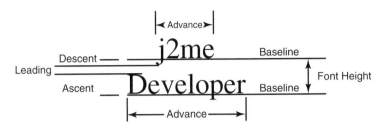

Figure 9–18   Font metrics

The advance is the total "distance" occupied by a character or string of characters. The advance is more than just the width of the individual characters, it also takes into consideration the gap between characters. The advance is useful when centering or otherwise horizontally aligning text.

Unlike the FontMetrics class in J2SE, MIDP does not include methods to obtain values for all metrics. However, the most common metrics for a font are available (see Table 9.18).

getHeight() returns the font height. Included is the leading, which provides for a gap between successive lines of text. getBaselinePosition() returns the ascent, the distance from the baseline to the top of the tallest character. The remaining methods determine the advance (total length occupied) for a single character, array of characters, String and a sub-string of a String.

Table 9.18   Metrics Methods: javax.microedition.lcdui.Font

Method	Description
int **getHeight**()	Get font height (distance between baselines)
int **getBaselinePosition**()	Get font ascent (baseline to top of character)
int **charWidth**(char ch)	Get the advance for specific character
int **charsWidth**(char[] ch, int offset, int length)	Get the advance for a series of characters
int **stringWidth**(String str)	Get the advance for a String
int **substringWidth**(String str, int offset, int length)	Get the advance for a sub-string of a String

Using the Advance

The methods for determining the advance are available to help in aligning text. You can quickly determine how much "space" will be occupied by any given text. With this information, you can center text, draw around it, create tables holding text values, and so forth.

The significance of these methods goes unnoticed until the time comes that you need to align text. Once you find yourself in that position, you'll undergo a different appreciation for what these methods provide.

Anchor Point

There is just one last topic to cover before drawing text: the anchor point. When drawing text, in addition to providing the String to display, we also specify an x and y location. Given that the coordinate system begins in the upper left corner of the display, it would be a reasonable assumption that this x and y value would be an offset from that location.

That would work fine; however, to provide for additional flexibility and make it easier to align text, the concept of an anchor point was introduced. Anchor points are defined in pairs, just like x and y coordinates. The x (horizontal) values are LEFT, HCENTER and RIGHT. The y (vertical) values are TOP, BASELINE and BOTTOM.

Picture these pairs as points around an imaginary box, known as the bounding box, of the text you would like to draw (see Figure 9–19).

Table 9.19   Text Anchor Points: javax.microedition.lcdui.Graphics

Anchor Point	Description	Direction
LEFT	Left of text	Horizontal
HCENTER	Center of text	Horizontal
RIGHT	Right of text	Horizontal
TOP	Top of text	Vertical
BASELINE	Baseline of text	Vertical
BOTTOM	Bottom of text	Vertical

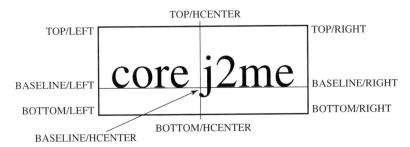

Figure 9–19 Anchor points around the bounding box of a text String

When you specify an anchor point what you are referring to is which location on the bounding box will be located at the x and y coordinate. We are putting the cart before the horse; however, to show an example using anchor points, let's look at the method `drawString()`.

```
g.drawString("core j2me", 0, 0 ,
                 Graphics.TOP | Graphics.LEFT);

g.drawString("core j2me", 0, 0 ,
                 Graphics.TOP | Graphics.HCENTER;
```

The first parameter is obvious—this is the text to draw. The next two values are the x and y coordinates. The last parameter is the anchor point. Anchor points are always specified in pairs, a vertical and horizontal value, combined using the logical OR operator (|).

The first call requests that the TOP/LEFT corner of the bounding box be located at 0,0. The second requests that the TOP/HCENTER of the bounding box be located at 0,0 (see Figures 9–20 and 9–21). To get a perspective of the

Figure 9–20 Anchor point TOP/LEFT on bounding box at 0,0

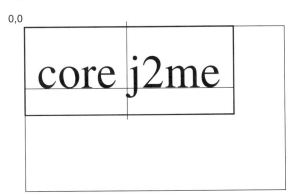

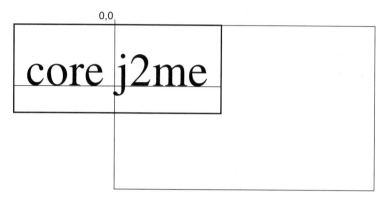

Figure 9–21   Anchor point TOP/HCENTER on bounding box at 0,0

coordinate system and the layout of the text, assume the light gray box represents the display.

Try this on for size:

```
g.drawString("core j2me",
             getWidth() / 2, getHeight() / 2,
             Graphics.BASELINE | Graphics.HCENTER);
```

This requests that the BASELINE/HCENTER of the bounding box be positioned at the center of the display (which is located by dividing both the screen width and height by 2). The end result, for all intents and purposes, is that the text is centered. (see Figure 9–22).

Figure 9–22   Centering text with anchor points

The idea behind anchor points is to make our life a little easier when laying out text. Be patient, it takes a little trial and error to get the feel for anchor points.

Drawing Text

At this point, with an understanding of fonts and anchor points, drawing text is nothing more than deciding which method to call. We can opt to draw a single character, an array (or subset of an array) of characters, a `String` or subset of a `String`.

Table 9.20   Drawing Text Methods: javax.microedition.lcdui.Graphics

Method	*Description*
void **drawChar**(char character, int x, int y, int anchor)	Draw one character
void **drawChars**(char[] data, int offset, int length, int x, int y, int anchor)	Draw an array (or subset) of characters
void **drawString**(String str, int x, int y, int anchor)	Draw a String
void **drawSubstring**(String str, int offset, int len, int x, int y, int anchor)	Draw a sub-string of a String
Font **getFont**()	Get the current Font
void setFont (Font font)	Set the current Font

Regardless of the method you choose, the implementation will align the text based on the x and y coordinates and the anchor point.

Example: Moving Text with Anchor Points

Let's run through an example that moves a text `String` around a `Canvas` by changing the anchor point (Example 9.6). For this MIDlet, x and y will always be positioned at the center of the display. The text will appear in various locations around this coordinate based on the anchor point.

For example, in Figure 9–23 the anchor point is BASELINE/HCENTER. This translates to: the location on the bounding box BASELINE/HCENTER will be at the center of the display (the x and y coordinate).

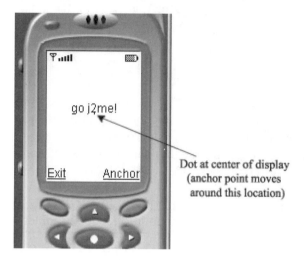

Figure 9–23   x and y at center of display; Anchor point baseline/hcenter

To choose an alternative anchor point, select the "Anchor" command on the display. You will be presented with a List of anchor point locations (see the left screen shot in Figure 9–24). Choosing "Top/Right" translates to: the location on the bounding box TOP/RIGHT will be at the center of the display (see the image on the right of Figure 9–24).

Figure 9–24   x and y at center of display. Anchor point top/right

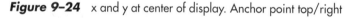

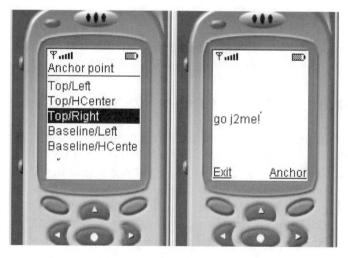

Example 9.6   Text.java

```
/*----------------------------------------------------
* Text.java
*
* Show various anchor points
*---------------------------------------------------*/
import javax.microedition.midlet.*;
import javax.microedition.lcdui.*;

public class Text extends MIDlet
{
  private Display   display;      // The display
  private TextCanvas canvas;      // Canvas to display text
  private AnchorPtList anchorPt;  // List to query for anchor point
  private int anchorPoint = Graphics.BASELINE | Graphics.HCENTER;

  public Text()
  {
    display = Display.getDisplay(this);
    canvas  = new TextCanvas(this);
    anchorPt = new AnchorPtList("Anchor point", List.IMPLICIT, this);
  }

  protected void startApp()
  {
    showCanvas();
  }

  protected void pauseApp()
  { }

  protected void destroyApp( boolean unconditional )
  { }

  public void showCanvas()
  {
    display.setCurrent(canvas);
  }

  public void showList()
  {
    display.setCurrent(anchorPt);
  }
```

(continued)

Example 9.6 *(Continued)*

```java
  public int getAnchorPoint()
  {
    return anchorPoint;
  }

  public void setAnchorPoint(int anchorPoint)
  {
    this.anchorPoint = anchorPoint;
  }

  public void exitMIDlet()
  {
    destroyApp(true);
    notifyDestroyed();
  }
}


/*--------------------------------------------------
 * Class TextCanvas
 *
 * Draw text at specified anchor point
 *--------------------------------------------------*/
class TextCanvas extends Canvas implements CommandListener
{
  private Command cmExit;  // Exit midlet
  private Command cmGetAnchorPt;
  private Text midlet;

  public TextCanvas(Text midlet)
  {
    this.midlet = midlet;

    // Create commands & listen for events
    cmExit = new Command("Exit", Command.EXIT, 1);
    cmGetAnchorPt = new Command("Anchor", Command.SCREEN, 2);

    addCommand(cmExit);
    addCommand(cmGetAnchorPt);
    setCommandListener(this);
  }
```

(continued)

Example 9.6 *(Continued)*

```
/*---------------------------------------------------
 * Draw text
 *-------------------------------------------------*/
protected void paint(Graphics g)
{
  int xcenter = getWidth() / 2,
      ycenter = getHeight() / 2;

  // Choose a font
  g.setFont(Font.getFont(Font.FACE_SYSTEM,
            Font.STYLE_PLAIN, Font.SIZE_MEDIUM));

  // Draw a dot at the center of the display
  g.drawLine(xcenter, ycenter, xcenter, ycenter);

  // x and y are always at the center of the display
  // Move the text around x and y based on the anchor point
  g.drawString("go j2me!",
               xcenter, ycenter, midlet.getAnchorPoint());
}

/*---------------------------------------------------
 * Exit midlet or show anchor point selection list
 *-------------------------------------------------*/
public void commandAction(Command c, Displayable d)
{
  if (c == cmExit)
    midlet.exitMIDlet();
  else if (c == cmGetAnchorPt)
  {
    midlet.showList();
  }
}
}

/*---------------------------------------------------
 * Class AnchorPtList
 *
 * List to query for an anchor point
 *-------------------------------------------------*/
```

(continued)

Example 9.6   *(Continued)*

```java
class AnchorPtList extends List implements CommandListener
{
  private Text midlet;

  public AnchorPtList(String title, int listType, Text midlet)
  {
    // Call list constructor
    super(title, listType);

    this.midlet = midlet;

    append("Top/Left", null);
    append("Top/HCenter", null);
    append("Top/Right", null);

    append("Baseline/Left", null);
    append("Baseline/HCenter", null);
    append("Baseline/Right", null);

    append("Bottom/Left", null);
    append("Bottom/HCenter", null);
    append("Bottom/Right", null);

    setCommandListener(this);
  }

  /*---------------------------------------------------
   * Commands to set anchor point
   *-------------------------------------------------*/
  public void commandAction(Command c, Displayable s)
  {
    switch (getSelectedIndex())
    {
      case 0:
          midlet.setAnchorPoint(Graphics.TOP | Graphics.LEFT);
        break;

      case 1:
          midlet.setAnchorPoint(Graphics.TOP | Graphics.HCENTER);
        break;
```

(continued)

Example 9.6 *(Continued)*

```
      case 2:
        midlet.setAnchorPoint(Graphics.TOP | Graphics.RIGHT);
        break;

      case 3:
        midlet.setAnchorPoint(Graphics.BASELINE | Graphics.LEFT);
        break;

      case 4:
        midlet.setAnchorPoint(Graphics.BASELINE | Graphics.HCENTER);
        break;

      case 5:
        midlet.setAnchorPoint(Graphics.BASELINE | Graphics.RIGHT);
        break;

      case 6:
        midlet.setAnchorPoint(Graphics.BOTTOM | Graphics.LEFT);
        break;

      case 7:
        midlet.setAnchorPoint(Graphics.BOTTOM | Graphics.HCENTER);
        break;

      case 8:
        midlet.setAnchorPoint(Graphics.BOTTOM | Graphics.RIGHT);
        break;

      default:
        midlet.setAnchorPoint(Graphics.BASELINE | Graphics.HCENTER);
    }

    midlet.showCanvas();
  }
}
```

This MIDlet consists of three classes:

Text: The main midlet. Allocates the Canvas and List components and displays each as requested.

TextCanvas: Extends the Canvas class and is home to the paint() method where the text is drawn based on the anchor point.

AnchorPtList: Extends the List class to display a selection of anchor points.

Focus your attention on paint(). Notice the x and y coordinates are always at the center of the display. We mark this location by drawing a tiny arc.

```
protected void paint(Graphics g)
{
    int xcenter = getWidth() / 2,
        ycenter = getHeight() / 2;

    // Choose a font
    g.setFont(Font.getFont(Font.FACE_SYSTEM,
            Font.STYLE_PLAIN, Font.SIZE_MEDIUM));

    // Draw a dot at the center of the display
    g.drawLine(xcenter, ycenter, xcenter, ycenter);

    // x and y are always at the center of the display
    // Move text around x and y based on anchor point
    g.drawString("go j2me!",
            xcenter, ycenter, midlet.getAnchorPoint());
}
```

Drawing Images

Drawing of images is not unlike drawing a line or text. There is an appropriately named method drawImage(). However, there's a catch. Look over the parameters for the method and see if anything comes to mind:

```
drawImage(Image, int x, int y, int anchor)
```

Table 9.21 Image Method: javax.microedition.lcdui.Graphics	
Method	*Description*
void **drawImage** (Image img, int x, int y, int anchor)	Draw an image

The concern has to do with the first parameter, which is a reference to an `Image` object. This implies, and correctly so, that we can't call `draw Image()` until we create an `Image`. Going one step further, if we create a mutable `Image`, which is nothing more than a block of memory, it has no content until drawn onto. It comes down to this: we need to lay the groundwork before calling `drawImage()`. Here are the basic steps:

Immutable Image

1. Allocate the image

```
Image im = Image.createImage("/imageTest.png");
```

2. Display the image

```
protected void paint(Graphics g)
{
  ...
   g.drawImage(im, 10, 10, Graphics.LEFT | Graphics.TOP);
  ...
}
```

Mutable Image

1. Allocate the image

```
Image im = Image.createImage(80, 20);
```

2. Create the image content (using arcs, rectangles, lines and text)

```
// Get Graphics object to draw onto image
Graphics graphics = im.getGraphics();

// Draw a filled rectangle
graphics.fillRoundRect(0, 0, 50, 50, 20, 20);

  . . .
```

3. Display the image

```
protected void paint(Graphics g)
{
  ...
   g.drawImage(im, 10, 10, Graphics.LEFT | Graphics.TOP);
  ...
}
```

Example: Immutable Image

Two examples are in order, one each for immutable and mutable images (see Example 9.7).

Example 9.7   ImmutableImage.java

```java
/*-----------------------------------------------------
 * ImmutableImage.java
 *
 * Draw immutable image on a canvas
 *-----------------------------------------------------*/
import javax.microedition.midlet.*;
import javax.microedition.lcdui.*;

public class ImmutableImage extends MIDlet
{
  private Display  display;      // The display
  private ImageCanvas canvas;    // Canvas

  public ImmutableImage()
  {
    display = Display.getDisplay(this);
    canvas  = new ImageCanvas(this);
  }

  protected void startApp()
  {
    display.setCurrent(canvas);
  }

  protected void pauseApp()
  { }

  protected void destroyApp(boolean unconditional)
  { }

  public void exitMIDlet()
  {
    destroyApp(true);
    notifyDestroyed();
  }
}
```

(continued)

Example 9.7 *(Continued)*

```
/*-----------------------------------------------
* Class ImageCanvas
*
* Draw immutable image
*-----------------------------------------------*/
class ImageCanvas extends Canvas implements CommandListener
{
  private Command cmExit;  // Exit midlet
  private ImmutableImage midlet;
  private Image im = null;

  public ImageCanvas(ImmutableImage midlet)
  {
    this.midlet = midlet;

    // Create exit command & listen for events
    cmExit = new Command("Exit", Command.EXIT, 1);
    addCommand(cmExit);
    setCommandListener(this);

    try
    {
      // Create immutable image
      im = Image.createImage("/image_bw.png");
    }
    catch (java.io.IOException e)
    {
      System.err.println("Unable to locate or read .png file");
    }
  }

  /*-----------------------------------------------
  * Draw immutable image
  *-----------------------------------------------*/
  protected void paint(Graphics g)
  {
    if (im != null)
      g.drawImage(im, 10, 10, Graphics.LEFT | Graphics.TOP);
  }

  public void commandAction(Command c, Displayable d)
  {
```

(continued)

Example 9.7   (Continued)

```
    if (c == cmExit)
      midlet.exitMIDlet();
  }
}
```

Inside the constructor for the `Canvas` an immutable image is read from a file resource.

```
// Create immutable image
im = Image.createImage("/image_bw.png");
```

The `paint()` method draws the image onto the `Canvas` (see Figure 9–25).

```
protected void paint(Graphics g)
{
  if (im != null)
    g.drawImage(im, 10, 10, Graphics.LEFT | Graphics.TOP);
}
```

Example: Mutable Image

Example 9.8 displays a mutable `Image`. However, there are a few additional steps. After allocating the `Image`, we will need to obtain a reference to a

Figure 9–25   Immutable image on Canvas

Graphics context and use that reference to create the Image content. At that point we can then call drawImage().

Example 9.8   MutableImage.java

```
/*-------------------------------------------------------
* MutableImage.java
*
* Draw mutable image on a canvas
*-----------------------------------------------*/
import javax.microedition.midlet.*;
import javax.microedition.lcdui.*;

public class MutableImage extends MIDlet
{
  private Display     display;      // The display
  private ImageCanvas canvas;       // Canvas

  public MutableImage()
  {
    display = Display.getDisplay(this);
    canvas  = new ImageCanvas(this);
  }

  protected void startApp()
  {
    display.setCurrent(canvas);
  }

  protected void pauseApp()
  { }

  protected void destroyApp(boolean unconditional)
  { }

  public void exitMIDlet()
  {
    destroyApp(true);
    notifyDestroyed();
  }
}
```

(continued)

Example 9.8 *(Continued)*

```
/*-------------------------------------------------
* Class ImageCanvas
*
* Draw mutable image
*-------------------------------------------------*/
class ImageCanvas extends Canvas implements CommandListener
{
  private Command cmExit;  // Exit midlet
  private MutableImage midlet;
  private Image im = null;
  private String message = "Core J2ME";

  public ImageCanvas(MutableImage midlet)
  {
    this.midlet = midlet;

    // Create exit command & listen for events
    cmExit = new Command("Exit", Command.EXIT, 1);
    addCommand(cmExit);
    setCommandListener(this);

    try
    {
      // Create mutable image
      im = Image.createImage(80, 20);

      // Get graphics object to draw onto the image
      Graphics graphics = im.getGraphics();

      // Specify a font face, style and size
      Font font = Font.getFont(Font.FACE_SYSTEM,
                               Font.STYLE_ITALIC,
                               Font.SIZE_MEDIUM);
      graphics.setFont(font);

      // Draw a filled (black) rectangle
      graphics.setColor(0, 0, 0);
      graphics.fillRoundRect(0,0,
                             im.getWidth()-1, im.getHeight()-1,
                             20, 20);

      // Center text horizontally in the image. Draw text in white
```

(continued)

Example 9.8   (Continued)

```
      graphics.setColor(255, 255, 255);
      graphics.drawString(message,
          (im.getWidth() / 2) - (font.stringWidth(message) / 2), 0,
          Graphics.TOP | Graphics.LEFT);
  }
  catch (Exception e)
  {
    System.err.println("Error during image creation");
  }
}


/*---------------------------------------------------
 * Draw mutable image
 *-------------------------------------------------*/
protected void paint(Graphics g)
{
  // Center the image on the display
  if (im != null)
    g.drawImage(im,
                getWidth() / 2, getHeight() / 2,
                Graphics.VCENTER | Graphics.HCENTER);
}

public void commandAction(Command c, Displayable d)
{
  if (c == cmExit)
    midlet.exitMIDlet();
}
}
```

The first step is to create a mutable image:

```
im = Image.createImage(80, 20);
```

Next, to draw onto the image, we need a reference to a `Graphics` object:

```
Graphics graphics = im.getGraphics();
```

The remaining code uses this object to draw a rounded (filled) rectangle and a text message onto the image. Remember, at this point the image is still not visible. It exists only in memory.

```
// Specify a font face, style and size
   Font font = Font.getFont(Font.FACE_SYSTEM,
                            Font.STYLE_ITALIC,
                            Font.SIZE_MEDIUM);
   graphics.setFont(font);

   // Draw a filled (black) rectangle
   graphics.setColor(0, 0, 0);
   graphics.fillRoundRect(0,0,
                          im.getWidth()-1, im.getHeight()-1,
                          20, 20);

   // Center text horizontally in the image. Draw text in white
   graphics.setColor(255, 255, 255);
   graphics.drawString(message,
      (im.getWidth() / 2) - (font.stringWidth(message) / 2), 0,
      Graphics.TOP | Graphics.LEFT);
```

The `paint()` method draws the image on the Canvas (see Figure 9–26).

```
protected void paint(Graphics g)
   {
      // Center the image on the display
      if (im != null)
        g.drawImage(im,
                    getWidth() / 2, getHeight() / 2,
                    Graphics.VCENTER | Graphics.HCENTER);
   }
```

Figure 9-26 Mutable image on Canvas

Table 9.22 Image Anchor Points: javax.microedition.lcdui.Graphics		
Anchor Point	*Description*	*Direction*
LEFT	Left of image	Horizontal
HCENTER	Center of image	Horizontal
RIGHT	Right of image	Horizontal
TOP	Top of image	Vertical
VCENTER	Center of image	Vertical
BOTTOM	Bottom of image	Vertical

One final note: when drawing images the last parameter specifies the anchor point.

```
g.drawImage(im, 10, 10, Graphics.TOP | Graphics.LEFT);
```

As with text, the anchor point is the location on the bounding box that is positioned at the specified x and y coordinates. For example, the aforementioned anchor point requests that the top left corner of the bounding box be located at the coordinates 10, 10.

Table 9.22 lists the horizontal and vertical anchor points available for images. Notice VCENTER has taken the place of BASELINE (see Table 9.19). An image does not have the notion of a baseline (as does text); however, an image does have a vertical center.

Figure 9–27 Image anchor points

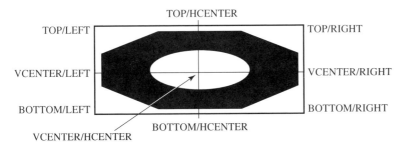

Take one last look at the `paint()` method for Example 9.7 and the output shown in Figure 9–26.

```
g.drawImage(im,
            getWidth() / 2, getHeight() / 2,
            Graphics.VCENTER | Graphics.HCENTER);
```

The `Image` is centered on the display by placing the anchor point at the vertical and horizontal center of the image and by requesting the x and y coordinates to be in the center of the `Canvas`, using `getWidth()` and `getHeight()`. In essence, the center of the `Image` is requested to be at the center of the `Canvas`. If you need a review of anchor points, refer back to "Anchor Point" in the section "Drawing Text."

Translating Coordinates

When defining the coordinate system we placed 0,0 at the upper left corner of the display (see the screen shot on the left in Figure 9–28).

Through a concept referred to as translation, a `Graphics` object can reference its origin (0,0) at a different location on the display. For example, on the right screen shot in Figure 9–28, the origin has been translated to the lower left corner.

Figure 9–28   Original coordinate system on left; translated on right

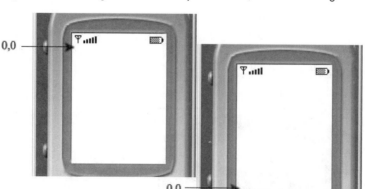

Table 9.23 Translation Methods: javax.microedition.lcdui.Graphics	
Method	*Description*
void **translate**(int x, int y)	Translate the origin (0, 0) for a Graphics object
int **getTranslateX**()	Get the current translated x coordinate
int **getTranslateY**()	Get the current translated y coordinate

Example: Moving an Image

Example 9.9 moves an image up/down and left/right on a Canvas by translating the origin of the Graphics object. The game actions LEFT, RIGHT, UP and DOWN trigger events where the translation occurs. Here is a partial listing of keyPressed() that shows the translation when selecting the DOWN action.

```
protected void keyPressed(int keyCode)
{
  switch (getGameAction(keyCode))
  {
    case UP:
      ...

    case DOWN:
      // If scrolling off the bottom, roll around to top
      if ((translatey + im.getHeight() + im.getHeight())
            > getHeight())
        translatey = 0;
      else
        translatey += im.getHeight();
      break;
    ...
  }
  repaint();
}
```

Before translating the y coordinate down, a check is made to see if another complete image can be displayed below the current location. If yes, update the translation point equal to the height of the image; otherwise, reset the translation point to zero, which will move the image back to the top of the display. Once the coordinate system has been translated, we request the display be updated through a call to repaint().

```
protected void paint(Graphics g)
{
  if (im != null)
  {
    // Clear the background
    g.setColor(255, 255, 255);
    g.fillRect(0, 0, getWidth(), getHeight());

    // Translate coordinates
    g.translate(translatex, translatey);

    // Always draw at 0,0
    g.drawImage(im, 0, 0, Graphics.LEFT | Graphics.TOP);
  }
}
```

The call to drawImage() always places the image at 0, 0 (for this example). Nothing has changed other than where the Graphics object considers its origin to be located.

Figure 9–29 shows an image drawn before any translation. Figure 9–30 shows the result of translating once down and once to the right. One important point: The amount of translation in each direction is based on the height and width of the image.

Figure 9–29 Original coordinate system (before translation)

0,0

Figure 9-30 Translation down and to right

Example 9.9   Translate.java

```
/*-----------------------------------------------
 * Translate.java
 *
 * Translate coordinate system
 *-----------------------------------------------*/
import javax.microedition.midlet.*;
import javax.microedition.lcdui.*;

public class Translate extends MIDlet
{
  private Display  display;          // The display
  private TranslateCanvas canvas;    // Canvas

  public Translate()
  {
    display = Display.getDisplay(this);
    canvas  = new TranslateCanvas(this);
  }

  protected void startApp()
  {
    display.setCurrent(canvas);
  }
```

(continued)

Example 9.9   (Continued)

```
  protected void pauseApp()
  { }

  protected void destroyApp(boolean unconditional)
  { }

  public void exitMIDlet()
  {
    destroyApp(true);
    notifyDestroyed();
  }
}

/*-------------------------------------------------
 * Class Translate
 *
 * Draw image using translated coordinates
 *-------------------------------------------------*/
class TranslateCanvas extends Canvas implements CommandListener
{
  private Command cmExit;  // Exit midlet
  private Translate midlet;
  private Image im = null;
  private int translatex = 0, translatey = 0;

  public TranslateCanvas(Translate midlet)
  {
    this.midlet = midlet;

    // Create exit command & listen for events
    cmExit = new Command("Exit", Command.EXIT, 1);
    addCommand(cmExit);
    setCommandListener(this);

    try
    {
      // Create immutable image
      im = Image.createImage("/bolt.png");
    }
    catch (java.io.IOException e)
    {
      System.err.println("Unable to locate or read .png file");
    }
  }
```

(continued)

Example 9.9 *(Continued)*

```
protected void paint(Graphics g)
{
  if (im != null)
  {
    // Clear the background
    g.setColor(255, 255, 255);
    g.fillRect(0, 0, getWidth(), getHeight());

    // Translate coordinates
    g.translate(translatex, translatey);

    // Always draw at 0,0
    g.drawImage(im, 0, 0, Graphics.LEFT | Graphics.TOP);
  }
}

public void commandAction(Command c, Displayable d)
{
  if (c == cmExit)
    midlet.exitMIDlet();
}

protected void keyPressed(int keyCode)
{
  switch (getGameAction(keyCode))
  {
    case UP:

      // If scrolling off the top, roll around to bottom
      if (translatey - im.getHeight() < 0)
        translatey = getHeight() - im.getHeight();
      else
        translatey -= im.getHeight();
      break;

    case DOWN:

      // If scrolling off the bottom, roll around to top
      if ((translatey + im.getHeight() + im.getHeight())
          > getHeight())
        translatey = 0;
```

(continued)

Example 9.9   (Continued)

```
        else
          translatey += im.getHeight();
        break;

    case LEFT:

        // If scrolling off the left, bring around to right
        if (translatex - im.getWidth() < 0)
          translatex = getWidth() - im.getWidth();
        else
          translatex -= im.getWidth();
        break;

    case RIGHT:

        // If scrolling off the right, bring around to left
        if ((translatex + im.getWidth() + translatex) > getWidth())
          translatex = 0;
        else
          translatex += im.getWidth();
        break;
    }
    repaint();
}
```

Clipping Regions

For each call we've made to paint(), the entire display has been redrawn.
A clipping region can be used to limit what is painted on the display. One important benefit is a reduction in the time to refresh the display.

Before we define a clipping region of our own, let's display an image along with information about the default clipping region.

```
Image im = Image.createImage("/bridge.png");
...
protected void paint(Graphics g)
{
  System.out.println("x: " + g.getClipX());
  System.out.println("y: " + g.getClipY());
```

Table 9.24 Clipping Methods: javax.microedition.lcdui.Graphics	
Method	*Description*
void **setClip**(int x, int y, int width, int height)	Set the clipping rectangle
void **clipRect**(int x, int y, int width, int height)	Intersect this rectangle with the current clipping rectangle to create a new clipping region
int **getClipX**()	Get x coordinate of the current clipping region
int **getClipY**()	Get y coordinate of the current clipping region
int **getClipHeight**()	Get height of the current clipping region
int **getClipWidth**()	Get width of the current clipping region

Figure 9–31 Unclipped image and the corresponding clipping coordinates

```
    System.out.println("width: " + g.getClipWidth());
    System.out.println("height: " + g.getClipHeight());
    g.drawImage(im, 0, 0, Graphics.LEFT | Graphics.TOP);
  }
```

That's interesting—there is already a clipping region defined, even before we call setClip(). The default is a clipping rectangle that consists of the entire display—x and y starting at 0,0 and width and height matching the values returned by Canvas.getWidth() and Canvas.getHeight().

Let's modify the clipping rectangle and see how this affects the output on the display.

```
protected void paint(Graphics g)
{
  g.setClip(25, 25, 45, 45);
  g.drawImage(im, 0, 0, Graphics.TOP | Graphics.LEFT);
}
```

Figure 9–32 shows how only the region of the display defined by the clipping rectangle has been painted.

Default Clipping Rectangle

The default clipping rectangle consists of the entire display. That is, x and y will be 0, the width will be equivalent to the value returned by `Canvas.getWidth()` and the height will be equivalent to the value returned by `Canvas.getHeight()`.

Example: View Port Game

Let's write a MIDlet that follows a similar path as the previous example. We'll use game actions to generate events; however, instead of translating the

Figure 9-32 Clipping region defined as 25, 25, 45, 45

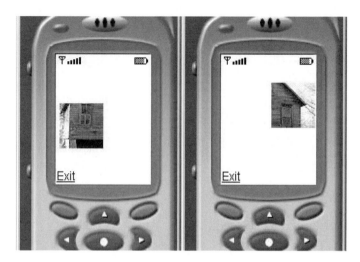

Figure 9–33 Clipping region moving around the Canvas

origin, we move the clipping region around the Canvas. This creates an intriguing "view port" that allows only a portion of the display to be seen at any one time.

To mimic a simple game—with the objective to guess what's on the display—we'll randomly determine the starting coordinates for the clipping region. The game actions LEFT, RIGHT, UP and DOWN will move the clipping region around the Canvas (see Figure 9–33). If at some point you would like to see the entire Image, select the FIRE game action (see Figure 9–34).

Figure 9–34 Reset the clipping region to the entire display

Example 9.10   Clip.java

```
/*-----------------------------------------------------
 * Clip.java
 *
 * Move a clipping region around a Canvas
 *---------------------------------------------------*/
import javax.microedition.midlet.*;
import javax.microedition.lcdui.*;
import java.util.*;

public class Clip extends MIDlet
{
  private Display  display;     // The display
  private ClipCanvas canvas;    // Canvas

  public Clip()
  {
    display = Display.getDisplay(this);
    canvas  = new ClipCanvas(this);
  }

  protected void startApp()
  {
    display.setCurrent(canvas);
  }

  protected void pauseApp()
  { }

  protected void destroyApp(boolean unconditional)
  { }

  public void exitMIDlet()
  {
    destroyApp(true);
    notifyDestroyed();
  }
}

/*-----------------------------------------------------
 * Class ClipCanvas
 *
 * Display the clipping region
 *---------------------------------------------------*/
```

(*continued*)

Example 9.10   (*Continued*)

```
class ClipCanvas extends Canvas implements CommandListener
{
  private Command cmExit;    // Exit
  private Clip midlet;       // Main midlet
  private Image im = null;   // Image to display
  private Random random;     // Get random number
  private int clipx = 0,  clipy = 0,   // View port
              clipw = 45, cliph = 45; // (clipping region)
  private int old_clipx = 0, old_clipy = 0; // Last clipping region

  public ClipCanvas(Clip midlet)
  {
    this.midlet = midlet;

    // Create exit command & listen for events
    cmExit = new Command("Exit", Command.EXIT, 1);
    addCommand(cmExit);
    setCommandListener(this);

    // Get random values for starting point
    random = new java.util.Random();

    // Make sure the entire clipping region is
    // visible on the display
    clipx = Math.min((getWidth() - clipw),
                    (random.nextInt() >>> 1) % getWidth());
    clipy = Math.min((getHeight() - cliph),
                    (random.nextInt() >>> 1) % getHeight());
    try
    {
      // Create immutable image
      im = Image.createImage("/house.png");
    }
    catch (java.io.IOException e)
    {
      System.err.println("Unable to locate or read .png file");
    }
  }

  protected void paint(Graphics g)
  {
  if (im != null)
  {
```

(*continued*)

Example 9.10   *(Continued)*

```
  // Clear only the previous clipping region
  g.setColor(255, 255, 255);
  g.fillRect(old_clipx, old_clipy, clipw, cliph);

  // Set the new clipping region
  g.setClip(clipx, clipy, clipw, cliph);

  // Draw image
  g.drawImage(im, 0, 0, Graphics.LEFT | Graphics.TOP);
  }
}

public void commandAction(Command c, Displayable d)
{
  if (c == cmExit)
    midlet.exitMIDlet();
}

protected void keyPressed(int keyCode)
{
  // Save the last clipping region
  old_clipx = clipx;
  old_clipy = clipy;

  switch (getGameAction(keyCode))
  {
    case UP:
      // Move clipping region up 3 pixels
      if (clipy > 0)
        clipy = Math.max(0, clipy - 3);
      break;

    case DOWN:
      // Move clipping region down 3 pixels
      if (clipy + cliph < getHeight())
        clipy = Math.min(getHeight(), clipy + 3);
      break;

    case LEFT:
      // Move clipping region left 3 pixels
      if (clipx > 0)
        clipx = Math.max(0, clipx - 3);
      break;
```

(continued)

Example 9.10   (Continued)

```
    case RIGHT:
      // Move clipping region right 3 pixels
      if (clipx + clipw < getWidth())
        clipx = Math.min(getWidth(), clipx + 3);
     break;

    case FIRE:
      // Show the whole screen by reseting
      // the clipping region to the entire display
      clipx = clipy = 0;
      clipw = getWidth();
      cliph = getHeight();
  }
   repaint();
  }
}
```

Let's touch on a few pieces of code. Inside the constructor `ClipCanvas()` we create a random starting location:

```
public ClipCanvas(Clip midlet)
  {
    ...

    // Get random values for starting point
    random = new java.util.Random();

    // Make sure the entire clipping region is
    // visible on the display
    clipx = Math.min((getWidth() - clipw),
                     (random.nextInt() >>> 1) % getWidth());
    clipy = Math.min((getHeight() - cliph),
                     (random.nextInt() >>> 1) % getHeight());

    ...
  }
```

Notice in Figure 9–33 that the clipping region is always the same size and fits in its entirety on the display. Here are the steps to ensure this outcome:

1. The random value must not be negative. Thus we shift a zero into the sign bit of the random number.

2. The random value must be in the range 0 to the width of the display for the x coordinate, and 0 to the height of the display for the y coordinate. We obtain a value in the appropriate range using the mod operator (%) applied to the value returned from Step 1.

    At this point, for the x coordinate, we have a number that is between 0 and the width of the display. We have a corresponding y value, between 0 and the height of the display.

3. The x coordinate must take into consideration the width of the clipping region (`clipw`) and the y coordinate must consider the height of the clipping region (`cliph`)

    ```
    getWidth()   - clipw
    getHeight()  - cliph
    ```

Using the minimum value between the results of Step 2 and Step 3 we know the entire clipping region will be visible on the display.

Each movement of the clipping region requires the display to be cleared. There are two options: We can take the easy way out and clear the entire display or we can take a moment and write a few extra lines of code and have a much more efficient solution. Choosing the latter is as simple as the following two steps:

1. Save the current clipping region inside `keypressed()` before defining the new clipping region:

    ```
    protected void keyPressed(int keyCode)
    {
      // Save the last clipping region
      old_clipx = clipx;
      old_clipy = clipy;
      ...
    }
    ```

2. Inside `paint()` fill a rectangle that matches the old clipping region

    ```
    protected void paint()
    {
      ...
      // Clear only the previous clipping region
    ```

```
    g.setColor(255, 255, 255);
    g.fillRect(old_clipx, old_clipy, clipw, cliph);
    ...
}
```

If you find this simple MIDlet in the least bit intriguing, you could make this a much more captivating game by randomly choosing an image. Keeping count of the moves and providing a means to guess what's on the display would also be a nice addition.

CREATING
A DISPLAYER
MANAGER

Topics in this Chapter

- Animation MIDlet

- Display Manager API

- Animating a Series of Images

- Source Code

Chapter 10

We've had it easy up to this point. All examples have made use of only one or two `Displayable` objects. As the complexity of your MIDlets grows, so does managing the transition between `Displayable` components. As a review, the `Displayable` hierarchy is shown here.

Displayable	(public abstract class Displayable)
Screen	(public abstract class Screen extends Displayable)
Form	(public class Form extends Screen)
List	(public class List extends Screen implements Choice)
TextBox	(public class TextBox extends Screen)
Alert	(public class Alert extends Screen)
Canvas	(public abstract class Canvas extends Displayable)

There's little to no challenge to move from a `Form` to a `List`, and back again. However, in the development of a production application there may be transitions between any number of `Displayables`. For example, imagine a MIDlet that presented a `List` of three elements. Each element could invoke a unique `Displayable`, say a `Form`, `Canvas` and `TextBox`. Upon selecting the Form, it could invoke another List of Displayables, each of those . . . you get the picture.

Making the calls "moving forward" is not much of a issue. The challenge comes when you need to unwind back through the Displayables. If you are not much for object-oriented programming and would opt to use public variables and methods, solving this dilemma is not too difficult (other than dealing with a mess of "global" data). Hopefully you lean toward good data design and keep public variables and methods to a minimum. If this is the case, working back through the hierarchy is a little more taxing.

The DisplayManager class was written out of my own frustration when working with MIDlets that had numerous Displayables and rather involved application logic. I found that the deeper I drilled down, the more challenging it was to work my way back out.

The beauty of the DisplayManager is in its simplicity. It does little more than leave a trail as you advance through various Displayables. This unassuming trail, however, makes moving back through Displayables a piece of cake.

Origin of the Display Manager

It deserves repeating that the DisplayManager class is **not** part of MIDP. This is a class I designed and developed to help manage moving between Displayable objects.

Animation MIDlet

In this chapter we'll kill two birds with one stone. Not only will we create a solution to manage Displayable objects, we'll also learn how to perform simple animation. Figure 10–1 shows a glimpse of the animated clock that we'll create.

To tie this example in with the intent of this chapter, in addition to the Canvas that displays the animation, there will be two Displayables, each to facilitate configuration of the clock (viz, starting, stopping and adjusting the speed at which the arm of the clock spins). This will give a nesting of

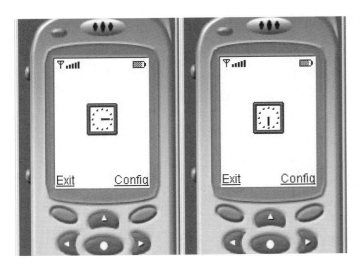

Figure 10–1   Animation of a clock

several `Displayables` to help illustrate when/why you may opt to use to the `DisplayManager` (or write something similar of your own).

Figure 10–2 shows a `List` that is displayed when selecting "Config" from the main animation (Figure 10–1). From this point you can either return to the animation ("Back"), start or stop the animation or choose to set the sleep interval of the `Thread` running the animation.

Choosing the first option will bring up the `Form` shown on the left screen shot in Figure 10–3. The `Form` contains a `Gauge` to adjust the speed of the

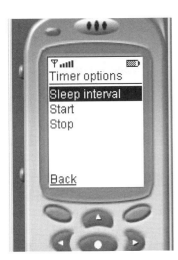

Figure 10–2   Configuration options
(using a List)

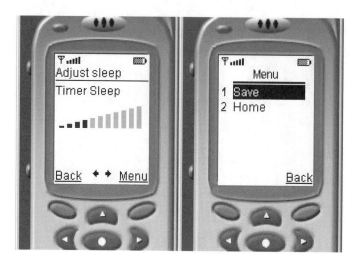

Figure 10–3   Setting the sleep interval using a Form and Gauge

animation. In actuality, it sets the amount of time the animation thread sleeps between repaints of the display. The higher the value on the Gauge, the longer the delay.

On the right of Figure 10–3 are three options:

- Back: return to the gauge.
- Save: save current setting of gauge and return to timer options (Figure 10–2).
- Home: return to the animation (Figure 10–1).

Application Design

The 20,000 foot view of the animation MIDlet is shown in Figure 10–4.

AnimatedTimer is the main MIDlet class. As you'll see, this class does little more than initialize the other components and manage the interface with the application manager.

cvTimer correlates to the screen shot in Figure 10–1. From here you can exit the MIDlet or choose to view the list component lsOptions to configure the animation. When moving to lsOptions, notice the reference to pushDisplayable(). This is our first meeting with the Display-

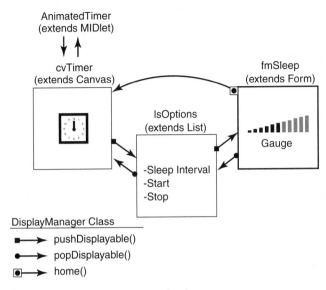

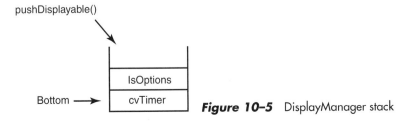

Figure 10-4 Animation MIDlet design

Manager class. This call translates to pushing a reference to the current `Displayable` (`cvTimer`) onto a stack.

From `lsOptions`, you can move back to `cvTimer` or display the form `fmSleep` to configure the sleep interval of the animation Thread. When moving to `fmSleep`, once again, we push the current `Displayable` onto a stack.

Although we are getting a little ahead of ourselves as far as how the `DisplayManager` works internally, it deserves a look at how the `DisplayManager`'s internal stack may look at this point (see Figure 10–5).

Now we can unwind our forward progress. From `fmSleep` you can return to `lsOptions` or head directly to `cvTimer`. If you choose the former, simply pop the topmost displayable off the stack, `popDisplayable()`. An additional call to this same method will return you to `cvTimer`.

Figure 10-5 DisplayManager stack

From `fmSleep` there is a shortcut to return directly to `cvTimer`. Calling the method `home()` pops all `Displayable` objects off the stack. The "main" `Displayable`, defined when creating the `DisplayManager`, is then shown on the display.

Display Manager API

With the application design fresh in your mind, and a picture of how to move between components, this is a good time to familiarize ourselves with the `DisplayManager` class.

As previously mentioned, the `DisplayManager` is implemented as a stack (`java.util.Stack`). This class has only three methods, and an equally small code size, weighing in at less than 70 lines.

Table 10.1   Display Manager Methods

Method	Description
Constructor	
DisplayManager(Display display, Displayable mainDisplayable)	Create a new display manager
Methods	
void **pushDisplayable**(Displayable newDisplayable)	Push a Displayable object on to the stack
void **popDisplayable**()	Pop a Displayable object off the stack
void **home**()	Pop all Displayable objects and return to the "main" Displayable object

Example 10.1   DisplayManager.java

```
/*----------------------------------------------------
 * Use a stack to push and pop displayable objects
 *
 * public void pushDisplayable(Displayable)
 * public void popDisplayable()
```

(continued)

Example 10.1   (*Continued*)

```
* public void home()
*------------------------------------------------*/
import javax.microedition.lcdui.*;
import java.util.*;

public class DisplayManager extends Stack
{
  private Display display;        // Reference to Display object
  private Displayable mainDisplayable; // Main displayable for MIDlet
  private Alert alStackError;  // Alert for error conditions

/*-------------------------------------------------
* Display manager constructor
  *------------------------------------------------*/
  public DisplayManager(Display display,
                    Displayable mainDisplayable)
  {
    // Only one display object per midlet, this is it
    this.display = display;
    this.mainDisplayable = mainDisplayable;

    // Create an alert displayed when an error occurs
    alStackError = new Alert("Displayable Stack Error");
    alStackError.setTimeout(Alert.FOREVER);  // Modal
  }

  /*-------------------------------------------------
  * Push the current displayable onto stack and set
  * the passed in displayable as active
  *------------------------------------------------*/
  public void pushDisplayable(Displayable newDisplayable)
  {
    push(display.getCurrent());
    display.setCurrent(newDisplayable);
  }

  /*-------------------------------------------------
  * Return to the main displayable object of MIDlet
  *------------------------------------------------*/
  public void home()
  {
```

(continued)

Example 10.1   *(Continued)*

```java
  while (elementCount > 1)
    pop();
  display.setCurrent(mainDisplayable);
}


/*--------------------------------------------------
 * Pop displayable from stack and set as active
 *------------------------------------------------*/
public void popDisplayable()
{
  // If the stack is not empty, pop next displayable
  if (empty() == false)
    display.setCurrent((Displayable) pop());
  else
    // On error show an alert
    // Once acknowldeged, set 'mainDisplayable' as active
    display.setCurrent(alStackError, mainDisplayable);
}
}
```

The constructor keeps a reference to a `Display` object (of which there is only one per MIDlet) and the `Displayable` (`Canvas`, `Form`, `TextBox`, etc.) that is considered the main user interface. An `Alert` component is also initialized and will be used to present a dialog box if an error occurs. The following code sets a `Form` as the main `Displayable` when creating the `DisplayManager`.

```java
Form fmMain = new Form("Form Stuff");
Display display = Display.getDisplay(this);

// Create a display manager object
DisplayManager displayMgr = new DisplayManager(display, fmMain);
```

To create the trail of components as we move from one `Displayable` to another, we call `pushDisplayable()`. Refer back to Figure 10–4. Notice the call to this method when moving from `cvTimer` to `lsOptions`.

```java
    // Push current displayable and show the options list
    pushDisplayable(lsOptions);
```

The current `Displayable` (`cvTimer`) will be placed onto the stack and the `Displayable` passed in (`lsOptions`) will be shown on the display.

```
/*-----------------------------------------------
 * Push the current displayable onto stack and set
 * the passed in displayable as active
 *-----------------------------------------------*/
public void pushDisplayable(Displayable newDisplayable)
{
  push(display.getCurrent());
  display.setCurrent(newDisplayable);
}
```

Assuming there is sufficient memory, you can push as many objects as you like onto the stack.

To reverse the process and display each component on the stack, one by one, call `popDisplayable()`.

```
public void popDisplayable()
{
  // If the stack is not empty, pop next displayable
  if (empty() == false)
    display.setCurrent((Displayable) pop());
  else
    // On error show an alert
    // Once acknowldeged, set 'mainDisplayable' as active
    display.setCurrent(alStackError, mainDisplayable);
}
```

Once we satisfy the check that the stack is not empty, the topmost element is popped off the stack and set as the current `Displayable`.

There is one last method available—`home()`. In the animation MIDlet we call this method from the form `fmSleep` when a user requests to move directly back to `cvTimer`, bypassing `lsOptions` (see Figure 10–3). This method empties the stack and displays the "main" `Displayable` object (as defined when creating the display manager class).

```
public void home()
{
  while (elementCount > 1)
    pop();
  display.setCurrent(mainDisplayable);
}
```

Figure 10–6 Individual images making up animation

Animating a Series of Images

A common approach to creating animation is to display a sequence of images, one after another. Showing each image for only a fraction of a second makes the images appear animated.

There are two options for storing the images, the first of which is to save each as a separate resource (see Figure 10–6).

The second option is to tie all the images together into one (see Figure 10–7).

Whether multiple images are stored across or up and down is of no significance. What is relevant is the extra work that we've created for ourselves. We've now got to determine the offset of each image in the sequence. The upside is that the extra effort pays off in that we only need to read, store and manage one resource. This will more than likely also be a boon to performance.

If you look to Figure 10–8 you'll see a conceptual view of our animated clock. The light gray box represents the display. The smaller box in the middle is a clipped region of the display.

To create the effect of the clock moving, we'll translate the coordinate system so the image is, in essence, slid (right to left) over the clipped region. After each translation, we repaint the display. Once the end of the sequence is reached, it will start again with the first image.

For the following discussion, `viewport_x` and `viewport_y` represent the x and y coordinates of the clipping region, which will be centered on the display. The height and width of the clipping region are equal to the height and width of one image in the series.

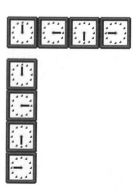

Figure 10–7 Images of an animation stored as one image

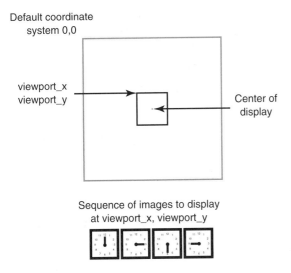

Default coordinate system 0,0

viewport_x
viewport_y

Center of display

Sequence of images to display
at viewport_x, viewport_y

Figure 10–8   Viewport (clipping region) at the center of the display

Figures 10–9 and 10–10 may help to visualize how the origin of the graphics context is translated. For the first image, 0,0 will be translated to the same coordinates as the clipping region—`viewport_x`, `viewport_y`.

For each successive image in the series, the origin will be translated to the left, in effect moving the next image in the sequence over the clipping region. Remember, `paint()` only displays what is viewable in the clipping region (see Figure 10–10).

Figure 10–9   For the first image, translate 0,0 to viewport_x, viewport_y

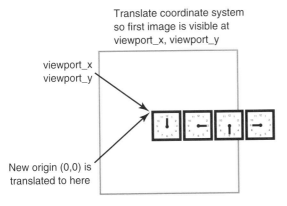

Translate coordinate system
so first image is visible at
viewport_x, viewport_y

viewport_x
viewport_y

New origin (0,0) is
translated to here

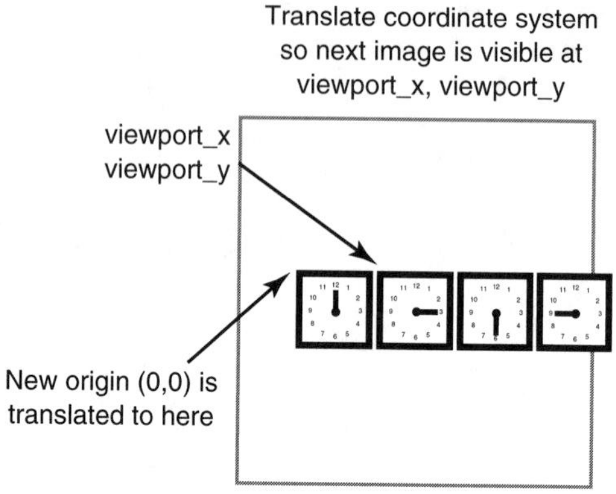

Translate coordinate system
so next image is visible at
viewport_x, viewport_y

viewport_x
viewport_y

New origin (0,0) is
translated to here

Figure 10–10 For each successive image, translate 0,0 to the left

Upon reaching the last image, the translation coordinates are reset to match viewport_x and viewport_y and the cycle is repeated.

One last note: The Canvas that displays the animation will implement the Thread class. This thread will be responsible for calling repaint() at regular intervals to display the images.

In Chapter 13 we will revisit animation using the Timer and Timer-Task classes that are included in the MIDP.

Source Code

Example 10.2   AnimatedTimer.java

```
/*-------------------------------------------------
 * Main midlet.
 * Shows canvas with an animated timer. Includes
 * configuration options to start/stop the timer
 * and to adjust the sleep interval of the thread
 *-------------------------------------------------*/
import javax.microedition.midlet.*;
import javax.microedition.lcdui.*;

public class AnimatedTimer extends MIDlet
{
```

(continued)

Example 10.2   *(Continued)*

```
private Display  display;           // The display
protected TimerCanvas cvTimer;      // Canvas to display timer
protected OptionsList lsOptions;    // List to change timer options
protected SleepForm fmSleep;        // Form w/gauge to set timer sleep
protected DisplayManager displayMgr; // Class to manage screens

public AnimatedTimer()
{
  display = Display.getDisplay(this);
  cvTimer  = new TimerCanvas(this);
  lsOptions = new OptionsList("Timer options",
                             List.IMPLICIT, this);
  fmSleep = new SleepForm("Adjust sleep", this);

  // Create a display manager object
  displayMgr = new DisplayManager(display, cvTimer);
}

protected void startApp()
{
  // Start with the canvas
  display.setCurrent(cvTimer);
}

protected void pauseApp()
{ }

protected void destroyApp( boolean unconditional )
{ }

public void exitMIDlet()
{
  destroyApp(true);
  notifyDestroyed();
}
}
```

Example 10.3   TimerCanvas.java

```
/*----------------------------------------------------
* Class TimerCanvas
*
* Animate a sequence of images to simulate
* a moving timer
*----------------------------------------------------*/
import javax.microedition.lcdui.*;

public class TimerCanvas extends Canvas
                    implements Runnable, CommandListener
{

   private AnimatedTimer midlet;    // Main midlet
   private Command cmExit;          // Exit midlet
   private Command cmOptions;       // Display options list
   private Image im  = null;        // Sequence of images
   private int imageCount = 4;      // Four images in the sequence
   private int imageWidth;          // Width of one image in sequence
   private int imageHeight;         // Height of one image in sequence
   private int imageIndex;          // Current image in the sequence
   private int translate_x;         // Translated x and y
   private int translate_y;
   private int viewport_x;          // Location of the viewport
   private int viewport_y;
   private boolean active = false;  // Timer active?
   private boolean requestedToStop = false; // Request to stop timer
   private int sleepTime = 400; // Current sleep time (milliseconds)

   public TimerCanvas(AnimatedTimer midlet)
   {
     // Call canvas constructor
     super();

     // Save reference to MIDlet so we can
     // access the display manager class
     this.midlet = midlet;

     // Create commands & listen for events
     cmExit = new Command("Exit", Command.EXIT, 1);
     cmOptions = new Command("Config", Command.SCREEN, 2);
     addCommand(cmExit);
     addCommand(cmOptions);
```

(continued)

Example 10.3 *(Continued)*

```
    setCommandListener(this);
}


/*-------------------------------------------------
 * Application manager is about to display canvas
 *-----------------------------------------------*/
protected void showNotify()
{
  if (im == null)
  {
    try
    {
      // Read the png from a file and get width and
      // height of one image in the sequence
      im = Image.createImage("/timer.png");
      imageHeight = im.getHeight();
      imageWidth = im.getWidth() / imageCount;

      // Get the coordinates for x/y of viewport
      // Viewport is centered on the display
      viewport_x = (getWidth() / 2 ) - (imageWidth / 2);
      viewport_y = (getHeight() / 2 ) - (imageHeight / 2);

      // Set first translated coordinate to match viewport
      translate_x = viewport_x;
      translate_y = viewport_y;
    }
    catch (Exception e)
    {
      System.err.println("Unable to read png file.");
    }

    // Begin with the first image in the sequence
    imageIndex = 0;
  }

  // If the user has not requested to stop the timer...
  if (!requestedToStop)
    active = true;

  new Thread(this).start();
}
```

(continued)

Example 10.3   (Continued)

```
/*--------------------------------------------------
* Application manager is no longer displaying canvas
*-------------------------------------------------*/
protected void hideNotify()
{
  active = false;
}


/*--------------------------------------------------
* Draw next timer in sequence
*-------------------------------------------------*/
protected void paint(Graphics g)
{
  if (im != null)
  {
    // Viewport at center of display
    g.setClip(viewport_x, viewport_y, imageWidth, imageHeight);

    // Draw image at translated coordinates
    g.drawImage(im, translate_x, translate_y,
                Graphics.TOP | Graphics.LEFT);
  }
}


/*--------------------------------------------------
* Loop forever, translating image coordinates
*-------------------------------------------------*/
public void run()
{
  try
  {
    while (active)
    {
      Thread.sleep(sleepTime);
      repaint();

      // Reached the last image in sequence
      if (imageIndex == imageCount - 1)
      {
        // Reset translated coordinates
        translate_x = viewport_x;
        translate_y = viewport_y;
```

(continued)

Example 10.3   (Continued)

```
      }
      else
      {
        // Translate coordinate system to the left
        translate_x -= imageWidth;
      }

      // Which image in the sequence is next
      imageIndex = (imageIndex + 1) % imageCount;
    }
  }
  catch (InterruptedException e)
  {
  }
}

/*----------------------------------------------------
 * Called from the "Config" options menu
 *--------------------------------------------------*/
public void startTimer()
{
  requestedToStop = false;
  active = true;
  repaint();
}

/*----------------------------------------------------
 * Called from the "Config" options menu
 *--------------------------------------------------*/
public void stopTimer()
{
  requestedToStop = true;
  active = false;
  repaint();
}

/*----------------------------------------------------
 * Called from form/gauge to adjust sleep
 *--------------------------------------------------*/
public void setSleep(int sleepTime)
{
```

(continued)

Example 10.3   (Continued)

```
    this.sleepTime = sleepTime;
  }


  /*--------------------------------------------------
   * Called from form/gauge to adjust sleep
   *-------------------------------------------------*/
  public int getSleep()
  {
    return sleepTime;
  }


  /*--------------------------------------------------
   * Command event handling
   *-------------------------------------------------*/

  public void commandAction(Command c, Displayable s)
  {
    if (c == cmOptions)
    {
      // Push current displayable and show the options list
      midlet.displayMgr.pushDisplayable(midlet.lsOptions);
    }
    else if (c == cmExit)
    {
      midlet.exitMIDlet();
    }
  }
}
```

Example 10.4   OptionsList.java

```
/*--------------------------------------------------
 * Class OptionsList
 *
 * List to provide options for configuring of timer
 *-------------------------------------------------*/
import javax.microedition.lcdui.*;

class OptionsList extends List implements CommandListener
{
```

(continued)

Example 10.4 *(Continued)*

```java
private AnimatedTimer midlet; // Main midlet
private Command cmBack;

public OptionsList(String title, int listType, AnimatedTimer midlet)
{
  // Call list constructor
  super(title, listType);

  // Save reference to MIDlet so we can
  // access the display manager class
  this.midlet = midlet;

  // Create the list entries
  append("Sleep interval", null);
  append("Start", null);
  append("Stop", null);

  // Create command and listen for events
  cmBack = new Command("Back", Command.BACK, 1);
  addCommand(cmBack);
  setCommandListener(this);
}

/*-------------------------------------------------
 * Command event handling
 *-------------------------------------------------*/
public void commandAction(Command c, Displayable s)
{
  // Event generated by the implicit list
  if (c == List.SELECT_COMMAND)
  {
    switch (getSelectedIndex())
    {
      case 0:
        // Push current displayable and show the form
        // to adjust the timer sleep
        midlet.displayMgr.pushDisplayable(midlet.fmSleep);
        break;

      case 1:
        // Start timer and return to previous displayable
        midlet.cvTimer.startTimer();
```

(continued)

Example 10.4 (Continued)

```
            midlet.displayMgr.popDisplayable();
            break;

        case 2:
            // Stop timer and return to previous displayable
            midlet.cvTimer.stopTimer();
            midlet.displayMgr.popDisplayable();
            break;
        }
      }
      else if (c == cmBack)
      {
        // Return to previous displayable
        midlet.displayMgr.popDisplayable();
      }
    }
}
```

Example 10.5 SleepForm.java

```
/*--------------------------------------------------
 * Class SleepForm
 *
 * Form with gauge to adjust sleep interval of timer
 *--------------------------------------------------*/
import javax.microedition.lcdui.*;

public class SleepForm extends Form implements CommandListener
{
    private AnimatedTimer midlet; // Main midlet
    private Command cmBack,        // Back to options list
                    cmHome,        // Go to main displayable (canvas)
                    cmSave;        // Save new sleep time
    private Gauge gaSleep;         // Gauge to adjust sleep

    public SleepForm(String title, AnimatedTimer midlet)
    {
        // Call the form constructor
        super(title);
```

(continued)

Example 10.5   (Continued)

```
    // Save reference to MIDlet so we can
    // access the display manager class
    this.midlet = midlet;

    // Commands
    cmSave = new Command("Save", Command.SCREEN, 1);
    cmBack = new Command("Back", Command.BACK, 2);
    cmHome = new Command("Home", Command.SCREEN, 2);

    // Gauge to adjust the length of timer sleep
    gaSleep = new Gauge("Timer Sleep", true, 100, 1000);

    // Set to current sleep. Gauge holds values 0 to 100,
    // divide the current sleep (milliseconds) by 10
    gaSleep.setValue(midlet.cvTimer.getSleep() / 10);

    // Add to form and listen for events
    append(gaSleep);
    addCommand(cmSave);
    addCommand(cmBack);
    addCommand(cmHome);
    setCommandListener(this);
}

/*----------------------------------------------------
 * Command event handling
 *---------------------------------------------------*/
public void commandAction(Command c, Displayable s)
{
    if (c == cmSave)
    {
        // Gauge returns a value between 0 and 100
        // We want milliseconds, so multiply by 10
        midlet.cvTimer.setSleep(gaSleep.getValue() * 10);

        // Return to main midlet
        midlet.displayMgr.home();

    }
    else if (c == cmBack)
    {
        // Pop the last displayable off the stack
```

(*continued*)

Example 10.5   (Continued)

```
    midlet.displayMgr.popDisplayable();
  }
  else if (c == cmHome)
  {
    // Return to main midlet
    midlet.displayMgr.home();
  }
  }
}
```

Example 10.6   DisplayManager.java

```
/*-------------------------------------------------
* Use a stack to push and pop displayable objects
*
* public void pushDisplayable(Displayable)
* public void popDisplayable()
* public void home()
*-------------------------------------------------*/
import javax.microedition.lcdui.*;
import java.util.*;

public class DisplayManager extends Stack
{
  private Display display;       // Reference to Display object
  private Displayable mainDisplayable; // Main displayable for MIDlet
  private Alert alStackError;   // Alert for error conditions

  public DisplayManager(Display display, Displayable mainDisplayable)
  {
    // Only one display object per midlet, this is it
    this.display = display;
    this.mainDisplayable = mainDisplayable;

    // Create an alert displayed when an error occurs
    alStackError = new Alert("Displayable Stack Error");
    alStackError.setTimeout(Alert.FOREVER);   // Modal
  }
```

(continued)

Example 10.6 (*Continued*)

```
/*--------------------------------------------------
 * Push the current displayable onto stack and set
 * the passed in displayable as active
 *------------------------------------------------*/
public void pushDisplayable(Displayable newDisplayable)
{
  push(display.getCurrent());
  display.setCurrent(newDisplayable);
}


/*--------------------------------------------------
 * Return to the main displayable object of MIDlet
 *------------------------------------------------*/
public void home()

{
  while (elementCount > 1)
    pop();
  display.setCurrent(mainDisplayable);
}


/*--------------------------------------------------
 * Pop displayable from stack and set as active
 *------------------------------------------------*/
public void popDisplayable()
{
  // If the stack is not empty, pop next displayable
  if (empty() == false)
    display.setCurrent((Displayable) pop());
  else
    // On error show an alert
    // Once acknowldeged, set 'mainDisplayable' as active
    display.setCurrent(alStackError, mainDisplayable);
}
}
```

RECORD MANAGEMENT SYSTEM (RMS)

Topics in this Chapter

- Persistent Storage Through the Record Store
- Navigating with RecordEnumeration
- Sorting with RecordComparator
- Searching with RecordFilter
- Notification of Changes with RecordListener
- Exception Handling

Chapter 11

We can cover a lot of miles with the concepts we've covered up to this point. However, we are missing a significant capability that will eventually catch up with us. In fact, it is so ingrained into our daily computing we often take this concept for granted. I am referring to storing and retrieving of data. Whether the information is as simple as application preferences or as comprehensive as a product catalog, we need a way to manage application-related data.

In desktop computing the options are obvious, CD-ROM, local drive, network drive, and so forth. It becomes a little more challenging with mobile devices. There are size and performance concerns, not to mention the differences between manufacturers as far as support (or lack of) for file systems and networking.

The Record Management System (RMS) is a persistent storage environment within the MIDP. This chapter describes how you can read, write, sort and search data within a RMS.

Persistent Storage Through the Record Store

As an alternative to using a file system, the RMS uses non-volatile memory to store information. This record-oriented database, often referred to as a flat-file, can be thought of as a series of rows in a table, with a unique identifier for each row (see Table 11.1).

Table 11.1 Record Store	
Record ID	*Data*
1	Array of bytes
2	Array of bytes
3	Array of bytes
...	...

Each **record** consists of a **record id,** an integer value that plays the role of primary key for the database and an array of bytes for storing the record data. A collection of records is known as a **record store.**

A MIDlet can have any number of record stores (including none), where each is uniquely identified by its name. This idea needs to be carried one step further—if a MIDlet is part of MIDlet suite, record store names must also be unique within the suite.

Naming Record Stores

Each record store name can consist of up to 32 Unicode (16-bit) characters. Names are case sensitive. Names must be unique within a MIDlet suite.

MIDlets that are packaged within a suite can access not only the record stores they create, but also those of other MIDlets in the suite. Figure 11–1 illustrates this concept.

MIDLET SUITE ONE

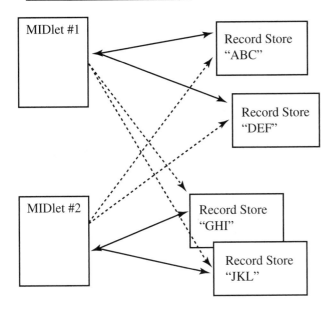

MIDLET SUITE TWO

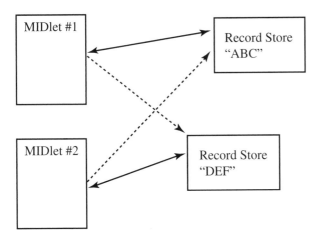

Figure 11-1 MIDlet access to record stores. *The solid lines indicate access to record stores the MIDlet has created. Dashed lines represent access to record stores created by a different MIDlet within the same suite.*

Within "MIDlet Suite One," MIDlet #1 and MIDlet #2 can access all four record stores available as part of the suite. The same applies to "Suite Two." However, MIDlets in Suite One cannot access the record stores of Suite Two.

Record store names within a suite must be unique. That is, Suite One must have all unique record store names. However, record store names in one suite may be duplicated in another. For example, Suite One and Suite Two both have record stores with the name "ABC" and "DEF."

There are two values maintained by a record store that may be helpful for tracking database usage. Each is updated when a record is added, deleted or changed:

1. ***Version number*** is an integer value. Unfortunately, the starting value when creating a new record is not defined by the API. If you need to track version numbers, you can query the record store immediately after creation using `getVersion()` to determine the starting value.

2. ***Date and time stamp*** is a long integer that represents the number of milliseconds since midnight January 1st, 1970. You can query this value by calling `getLastModified()`.

Whenever a request is made to modify the record store, it is done in one fell swoop. That is, once a change is underway it is guaranteed to be completed before another begins. If a request(s) is made to update the record store while an operation is in progress, it will be queued, waiting for the current operation to finish.

Removing Record Stores

If a MIDlet suite is removed from a device, all record stores will be deleted as well.

Record Store API

This class is the heart of the RMS. Through this class we create, update, query and delete record stores (see Table 11.2).

Table 11.2 RecordStore Class: javax.microedition.rms.RecordStore	
Method	*Description*
Constructors	
No constructor. See openRecordStore()	
Methods	
static RecordStore **openRecordStore**(String recordStoreName, boolean createIfNecessary)	Open record store. Optionally, create the store if it does not already exist.
void **closeRecordStore**()	Close record store.
static void **deleteRecordStore**(String recordStoreName)	Delete record store.
static String[] **listRecordStores**()	List record stores in MIDlet suite.
int **addRecord**(byte[] data, int offset, int numBytes)	Add a record.
void **setRecord**(int recordId, byte[] newData, int offset, int numBytes)	Set (replace) data in a record.
void **deleteRecord**(int recordId)	Delete a record.
byte[] **getRecord**(int recordId)	Get byte array containing record data.
int **getRecord**(int recordId, byte[] buffer, int offset)	Get contents of record into byte array parameter copying data from specified offset.
int **getRecordSize**(int recordId)	Size in bytes of a record.
int **getNextRecordID**()	The number of the next record when adding a new record to the store.
int **getNumRecords**()	Number of records in the record store.
long **getLastModified**()	Last modified date of the record store.
int **getVersion**()	Record store version number.
String **getName**()	Name of the record store.

(continued)

Table 11.2 (Continued)	
int **getSize**()	Total bytes occupied by record store.
int **getSizeAvailable**()	Current space (bytes) available for records. This will change as records are added/deleted.

RecordEnumeration **enumerateRecords**(
    RecordFilter filter,
    RecordComparator comparator,
    boolean keepUpdated)
	Build an enumeration for traversing records in the record store.

void **addRecordListener** (RecordListener listener)	Add a listener to detect record store changes.
void **removeRecordListener** (RecordListener listener)	Remove listener.

Example: Read and Write Records

Now that we understand the basics of RMS, let's walk through two examples. Each will create a record store, write several records, read back those same records and delete the record store. The difference lies with how the data is manipulated before and after writing. More on that in a minute.

We have two methods to write data into a record store:

```
public int addRecord (byte[] data, int offset, int numBytes)

public void setRecord (int recordId, byte[] newData,
                       int offset, int numBytes)
```

Regardless of which we choose, each accepts an array of bytes as the input. What will vary for our two examples is how we manage the array of data, for both reading and writing records.

In our first example (Example 11.1), we will write `String` objects into the record store.

Figure 11–2 shows the contents of the two records that were read from the record store.

I've gone ahead and written several convenience methods for managing the record store. These include opening, closing and deleting. Each method

Example 11.1   ReadWrite.java

```
/*-------------------------------------------------
 * ReadWrite.java
 *
 * Read and write to the record store.
 *
 * No GUI interface, all output is to the console
 *-------------------------------------------------*/
import java.io.*;
import javax.microedition.midlet.*;
import javax.microedition.rms.*;

public class ReadWrite extends MIDlet
{
  private RecordStore rs = null;
  static final String REC_STORE = "db_1";

  public ReadWrite()
  {
    openRecStore();    // Create the record store

    // Write a few records and read them back
    writeRecord("J2ME and MIDP");
    writeRecord("Wireless Technology");
    readRecords();

    closeRecStore();  // Close record store
    deleteRecStore(); // Remove the record store
  }

  public void destroyApp( boolean unconditional )
  {
  }

  public void startApp()
  {
    // There is no user interface, go ahead and shutdown
    destroyApp(false);
    notifyDestroyed();
  }

  public void pauseApp()
  {
  }
```

(continued)

Example 11.1 *(Continued)*

```java
public void openRecStore()
{
  try
  {
    // Create record store if it does not exist
    rs = RecordStore.openRecordStore(REC_STORE, true );
  }
  catch (Exception e)
  {
    db(e.toString());
  }
}

public void closeRecStore()
{
  try
  {
    rs.closeRecordStore();
  }
  catch (Exception e)
  {
    db(e.toString());
  }
}

public void deleteRecStore()
{
  if (RecordStore.listRecordStores() != null)
  {
    try
    {
      RecordStore.deleteRecordStore(REC_STORE);
    }
    catch (Exception e)
    {
      db(e.toString());
    }
  }
}

public void writeRecord(String str)
```

(continued)

Example 11.1   *(Continued)*

```
  {
    byte[] rec = str.getBytes();

    try
    {
      rs.addRecord(rec, 0, rec.length);
    }
    catch (Exception e)
    {
      db(e.toString());
    }
  }

  public void readRecords()
  {
    try
    {
      byte[] recData = new byte[50];
      int len;

      for (int i = 1; i <= rs.getNumRecords(); i++)
      {
        len = rs.getRecord( i, recData, 0 );
        System.out.println("Record #" + i + ": " +
                           new String(recData, 0, len));
        System.out.println("-----------------------------");
      }
    }
    catch (Exception e)
    {
      db(e.toString());
    }
  }


  /*----------------------------------------------------
   * Simple message to console for debug/errors
   * When used with Exceptions we should handle the
   * error in a more appropriate manner.
   *--------------------------------------------------*/
  private void db(String str)
  {
    System.err.println("Msg: " + str);
  }
}
```

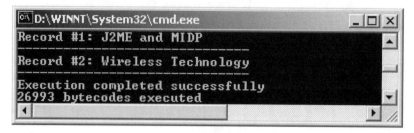

Figure 11–2   Reading and writing String objects

is self-explanatory. Here is the method to open a record store, which will create the store if it does not already exist:

```
public void openRecStore()
{
  try
  {
  // The second parameter indicates that the record store
    // should be created if it does not exist
    rs = RecordStore.openRecordStore(REC_STORE, true );
  }
  catch (Exception e)
  {
    db(e.toString());
  }
}
```

I have taken a shortcut in handling exceptions. Notice that I trap all exceptions with one catch. This obviously skirts around the issue of dealing with error conditions. However, later in this chapter (in the Section "Catching Exceptions") we introduce all the RMS exceptions and show how to appropriately manage these errors.

Let's focus on the code to write and read records. Inside `write-Record()` we need to convert the `String` object passed in to an array of bytes. We can now pass this array as a parameter to `addRecord()`.

```
byte[] rec = str.getBytes();
...
rs.addRecord(rec, 0, rec.length);
```

Reading from the record store is not a great deal different. Inside `read-Records()` we set up an array of bytes to hold the record data and call `getRecord()`.

```
byte[] recData = new byte[50];
...
len = rs.getRecord( i, recData, 0 );
```

Worth mentioning is the size of array that will hold the record data—I simply allocated an array that I knew was large enough. It may not always be as simple as this. If you did not write the records yourself, you may not be privy to the contents (length) of each record. With a minor tweak we can make this code a little more robust. Let's check the length of the data in the record before we actually read it from the store. This will give us an opportunity to resize the destination array. Change the for loop inside read-Records() to the following:

```
for (int i = 1; i <= rs.getNumRecords(); i++)
{
   if (rs.getRecordSize(i) > recData.length)
     recData = new byte[rs.getRecordSize(i)];

len = rs.getRecord(i, recData, 0);
System.out.println("Record #" + i + ": " +
                       new String(recData, 0, len));
System.out.println("----------------------------");
}
```

Example: Read and Write Records with Streams

If you plan to read and write only text to the record store, at this point you've got all you need. It may not be the most efficient or fastest way to manage data, but it does work. There is a much preferred means to read and write data, which leads us to our next example.

The code in Example 11.2 is similar to the previous example in that it writes and reads a few records to the record store. However, there are two main differences. First, we'll write more than straight text. Specifically, we will store Java data types including a String, int, and a boolean. Second, we'll use Java streams for both reading and writing. Not only will we have additional flexibility for writing any type of data, we also increase the efficiency with which data is written to and read from the record store.

Example 11.2   ReadWriteStreams.java

```java
/*-------------------------------------------------
 * ReadWriteStreams.java
 *
 * Use streams to read and write Java data types
 * to the record store.
 *
 * No GUI interface, all output is to the console
 *-------------------------------------------------*/

import java.io.*;
import javax.microedition.midlet.*;
import javax.microedition.rms.*;

public class ReadWriteStreams extends MIDlet
{
  private RecordStore rs = null;        // Record store
  static final String REC_STORE = "db_1"; // Name of record store

  public ReadWriteStreams()
  {
    openRecStore();    // Create the record store

    writeTestData();   // Write a series of records
    readStream();      // Read back the records

    closeRecStore();   // Close record store
    deleteRecStore();  // Remove the record store
  }

  public void destroyApp( boolean unconditional )
  {
  }

  public void startApp()
  {
    // There is no user interface, go ahead and shutdown
    destroyApp(false);
    notifyDestroyed();
  }

  public void pauseApp()
  {
  }
```

(continued)

Example 11.2   (Continued)

```java
public void openRecStore()
{
  //See Example 11-1
}

public void closeRecStore()
{
  //See Example 11-1
}

public void deleteRecStore()
{
  //See Example 11-1
}

/*--------------------------------------------------
 * Create three arrays to write to record store
 *----------------------------------------------*/
public void writeTestData()
{
  String[] strings = {"Text 1", "Text 2"};
  boolean[] booleans = {false, true};
  int[] integers = {1 , 2};

  writeStream(strings, booleans, integers);
}

/*--------------------------------------------------
 * Write to record store using streams.
 *----------------------------------------------*/
public void writeStream(String[] sData, boolean[] bData,
                        int[] iData)
{
  try
  {
    // Write data into an internal byte array
    ByteArrayOutputStream strmBytes =
            new ByteArrayOutputStream();

    // Write Java data types into the above byte array
    DataOutputStream strmDataType =
            new DataOutputStream(strmBytes);
```

(continued)

Example 11.2 *(Continued)*

```
byte[] record;

for (int i = 0; i < sData.length; i++)
{
  // Write Java data types
  strmDataType.writeUTF(sData[i]);
  strmDataType.writeBoolean(bData[i]);
  strmDataType.writeInt(iData[i]);

  // Clear any buffered data
  strmDataType.flush();

  // Get stream data into byte array and write record
  record = strmBytes.toByteArray();
  rs.addRecord(record, 0, record.length);

  // Toss any data in the internal array so writes
  // starts at beginning (of the internal array)
  strmBytes.reset();
}

strmBytes.close();
strmDataType.close();

}
catch (Exception e)
{
  db(e.toString());
}
}

/*--------------------------------------------------
 * Read from the record store using streams
 *------------------------------------------------*/
public void readStream()
{
  try
  {
    // Careful: Make sure this is big enough!
    // Better yet, test and reallocate if necessary
    byte[] recData = new byte[50];
```

(continued)

Example 11.2   *(Continued)*

```
    // Read from the specified byte array
    ByteArrayInputStream strmBytes =
            new ByteArrayInputStream(recData);

    // Read Java data types from the above byte array
    DataInputStream strmDataType =
            new DataInputStream(strmBytes);

    for (int i = 1; i <= rs.getNumRecords(); i++)
    {
      // Get data into the byte array
      rs.getRecord(i, recData, 0);

      // Read back the data types
      System.out.println("Record #" + i);
      System.out.println("UTF: " + strmDataType.readUTF());
      System.out.println("Boolean: " +
                      strmDataType.readBoolean());
      System.out.println("Int: " + strmDataType.readInt());
      System.out.println("-------------------");

      // Reset so read starts at beginning of array
      strmBytes.reset();
    }

    strmBytes.close();
    strmDataType.close();

  }
  catch (Exception e)
  {
    db(e.toString());
  }
}

/*----------------------------------------------------
 * Simple message to console for debug/errors
 * When used with Exceptions we should handle the
 * error in a more appropriate manner.
 *----------------------------------------------------*/
private void db(String str)
```

(continued)

Example 11.2   (Continued)

```
{
   System.err.println("Msg: " + str);
}
}
```

Before we see the output of this MIDlet, let's look over the code for writing to the record store. First, we create and populate several arrays for the data we want to write:

```
public void writeTestData()
{
   String[] strings = {"Text 1", "Text 2"};
   boolean[] booleans = {false, true};
   int[] integers = {1 , 2};

   writeStream(strings, booleans, integers);
}
```

Once we have all the data prepared, we call writeStream() to do the actual work of writing to the record store.

```
// Write data into an internal byte array
ByteArrayOutputStream strmBytes = new ByteArrayOutputStream();

// Write Java data types into the above byte array
DataOutputStream strmDataType = new DataOutputStream(strmBytes);

byte[] record;

for (int i = 0; i < sData.length; i++)
{
   // Write Java data types
   strmDataType.writeUTF(sData[i]);
   strmDataType.writeBoolean(bData[i]);
   strmDataType.writeInt(iData[i]);

   // Clear any buffered data
   strmDataType.flush();

   // Get stream data into byte array and write record
```

```
    record = strmBytes.toByteArray();
    rs.addRecord(record, 0, record.length);

    // Toss any data in the internal array so writes
    // starts at beginning (of the internal array)
    strmBytes.reset();
}
```

We've created two streams: `strmBytes` is an array that is managed internally by Java. This is our byte array that will hold that the data we'll eventually write to the record store.

To this stream we have added a filter: `strmDataType`. This class includes methods for writing Java primitive data types. The end result is that, the internal byte array will consist of portable binary data. Thus, when we reverse the process and read the data back, we are assured to get the same information, in the same format. That is, if we write an integer into the byte array, regardless of how the system running the JVM represents an integer (16 bits, 32 bits, etc.), we are guaranteed to get the expected results.

Once the streams are in place we call the appropriate methods based on the type of data we choose to write. Next, we flush the stream, which writes any buffered data to the stream. We're nearly there. All we have to do at this point is get the data from the stream into a byte array and add the record.

There is one small, yet very important detail that we must take care of before we can write another record. We need to clear the internal array that is being managed by our byte stream, `strmBytes`.

```
strmBytes.reset();
```

If we overlook this, the next write operation:

```
strmDataType.writeUTF("Text 2");
```

will append to the current byte array. The next record would contain all the data we've accumulated up to this point.

Reading the data back from the record store is almost as simple as changing our output streams to input streams. Almost.

```
byte[] recData = new byte[50];

// Read from the specified byte array
ByteArrayInputStream strmBytes = new
ByteArrayInputStream(recData);

// Read Java data types from the above byte array
DataInputStream strmDataType = new DataInputStream(strmBytes);
```

```
for (int i = 1; i <= rs.getNumRecords(); i++)
{
  // Get data into the byte array
  rs.getRecord(i, recData, 0);

  // Read back the data types
  System.out.println("Record #" + i);
  System.out.println("UTF: " + strmDataType.readUTF());
  System.out.println("Boolean: " + strmDataType.readBoolean());
  System.out.println("Int: " + strmDataType.readInt());
  System.out.println("--------------------");

  // Reset so read starts at beginning of array
  strmBytes.reset();
}
```

I've allocated a byte array to hold our data, `recData`. If you skip down a few lines, you'll notice this array is where the record store will write the contents of each record:

```
// Get data into the byte array
rs.getRecord(i, recData, 0);
```

After this call, `recData` contains exactly what we wrote to the record store a moment ago. If you recall, that was a binary stream of data, specifically, Java primitive data types. Without a little help we can't use this data as it exists. Here's where we introduce `ByteArrayInputStream` and `DataInputStream`. Notice the declarations for each:

```
// Read from the specified byte array
ByteArrayInputStream strmBytes = new ByteArrayInputStream(recData);

// Read Java data types from the above byte array
DataInputStream strmDataType = new DataInputStream(strmBytes);
```

The byte array stream, `strmBytes`, references the array (`recData`) that the record store will write data into. The data input stream, `strmDataType`, which reads Java primitive types, references the byte stream. We now have everything in place to read back our data just as it was written.

```
System.out.println("UTF: " + strmDataType.readUTF());
System.out.println("Boolean: " + strmDataType.readBoolean());
System.out.println("Int: " + strmDataType.readInt());
```

The output for this MIDlet is shown in Figure 11–3.

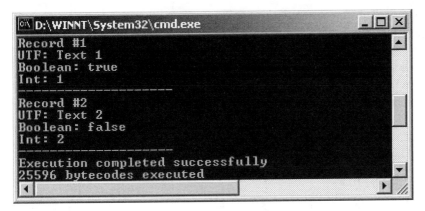

Figure 11-3 Reading and writing Java primitive data types

Java Primitives

Although this seems quite obvious, when using `DataOutputStream` and `DataInputStream` you need to write and read in the same order and format. For example, if you write a text string, a boolean value and an integer, you must read back a text string, boolean value and an integer. If you aren't getting the expected results when using these streams, look carefully to see that you are reading and writing data in the same sequence.

Navigating with RecordEnumeration

In the previous example we perused records in the record store using a simple loop:

```
for (int i = 1; i <= rs.getNumRecords(); i++)
{
  rs.getRecord(i, recData, 0);
  ...
}
```

This works fine for simple iterations. However, if you would like to sort and/or search records we need to move up to a record enumerator.

The `RecordEnumeration` (A.K.A enumerator) class provides methods for moving forward and back through a record store. What makes the enumerator so powerful is that the iteration can take into account the results of a filter (to search) and/or a comparator (to sort). For example, you can set up a filter to only return records that contain a specific substring. Or, you might prefer to enumerate through the records, sorting alphabetically.

Setting up an enumerator takes only a few lines. Assuming the variable `rs` references an existing and open record store, here is a loop to move through all the records:

```
RecordEnumeration re = rs.enumerateRecords(null,null,false);
while (re.hasNextElement())
{
  // Get the next record into a String
  String str = new String(re.nextRecord());

  ... do something ...
}
```

There are two key methods for moving through a record store with an enumerator: `nextRecord()` to move forward, `previousRecord()` to move back. If you need to start at the end and move toward the front, create an enumerator and have as your first call `previousRecord()`, which will return the last record. Each subsequent call will move you one element closer to the front.

An enumerator maintains in internal index of the record store. If at any point the record store changes, it may be possible that the enumerator will no longer return the correct results. As an example, assume that you create an enumerator to return records that are sorted. At a later point in the application, a new record is added. This new record may upset the balance and affect what the "new" proper sort order is. The enumerator has a method to re-index, which will take into consideration any changes that may have occurred within the record store.

As far as when to re-index:

1. You can make calls to `reindex()` whenever you update, delete or add a record. This will work fine, as long as you are thorough and sure not to leave any holes, which may cause the enumerator to get out of sync.

2. A record listener can be established to notify you of changes to the record store. Whenever a change occurs, the listener will call one of three methods, depending on whether the change was an add, delete or update. Within the method called, you can re-index the record store. We'll discuss this in more detail in the next section.

RecordEnumeration API

Table 11.3	RecordEnumeration Interface: javax.microedition.rms.RecordEnumeration

Method	Description
No constructor. See `enumerateRecords()` in `RecordStore` class, Table 11.2	
Methods	
int **numRecords**()	Number of records in the enumeration (result set)
byte[] **nextRecord**()	Get the next record in result set
int **nextRecordId**()	Get ID of the next record number in result set
byte[] **previousRecord**()	Get previous record in result set
int **previousRecordId**()	Get ID of previous record in result set
boolean **hasNextElement**()	Does enumeration have more records going forward?
boolean **hasPreviousElement**()	Does enumeration have more records going backward?
void **keepUpdated**(boolean keepUpdated)	Set whether enumeration will re-index as record store changes
boolean **isKeptUpdated**()	Will enumeration re-index as record store changes?
void **rebuild**()	Rebuild enumeration index
void **reset**()	Reset enumeration to beginning
void **destroy**()	Free all resources held by the enumeration

Sorting with RecordComparator

RecordComparator is a Java interface. You implement this interface when you would like the enumerator to return records in sorted order.

Here is a simple class that implements the interface.

```
public class Comparator implements RecordComparator
{
  public int compare(byte[] rec1, byte[] rec2)
  {
    String str1 = new String(rec1), str2 = new String(rec2);

    int result = str1.compareTo(str2);
    if (result == 0)
      return RecordComparator.EQUIVALENT;
    else if (result < 0)
      return RecordComparator.PRECEDES;
    else
      return RecordComparator.FOLLOWS;
  }
}
```

Notice the return values. There are three pre-defined values that you must use (see Table 11.4). This class becomes part of the enumeration process with the following.

```
// Create a new comparator for sorting
Comparator comp = new Comparator();

// Reference the comparator when creating the result set
RecordEnumeration re = rs.enumerateRecords(null,comp,false);
// Iterate through the sorted results
while (re.hasNextElement())
{
String str = new String(re.nextRecord());
...
}
```

The enumerator references the compare() inside Comparator to sort the records in the record store.

Table 11.4	RecordComparator Types: javax.microedition.rms.RecordComparator

Value	*Description*
EQUIVALENT	The records passed to compare() method are equivalent
FOLLOWS	Based on the sort algorithm in the compare() method, the first parameter follows the second
PRECEDES	Based on the sort algorithm in the compare() method, the first parameter precedes the second

RecordComparator API

Table 11.5	RecordComparator Interface: javax.microedition.rms.RecordComparator

Method	*Description*
int **compare**(byte[] rec1, byte[] rec2)	Compare records to determine sort order. See Table 11.4 for return values.

Example: Simple String Sort

Let's head back to Example 11.1 and add a comparator class (see Example 11.3) for sorting the records in the record store.

Example 11.3   SimpleSort.java

```
/*-----------------------------------------------
* SimpleSort.java
*
* No GUI interface, all output is to the console
*-----------------------------------------------*/
import java.io.*;
```

(continued)

Example 11.3 *(Continued)*

```
import javax.microedition.midlet.*;
import javax.microedition.rms.*;

public class SimpleSort extends MIDlet
{
  private RecordStore rs = null;
  static final String REC_STORE = "db_1";

  public SimpleSort()
  {
    openRecStore();   // Create the record store

    // Write a few records
    writeRecord("Sand Wedge");
    writeRecord("One Wood");
    writeRecord("Putter");
    writeRecord("Five Iron");

    // Read back with enumerator, sorting the results
    readRecords();

    closeRecStore();  // Close record store
    deleteRecStore(); // Remove the record store
  }

  public void destroyApp( boolean unconditional )
  {
  }

  public void startApp()
  {
    // There is no user interface, go ahead and shutdown
    destroyApp(false);
    notifyDestroyed();
  }

  public void pauseApp()
  {
  }

  public void openRecStore()
  {
```

(continued)

Example 11.3   (Continued)

```java
    // See Example 11-1
  }

  public void closeRecStore()
  {
    // See Example 11-1
  }

  public void deleteRecStore()
  {
    // See Example 11-1
  }

  public void writeRecord(String str)
  {
    byte[] rec = str.getBytes();

    try
    {
      rs.addRecord(rec, 0, rec.length);
    }
    catch (Exception e)
    {
      db(e.toString());
    }
  }

  public void readRecords()
  {
    try
    {
      if (rs.getNumRecords() > 0)
      {
        Comparator comp = new Comparator();

        RecordEnumeration re = rs.enumerateRecords(null,
                                          comp, false);
        while (re.hasNextElement())
        {
          String str = new String(re.nextRecord());
```

(continued)

Example 11.3   (Continued)

```
            System.out.println(str);
            System.out.println("-----------------------------");
        }
      }
    }
    catch (Exception e)
    {
        db(e.toString());
    }
  }

  /*--------------------------------------------------
   * Simple message to console for debug/errors
   * When used with Exceptions we should handle the
   * error in a more appropriate manner.
   *------------------------------------------------*/
  private void db(String str)
  {
    System.err.println("Msg: " + str);
  }
}


/*--------------------------------------------------
| Comparator.java
|
| Compares two records to determine sort order
*------------------------------------------------*/
class Comparator implements RecordComparator
{
  public int compare(byte[] rec1, byte[] rec2)
  {
    String str1 = new String(rec1), str2 = new String(rec2);

    int result = str1.compareTo(str2);
    if (result == 0)
      return RecordComparator.EQUIVALENT;
    else if (result < 0)
      return RecordComparator.PRECEDES;
    else
      return RecordComparator.FOLLOWS;
  }
}
```

If you step inside readRecords() you'll see the code for allocating a new Comparator and the reference to this new object when creating a RecordEnumeration.

```
Comparator comp = new Comparator();
RecordEnumeration re = rs.enumerateRecords(null,
                            comp, false);
while (re.hasNextElement())
{
    ...
}
```

When the enumerator creates its internal index of the record store, it will use the compare() function that we provided inside the class Comparator. Figure 11–4 shows the contents of the record store after sorting.

It's obvious this example works just fine, so why does the enumerator require a separate class for comparing records? Would it be possible for the enumerator to have a string sorting algorithm all of its own? Well, it could, in theory.

Inside the compare() method is a reference to compareTo() which is a method inside the String class.

```
int result = str1.compareTo(str2);
```

This is easy enough, assuming the data in a record is always text, as it was in this example. However, if you recall Example 11.2, we wrote several Java data types into **each** record. The code looked something similar to this:

```
// Write Java data types to stream
strmDataType.writeUTF("Text 1");
strmDataType.writeBoolean(true);
strmDataType.writeInt(1);
```

Figure 11–4 Sorted records using an Enumerator with RecordComparator

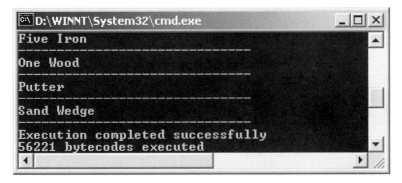

Each of these calls writes to a stream, in binary format. The contents of the stream are then written to an array, which is in turn added to a record in the record store.

```
// Get stream data into an array
record = strmBytes.toByteArray();

// Write the array to a record
rs.addRecord(record, 0, record.length);
```

Our simple sort method will fail miserably when trying to sort this (binary) data. If we choose to sort records that contain more than one simple data type, we need to write a compare() method that can extract and sort the appropriate data from each record; hence, the reason the enumerator supports a separate class for sorting.

Example: String Sort with Compound Records

More often than not, you'll store multiple "fields" of data within a single record as we did in Example 11.2 (storing a String, boolean and int). When a record has multiple data types stored within it (what I'll refer to as a compound record), there may be more than one field that would be appropriate for sorting. Reasonable sorting choices for Example 11.2 could be either the text or the integer. It all depends on the needs of the application.

The next two examples will implement the RecordComparator interface and each will sort a record that contains multiple Java data types. The examples will use the same set of data; however, one will sort based on a String, and one will sort based on an int. To be consistent with Example 11.2, each record will consist of a String, boolean and int. Here are the arrays that will make up each record:

```
String[] pets = {"duke", "tiger", "spike", "beauregard"};
boolean[] dog = {true, false, true, true};
int[] rank = {3, 0, 1, 2};
```

Once written to the record store, the contents of the records will look something like:

```
Record #1
"duke" true 3

Record #2
"tiger" false 0
```

```
Record #3
"spike" true 1

Record #4
"beauregard" true 2
```

Can you see the sorting problem we've created for ourselves? Because the data no longer contains pure text, a simple `String.compareTo()` on the contents of an entire record is not sufficient to sort the data.

We need to extract from each record the "field" that we wish to use as the sort criteria. Example 11.4 will extract and sort based on the `String` at the beginning of each record. Example 11.5 will extract and sort based on the `int` at the end of each record.

Example 11.4   StringSort.java

```
/*---------------------------------------------------
 * StringSort.java
 *
 * Sort records that contain multiple Java
 * data types. Sort using String type.
 *
 * Uses: Streams, Enumeration, RecordComparator
 *
 * No GUI interface, all output is to the console
 *---------------------------------------------------*/

import java.io.*;
import javax.microedition.midlet.*;
import javax.microedition.rms.*;

public class StringSort extends MIDlet
{
  private RecordStore rs = null;     // Record store
  static final String REC_STORE = "db_3"; // Name of record store

  public StringSort()
  {
    openRecStore();    // Create the record store

    writeTestData();   // Write a series of records
    readStream();      // Read back the records
```

(continued)

Example 11.4   (*Continued*)

```
  closeRecStore();  // Close record store
  deleteRecStore(); // Remove the record store
}

public void destroyApp( boolean unconditional )
{
}

public void startApp()
{
  // There is no user interface, go ahead and shutdown
  destroyApp(false);
  notifyDestroyed();
}

public void pauseApp()
{
}

public void openRecStore()
{
    // See Example 11-1
}

public void closeRecStore()
{
  // See Example 11-1
}

public void deleteRecStore()
{
  // See Example 11-1
}

/*-------------------------------------------------
 * Create three arrays to write to record store
 *-----------------------------------------------*/
public void writeTestData()
{
 String[] pets = {"duke", "tiger", "spike", "beauregard"};
 boolean[] dog = {true, false, true, true};
 int[] rank = {3, 0, 1, 2};
```

(*continued*)

Example 11.4   *(Continued)*

```java
  writeStream(pets, dog, rank);
}


/*-------------------------------------------------
 * Write to record store using streams.
 *------------------------------------------------*/
public void writeStream(String[] sData, boolean[] bData,
                        int[] iData)
{
  try
  {
     // Write data into an internal byte array
     ByteArrayOutputStream strmBytes =
             new ByteArrayOutputStream();

     // Write Java data types into the above byte array
     DataOutputStream strmDataType =
             new DataOutputStream(strmBytes);

     byte[] record;

     for (int i = 0; i < sData.length; i++)
     {
       // Write Java data types
       strmDataType.writeUTF(sData[i]);
       strmDataType.writeBoolean(bData[i]);
       strmDataType.writeInt(iData[i]);

       // Clear any buffered data
       strmDataType.flush();

       // Get stream data into byte array and write record
       record = strmBytes.toByteArray();
       rs.addRecord(record, 0, record.length);

       // Toss any data in the internal array so writes
       // starts at beginning (of the internal array)
       strmBytes.reset();
     }

     strmBytes.close();
     strmDataType.close();

  }
```

(continued)

Example 11.4   *(Continued)*

```
  catch (Exception e)
  {
    db(e.toString());
  }
}

/*--------------------------------------------------
* Read from the record store using streams
*--------------------------------------------------*/
public void readStream()
{
  try
  {
    // Careful: Make sure this is big enough!
    // Better yet, test and reallocate if necessary
    byte[] recData = new byte[50];

     // Read from the specified byte array
    ByteArrayInputStream strmBytes =
            new ByteArrayInputStream(recData);

    // Read Java data types from the above byte array
    DataInputStream strmDataType =
            new DataInputStream(strmBytes);

    if (rs.getNumRecords() > 0)
    {
      ComparatorString comp = new ComparatorString();

      int i = 1;
      RecordEnumeration re = rs.enumerateRecords(null,
                               comp, false);
      while (re.hasNextElement())
      {
        // Get data into the byte array
        rs.getRecord(re.nextRecordId(), recData, 0);

        // Read back the data types
        System.out.println("Record #" + i++);

        System.out.println("Name: " + strmDataType.readUTF());
        System.out.println("Dog: " + strmDataType.readBoolean());
```

(continued)

Example 11.4   *(Continued)*

```
         System.out.println("Rank: " + strmDataType.readInt());
         System.out.println("--------------------");

         // Reset so read starts at beginning of array
         strmBytes.reset();
       }

       comp.compareStringClose();

     // Free enumerator
       re.destroy();
     }

     strmBytes.close();
     strmDataType.close();

   }
   catch (Exception e)
   {
     db(e.toString());
   }
 }


 /*----------------------------------------------------
  * Simple message to console for debug/errors
  * When used with Exceptions we should handle the
  * error in a more appropriate manner.
  *--------------------------------------------------*/
 private void db(String str)
 {
   System.err.println("Msg: " + str);
 }
}


/*----------------------------------------------------
 | Compares two strings to determine sort order
 | Each record passed in contains multiple Java data
 | types - use only the String data for sorting
 *--------------------------------------------------*/
class ComparatorString implements RecordComparator
{
  private byte[] recData = new byte[10];
```

(continued)

Example 11.4   *(Continued)*

```java
// Read from a specified byte array
private ByteArrayInputStream strmBytes = null;

// Read Java data types from the above byte array
private DataInputStream strmDataType = null;

public void compareStringClose()
{
  try
  {
    if (strmBytes != null)
      strmBytes.close();
    if (strmDataType != null)
      strmDataType.close();
  }
  catch (Exception e)
  {}
}

public void compareStringClose()
{
  try
  {
    strmBytes.close();
    strmDataType.close();
  }
  catch (Exception e)
  {}
}

public int compare(byte[] rec1, byte[] rec2)
{
  String str1, str2;

  try
  {
    // If either record is larger than our buffer, reallocate
    int maxsize = Math.max(rec1.length, rec2.length);
    if (maxsize > recData.length)
      recData = new byte[maxsize];
```

(continued)

Example 11.4 (Continued)

```
      // Read record #1
      // Only need one read because the string to
      // sort on is the first "field" in the record
      strmBytes = new ByteArrayInputStream(rec1);
      strmDataType = new DataInputStream(strmBytes);
      str1 = strmDataType.readUTF();

      // Read record #2
      strmBytes = new ByteArrayInputStream(rec2);
      strmDataType = new DataInputStream(strmBytes);
      str2 = strmDataType.readUTF();

      // Compare record #1 and #2
      int result = str1.compareTo(str2);
      if (result == 0)
        return RecordComparator.EQUIVALENT;
      else if (result < 0)
        return RecordComparator.PRECEDES;
      else
        return RecordComparator.FOLLOWS;

    }
    catch (Exception e)
    {
      return RecordComparator.EQUIVALENT;
    }
  }
}
}
```

The majority of the MIDlet is nearly identical to Example 11.2. What has changed is the addition of a class that implements RecordComparator. More specifically, a compare() method that is aware of the sequence of data in each record and can extract that which is required to properly compare records.

The first "field" in each record is the String we would like to use as the basis for sorting. Read the String from each record using readUTF(), then call compareTo() in the String class to determine the relative sort order of the records.

```
// Read record #1
// Only need one read because the string to
// sort on is the first "field" in the record
```

```
strmBytes = new ByteArrayInputStream(rec1);
strmDataType = new DataInputStream(strmBytes);
str1 = strmDataType.readUTF();

// Read record #2
strmBytes = new ByteArrayInputStream(rec2);
strmDataType = new DataInputStream(strmBytes);
str2 = strmDataType.readUTF();

// Compare record #1 and #2
int result = str1.compareTo(str2);
if (result == 0)
  return RecordComparator.EQUIVALENT;
else if (result < 0)
  return RecordComparator.PRECEDES;
else
  return RecordComparator.FOLLOWS;
```

Take a moment to look at Figure 11–5. Notice that the records are sorted based on the "Name," which is the String we wrote in each record.

Figure 11–5   Records with multiple Java data types, sorted by "Name"

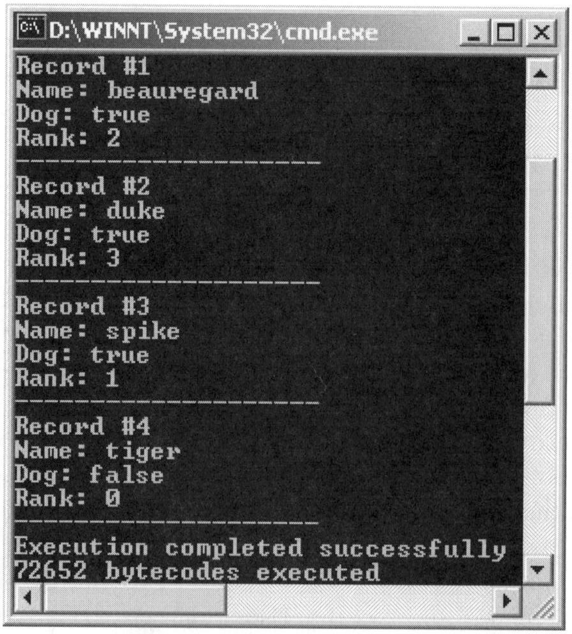

Example: Integer Sort with Compound Records

Using the same data as in the previous example, let's complicate things just a bit. Whereas the previous example sorted based on the String at the beginning of the record, the next example will sort based on the int located at the end of the record (see Example 11.5).

Part of the beauty of object-oriented code is that with a good design up-front, changes need not impart drastic rewrites. With this next example, for the most part, all that has changed is the class that implements the Record-Comparator, extracting and comparing integers instead of strings.

As a refresher, here is the data that was used to create each record in the previous example:

```
String[] pets = {"duke", "tiger", "spike", "beauregard"};
boolean[] dog = {true, false, true, true};
int[] rank = {3, 0, 1, 2};
```

Once written to the record store, the contents of the records will look something like:

```
Record #1
"duke" true 3

Record #2
"tiger" false 0

Record #3
"spike" true 1

Record #4
"beauregard" true 2
```

Example 11.5   IntSort.java

```
/*-------------------------------------------------
 * IntSort.java
 *
 * Sort records that contain multiple Java
 * data types. Sort using integer type.
 *
 * Uses: Streams, Enumeration, RecordComparator
```

(continued)

Example 11.5   *(Continued)*

```
*
* No GUI interface, all output is to the console
*-------------------------------------------------*/

import java.io.*;
import javax.microedition.midlet.*;
import javax.microedition.rms.*;

public class IntSort extends MIDlet
{
  private RecordStore rs = null;          // Record store
  static final String REC_STORE = "db_4"; // Name of record store

  public IntSort()
  {
    openRecStore();   // Create the record store

    writeTestData();  // Write a series of records
    readStream();     // Read back the records

    closeRecStore();  // Close record store
    deleteRecStore(); // Remove the record store
  }

  public void destroyApp( boolean unconditional )
  {
  }

  public void startApp()
  {
    // There is no user interface, go ahead and shutdown
    destroyApp(false);
    notifyDestroyed();
  }

  public void pauseApp()
  {
  }
```

(continued)

Example 11.5   *(Continued)*

```
public void openRecStore()
{
  // See Example 11-1
}

public void closeRecStore()
{
  // See Example 11-1
}

public void deleteRecStore()
{
  // See Example 11-1
}

/*-------------------------------------------------
 * Create three arrays to write to record store
 *-----------------------------------------------*/
public void writeTestData()
{
 String[] pets = {"duke", "tiger", "spike", "beauregard"};
 boolean[] dog = {true, false, true, true};
 int[] rank = {3, 0, 1, 2};

 writeStream(pets, dog, rank);
}

/*-------------------------------------------------
 * Write to record store using streams.
 *-----------------------------------------------*/
public void writeStream(String[] sData, boolean[] bData,
                        int[] iData)
{
  try
  {
     // Write data into an internal byte array
    ByteArrayOutputStream strmBytes =
            new ByteArrayOutputStream();

     // Write Java data types into the above byte array
    DataOutputStream strmDataType =
            new DataOutputStream(strmBytes);
```

(continued)

Example 11.5   (Continued)

```
    byte[] record;

    for (int i = 0; i < sData.length; i++)
    {
      // Write Java data types
      strmDataType.writeUTF(sData[i]);
      strmDataType.writeBoolean(bData[i]);
      strmDataType.writeInt(iData[i]);

      // Clear any buffered data
      strmDataType.flush();

      // Get stream data into byte array and write record
      record = strmBytes.toByteArray();
      rs.addRecord(record, 0, record.length);

      // Toss any data in the internal array so writes
      // starts at beginning (of the internal array)
      strmBytes.reset();
    }

    strmBytes.close();
    strmDataType.close();

  }
  catch (Exception e)
  {
    db(e.toString());
  }
}

/*--------------------------------------------------
 * Read from the record store using streams
 *--------------------------------------------------*/
public void readStream()
{
  try
  {
    // Careful: Make sure this is big enough!
    // Better yet, test and reallocate if necessary
    byte[] recData = new byte[50];
```

(continued)

Example 11.5 *(Continued)*

```
 // Read from the specified byte array
ByteArrayInputStream strmBytes =
          new ByteArrayInputStream(recData);

// Read Java data types from the above byte array
DataInputStream strmDataType =
          new DataInputStream(strmBytes);

if (rs.getNumRecords() > 0)
{
  ComparatorInt comp = new ComparatorInt();

  int i = 1;
  RecordEnumeration re = rs.enumerateRecords(null,
                                  comp, false);
  while (re.hasNextElement())
  {
    // Get data into the byte array
    rs.getRecord(re.nextRecordId(), recData, 0);

    // Read back the data types
    System.out.println("Record #" + i++);

    System.out.println("Name: " + strmDataType.readUTF());
    System.out.println("Dog: " + strmDataType.readBoolean());
    System.out.println("Rank: " + strmDataType.readInt());
    System.out.println("--------------------");

    // Reset so read starts at beginning of array
    strmBytes.reset();
  }

  comp.compareIntClose();

// Free enumerator
  re.destroy();
}

strmBytes.close();
strmDataType.close();
```

(continued)

Example 11.5   (Continued)

```
        }
        catch (Exception e)
        {
            db(e.toString());
        }
    }

    /*--------------------------------------------------
     * Simple message to console for debug/errors
     * When used with Exceptions we should handle the
     * error in a more appropriate manner.
     *----------------------------------------------*/
    private void db(String str)
    {
        System.err.println("Msg: " + str);
    }
}

/*--------------------------------------------------
| Compares two integers to determine sort order
| Each record passed in contains multiple Java data
| types - use only the integer data for sorting
*----------------------------------------------*/
class ComparatorInt implements RecordComparator
    {
    private byte[] recData = new byte[10];

    // Read from a specified byte array
    private ByteArrayInputStream strmBytes = null;

    // Read Java data types from the above byte array
    private DataInputStream strmDataType = null;

    public void compareIntClose()
    {
        try
        {
            if (strmBytes != null)
                strmBytes.close();
            if (strmDataType != null)
                strmDataType.close();
        }
```

(continued)

Example 11.5 *(Continued)*

```java
  catch (Exception e)
  {}
}

public int compare(byte[] rec1, byte[] rec2)
{
  int x1, x2;

  try
  {
    // If either record is larger than our buffer, reallocate
    int maxsize = Math.max(rec1.length, rec2.length);
    if (maxsize > recData.length)
      recData = new byte[maxsize];

    // Read record #1
    // We want the integer from the record, which is
    // the last "field" thus we must read the String
    // and boolean to get to the integer
    strmBytes = new ByteArrayInputStream(rec1);
    strmDataType = new DataInputStream(strmBytes);
    strmDataType.readUTF();
    strmDataType.readBoolean();
    x1 = strmDataType.readInt();  // Here's our data

    // Read record #2
    strmBytes = new ByteArrayInputStream(rec2);
    strmDataType = new DataInputStream(strmBytes);
    strmDataType.readUTF();
    strmDataType.readBoolean();
    x2 = strmDataType.readInt();  // Here's our data

    // Compare record #1 and #2
    if (x1 == x2)
      return RecordComparator.EQUIVALENT;
    else if (x1 < x2)
      return RecordComparator.PRECEDES;
    else
      return RecordComparator.FOLLOWS;

  }
  catch (Exception e)
```

(continued)

Example 11.5   *(Continued)*

```
  {
     return RecordComparator.EQUIVALENT;
  }
 }
}
```

Here is the bulk of the code that has been changed:

```
// Read record #1
// We want the integer from the record, which is
// the last "field" thus we must read the String
// and boolean to get to the integer
strmBytes = new ByteArrayInputStream(rec1);
strmDataType = new DataInputStream(strmBytes);
strmDataType.readUTF();
strmDataType.readBoolean();
x1 = strmDataType.readInt();  // Here's our data

// Read record #2
strmBytes = new ByteArrayInputStream(rec2);
strmDataType = new DataInputStream(strmBytes);
strmDataType.readUTF();
strmDataType.readBoolean();
x2 = strmDataType.readInt();  // Here's our data

// Compare record #1 and #2
if (x1 == x2)
   return RecordComparator.EQUIVALENT;
else if (x1 < x2)
   return RecordComparator.PRECEDES;
else
   return RecordComparator.FOLLOWS;.
```

We are attempting to sort based on the integer that is located at the end of each record. To get to that location, we need to read the `String` and `boolean` that are stored prior to that position. Once we have the integers from each record, the comparison code itself is trivial. Compare the output of Figure 11–5 and Figure 11–6. The former sorts by "Name" (`String`); the latter by "Rank" (`int`).

The `RecordComparator` is a necessity for all but the simplest of records. You can provide an endless variety of sorting options if you are will-

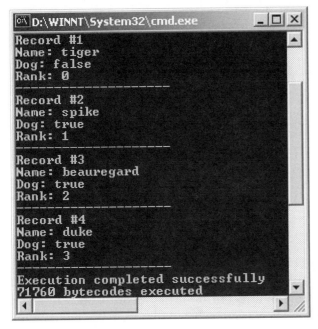

Figure 11-6 Records with multiple Java data types, sorted by "Rank" (integer)

ing to extract the necessary record "fields" and write a few lines of code comparing those same values.

Searching with RecordFilter

In addition to sorting records (using `RecordComparator`), an enumerator can filter records. There is a subtle difference, however. When using `RecordComparator` all records in a record store are in the result set. With a `RecordFilter`, only those records that match the filter criteria will become part of the enumerator result set.

Following is a class that implements the `RecordFilter` interface.

```
class SearchFilter implements RecordFilter
{
  private String searchText = null;

  public SearchFilter(String searchText)
  {
```

```
    // This is the text to search for
    this.searchText = searchText.toLowerCase();
}

public boolean matches(byte[] candidate)
{
    String str = new String(candidate).toLowerCase();

    // Look for a match
    if (searchText != null && str.indexOf(searchText) != -1)
        return true;
    else
        return false;
    }
}
```

When an instance of this class is created we save the desired search text in a private variable. This text is then used when the enumerator calls the matches() method, passing in a record from the record store. Here is a small piece of code that shows how you create a reference between the filter and an enumerator.

```
// Create a new search filter
SearchFilter search = new SearchFilter("search text");

// Reference the filter when creating the result set
RecordEnumeration re =
    rs.enumerateRecords(search,null,false);

// If there is at least one record in result set, a match
    was found
if (re.numRecords() > 0)
    // Do something
```

RecordFilter API

Table 11.6   RecordFilter Interface: javax.microedition.rms.RecordFilter

Method	*Description*
boolean **matches**(byte[] candidate)	Search a record for a specific value

Example: Simple String Search

Two examples follow that use a `RecordFilter` to search the record store. Both MIDlets display a `Form` and a provide a `TextField` for entering the desired search string. The results of the first MIDlet are shown in Figure 11–7.

The reason for two examples is to keep a consistent pace with other examples we've created in this chapter. The first will write/search records that contain only pure text, which we accomplish by writing a `String` object into each record. The second example will use streams to write/search the record store. In this case, each record will consist of a `String`, a `boolean` and an `int`. This example is probably a little more realistic in the sense that it will more closely mimic what types of data you may actually store. In addition, it proves to be a little more thought-provoking.

Example 11.6   SimpleSearch.java

```
/*-------------------------------------------------
* SimpleSearch.java
*
* Display a Form and Textbox for searching records
* Each record contains a String object.
*
* Uses: Enumeration, RecordFilter
*-------------------------------------------------*/

import java.io.*;
import javax.microedition.midlet.*;
import javax.microedition.rms.*;
import javax.microedition.lcdui.*;

public class SimpleSearch extends MIDlet implements CommandListener
{
    private Display display;            // Reference to Display object
    private Form fmMain;                 // The main form
    private StringItem siMatch;          // The matching text, if any
    private Command cmFind;              // Command to search record store
    private Command cmExit;              // Command to insert items
    private TextField tfFind;            // Search text as requested by user
    private RecordStore rs = null;       // Record store
    static final String REC_STORE = "db_6"; // Name of record store
```

(continued)

Example 11.6   *(Continued)*

```java
public SimpleSearch()
{
  display = Display.getDisplay(this);

  // Define textfield, stringItem and commands
  tfFind = new TextField("Find", "", 10, TextField.ANY);
  siMatch = new StringItem(null, null);
  cmExit = new Command("Exit", Command.EXIT, 1);
  cmFind = new Command("Find", Command.SCREEN, 2);

  // Create the form, add commands
  fmMain = new Form("Record Search");
  fmMain.addCommand(cmExit);
  fmMain.addCommand(cmFind);

  // Append textfield and stringItem
  fmMain.append(tfFind);
  fmMain.append(siMatch);

  // Capture events
  fmMain.setCommandListener(this);

  //--------------------------------
  // Open and write to record store
  //--------------------------------
  openRecStore();   // Create the record store
  writeTestData();  // Write a series of records
}

public void destroyApp( boolean unconditional )
{
  closeRecStore();   // Close record store
}

public void startApp()
{
  display.setCurrent(fmMain);
}

public void pauseApp()
{
}
```

(continued)

Example 11.6   (*Continued*)

```
public void openRecStore()
{
  // See Example 11-1
}

public void closeRecStore()
{
  // See Example 11-1
}

/*-----------------------------------------------
 * Create array of data to write into record store
 *-----------------------------------------------*/
public void writeTestData()
{
  String[] golfClubs = {
                "Wedge...good from the sand trap",
                "One Wood...off the tee",
                "Putter...only on the green",
                "Five Iron...middle distance"};
  writeRecords(golfClubs);
}


/*-----------------------------------------------
 * Write to record store.
 *-----------------------------------------------*/
public void writeRecords(String[] sData)
{
  byte[] record;

  try
  {
    // Only add the records once
    if (rs.getNumRecords() > 0)
      return;

    for (int i = 0; i < sData.length; i++)
    {
      record = sData[i].getBytes();
```

(*continued*)

Example 11.6   *(Continued)*

```java
      rs.addRecord(record, 0, record.length);
    }
  }
  catch (Exception e)
  {
    db(e.toString());
  }
}

/*-------------------------------------------------
 * Search using enumerator and record filter
 *-----------------------------------------------*/
private void searchRecordStore()
{
  try
  {
    // Record store is not empty
    if (rs.getNumRecords() > 0)
    {
      // Setup the search filter with the user requested text
      SearchFilter search =
            new SearchFilter(tfFind.getString());

      RecordEnumeration re =
            rs.enumerateRecords(search, null, false);

      // A match was found using the filter
      if (re.numRecords() > 0)
        // Show match in the stringItem on the form
        siMatch.setText(new String(re.nextRecord()));

      re.destroy();    // Free enumerator
    }
  }
  catch (Exception e)
  {
    db(e.toString());
  }
}

public void commandAction(Command c, Displayable s)
{
```

(continued)

Example 11.6 *(Continued)*

```
  if (c == cmFind)
  {
    searchRecordStore();
  }
  else if (c == cmExit)
  {
    destroyApp(false);
    notifyDestroyed();
  }
}


/*----------------------------------------------------
 * Simple message to console for debug/errors
 * When used with Exceptions we should handle the
 * error in a more appropriate manner.
 *----------------------------------------------------*/
private void db(String str)
{
  System.err.println("Msg: " + str);
}
}


/*----------------------------------------------------
 * Search for text within a record
 * Each record passed in contains only text (String)
 *----------------------------------------------------*/
class SearchFilter implements RecordFilter
{
  private String searchText = null;

  public SearchFilter(String searchText)
  {
    // This is the text to search for
    this.searchText = searchText.toLowerCase();
  }

  public boolean matches(byte[] candidate)
  {
    String str = new String(candidate).toLowerCase();

    // Look for a match
    if (searchText != null && str.indexOf(searchText) != -1)
```

(continued)

Example 11.6   (Continued)

```
        return true;
    else
        return false;
    }
}
```

At the top of the example you'll see the standard stuff—allocating the components and setting up the event listener. There are also a few lines for writing records to the record store. The text written to the store is simply an array of strings:

```
String[] golfClubs = {
                    "Wedge...good from the sand trap",
                    "One Wood...off the tee",
                    "Putter...only on the green",
                    "Five Iron...middle distance"};
```

Before writing the `searchFilter` class that implements the `Record-Filter` interface, let's see how our enumerator in this example differs from the previous example.

```
// Setup the search filter with the user requested text
SearchFilter search = new SearchFilter(tfFind.getString());

RecordEnumeration re =rs.enumerateRecords(search,null,false);

// A match was found using the filter
if (re.numRecords() > 0)
    siMatch.setText(new String(re.nextRecord()));
```

First, we must allocate an instance of `SearchFilter`. Notice the constructor has a parameter that accepts the user-requested search text. Next, we create an enumerator with a reference to this class. If the result set of the enumeration has more than zero records, we know there was at least one match and we set the `StringItem` text.

At the bottom of the example is where you'll find the `SearchFilter` class. Notice the constructor saves the search text that was requested by the user. This text is then available to the method `matches()`, which is called by the enumerator during its initialization. This method will be called once for each record in the record store. Only those records that match the filter will be included in result set.

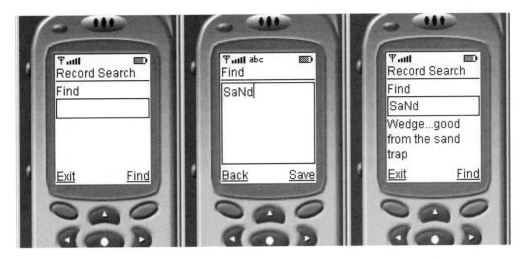

Figure 11-7 Searching for records

Figure 11–7 shows a series of screen shots, walking through a search of the record store. Notice the search is *not* case sensitive. Head back to the code and see why that is.

Example: String Search with Compound Records

Example 11.7 differs little from what we've just written. What has changed is the type of data that we write, and how that same data is placed into the record store.

The data that will make up the records for this example is much more comprehensive:

```
String[] pets = {"duke - big, goofy golden retriever",
                 "tiger - we found in a field",
                 "spike - loves chasing car tires",
                 "beauregard - barks at everything"};
boolean[] dog = {true, false, true, true};
int[] rank = {3, 0, 1, 2};
```

Obviously, we'll need a little more smarts when we read and search the record store.

Example 11.7 SearchStreams.java

```
/*--------------------------------------------------
 * SearchStreams.java
 *
 * Display a Form and Textbox for searching records
 * Each record contains multiple Java data types -
 * (String, boolean and integer). Use the String
 * data for searching
 *
 * Uses: Enumeration, RecordFilter
 *--------------------------------------------------*/

import java.io.*;
import javax.microedition.midlet.*;
import javax.microedition.rms.*;
import javax.microedition.lcdui.*;

public class SearchStreams extends MIDlet implements CommandListener
{
  private Display display;       // Reference to Display object
  private Form fmMain;           // The main form
  private StringItem siMatch;    // The matching text, if any
  private Command cmFind;        // Command to search record store
  private Command cmExit;        // Command to insert items
  private TextField tfFind;      // Search text
  private RecordStore rs = null;          // Record store
  static final String REC_STORE = "db_7"; // Name of record store

  public SearchStreams()
  {
    display = Display.getDisplay(this);

    // Define textfield, stringItem and commands
    tfFind = new TextField("Find", "", 10, TextField.ANY);
    siMatch = new StringItem(null, null);
    cmExit = new Command("Exit", Command.EXIT, 1);
    cmFind = new Command("Find", Command.SCREEN, 2);

    // Create the form, add commands
    fmMain = new Form("Record Search");
    fmMain.addCommand(cmExit);
    fmMain.addCommand(cmFind);
```

(continued)

Example 11.7 *(Continued)*

```
  // Append textfield and stringItem
  fmMain.append(tfFind);
  fmMain.append(siMatch);

  // Capture events
  fmMain.setCommandListener(this);

  //-------------------------------
  // Open and write to record store
  //-------------------------------
  openRecStore();   // Create the record store
  writeTestData();  // Write a series of records
}

public void destroyApp( boolean unconditional )
{
  closeRecStore();  // Close record store
}

public void startApp()
{
  display.setCurrent(frmMain);
}

public void pauseApp()
{
}

public void openRecStore()
{
  // See Example 11-1
}

public void closeRecStore()
{
  // See Example 11-1
}

/*----------------------------------------------------
 * Create three arrays to write into record store
 *--------------------------------------------------*/
public void writeTestData()
{
```

(continued)

Example 11.7   *(Continued)*

```
String[] pets = {"duke - big, goofy golden retriever",
                 "tiger - we found in a field",
                 "spike - loves chasing car tires",
                 "beauregard - barks at everything"};
boolean[] dog = {true, false, true, true};
int[] rank = {3, 0, 1, 2};

writeStream(pets, dog, rank);
}


/*---------------------------------------------------
* Write to record store using streams.
*-------------------------------------------------*/
public void writeStream(String[] sData, boolean[] bData,
                        int[] iData)
{
  try
  {
    // Only add the records once
    if (rs.getNumRecords() > 0)
      return;

     // Write data into an internal byte array
    ByteArrayOutputStream strmBytes =
            new ByteArrayOutputStream();

    // Write Java data types into the above byte array
    DataOutputStream strmDataType =
            new DataOutputStream(strmBytes);

    byte[] record;

    for (int i = 0; i < sData.length; i++)
    {
      // Write Java data types
      strmDataType.writeUTF(sData[i]);
      strmDataType.writeBoolean(bData[i]);
      strmDataType.writeInt(iData[i]);

      // Clear any buffered data
      strmDataType.flush();
```

(continued)

Example 11.7   *(Continued)*

```
      // Get stream data into byte array and write record
      record = strmBytes.toByteArray();
      rs.addRecord(record, 0, record.length);

      // Toss any data in the internal array so writes
      // starts at beginning (of the internal array)
      strmBytes.reset();
    }

    strmBytes.close();
    strmDataType.close();
  }
  catch (Exception e)
  {
    db(e.toString());
  }
}

/*-------------------------------------------------
 * Search using enumerator and record filter
 *-----------------------------------------------*/
private void searchRecordStore()
{
  try
  {
    // Record store is not empty
    if (rs.getNumRecords() > 0)
    {
      // Setup the search filter with the user requested text
      SearchFilter search =
            new SearchFilter(tfFind.getString());

      RecordEnumeration re =
            rs.enumerateRecords(search, null, false);

      // A match was found using the filter
      if (re.numRecords() > 0)
      {
        // Read from the specified byte array
        ByteArrayInputStream strmBytes =
              new ByteArrayInputStream(re.nextRecord());
```

(continued)

Example 11.7   *(Continued)*

```
            // Read Java data types from the above byte array
            DataInputStream strmDataType =
                    new DataInputStream(strmBytes);

            // Show matching result in stringItem component on form
            siMatch.setText(strmDataType.readUTF());

            search.searchFilterClose(); // Close record filter
            strmBytes.close();          // Close stream
            strmDataType.close();       // Close stream
            re.destroy();               // Free enumerator
        }
      }
    }
    catch (Exception e)
    {
      db(e.toString());
    }
  }

  public void commandAction(Command c, Displayable s)
  {
    if (c == cmFind)
    {
      searchRecordStore();
    }
    else if (c == cmExit)
    {
      destroyApp(false);
      notifyDestroyed();
    }
  }


  /*--------------------------------------------------
   * Simple message to console for debug/errors
   * When used with Exceptions we should handle the
   * error in a more appropriate manner.
   *--------------------------------------------------*/
  private void db(String str)
  {
    System.err.println("Msg: " + str);
  }
}
```

(continued)

Example 11.7   (Continued)

```
/*-------------------------------------------------
 * Search for text within a record
 * Each record passed in contains multiple Java data
 * types (String, boolean and integer)
 *-------------------------------------------------*/
class SearchFilter implements RecordFilter
{
  private String searchText = null;

   // Read from a specified byte array
  private ByteArrayInputStream strmBytes = null;

  // Read Java data types from the above byte array
  private DataInputStream strmDataType = null;

  public SearchFilter(String searchText)
  {
    // This is the text to search for
    this.searchText = searchText.toLowerCase();
  }

  // Cleanup
  public void searchFilterClose()
  {
    try
    {
      if (strmBytes != null)
        strmBytes.close();
      if (strmDataType != null)
        strmDataType.close();
    }
    catch (Exception e)
    {}
  }

  public boolean matches(byte[] candidate)
  {
    String str = null;

    try
    {
```

(continued)

Example 11.7   *(Continued)*

```
        strmBytes = new ByteArrayInputStream(candidate);
        strmDataType = new DataInputStream(strmBytes);

        // Although 3 pieces of data were written to
        // the record (String, boolean and integer)
        // we only need one read because the string to
        // search is the first "field" in the record
        str = strmDataType.readUTF().toLowerCase();
    }
    catch (Exception e)
    {
        return false;
    }

    // Look for a match
    if (str != null && str.indexOf(searchText) != -1)
        return true;
    else
        return false;
    }
}
```

Once again, the basics are the same: set up the Form, TextField and Command objects. When writing to the record store, we use streams to write each array element as a primitive Java data type, for example:

```
        strmDataType.writeUTF(sData[i]);         // Write Strings
        strmDataType.writeBoolean(bData[i]);     // Write booleans
        strmDataType.writeInt(iData[i]);         // Write integers
```

Inside searchRecordStore() is where we create the search filter and enumerator. Before going into the specifics of this method, let's review the code inside SearchFilter, the class that implements the Record-Filter interface.

As with the previous example, we save the search text into a local variable:

```
        this.searchText = searchText.toLowerCase();
```

The method matches() is called by the enumerator for each record in the record store. To get the data in the same format as it was written to the record, we need to create two streams—one that references the byte array with the incoming data and another to read Java data types from the previous stream:

```
strmBytes = new ByteArrayInputStream(candidate);
strmDataType = new DataInputStream(strmBytes);
```

Although we've written three pieces of data into each record (`String`, `boolean`, `int`) our search only applies to the first "field," the `String`. So we extract the `String` and store it in a local variable:

```
str = strmDataType.readUTF().toLowerCase();
```

The remainder of the code is straightforward. Compare the text from the record with the text in the variable `searchText`, which we saved when we created the filter:

```
if (str != null && str.indexOf(searchText) != -1)
    return true;
  else
    return false;
```

We can finish this discussion by looking back at `searchRecord-Store()`. If the enumerator has more than 0 records as part of the result set, we know there was a successful match between the text the user requested and one or more records in the record store:

```
if (re.numRecords() > 0)
{
  // Read from the specified byte array
  ByteArrayInputStream strmBytes =
      new ByteArrayInputStream(re.nextRecord());

  // Read Java data types from the above byte array
  DataInputStream strmDataType =
      new DataInputStream(strmBytes);

  // Show matching result in stringItem component on form
  siMatch.setText(strmDataType.readUTF());

  ...
}
```

Before we can display the text from the record (on the form), once again we need to extract the data in the same format in which it was written. We do this by setting up the necessary streams, reading the `String` from the record and adding the resulting text into the `StringItem` on the form (see Figure 11–8).

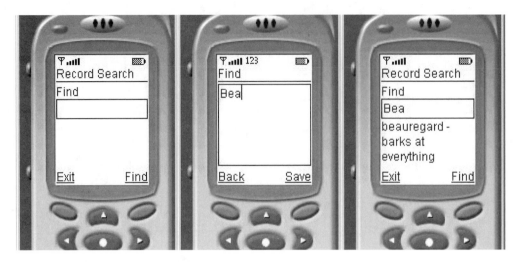

Figure 11-8   Searching compound records

Notification of Changes with RecordListener

At times you may find it helpful to be notified when a record has been added, deleted or updated. For instance, a MIDlet could store application preferences to persistent storage. When a user makes a change to their preferences, it may be handy to be aware of this fact, so the MIDlet can make any necessary adjustments on the fly, so to speak.

Or how about this idea? We have a MIDlet that maintains an internal list of contact information (name, email address, etc.). The list can be used at anytime by the MIDlet; for example, when a user is writing an email they may need to search for a specific email address. Let's say that somewhere on a remote server is a master list of contacts (updated from a separate source). When a change is made in the master, we'd like the MIDlet to be updated as well.

Here's a thought—the MIDlet could periodically poll the remote server. If the two lists are not identical, a background process could add, delete or update the record store as necessary. With this listener in place, once any change has been detected, the MIDlet could re-read the contact information from the (now current) record store and update its internal list.

The RecordListener operates as do the other listeners we've discussed. If you register a listener, when an event occurs a method is called to notify you of the change. For this interface, the methods are `record Added()`, `recordChanged()` and `recordDeleted()`. Which is called obviously depends on what change occurred in the record store.

RecordListener API

Table 11.7   RecordListener Interface: javax.microedition.rms.RecordListener

Method	Description
void **recordAdded**(RecordStore recordStore, int recordId)	Called when record is added
void **recordChanged**(RecordStore recordStore, int recordId)	Called when record is changed
void **recordDeleted**(RecordStore recordStore, int recordId)	Called when record is deleted

Examples: Capturing Changes

Example 11.8 is merely a skeleton that shows calls to the various listeners of the RMS. Up front we open a record store and add a listener to that same store. Then we proceed to add, update and delete a record. Each of these actions will trigger the listener to call the appropriate method, where we commence to print a message showing that we arrived.

Example 11.8   RmsListener.java

```
/*-------------------------------------------------
 * RmsListener.java
 *
 * Test the RMS listener methods
 *
 * No GUI interface, all output is to the console
 *-------------------------------------------------*/
import java.io.*;
import javax.microedition.midlet.*;
import javax.microedition.rms.*;

public class RmsListener extends MIDlet
{
  private RecordStore rs = null;
  static final String REC_STORE = "db_8";
```

(continued)

Example 11.8   (Continued)

```java
public RmsListener()
{
  // Open record store and add listener
  openRecStore();
  rs.addRecordListener(new TestRecordListener());

  // Initiate actions that will wake up the listener
  writeRecord("J2ME and MIDP");
  updateRecord("MIDP and J2ME");
  deleteRecord();

  closeRecStore();  // Close record store
  deleteRecStore(); // Remove the record store
}

public void destroyApp( boolean unconditional )
{
}

public void startApp()
{
  // There is no user interface, go ahead and shutdown
  destroyApp(false);
  notifyDestroyed();
}

public void pauseApp()
{
}

public void openRecStore()
{
  // See Example 11-1
}

public void closeRecStore()
{
  // See Example 11-1
}

public void deleteRecStore()
{
  // See Example 11-1
}
```

(continued)

Example 11.8 *(Continued)*

```java
public void writeRecord(String str)
{
  byte[] rec = str.getBytes();

  try
  {
    rs.addRecord(rec, 0, rec.length);
  }
  catch (Exception e)
  {
    db(e.toString());
  }
}

public void updateRecord(String str)
{
  try
  {
    rs.setRecord(1, str.getBytes(), 0, str.length());
  }
  catch (Exception e)
  {
    db(e.toString());
  }
}

public void deleteRecord()
{
  try
  {
    rs.deleteRecord(1);
  }
  catch (Exception e)
  {
    db(e.toString());
  }
}

/*-------------------------------------------------
 * Simple message to console for debug/errors
 * When used with Exceptions we should handle the
 * error in a more appropriate manner.
 *-------------------------------------------------*/
public void db(String str)
```

(continued)

Example 11.8   (Continued)

```
  {
    System.err.println("Msg: " + str);
  }
}

/*------------------------------------------------
* Listen for updates to the record store
*------------------------------------------------*/
class TestRecordListener implements RecordListener
{
  public void recordAdded(RecordStore recordStore, int recordId)
  {
    try
    {
        System.out.println("Record with ID#: " + recordId +
                           "added to RecordStore: " +
                           recordStore.getName());
    }
    catch (Exception e)
    {
        System.err.println(e);
    }
  }

  public void recordDeleted(RecordStore recordStore, int recordId)
  {
    try
    {
        System.out.println("Record with ID#: " + recordId +
                           "deleted from RecordStore: " +
                           recordStore.getName());
    }
    catch (Exception e)
    {
        System.err.println(e);
    }
  }

  public void recordChanged(RecordStore recordStore, int recordId)
  {
    try
    {
        System.out.println("Record with ID#: " + recordId +
                           "changed in RecordStore: " +
                           rs.getName());
```

(continued)

Example 11.8   (Continued)

```
      }
      catch (Exception e)
      {
          System.err.println(e);
      }
    }
}
```

Figure 11–9 shows the console output from the listener methods.

Figure 11–9   Output of Record Store listener methods

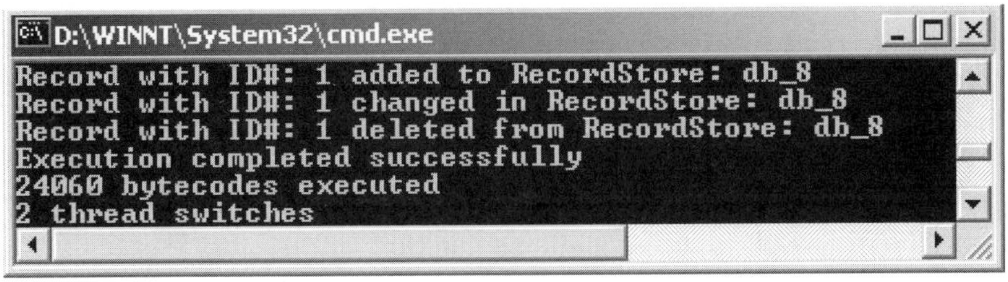

Exception Handling

There are five exceptions that are specific to the RMS. As expected, each is inherited from the class java.lang.Throwable. All five exceptions are listed next, along with a brief description and the constructor methods in the event your application code needs to create/throw an RMS-related exception.

InvalidRecordIDException

Used to indicate an invalid record number. For example, if Record-Store.getRecord(int) is called with a record that does not exist in the record store, this exception will be thrown.

```
    public InvalidRecordIDException(String message)
    public InvalidRecordIDException()
```

RecordStoreException

A general exception indicating an error with the record store.

```
public RecordStoreException()
public RecordStoreException(String message)
```

RecordStoreFullException

Signals the record store is full. For example, if `RecordStore.add Record(byte[], int, int)` is called to add a new record, this exception will be thrown if the record store has reached its maximum capacity.

```
public RecordStoreFullException()
public RecordStoreFullException(String message)
```

RecordStoreNotFoundException

Indicates the record store name does not exist. For example, calling `RecordStore.deleteRecordStore(String)` with an invalid record store name will result in this exception being thrown.

```
public RecordStoreNotFoundException()
public RecordStoreNotFoundException(String message)
```

RecordStoreNotOpenException

Used to indicate that the requested record store is not open. For example, if `RecordStore.getNumRecords()` is called prior to opening the record store, this exception will be thrown.

```
public RecordStoreNotOpenException()
public RecordStoreNotFoundOpen(String message)
```

Catching Exceptions

To keep the examples in this chapter focused on the concepts presented, I've done the absolute minimum to appease the Java compiler when dealing with exceptions. Typical code has simply caught every type of exception and written a message to the console:

```
RecordStore rs;
    try
    {
       rs.closeRecordStore();
    }
    catch (Exception e)
    {
       db(e.toString());
    }

    ...

  private void db(String str)
  {
     System.err.println("Msg: " + str);
  }
```

Many record store methods throw exceptions. Any production application will need to implement a more robust means of dealing with problems as they arise. All exceptions should be caught and handled in an appropriate manner, depending on the type of error. Ideally, the aforementioned code should look a little more like the following:

```
try
{
  rs.closeRecordStore();
}
catch (RecordStoreNotOpenException e)
{
  do something here...
}
catch (RecordStoreException e2)
{
  do something else here...
}
catch (Exception e3)
{
  other error condition...
}
```

The missing code ("do something here") will be dependent on the error that occurred. For example, if the record store was not open, it may be as simple as calling a method to open the record store and retrying the operation. If the error is more on the esoteric side (as with the `RecordStore-Exception`), you may need to notify the user and ask how they would like to proceed.

TODO LIST
EXAMPLE:PART I

Topics in this Chapter

Chapter 12

At this point in the book we have covered a great deal of information regarding how to write J2ME MIDlets. Although there are still a few topics to review before we have covered all the MIDP has to offer, it's a good time to write an application that ties together much of what we've learned.

I don't know about you, but I simply cannot live without my todo list. Well, I suppose I could live, it would just be in a fog. Given my paper version follows me everywhere, I thought this would be an ideal MIDlet to have on a mobile device. To be useful, the MIDlet would need to provide the same capabilities as a paper list (viz, adding new items, removing completed items and setting priorities).

Using the Todo List

It's easiest to get a feel for this MIDlet by walking through a few screen shots. Figure 12–1 shows the main todo list. You'll notice you can look at the todo list with or without priorities.

429

Figure 12–1 Todo list—without and with priorities

Selecting the "Menu" option will bring up the screen shown in Figure 12–2. We can either add a new todo item or view/change the application preferences.

If you choose to add a new item to your todo list, the screen shown in Figure 12–3 will appear. There is just enough detail on the display to make out that this screen consists of a `Form` with a `TextField` and `ChoiceGroup`.

There are a total of five priorities that we can choose from. Anywhere from "Today" to "Someday" (see Figure 12–4).

Figure 12–2 Todo menu options

Figure 12–3 Add todo item; Form containing a TextField and ChoiceGroup

Heading back to Figure 12–2 and selecting the "Preferences" option from the menu, we will be presented with the screen as shown in Figure 12–5. Here we choose whether or not we would like the items sorted by priority (if not, they appear in the order entered). We can also opt to have priorities listed next to each item.

A couple of thoughts—if you look back at Figure 12–1 (on the right) you'll notice that priorities are shown as integers. However, if you look at Figure 12-4 you'll see that priority selection is done using a text string. I found it much more intuitive to enter priorities by selecting from options that closely

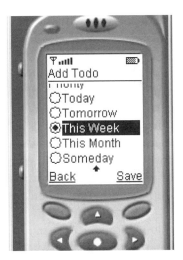

Figure 12–4 Priority selection

Figure 12–5 Select application preferences

match how I think. That is, this must be done today, that can wait until tomorrow, and so forth.

When I write a todo list on paper and pencil I generally list them from most important to least. And no, I don't assign them numbers, but it generally works out to the same as shown here. That is, most important on top, least important at the bottom.

Obviously, due to constraints of the display, we can't show the priority text next to each item; thus, internally we track them as numbers and this is what we display on the list.

Interface Design

One of the beauties of the MIDP is its simplicity. You can quickly get your hands around the components and have a good sense of just what capability each can offer and how they can work together. After writing only a few MIDlets, chances are you will be able to visualize the components, and it will become almost second nature to lay out simple application designs in your head.

However, that simplicity is a double-edged sword. As your programming projects become more complex, with more sophisticated user interface needs, you'll find yourself clamoring for more robust and comprehensive components.

There are various options to work around the limitations of the component library. First, you can write your own components, building off what is already available through the MID libraries or writing what you need from scratch. Second, as with most any new technology, there are individuals and businesses working feverishly to provide tools and components. I have no doubt in the near future there will be an abundance of software supporting MIDP development. However, to keep the focus on the components addressed within this book, we will use only those found within MIDP.

As I led you to believe just a moment ago, the user interface for this MIDlet is quite simple, with the main user interface consisting of only three forms (see Figure 12–6).

Main Form

The focal point of interaction for the MIDlet is fmMain. Figure 12–1 shows this Form along with the corresponding ChoiceGroup (the todo list) and Command objects (adding and setting preferences).

Figure 12–6 Todo List GUI interface design

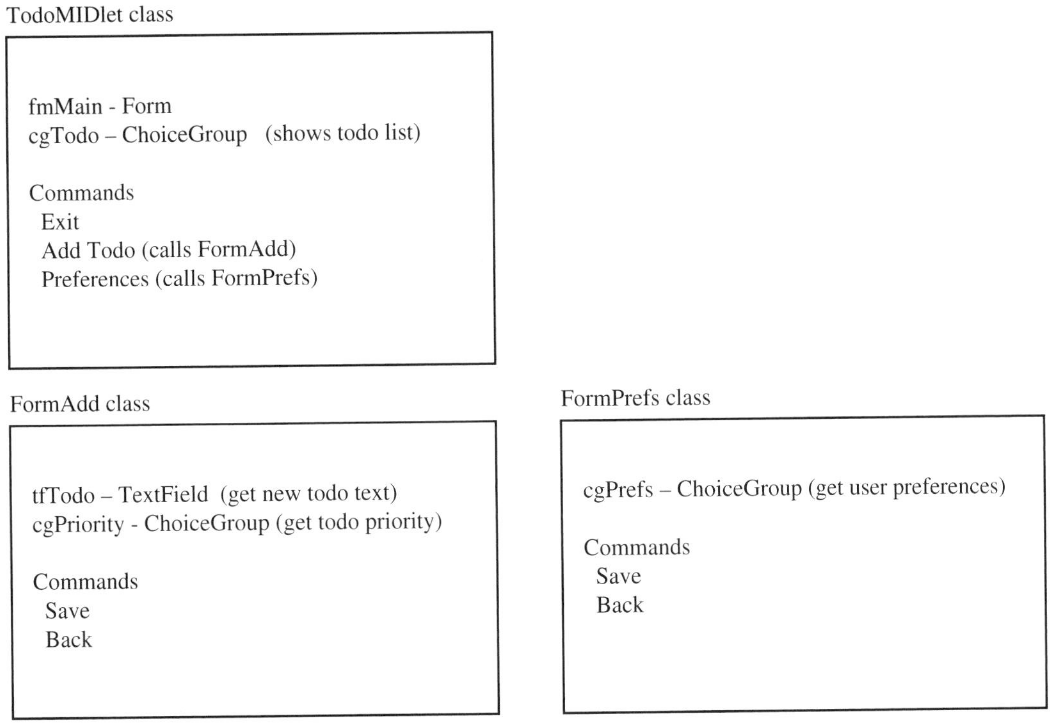

TodoMIDlet class

```
fmMain - Form
cgTodo – ChoiceGroup   (shows todo list)

Commands
  Exit
  Add Todo (calls FormAdd)
  Preferences (calls FormPrefs)
```

FormAdd class

```
tfTodo – TextField  (get new todo text)
cgPriority - ChoiceGroup (get todo priority)

Commands
  Save
  Back
```

FormPrefs class

```
cgPrefs – ChoiceGroup (get user preferences)

Commands
  Save
  Back
```

Add Todo Item From

When adding a new todo item, `FormAdd` will be invoked. Within this form we show a `TextField` for getting the todo item text and a `ChoiceGroup` for selecting the todo item priority. There are also two `Commands`—one to save the new item and one to return to the main form with no change (see Figure 12–3).

Update Preferences Form

When we choose to update the application preferences, `FormPrefs` will be presented. This form consists of a `ChoiceGroup` for selecting sort order and deciding whether or not to show priorities on the todo list. As with `FormAdd`, there is one `Command` to save the preferences and another to return to the main form with no change (see Figure 12–5).

Data Design

From the GUI design point of view this MIDlet is quite straightforward. However, don't let this fool you into thinking the code itself is trivial. It's not rocket science either, but there is a fair amount code to maintain the internal data structures, manage the record store and handle events, all while trying to conserve and re-use resources as much as possible.

As with most any programming project there is no one preferred way to design and implement the application. I chose a design that would not only solve the problem at hand but provide flexibility for future changes and enhancements. Here is what I came up with.

Record Stores

There are two record stores, one to hold todo items and another to store application preferences.

```
private RecordStore rsTodo;
private RecordStore rsPref;
private static final String REC_STORE_TODO = "TodoList";
private static final String REC_STORE_PREF = "TodoPrefs";
```

`rsTodo` stores individual records for a todo item. There may be any number of records in this store (including zero). Each todo item has not only the text (for example, "buy gas") it also has a priority ("Today," "Tomorrow," etc.). We store the priority as an integer and the text as a String. Each record has the following internal format:

rsTodo Record

Integer	String

Priority   Todo Text

Remember, each record is actually written to the record store as an array of bytes. The aforementioned display is just an abstraction that we use at the application level. When the user enters a priority (as an integer) and the todo text (as a String), we will actually convert these into an array of bytes prior to writing to the record store.

rsPrefs hold the user preferences regarding sorting and whether or not to show priorities on the todo list. This record store will always have just one record. The record will look as follows:

rsPrefs Record

Boolean	Boolean

Sort by priority   Show priorities

These two "fields" are populated from variables maintained with the current user preferences.

```
private boolean flagSortByPriority = false, // Sort by priority?
                flagShowPriority = true;    // Show priorities ?
```

While on the subject of record stores, let's look at how we sort todo items. If you recall when learning about the RMS, there is a RecordEnumeration class for looping through the record store. When you define an enumeration, you can also make a reference to a RecordComparator class to specify the sort order of records returned by the enumeration.

That sounds a little better than it actually is. We still need to write the sorting algorithm, however, the enumeration will feed us records in the order provided by our sorting code. This is very handy—we decide what it means to sort a record (e.g., by comparing the priority "fields" in the record) and the enumeration does the rest. We'll see the class that implements the sorting code in the next section.

Classes

There are six classes that go into creating our todo MIDlet. We can actually learn a great deal about the application design simply by looking over the class declarations. Following is a brief description of each class.

TodoMIDlet

This is the main class for the MIDlet.

```
public class TodoMIDlet extends MIDlet
            implements ItemStateListener, CommandListener
```

From the declaration it's obvious that this class can handle `Command` events as well as listen for events from an `Item`. For the latter, this is a `ChoiceGroup` that represents the list of todo items. When a user selects an entry on their todo list, the method `itemStateChanged()` will be called. Within this method we will write the code to remove the selected item.

TodoItem

Each todo item, including its text, priority and associated record id in the record store (more on this field in a minute), are stored in an instance of `TodoItem` class.

```
public class TodoItem
{
  private int priority;
  private String text;
  private int recordId;
  ...
}
```

To keep track of multiple items I choose to use a vector—a simple data structure that can hold any type of object. A vector (`java.util.Vector`) is nothing more than an array. One benefit of a vector is that all the code for manipulating the indivdual elements is handled for you, to name a few: adding, deleting, retrieving and even resizing to accommodate more elements.

In a moment, we'll talk about how the vector, record store and the `ChoiceGroup` holding the todo items are kept synchronized during the lifetime of the application.

FormAdd

This form is for adding a new todo item to the list. We extend the `Form` class and implement the `CommandListener` interface.

```
public class FormAdd extends Form implements CommandListener
```

If for nothing else, a good reason to subclass `Form` is so we can encapsulate the event handling. This class will have its own `commandAction()` method to process events, those events that are triggered by interacting with the commands on this form only. This simple idea carried throughout your application can greatly simplify event handling code in the main midlet.

If we defined this form within the main MIDlet (without subclassing), the `commandAction()` method would need to decipher what `Displayable` (which `Form`, `List`, `TextBox`, etc.) generated the event and then further break that down into which command was invoked. It's not that the code would be difficult to write. It's just that we can break the application into smaller, more manageable chunks. Each chunk is self-sufficient in that it provides its own handling of data and deals with only the events it is interested in.

FormPrefs

This form follows the same logic as the previous. Extend the `Form` class and provide event handling specific to this form.

```
public class FormPrefs extends Form implements CommandListener
```

ComparatorInt

When creating an enumeration to loop through records in the RMS, we can define a comparator class to assist with sorting. This class provides a method that is called by the enumeration to sort records.

```
public class ComparatorInt implements RecordComparator
{
  ...
  public int compare(byte[] rec1, byte[] rec2)
  {
   // compare the priority of each record
    ...
  }
}
```

The method `compare()` is passed two byte arrays. Each array holds the contents of a record from the record store. This method is where we write our application logic for sorting. It is our responsibility to understand the format of the data in each array and provide an algorithm that can determine which record precedes the other.

DisplayManager

In Chapter 10 we created the class `DisplayManager` to help manage `Displayable` objects (`Form`, `TextBox`, `Canvas`, etc.) as we move about through our application. This class has methods to push and pop objects using a stack. The idea is that, we can create as many `Displayable` objects as we need and call them one after another, always pushing the current `Displayable` onto the stack. When we want to work our way back out, all we need to do is to pop them, one by one, off the stack.

```
public class DisplayManager extends Stack
```

Data Flow

When this MIDlet is running, a `ChoiceGroup` displays the various todo items. When inactive the todo list remains intact in persistent storage. I mentioned previously that each todo item is stored in an instance of `TodoItem`.

```
public class TodoItem
{
  private int priority;
  private String text;
  private int recordId;
  ...
}
```

I also pointed out that we store these items in a vector. Wouldn't it be easier to read the items from the record store and write them directly to the choicegroup? Why do we need to keep each item in the RMS, a vector and also in a choicegroup? There are several reasons; let's look at the most obvious.

Mapping between RMS, Vector and ChoiceGroup

We need a means to map each record in the record store with an entry in the choicegroup. For example, if a user chooses to delete a todo item, it's a simple matter to remove the entry from the choicegroup. However, removing the correct entry from the record store may prove to be more challenging.

The RMS maintains a record id for each record in the store. The first record is 1, the next is 2, and so forth. However, record ids are NOT reused! For example, if you have records with the ids 1, 2 and 3, and you proceed to delete record id 2, the next record inserted will have record id 4. Thus, your new record ids are 1, 3 and 4.

This makes it challenging when trying to figure out which entry in the record store corresponds to which entry in the choicegroup. It is not as simple as "if I delete the choicegroup item 5, I can delete record id number 5." That would be nice.

Here is what we'll do instead. We will have a vector that holds a `TodoItem` for each entry in the record store. At application startup, we'll create the vector from the records in the store. In addition to reading the text and priority from each record, we'll also keep a reference to the record id inside the `TodoItem`. Once the vector is complete, we create the choicegroup from the entries in the vector.

When a choicegroup element (todo item) is deleted, there is a one-to-one mapping into the vector. With this mapping we can get the corresponding `TodoItem` (object) from the vector. We can now look up the record id that we stored previously, and remove it from the record store. We will then re-build the vector from the record store and re-build the choicegroup from the vector. This process assures us that the record store, vector and choicegroup are all in sync.

There's an additional benefit to using a vector to hold an instance of `TodoItem` for each element on the todo list—we can easily add fields to provide for additional functionality. For example, we could store a category and due date for each item by simply updating the `TodoItem` class:

```
public class TodoItem
{
   private int priority;
   private String text;
   private int recordId;
   private String category;
   private Date dueDate;
   ...
}
```

Streams

When reading and writing to the record store the preferred approach is through a stream. Given the record store will more than likely be accessed many times while the MIDlet is running, it makes sense to allocate our input and output streams only once.

```
//-------------------------------------------------
// Re-use these input streams throughout the MIDlet
//-------------------------------------------------
// Read from a specified byte array
private ByteArrayInputStream istrmBytes = null;
// Read Java data types from the above byte array
private DataInputStream istrmDataType = null;
// If you change length of a todo entry, bump this
byte[] recData = new byte[25];

//-------------------------------------------------
// Re-use these output streams throughout the MIDlet
//-------------------------------------------------
// Write data into an internal byte array
ByteArrayOutputStream ostrmBytes = null;
// Write Java data types into the above byte array
DataOutputStream ostrmDataType = null;
```

We can reuse these streams throughout the application, as long as we reset them prior to each use, which is as simple as shown here:

```
istrmBytes.reset();

ostrmBytes.reset();
```

Application Logic

In my world the fun part is writing code. All the GUI and data design stuff is for the birds, or at least I wish it was. I have to do my best to hold back from jumping in and just cranking out the code. However, experience has taught me well. If the design is properly thought through upfront, you run into fewer bricks walls and thereby end up re-writing less code. (For some reason, re-writing code lacks the appeal of writing it correctly the first time.) With that in mind, let's think through the flow of this application.

Startup

We begin inside the `TodoMIDlet` constructor, creating the main form, choicegroup and event handling commands. We also open the record store, read the user preferences from the same and initialize the input and output streams.

As the final steps, we construct the vector of todo items from the record store and create the todo list by building a choicegroup from the vector. When requested by the application manager, we display the main form:

```
public void startApp ()
{
  display.setCurrent(fmMain);
}
```

Add Items

When a user chooses to add a new todo item by selecting "Add Todo" (see Figure 12–2) the following method is called.

```
public void commandAction(Command c, Displayable d)
{
  ...
  // Push current displayable onto stack
  displayMgr.pushDisplayable(display.getCurrent());

  if (c == cmAdd)
  {
    // Reset the textfield and choicegroup
    // on the 'add todo' form
    fmAdd.txfTodo.setString("");
    fmAdd.chgPriority.setSelectedIndex(0, true);

    // Show 'add todo' form
    display.setCurrent(fmAdd);
  }
  ...
}
```

Here we store a reference to the current `Form` (`Displayable`) that is currently shown on the mobile device display. We do this by pushing the current `Displayable` onto the display manager stack. We also initialize the `TextBox` and `ChoiceGroup` for the todo item text and priority, respectively. The last step is to set the current `Displayable` to the `Form` (`fmAdd`) for adding a todo item.

`fmAdd` manages its own event handling; that is, it has a `commandAction()` method. It looks as follows:

```
public void commandAction(Command c, Displayable s)
{
  if (c == cmSave)
  {
    midlet.addTodoItem(cgPriority.getSelectedIndex() +
                  1, tfTodo.getString());
  }

  // Any other event and we go back to the main form...
  // Pop the last displayable off the stack
  midlet.displayMgr.popDisplayable();
}
```

If the user requests to save the current todo item (see Figure 12–3), we call a method inside the main MIDlet to add the item to the vector, RMS and the choicegroup. Otherwise we simply pop the last displayable off the stack to return to the main form.

Delete Items

When the user would like to delete a todo element they select the element in the todo list (choicegroup; see Figure 12–1). Call to mind how we detect events with objects that are subclasses of `Item` (`ChoiceGroup`, `DataField`, `TextField`, etc.). This is done using an `itemStateListener`, which calls the method `itemStateChanged()` when an event occurs:

```
public void itemStateChanged(Item item)
{
  ...
  // Determine which it was selected
  ...
  // Get the todo Item at that location
  TodoItem todoitem = (TodoItem) vecTodo.elementAt(i);
  ...
  // Delete from rms
  rsTodo.deleteRecord(todoitem.getRecordId());
  ...
  // Delete from vector
```

```
vecTodo.removeElementAt(i);
...

// Read rms into vector
writeRMS2Vector();

// Rebuild todo list
rebuildTodoList();
}
```

We determine which item the user selected and proceed to delete the record from the record store and the vector. Once this is done, we rebuild the todo list (choicegroup).

Change Preferences

When presenting the form for changing user preferences (FormPrefs. Java) it would be nice to display the current application settings (see Figure 12–5). We can accomplish this, inside TodoMIDLet class, by creating an array of booleans and populating with the current values of the preference variables:

```
public void commandAction(Command c, Displayable d)
{
  ...
  // Push current displayable onto stack
  displayMgr.pushDisplayable(display.getCurrent());

  ...
  else if (c == cmPrefs)
  {
    boolean flags[] = {flagSortByPriority, flagShowPriority};

    // Show preferences form passing in current
    // preference settings
    display.setCurrent(new formPrefs("Preferences",this,flags));
  }
  ...
}
```

We pass the array (flags) to the constructor when creating the form to display user preferences. Within the constructor we create a new choice-group and set the status of the choice group entries using the array.

```
public FormPrefs(String title, todoMIDlet midlet,
                 boolean flags[])
```

```
    {
        ...
        // Choicegroup for sort order and showing priority
        cgPrefs = new ChoiceGroup("Preferences", Choice.MULTIPLE);
        cgPrefs.append("Sort by Priority", null);
        cgPrefs.append("Show Priority", null);

        // Set the current status of each entry
        cgPrefs.setSelectedFlags(flags);

        ...
    }
```

That's it. We're ready to write the code.

Source Code

Example 12.1 TodoMIDlet.java

```
/*-------------------------------------------------
| TodoMIDlet.java
|
| The main class for todo list MIDlet
*-------------------------------------------------*/
import java.io.*;
import java.util.*;
import javax.microedition.midlet.*;
import javax.microedition.lcdui.*;
import javax.microedition.rms.*;

public class TodoMIDlet extends MIDlet implements ItemStateListener,
                                                  CommandListener
{
    private Display display;        // Our display
    private Form fmMain;            // Main Form
    private FormAdd fmAdd;          // Form to add todo item
    private Command cmAdd,          // Command to add todo
                    cmPrefs,        // Command to set preferences
                    cmExit;         // Command to exit
    private Vector vecTodo;         // The "master" list of todo items
    private ChoiceGroup cgTodo;     // Todo items (read from vecTodo)
```

(continued)

Example 12.1 *(Continued)*

```
protected DisplayManager displayMgr;  // Class to help manage screens

//-------------------------------------------------
// Record Stores. One for todo, one for preferences
//-------------------------------------------------
private RecordStore rsTodo;
private RecordStore rsPref;
private static final String REC_STORE_TODO = "TodoList";
private static final String REC_STORE_PREF = "TodoPrefs";
private boolean flagSortByPriority = false, // Sort by priority?
                flagShowPriority = true;     // Show priorities ?

//-------------------------------------------------
// Re-use these input streams throughout the MIDlet
//-------------------------------------------------
// Read from a specified byte array
private ByteArrayInputStream istrmBytes = null;
// Read Java data types from the above byte array
private DataInputStream istrmDataType = null;
// If you change length of a todo entry, bump this
byte[] recData = new byte[25];

//-------------------------------------------------
// Re-use these output streams throughout the MIDlet
//-------------------------------------------------
// Write data into an internal byte array
ByteArrayOutputStream ostrmBytes = null;
// Write Java data types into the above byte array
DataOutputStream ostrmDataType = null;

//-------------------------------------------------
// Record Enumerator and compare class
//-------------------------------------------------
private RecordEnumeration enum = null;
private ComparatorInt comp = null;

/*-------------------------------------------------
 * MIDlet constructor.
 *-----------------------------------------------*/
public TodoMIDlet()
{
  display = Display.getDisplay(this);
```

(continued)

Example 12.1 *(Continued)*

```
// Create 'main' and 'add todo item' forms
// Form for setting prefs is in commandAction()
fmMain = new Form("Todo List");
fmAdd = new FormAdd("Add Todo", this);

// Todo list and vector
cgTodo = new ChoiceGroup("", Choice.MULTIPLE);
vecTodo = new Vector();

// Commands
cmAdd = new Command("Add Todo", Command.SCREEN, 2);
cmPrefs = new Command("Preferences", Command.SCREEN, 3);
cmExit = new Command("Exit", Command.EXIT, 1);

// Add all to form and listen for events
fmMain.addCommand(cmAdd);
fmMain.addCommand(cmPrefs);
fmMain.addCommand(cmExit);
fmMain.append(cgTodo);
fmMain.setCommandListener(this);
fmMain.setItemStateListener(this);

// Create a display manager object
displayMgr = new DisplayManager(display, fmMain);

// Open/create the record stores
rsTodo = openRecStore(REC_STORE_TODO);
rsPref = openRecStore(REC_STORE_PREF);

// Initialize the streams
initInputStreams();
initOutputStreams();

// Read preferences from rms
refreshPreferences();

// Initialize the enumeration for todo rms
initEnumeration();

// Read rms into vector
writeRMS2Vector();
```

(continued)

Example 12.1 *(Continued)*

```
  // Build the todo list (choice group)
  rebuildTodoList();
}

/*----------------------------------------------------
* Show the main Form
*--------------------------------------------------*/
public void startApp ()
{
  display.setCurrent(fmMain);
}

/*----------------------------------------------------
* Shutting down. Cleanup all we created
*--------------------------------------------------*/
public void destroyApp (boolean unconditional)
{
  // Cleanup for enumerator
  if (comp != null)
    comp.compareIntClose();
  if (enum != null)
    enum.destroy();

  // Cleanup streams
  try
  {
    if (istrmDataType != null)
      istrmDataType.close();

    if (istrmBytes != null)
      istrmBytes.close();

    if (ostrmDataType != null)
      ostrmDataType.close();

    if (ostrmBytes != null)
      ostrmBytes.close();
  }
  catch (Exception e)
  {
    db(e.toString());
  }
```

(continued)

Example 12.1 (Continued)

```
  // Cleanup rms
  closeRecStore(rmsTodo);
  closeRecStore(rmsPref);
}

/*---------------------------------------------------
 * No pause code necessary
 *-------------------------------------------------*/
public void pauseApp ()
{ }


/*---------------------------------------------------
 * Open input streams
 *-------------------------------------------------*/
private void initInputStreams()
{
  istrmBytes = new ByteArrayInputStream(recData);
  istrmDataType = new DataInputStream(istrmBytes);
}


/*---------------------------------------------------
 * Open output streams
 *-------------------------------------------------*/
private void initOutputStreams()
{
  ostrmBytes = new ByteArrayOutputStream();
  ostrmDataType = new DataOutputStream(ostrmBytes);
}


/*---------------------------------------------------
 * Initialize enumeration for todo rms
 *-------------------------------------------------*/
private void initEnumeration()
{
  // Are we to bother with sorting?
  if (flagSortByPriority)
    comp = new ComparatorInt();
  else
    // We must set this to null to clear out
    // any previous setting
    comp = null;

  try
  {
```

(continued)

Example 12.1 (*Continued*)

```
    enum = rsTodo.enumerateRecords(null, comp, false);
  }
  catch (Exception e)
  {
    db(e.toString());
  }
}

/*-------------------------------------------------
 * Open a record store
 *-----------------------------------------------*/
private RecordStore openRecStore(String name)
{
  try
  {
    // Open the Record Store, creating it if necessary
    return RecordStore.openRecordStore(name, true);
  }
  catch (Exception e)
  {
    db(e.toString());
    return null;
  }
}

/*-------------------------------------------------
 * Close a record store
 *-----------------------------------------------*/
private void closeRecStore(RecordStore rs)
{
  try
  {
    rs.closeRecordStore();
  }
  catch (Exception e)
  {
    db(e.toString());
  }
}

/*-------------------------------------------------
 * Delete a record store
 *-----------------------------------------------*/
```

(continued)

Example 12.1   (Continued)

```
private void deleteRecStore(String name)
{
  try
  {
    RecordStore.deleteRecordStore(name);
  }
  catch (Exception e)
  {
    db(e.toString());
  }
}

/*-----------------------------------------------------
* Write new todo item
*    - Write a new record into the rms
*    - Write a new item into the vector
*    - Recreate the vector from the rms (which will
*      use the proper sort (using rms enumeration)
*    - Rebuild todo list from vector
*-----------------------------------------------------*/
protected void addTodoItem(int priority, String text)
{
  try
  {
    // Toss any data in the internal array so writes
    // starts at beginning (of the internal array)
    ostrmBytes.reset();

    // Write priority and todo text
    ostrmDataType.writeInt(priority);
    ostrmDataType.writeUTF(text);

    // Clear any buffered data
    ostrmDataType.flush();

    // Get stream data into byte array and write record
    byte[] record = ostrmBytes.toByteArray();
    int recordId = rsTodo.addRecord(record, 0, record.length);

    // Create a new Todo item and insert it into our Vector
    TodoItem item = new TodoItem(priority, text, recordId);
    vecTodo.addElement(item);
```

(continued)

Example 12.1   (Continued)

```
  }
  catch (Exception e)
  {
    db(e.toString());
  }

  // Read rms into vector
  writeRMS2Vector();

  // Rebuild todo list
  rebuildTodoList();
}

/*------------------------------------------------
 * Save preferences to record store
 *---------------------------------------------*/
protected void savePreferences(boolean sort, boolean showSort)
{
  // No changes we made
  if (sort == flagSortByPriority && showSort == flagShowPriority)
    return;

  // Save the current sort status
  boolean previouslySorted = flagSortByPriority;
  boolean previouslyShowPriority = flagShowPriority;

  try
  {
    // Update prefs in private variables
    flagSortByPriority = sort;
    flagShowPriority = showSort;

    // Toss any data in the internal array so writes
    // starts at beginning (of the internal array)
    ostrmBytes.reset();

    // Write the sort order and keep completed flags
    ostrmDataType.writeBoolean(flagSortByPriority);
    ostrmDataType.writeBoolean(flagShowPriority);

    // Clear any buffered data
    ostrmDataType.flush();
```

(continued)

Example 12.1   *(Continued)*

```
   // Get stream data into byte array and write record
   byte[] record = ostrmBytes.toByteArray();

   // Always write preferences at first record
   // We cannot request to set the first record unless
   // the record store has contents.
   // If empty => add a record
   // If not   => overwrite the first record
   if (rsPref.getNumRecords() == 0)
     rsPref.addRecord(record, 0, record.length);
   else
     rsPref.setRecord(1, record, 0, record.length);
  }
  catch (Exception e)
  {
    db(e.toString());
  }

  // If the sort order was changed, rebuild enumeration
  if (previouslySorted != flagSortByPriority)
    initEnumeration();

  // If we are going from non-sorted to sorted
  // or changing whether or not to show priority
  // then we must update what's currently displayed
  if ((!previouslySorted && flagSortByPriority) ||
      (previouslyShowPriority != flagShowPriority))
  {
    // Read rms into vector
    writeRMS2Vector();

    // Rebuild todo list
    rebuildTodoList();
  }
}

/*-------------------------------------------------
 * Read preferences from record store
 *-------------------------------------------------*/
private void refreshPreferences()
{
  try
```

(continued)

Example 12.1   (Continued)

```
  {
    // Record store is empty
    if (rsPref.getNumRecords() == 0)
    {
      // Write into the store the default preferences
      savePreferences(flagSortByPriority, flagShowPriority);
      return;
    }

    // Reset input back to the beginning
    istrmBytes.reset();

    // Read configuration data stored in the first record
    rsPref.getRecord(1, recData, 0);
    flagSortByPriority = istrmDataType.readBoolean();
    flagShowPriority = istrmDataType.readBoolean();

    System.out.println("Sort: " + flagSortByPriority);
    System.out.println("Show: " + flagShowPriority);
  }
  catch (Exception e)
  {
    db(e.toString());
  }
}

/*-------------------------------------------------
 * Create the vector from record store contents
 *-----------------------------------------------*/
private void writeRMS2Vector()
{
  // Cleanout the vector
  vecTodo.removeAllElements();

  try
  {
    // Rebuild enumeration for any changes
    enum.rebuild();

    while (enum.hasNextElement())
    {
      // Reset input back to the beginning
```

(continued)

Example 12.1   (*Continued*)

```
        istrmBytes.reset();

        // Get data into the byte array
        int id = enum.nextRecordId();
        rsTodo.getRecord(id, recData, 0);

        // Create a new Todo item and insert it into our Vector
        TodoItem item = new TodoItem(istrmDataType.readInt(),
                                     istrmDataType.readUTF(), id);
        vecTodo.addElement(item);
      }
    }
    catch (Exception e)
    {
      db(e.toString());
    }
  }

  /*-------------------------------------------------
   * Store the current vector contents to the rms
   *-----------------------------------------------*/
  private void writeVector2RMS()
  {
    try
    {
      byte[] record;

      for (int i = 0; i < vecTodo.size(); i++)
      {
        TodoItem item = (TodoItem) vecTodo.elementAt(i);

        int priority = item.getPriority();
        String text = item.getText();

        // Toss any data in the internal array so writes
        // starts at beginning (of the internal array)
        ostrmBytes.reset();

        // Write priority and todo text
        ostrmDataType.writeInt(priority);
        ostrmDataType.writeUTF(text);
```

(*continued*)

Example 12.1   (*Continued*)

```
      // Clear any buffered data
      ostrmDataType.flush();

      // Get stream data into byte array and write record
      record = ostrmBytes.toByteArray();
      rsTodo.addRecord(record, 0, record.length);
    }
  }
  catch (Exception e)
  {
    db(e.toString());
  }
}


/*-------------------------------------------------
 * Rebuild todo list (ChoiceGroup) from the Vector
 *-----------------------------------------------*/
protected void rebuildTodoList()
{
  // Clear out the ChoiceGroup.
  for (int i = cgTodo.size(); i > 0; i--)
    cgTodo.delete(i - 1);

  TodoItem item;
  int priority;
  String text;
  StringBuffer sb;

  for (int i = 0; i < vecTodo.size(); i++)
  {
    // Get a todo item from vector
    item = (TodoItem) vecTodo.elementAt(i);

    // Read values from todoitem class
    priority = item.getPriority();
    text = item.getText();

    // Are we are to show priority as part of the text?
    sb = new StringBuffer((flagShowPriority ?
                    (Integer.toString(priority) + "-"): ""));
    sb.append(text);
```

(*continued*)

Example 12.1 (*Continued*)

```
    // Append to todo choicegroup
    cgTodo.append(sb.toString(), null);
  }
}


/*-------------------------------------------------
 * This method is called when a todo item has been
 * selected in the choicegroup. We treat this as
 * a request to delete the item
 *-----------------------------------------------*/
public void itemStateChanged(Item item)
{
  ChoiceGroup cg;

  // Cast the item to a ChoiceGroup type
  cg = (ChoiceGroup) item;

  // Create an array that mirrors the ChoiceGroup
  // and populate with those items selected
  boolean selected[] = new boolean[cg.size()];
  cg.getSelectedFlags(selected);

  // Unfortunately, there is no (easy) way to determine
  // which item in the choiceGroup was "clicked" to
  // initiate this event. The best we can do is look at
  // each entry and determine its current selection state

  // For each element, see if it is selected
  // If so, delete it. Once we have found a selected
  // item, we can exit - there will never be more than
  // one item selected at any time
  for (int i = 0; i < cg.size(); i++)
  {
    if (selected[i])
    {
      // Get the record id from the todoItem
      // and delete record from rms
      TodoItem todoitem = (TodoItem) vecTodo.elementAt(i);
      try
      {
        rsTodo.deleteRecord(todoitem.getRecordId());
      }
    }
```

(*continued*)

Example 12.1   (Continued)

```
      catch (Exception e)
      {
         db(e.toString());
      }
      break;
   }
}

  // Read rms into vector
  writeRMS2Vector();

  // Rebuild todo list
  rebuildTodoList();
}


/*--------------------------------------------------
 * Process events for the main form
 *-------------------------------------------------*/
public void commandAction(Command c, Displayable d)
{
  if (c == cmExit)
  {
    destroyApp(false);
    notifyDestroyed();
  }
  else
  {
    if (c == cmAdd)
    {
      // Reset the textfield and choicegroup
      // on the 'add todo' form
      fmAdd.tfTodo.setString("");
      fmAdd.cgPriority.setSelectedIndex(0, true);

      // Push current displayable and activate 'add todo' form
      displayMgr.pushDisplayable(fmAdd);
    }
    else if (c == cmPrefs)
    {
      boolean flags[] = {flagSortByPriority, flagShowPriority};
```

(continued)

Example 12.1   (Continued)

```
      // Push current displayable and show preferences form
      // passing in current preference settings
        displayMgr.pushDisplayable(new FormPrefs("Preferences",
                                    this, flags));
      }
    }
  }


  /*------------------------------------------------
   * Simple message to console for debug/errors
   *----------------------------------------------*/
  private void db(String str)
  {
    System.err.println("Msg: " + str);
  }
}
```

Example 12.2   ComparatorInt.java

```
/*-----------------------------------------------
| ComparatorInt.java
|
| Sorts rms records based on todo item priority
| Provides compare() method for RecordEnumerator
|
| Supporting class for todoMIDlet
*----------------------------------------------*/
import java.io.*;
import javax.microedition.rms.*;

public class ComparatorInt implements RecordComparator
{
  private byte[] record = new byte[10];

  // Read from a specified byte array
  private ByteArrayInputStream strmBytes = null;

  // Read Java data types from the above byte array
  private DataInputStream strmDataType = null;
```

(continued)

Example 12.2 *(Continued)*

```java
public void compareIntClose()
{
  try
  {
    if (strmBytes != null)
      strmBytes.close();
    if (strmDataType != null)
      strmDataType.close();
  }
  catch (Exception e)
  {}
}

public int compare(byte[] rec1, byte[] rec2)
{
  int x1, x2;

  try
  {
    // If either record is larger than our buffer, reallocate
    int maxsize = Math.max(rec1.length, rec2.length);
    if (maxsize > record.length)
      record = new byte[maxsize];

    // Read record #1
    // We want the priority which is first "field"
    strmBytes = new ByteArrayInputStream(rec1);
    strmDataType = new DataInputStream(strmBytes);
    x1 = strmDataType.readInt();

    // Read record #2
    strmBytes = new ByteArrayInputStream(rec2);
    strmDataType = new DataInputStream(strmBytes);
    x2 = strmDataType.readInt();

    // Compare record #1 and #2
    if (x1 == x2)
      return RecordComparator.EQUIVALENT;
    else if (x1 < x2)
      return RecordComparator.PRECEDES;
    else
      return RecordComparator.FOLLOWS;
```

(continued)

Example 12.2 *(Continued)*

```
    }
    catch (Exception e)
    {
      return RecordComparator.EQUIVALENT;
    }
  }
}
```

Example 12.3 FormAdd.java

```
/*---------------------------------------------------
| FormAdd.java
|
| Form for adding new todoitems
|
| Supporting class for TodoMIDlet
*---------------------------------------------------*/
import javax.microedition.lcdui.*;

public class FormAdd extends Form implements CommandListener
{
  private Command cmBack,
                  cmSave;
  protected TextField tfTodo;
  protected ChoiceGroup cgPriority;
  private TodoMIDlet midlet;

  public FormAdd(String title, TodoMIDlet midlet)
  {
    // Call the Form constructor
    super(title);

    // Save reference to MIDlet so we can access
    // the display manager class and rms
    this.midlet = midlet;

    // Commands
    cmSave = new Command("Save", Command.SCREEN, 1);
    cmBack = new Command("Back", Command.BACK, 2);
```

(continued)

Example 12.3   *(Continued)*

```
  // Create textfield for entering todo items
  tfTodo = new TextField("Todo", null, 15, TextField.ANY);

  // Create choicegroup and append options (no images)
  cgPriority = new ChoiceGroup("Priority", Choice.EXCLUSIVE);
  cgPriority.append("Today", null);
  cgPriority.append("Tomorrow", null);
  cgPriority.append("This Week", null);
  cgPriority.append("This Month", null);
  cgPriority.append("Someday", null);

  // Add stuff to form and listen for events
  addCommand(cmSave);
  addCommand(cmBack);
  append(tfTodo);
  append(cgPriority);
  setCommandListener(this);
}

public void commandAction(Command c, Displayable s)
{
  if (c == cmSave)
  {
    // Add a new todo item
    // Notice we bump priority by 1. This is because the
    // choicegroup entries start at zero. We would like
    // the records in the rms to store priorities starting
    // at 1. Thus, if a user requests to display priorities
    // on the todo list, the highest priority is 1 (not zero)
    midlet.addTodoItem(cgPriority.getSelectedIndex() + 1,
                tfTodo.getString());
  }

  // Any other event and we go back to the main form...
  // Pop the last displayable off the stack
  midlet.displayMgr.popDisplayable();
  }
}
```

Example 12.4   FormPrefs.java

```
/*----------------------------------------------------
| FormPrefs.java
|
| Form for specifying user preferences
|
| Supporting class for TodoMIDlet
*---------------------------------------------------*/
import javax.microedition.lcdui.*;

public class FormPrefs extends Form implements CommandListener
{
   private Command cmBack,
                   cmSave;
   private TodoMIDlet midlet;
   private ChoiceGroup cgPrefs;

   public FormPrefs(String title, TodoMIDlet midlet, boolean flags[])
   {
      // Call the Form constructor
      super(title);

      // Save reference to MIDlet so we can access
      // the display manager class and rms
      this.midlet = midlet;

      // Commands
      cmSave = new Command("Save", Command.SCREEN, 1);
      cmBack = new Command("Back", Command.BACK, 2);

      // Choicegroup for sort order and showing priority
      cgPrefs = new ChoiceGroup("Preferences", Choice.MULTIPLE);
      cgPrefs.append("Sort by Priority", null);
      cgPrefs.append("Show Priority", null);

      // Set the current status of each entry
      cgPrefs.setSelectedFlags(flags);

      // Add to form and listen for events
      append(cgPrefs);
      addCommand(cmBack);
      addCommand(cmSave);
      setCommandListener(this);
   }
```

(continued)

Example 12.4   *(Continued)*

```java
  public void commandAction(Command c, Displayable s)
  {
    if (c == cmSave)
    {
      // Save the preferences
      midlet.savePreferences(cgPrefs.isSelected(0),
                             cgPrefs.isSelected(1));
    }
    // Any other event and we go back to the main form...
    // Pop the last displayable off the stack
    midlet.displayMgr.popDisplayable();
  }
}
```

Example 12.5   TodoItem.java

```java
/*-------------------------------------------------
| TodoItem.java
|
| Holds data/methods for a single todo item
| Supporting class for TodoMIDlet
*-------------------------------------------------*/
public class TodoItem
{
  private int priority;
  private String text;
  private int recordId;

  public TodoItem(int priority, String text, int recordId)
  {
    this.priority = priority;
    this.text = text;
    this.recordId = recordId;
  }

  public int getPriority()
  {
    return priority;
  }
  public void setPriority(int priority)
  {
```

(continued)

Example 12.5   (Continued)

```java
    this.priority = priority;
  }
  public String getText()
  {
    return text;
  }

  public void setText(String text)
  {
    this.text = text;
  }

  public int getRecordId()
  {
    return recordId;
  }
}
```

Example 12.6   DisplayManager.java

```java
/*----------------------------------------------------
 * Use a stack to push and pop displayable objects
 *
 * public void pushDisplayable(Displayable)
 * public void popDisplayable()
 * public void home()
 *------------------------------------------------*/
import javax.microedition.lcdui.*;
import java.util.*;

public class DisplayManager extends Stack
{
  private Display display;       // Reference to Display object
  private Displayable mainDisplayable; // Main displayable
  private Alert alStackError;   // Alert for error conditions

/*----------------------------------------------------
 * Display manager constructor
   *------------------------------------------------*/
  public DisplayManager(Display display,
                        Displayable mainDisplayable)
```

(continued)

Example 12.6   (Continued)

```
{
  // Only one display object per midlet, this is it
  this.display = display;
  this.mainDisplayable = mainDisplayable;

  // Create an alert displayed when an error occurs
  alStackError = new Alert("Displayable Stack Error");
  alStackError.setTimeout(Alert.FOREVER);   // Modal
}

/*-----------------------------------------------
 * Push the current displayable onto stack and set
 * the passed in displayable as active
 *-----------------------------------------------*/
public void pushDisplayable(Displayable newDisplayable)
{
  push(display.getCurrent());
  display.setCurrent(newDisplayable);
}

/*-----------------------------------------------
 * Return to the main displayable object of MIDlet
 *-----------------------------------------------*/
public void home()
{
  while (elementCount > 1)
    pop();
  display.setCurrent(mainDisplayable);
}

/*-----------------------------------------------
 * Pop displayable from stack and set as active
 *-----------------------------------------------*/
public void popDisplayable()
{
  // If the stack is not empty, pop next displayable
  if (empty() == false)
    display.setCurrent((Displayable) pop());
  else
    // On error show an alert
    // Once acknowldeged, set 'mainDisplayable' as active
    display.setCurrent(alStackError, mainDisplayable);
  }
}
```

SCHEDULING TASKS

Topics in this Chapter

Chapter 13

Java version 1.3 added two classes—`Timer` and `TimerTask`—to facilitate running of tasks in a background thread. Included as part of the `Timer` are an abundance of scheduling options, ranging from running a task once to repeating a task at regular intervals. It is surprisingly easy to use these classes. The only trick is to get your hands around the scheduling methods, deciding which is appropriate for your application.

The general concept is quite straightforward. We have a timer and a task. The timer specifies when a task is to be executed and the task is what is to be done. For example, we may have timer that "goes off" every second. The task updates a clock.

The classes `Timer` and `TimerTask` work hand-in-hand. One cannot exist without the other. If we toss out all the fluff, it comes down to the following:

Timer class: Scheduling when a task will occur
TimerTask class: Performing a task

Timer

There are six scheduling methods available in the `Timer` class. This may seem a little excessive, but each has a clearly defined purpose and once we walk through the specifics, you'll understand why there is such an abundance of options.

Scheduling One-Time Tasks

Let's start with two very simple ways to schedule a task:

1. Execute a task after a specific number of milliseconds

    ```
    public void schedule (TimerTask task, long delay)
    ```

2. Execute a task at a specific date

    ```
    public void schedule (TimerTask task, Date time)
    ```

Each of these timers executes a task just once. For the first case, this might be used as a countdown timer. For example, if you want to be notified 20 minutes from the current time (e.g., when your brownies need to come out of the oven), this timer would work just fine. However, if you need to be notified at a specific time in the future, such as this Thursday at 1 p.m., you would opt for the second case.

Scheduling Repeating Tasks

There are four remaining methods; each is a different variation for scheduling repeating tasks. We have two general types:

1. **Fixed-delay:** Each execution of a task is based solely on how long it was since the previous task finished.

    Let's say we create a timer that is to run a task every 60 seconds. In a perfect world, the task will run, as requested, every minute. Here's the downfall: If the timer is delayed, the execution of the task will also be delayed. For example, if the Java garbage collector happens to run in between tasks, it may be more than 60 seconds before the next task is executed. Once the task is run, it will be another 60 seconds (at a minimum) before an additional task can occur. This ends up creating a cascading effect.

You can imagine that if such a timer were used to execute a task updating a clock, the accuracy of the clock would be suspect. The longer the clock runs, the more inaccurate it may become.

These timers are well-suited to tasks where consistency is more important than accuracy. During a game when moving images around on the screen, we would be more concerned with the smoothness of the image movement than the actual time at which one task (move) finished and another task (move) started.

2. **Fixed-rate:** Each execution of a task is based on when the first task started and the requested delay between tasks.

Let's create the same timer as earlier, one that is to execute a task every 60 seconds. If more than one minute goes by before the system can execute the task, there will be repeated calls to the task to "catch up" for any lost time.

These timers are best when accuracy is very important. For example, if a task needs to occur every hour on the hour, this type of scheduling would be preferred.

You choose either fixed-rate or fixed-delay to establish how repeated tasks are managed. What has not been addressed is when does the first task occur, for either fixed-rate or fixed-delay.

A reasonable guess, based on the options we have for one-time tasks, is that the first task is executed either at a specific time in the future or after a specific number of milliseconds have elapsed. This is exactly right.

Here's a quick summary of the logic behind each of the remaining four methods for scheduling tasks:

1. Fixed-delay that starts in "n" number of milliseconds
2. Fixed-delay that starts at a specific date
3. Fixed-rate that starts in "n" number of milliseconds
4. Fixed-rate that starts at a specific date

If all this seems a little fuzzy, refer to Figure 13–1. I have created a hierarchy of sorts to help decide which scheduling method is most suitable. Start at the top of the chart and head either left or right based on when you would like the first task to be executed. From there, choose whether it is a one-time, fixed-delay or fixed-rate task(s).

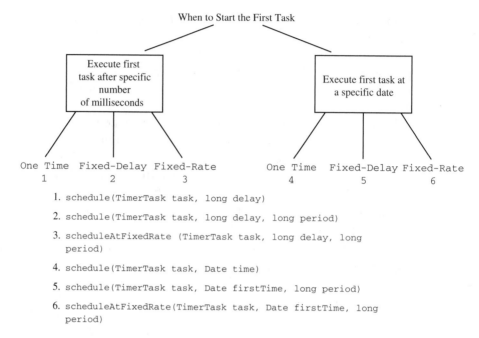

1. schedule(TimerTask task, long delay)

2. schedule(TimerTask task, long delay, long period)

3. scheduleAtFixedRate (TimerTask task, long delay, long period)

4. schedule(TimerTask task, Date time)

5. schedule(TimerTask task, Date firstTime, long period)

6. scheduleAtFixedRate(TimerTask task, Date firstTime, long period)

Figure 13-1   Six options for scheduling tasks

If we choose a repeating schedule (2, 3, 5 or 6), the time **between** repeated tasks is always specified in milliseconds, which is represented by the variable period shown above.

Timer API

Table 13.1 Timer Class: java.utli.Timer	
Method	*Description*
Constructors	
Timer()	Create timer
Methods	
void **cancel**()	Ends the timer and any scheduled tasks

(continued)

Table 13.1 (Continued)	
void **schedule**(TimerTask task, long delay)	Schedule a task to occur after a delay
void **schedule**(TimerTask task, long delay, long period)	Schedule a fixed-delay repeating task that starts after a delay
void **scheduleAtFixedRate**(TimerTask task, long delay, long period)	Schedule a fixed-rate repeating task that starts after a delay
void **schedule**(TimerTask task, Date time)	Schedule a task to occur on specific date
void **schedule**(TimerTask task, Date firstTime, long period)	Schedule a fixed-delay repeating task that starts on specific date
void **scheduleAtFixedRate**(TimerTask task, Date firstTime, long period)	Schedule fixed-rate repeating task that starts on specific date

TimerTask

Now that we know how to schedule a task, let's take a closer look inside a task. Observe that each of the scheduling methods has as the first parameter a reference to a `TimerTask` object. The `TimerTask` class has just three methods, not including the constructor:

```
abstract void run()
public boolean cancel()
public long scheduledExecutionTime()
```

The `run()` method is abstract, meaning there is no body to this method inside the `TimerTask` class. This is where we write the code that actually carries out whatever it is this task is to provide. Here is a glimpse at the `TimerTask` class as it is defined in MID:

```
public abstract class TimerTask implements Runnable
{
  . . .
  public abstract void run();
  . . .
}
```

To create a task that will be called by a timer, extend `TimerTask` and write the body of code for the `run()` method.

Putting the Pieces Together

There are three steps to make all this work.

1. Create a `Timer` with the appropriate scheduling option
2. Create a class that extends `TimerTask`
3. Write the `run()` method inside the above class

Here's a block of code that creates a `Timer` that will execute a task after 1,000 milliseconds has elapsed.

```
// Allocate a timer
Timer tm = new Timer();

// Allocate a task
TodoTask tt = new TodoTask();

// Schedule the timer to execute in 1000 milliseconds
tm.schedule(tt, 1000);

...

private class TodoTask extends TimerTask
{
  public final void run()
  {
    do something.....
  }
}
```

TimerTask API

Table 13.2 TimerTask Class: java.util.TimerTask	
Method	*Description*
Constructors	
TimerTask()	Create timer task
Methods	
boolean **cancel**()	End the task

(continued)

Table 13.2 *(Continued)*

abstract void **run**()	Place code in this method to carry out the action of the task
long **scheduledExecutionTime**()	Time when the last run task was scheduled to occur

Example: Timer Template

Example 13.1 is about as humdrum a MIDlet as you'll ever write. However, it provides a helpful template that shows how simple it is to create a timer and the associated task, regardless of which scheduling option you need.

The logic is simple: Create a timer using one of the six scheduling methods and print a message on a form when the task is run. That's it.

Example 13.1   TimerTemplate.java

```
/*----------------------------------------------------
| TimerTemplate.java
|
| Test all six Timer scheduling options
*----------------------------------------------------*/
import java.util.*;
import javax.microedition.midlet.*;
import javax.microedition.lcdui.*;

public class TimerTemplate extends MIDlet implements CommandListener
{
   private Display display;          // Our display
   private Form fmMain;              // Main form
   private Command cmExit;           // Exit midlet
   private Command cmStop;           // Stop the timer
   private Timer tm;                 // Timer
   private TestTimerTask tt;         // Task
   private int count = 0;            // How many times has task run

   public TimerTemplate()
   {
     display = Display.getDisplay(this);
```

(continued)

Example 13.1   (Continued)

```
// Create main form
fmMain = new Form("Timer Test");
fmMain.append("waiting...\n");

// Create commands and add to form
cmExit = new Command("Exit", Command.EXIT, 1);
cmStop = new Command("Stop", Command.STOP, 2);
fmMain.addCommand(cmExit);
fmMain.addCommand(cmStop);
fmMain.setCommandListener(this);

//-------------------------------------------------------
// Option #1 - One time task with delayed start
// Create a timer that will go off in 5 seconds
//-------------------------------------------------------
tm = new Timer();
tt = new TestTimerTask();
tm.schedule(tt, 5000);

//-------------------------------------------------------
// Option #2 - Fixed-delay repeating task with delayed start
// Create a timer that will go off in 5 seconds
// Repeating every 3 seconds
//-------------------------------------------------------
//    tm = new Timer();
//    tt = new TestTimerTask();
//    tm.schedule(tt, 5000, 3000);

//-------------------------------------------------------
// Option #3 - Fixed-rate repeating task with delayed start
// Create a timer that will go off in 5 seconds
// Repeating every 3 seconds
//-------------------------------------------------------
//    tm = new Timer();
//    tt = new TestTimerTask();
//    tm.scheduleAtFixedRate(tt, 5000, 3000);

//-------------------------------------------------------
// Option #4 - One time task at specified date
// Create timer that starts at current date
//-------------------------------------------------------
```

(continued)

Example 13.1 *(Continued)*

```
//     tm = new Timer();
//     tt = new TestTimerTask();
//     tm.schedule(tt, new Date());

    //------------------------------------------------------
    // Option #5 - Fixed-delay repeating task starting
    //             at a specified date
    // Create timer that starts at current date
    // Repeating every 3 seconds
    //------------------------------------------------------
//     tm = new Timer();
//     tt = new TestTimerTask();
//     tm.schedule(tt, new Date(), 3000);


    //------------------------------------------------------
    // Option #6 - Fixed-rate repeating task starting
    //             at a specified date
    // Create timer that starts at current date
    // Repeating every 3 seconds
    //------------------------------------------------------
//     tm = new Timer();
//     tt = new TestTimerTask();
//     tm.scheduleAtFixedRate(tt, new Date(), 3000);
  }

  /*-------------------------------------------------
   * Show the main Form
   *-----------------------------------------------*/
  public void startApp ()
  {
    display.setCurrent(fmMain);
  }

  /*-------------------------------------------------
   * Shutting down. Cleanup all we created
   *-----------------------------------------------*/
  public void destroyApp (boolean unconditional)
  { }

  /*-------------------------------------------------
   * No pause code necessary
   *-----------------------------------------------*/
```

(continued)

Example 13.1   (Continued)

```
public void pauseApp ()
{ }

/*-------------------------------------------------
 * Process events for the main form
 *-----------------------------------------------*/
public void commandAction(Command c, Displayable d)
{
  if (c == cmStop)
  {
    tm.cancel();
  }
  else if (c == cmExit)
  {
    destroyApp(false);
    notifyDestroyed();
  }
}

/*-------------------------------------------------
 * TestTimerTask Class - Run the task
 *-----------------------------------------------*/
private class TestTimerTask extends TimerTask
{
  public final void run()
  {
    fmMain.append("run count: " + ++count + "\n");
  }
}
}
```

To test all six scheduling options you will need to add comment delimiters (*///*) to one block and remove them from another, compile, pre-verify and re-run. Figure 13–2 shows the output for a one-time task that was started after a 5-second delay (Option #1 from the code).

Unless something unusual occurs, or you have an amazing eye for accuracy, you won't notice a difference when running a fixed-rate versus a fixed-delay repeated task. This is fine, as it is not the intention. Instead, you now have a starting point for writing any type of scheduled timer and task. Figure 13–3 shows the output this MIDlet with a repeating task.

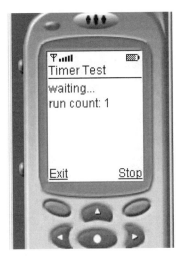

Figure 13–2   One-time task started
with a delay

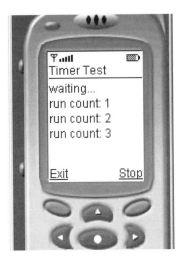

Figure 13–3   Repeating task

Example: Todo List MIDlet
Part II—Delay Timer

In Chapter 12 we created a todo list MIDlet that gave us options to add,
delete and sort items. If you took the time to compile and run the MIDlet
you noticed when you deleted an item, it immediately disappeared from the

Figure 13–4 Todo list before removing an item

list. There was no delay or warning, it was just gone. It leaves you with a "what the heck just happened?" kind of feeling.

To provide a little more reassurance when removing items, this example will add a few seconds of delay before updating the display. Figure 13–4 shows the todo list prior to deleting an item.

On the left screen shot in Figure 13–5 is the screen that appears during the timer delay. Notice the check ("X") by the item that was selected (to be deleted). The reason we can see this "X" has to do with how we apply the timer.

When a user selects an item to delete, the method `itemState-Changed()` is called. In the first version of the todo MIDlet (Chapter 12) this is where we deleted the item from the choicegroup. We then re-built the choicegroup without the item before the list was re-displayed. Therefore, the "X" never had a chance to be seen.

For this version the method `itemstateChanged()` has been modified to keep a reference to the item that initiated the event and to start a timer; we do not delete anything at this point.

```
public void itemStateChanged(Item item)
  {
    // Save the item
    // We use this in run() of the timer task
    deletedItem = item;

    // Create a timer that will go off in 2000 milliseconds
    tm = new Timer();
    tt = new TodoTask();
    tm.schedule(tt, 2000);
  }
```

Figure 13-5   Item to delete is selected (on left) and the new list (on right)

While waiting for the timer to start the task, the item selected in the choicegroup will appear as checked ("X"). See the screen-shot on the left in Figure 13–5. When the timer starts the task it will call the `run()` method in the `TodoTask` class. Here the item will be deleted from the record store. We'll then proceed to re-build the vector from the record store and re-build the choicegroup (todo list) from the vector. See Chapter 12 for specifics about the data design of the MIDlet.

```
public final void run()
{
  ...
  // ChoiceGroup selected values
  cg.getSelectedFlags(selected);

  for (int i = 0; i < cg.size(); i++)
  {
    // If we found the entry that was selected
    if (selected[i])
    {
      ...
      TodoItem todoItem = (TodoItem) vecTodo.elementAt(i);
      // Delete from the record store
      rsTodo.deleteRecord(todoitem.getRecordId());
    }
```

```
      }
      // Read rms into vector
      writeRMS2Vector();

      // Rebuild todo list
      rebuildTodoList();
    }
```

The new todo list appears on the right of Figure 13–5. The pause that was added gives a nice effect. The item to delete appears on the display as checked ("X"), then shortly thereafter (approximately 2 seconds) it is removed.

Example 13.2   TodoMIDet.java

Note: I have not included the entire source code. Follow the steps below to update the todo MIDlet written in Chapter 12.

```
1) Add to the declarations section

    private Timer tm;
    private TodoTask tt;
    private Item deletedItem;

2) New itemStateChanged() method

    public void itemStateChanged(Item item)
    {
      // Save the item
      // We use this in run() of the timer task
      deletedItem = item;

      // Create a timer that will go off in 2000 milliseconds
      tm = new Timer();
      tt = new TodoTask();
      tm.schedule(tt,2000);
    }

3) Add the following class inside the TodoMIDlet class

    /*-------------------------------------------------
     * TodoTask Class - Run the task
     *-----------------------------------------------*/
```

(*continued*)

Example 13.2   *(Continued)*

```java
private class TodoTask extends TimerTask
{
  public final void run()
  {
    ChoiceGroup cg;

    // Cast the deleted Item to a ChoiceGroup type
    // See itemStateChanged()
    cg = (ChoiceGroup) deletedItem;

    // Create an array that mirrors the ChoiceGroup
    // and populate with those items selected
    boolean selected[] = new boolean[cg.size()];
    cg.getSelectedFlags(selected);

    // Unfortunately, there is no (easy) way to determine
    // which item in the choiceGroup was "clicked" to
    // initiate this event. The best we can do is look at
    // each entry and determine its current selection state

    // For each element, see if it is selected
    // If so, delete it. Once we have found a selected
    // item, we can exit - there will never be more than
    // one item selected at any time
    for (int i = 0; i < cg.size(); i++)
    {
      if (selected[i])
      {
        // Get the record id from the todoItem
        // and delete record from rms
        TodoItem todoitem = (TodoItem) vecTodo.elementAt(i);
        try
        {
          rsTodo.deleteRecord(todoitem.getRecordId());
        }
        catch (Exception e)
        {
          db(e.toString());
        }
        break;
      }
    }
```

(continued)

Example 13.2   *(Continued)*

```
    // Read rms into vector
    writeRMS2Vector();

    // Rebuild todo list
    rebuildTodoList();
}
```

Example: Animation
with Timer/TimerTask

There are two general classifications of timers: those that execute a task one time and those that generate repeating tasks. Example 13.3 will schedule a timer to call a repeating task to move a ball around on a `Canvas`.

Whenever the timer interval has elapsed the task will change the position of the ball. Once the ball reaches an edge (top, bottom, left or right), it will bounce off in a different direction. To make it obvious when this occurs, the ball color will also be changed.

The following game actions (see Chapter 9) will be available to change the animation:

- Right will increase the size of the ball.
- Left will decrease the size of the ball.
- Fire resets the animation, clearing the background and changing the ball direction. The ball size will not be changed. This allows a user to restart and see how varying the ball size changes the animation.

Once the ball has changed directions "n" number of times (the default is 50), the screen will be cleared and the animation restarted. This gives a screen saver effect, which is nice if you leave it running on the device.

Each time the MIDlet is run (or re-started), a new trajectory (ball direction) will be randomly generated. Without this, the program would always display the same pattern.

Example 13.3   Animation.java

```
/*-----------------------------------------------------
* Animation.java
*
* Demonstrate simple animation using
* a Timer and TimerTask
*-------------------------------------------------*/
import java.util.*;
import javax.microedition.midlet.*;
import javax.microedition.lcdui.*;

public class Animation extends MIDlet
{
  private Display  display;            // The display
  private AnimationCanvas canvas;      // Canvas
  private Timer tm;                    // Timer
  private AnimateTimerTask tt;         // Task

  public Animation()
  {
    display = Display.getDisplay(this);
    canvas  = new AnimationCanvas(this);

    // Create and task that fires off every 1/10 second
    tm = new Timer();
    tt = new AnimateTimerTask(canvas);
    tm.schedule(tt, 0, 100);
  }

  protected void startApp()
  {
    display.setCurrent(canvas);
  }

  protected void pauseApp()
  { }

  protected void destroyApp(boolean unconditional)
  { }

  public void exitMIDlet()
  {
```

(continued)

Example 13.3   *(Continued)*

```
        destroyApp(true);

        notifyDestroyed();
    }
}


/*---------------------------------------------------
 * AnimationCanvas.java
 *
 * Show a ball that bounces around on a canvas
 * Each time we hit a wall we change the ball color
 * We also clear the screen after 'n' number of
 * hits against the wall
 * The "left" and "right" keys change the ball size
 * The "Fire" key resets the display, however,
 * it leaves the ball size the same.
 *---------------------------------------------------*/
import javax.microedition.midlet.*;
import javax.microedition.lcdui.*;
import java.util.*;

class AnimationCanvas extends Canvas implements CommandListener
{
    private Animation midlet;          // Main midlet
    private Command cmExit;            // Exit midlet
    private int     keyFire,           // Reset ball
                    keyRight,          // Increase ball radius
                    keyLeft;           // Decrease ball radius
    private boolean clearBackground = false; // Clear background
    private Random random;             // Random number
    int x_loc,                         // Current x & y locations
        y_loc,
        radius,                        // Ball radius
        red,                           // rgb colors
        green,
        blue,
        x_dir,                     // Next x & y positions of ball
        y_dir,
        start_x,                   // Where ball starts
        start_y,
        directionChanged = 0; // How many times we've hit a wall
    private static final int MAX_CHANGES = 50;
```

(continued)

Example 13.3   (Continued)

```
/*--------------------------------------------------
 * Constructor
 *--------------------------------------------------*/
public AnimationCanvas(Animation midlet)
{
  // Save reference to main midlet
  this.midlet = midlet;

  random = new java.util.Random();

  // Determine starting location and direction of ball
  init();
  radius = 7;

  // Create exit command and "Fire" key
  cmExit = new Command("Exit", Command.EXIT, 1);

  keyFire =  getKeyCode(FIRE);
  keyRight = getKeyCode(RIGHT);
  keyLeft = getKeyCode(LEFT);

  addCommand(cmExit);
  setCommandListener(this);
}


/*--------------------------------------------------
 * Paint a new ball, clearing the screen is asked
 *--------------------------------------------------*/
protected void paint(Graphics g)
{
  // Max edge hits, reset everything
  if (directionChanged > MAX_CHANGES)
    init();

  // Clear the background
  if (clearBackground)
  {
    g.setColor(255, 255, 255);
        g.fillRect(0, 0, getWidth(), getHeight());
    clearBackground = !clearBackground;
  }
```

(continued)

Example 13.3   *(Continued)*

```
  // Set color and draw another ball
  g.setColor(red, green, blue);
  g.fillArc( x_loc, y_loc, radius, radius, 0, 360);
}
/*----------------------------------------------------
 * Initialize starting location and direction of ball
 *--------------------------------------------------*/
private void init()
{
  // Start close to the middle
  x_loc = getWidth() / 2;
  y_loc = getHeight() / 2;

  // The direction the ball is heading
  x_dir = (random.nextInt() % 10);
  if (x_dir == 0)  x_dir = 1;

  y_dir = (random.nextInt() % 10);
  if (y_dir == 0)  y_dir = 1;

  directionChanged = 0;
  clearBackground = true;
  changeColor();
}

/*----------------------------------------------------
 * Change the colors.
 * I am counting on the implemention to substitute
 * a use-able color if any of these are out of the
 * devices supported range
 *--------------------------------------------------*/
protected void changeColor()
{
  // The shift is to remove any sign (negative) bit
  red = (random.nextInt() >>> 1) % 256;
  green = (random.nextInt() >>> 1) % 256;
  blue = (random.nextInt() >>> 1) % 256;
}

/*----------------------------------------------------
 * Event handling
 *--------------------------------------------------*/
```

(continued)

Example 13.3   *(Continued)*

```java
public void commandAction(Command c, Displayable d)
{
  if (c == cmExit)
    midlet.exitMIDlet();
}

/*-------------------------------------------------
 * Reset ball is "Fire" key is pressed
 *-----------------------------------------------*/
protected void keyPressed(int keyCode)
{
  // Restart
  if (keyCode == keyFire)
    init();
  // Decrease ball size
  else if (keyCode == keyLeft)
    radius = Math.max(1, --radius);
  else if (keyCode == keyRight)
  // Increase ball size
    radius = Math.min(getWidth() / 4, ++radius);
}
}

/*-------------------------------------------------
 * AnimateTimerTask.java
 *
 * Change the location of bouncing ball
 * on the canvas
 *-----------------------------------------------*/
import java.util.*;

class AnimateTimerTask extends TimerTask
{
  private AnimationCanvas canvas;

  public AnimateTimerTask(AnimationCanvas canvas)
  {
    this.canvas = canvas;
  }
```

(continued)

Example 13.3 *(Continued)*

```
/*----------------------------------------------------
 * Determine next location of the ball.
 * If the ball reaches any edge, change the color
 * Track how many times we've switced directions
 *----------------------------------------------------*/
public final void run()
{
  // If past the right edge or prior to left edge...
  if ((canvas.x_loc + canvas.radius + canvas.x_dir >
      canvas.getWidth()) ||
      (canvas.x_loc - canvas.radius + canvas.x_dir < 0))
  {
    canvas.x_dir = -canvas.x_dir;
    canvas.changeColor();
    canvas.directionChanged++;
  }

  // If past the bottom or before the top...
  if ((canvas.y_loc + canvas.radius + canvas.y_dir >
      canvas.getHeight()) ||
      (canvas.y_loc - canvas.radius + canvas.y_dir < 0))
  {
    canvas.y_dir = -canvas.y_dir;
    canvas.changeColor();
    canvas.directionChanged++;
  }

  // Update the new x and y locations
  canvas.x_loc += canvas.x_dir;
  canvas.y_loc += canvas.y_dir;

  canvas.repaint();

  }
}
```

It should be no surprise that the majority of the code for this MIDlet is in the canvas and the task. The MIDlet itself does little more than create the canvas, timer and task. Here is the bulk of the code:

```
//Constructor for the MIDlet
public Animation()
{
   display = Display.getDisplay(this);
   canvas  = new AnimationCanvas(this);

   // Create and task that fires off every 1/10 second
   tm = new Timer();
   tt = new AnimateTimerTask(canvas);
   tm.schedule(tt, 0, 100);
}
```

Before we look at how to move the ball, let's see what occurs each time a task is run. Inside the `run()` method of the class `AnimateTimerTask` we determine the next location of the ball. Before we can update the location, we need to see if the ball is about to hit an edge. This is done by adding the current location of the ball with the ball radius to see if any edge boundaries have been crossed.

```
// If past the right edge or prior to left edge...
if ((canvas.x_loc + canvas.radius + canvas.x_dir >
      canvas.getWidth()) ||
     (canvas.x_loc - canvas.radius + canvas.x_dir < 0))
{
  canvas.x_dir = -canvas.x_dir;
  canvas.changeColor();
  canvas.directionChanged++;
}

// If past the bottom or before the top...
if ((canvas.y_loc + canvas.radius + canvas.y_dir >
      canvas.getHeight()) ||
     (canvas.y_loc - canvas.radius + canvas.y_dir < 0))
{
  canvas.y_dir = -canvas.y_dir;
  canvas.changeColor();
  canvas.directionChanged++;
}
```

If any of these conditions are met, flip directions, request a change in the ball color and bump the counter of how many edges have been hit. Before leaving, set the new x and y locations of the ball and request the display to be repainted.

```
// Update the new x and y locations
canvas.x_loc += canvas.x_dir;
canvas.y_loc += canvas.y_dir;
canvas.repaint();
```

You can see that moving the ball is nothing more than adding an offset to the current x and y locations. For example, given a current x_loc of 10 and a current y_loc of 15, if x_dir is 3 and y_dir is 5, then:

new value of x_loc   10 + 3 = 13
new value of y_loc   15 + 5 = 15

The only time this gets a little weird is when you switch directions and are dealing with negative values for x_dir and y_dir. However, don't let that confuse you—the math and the logic are still the same.

The canvas class is the real workhorse. It is responsible for all event handling and painting of the display. We've seen most of the code before. However, there are a few lines worth mentioning.

Inside the init() method we get both the starting x and y location of the ball, and determine the ball direction.

```
private void init()
{
  // Start close to the middle
  x_loc = getWidth() / 2;
  y_loc = getHeight() / 2;

  // The direction the ball is heading
  x_dir = (random.nextInt() % 10);
  if (x_dir == 0)   x_dir = 1;

  y_dir = (random.nextInt() % 10);
  if (y_dir == 0)   y_dir = 1;

  directionChanged = 0;
  clearBackground = true;
  changeColor();
}
```

The statement (random.nextInt() % 10) generates a random value for the x and y direction. The mod operator (%) gives the remainder after dividing the random number by 10. This gives a final value in the range of –9 to +9. A value too large (or too small) will result in trying to draw the ball outside the boundaries of the display.

Following is the method to change the ball color.

```
protected void changeColor()
{
   // The shift is to remove any sign (negative) bit
   red = (random.nextInt() >>> 1) % 256;
   green = (random.nextInt() >>> 1) % 256;
   blue = (random.nextInt() >>> 1) % 256;
}
```

Color Support

To get the most bang for the buck this MIDlet needs to be run in color. If you are using Sun's MIDP implementation, you can change the color support of the emulator as outlined in the section "Create MIDP-HOME Environment Variable" in Chapter 4.

Once again, we use a random number and the mod operator. This gives a number in the range of -255 to 255. The >>> operator is a convenient (and

Figure 13–6 Animation MIDlet

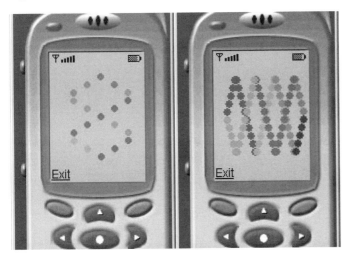

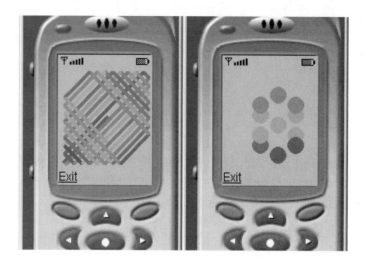

Figure 13–7 Animation MIDlet

fast) way to remove the sign bit. It does a right shift, moving a zero into the leftmost bit. The end result are color values between 0 and 255.

Figures 13–6 and 13–7 show several animation sequences created by this MIDlet.

GENERIC CONNECTION FRAMEWORK

Topics in this Chapter

- Connection Hierarchy
- HTTP Connection
  - Creating a Connection
  - Client Request
  - Server Response
  - Connection Information
  - Session Management with Java Servlets

Chapter 14

Weighing in at nearly 200 kilobytes, the 100+ classes and interfaces in J2SE java.io and java.net will exceed the resources available on many mobile devices. Beyond memory considerations, mobile devices will span the gamut in support for network protocols and file systems. To provide an extensible framework for i/o and networking, the GCF was developed.

The goal was not to devise a completely new set of classes, but rather to provide a subset of J2SE that is more in tune with the limitations and variations likely to be found on devices implementing MIDP.

Connection Hierarchy

The basic idea is to have one class, the `Connector`, that can create any type of connection, file, http, datagram, and so forth. The open method has the following form:

```
Connector.Open("protocol:address;parameters");
```

For example,

```
Connector.Open("http://www.some_web_address.com");
```

```
Connector.Open("socket://someaddress:1234");

Connector.Open("file://testdata.txt");
```

How the protocols are resolved is where the flexibility of the GCF comes into play. At runtime, `Connector` looks for the appropriate class that implements the requested protocol. This is done using `Class.forName()`. A request to open a HTTP connection in J2ME (using Sun's implementation) may look as follows:

```
Class.forName("com.sun.midp.io.j2me.http.Protocol");
```

If a class is found, an object is returned that implements a `Connection` interface. The `Connector` class and `Connection` interfaces are defined in CLDC. Figure 14–1 shows the classes that make up the `Connection` hierarchy, where each class is defined as an interface.

The actual implementation of the protocol(s) is at the Profile level. For example, in MIDP 1.0 the class `HttpConnection` supports a subset of HTTP version 1.1.[1] In Figure 14–1, notice `HttpConnection` extends `ContentConnection` and in turn provides over 20 methods for working specifically with HTTP.

Although `DatagramConnection` is included in the hierarchy, an implementation of MIDP is not required to support this protocol. We'll focus on HTTP, as it is the only requirement of MIDP.

Locating the Protocol Source Code

If you are using Sun's implementation of MIDP you can follow the path specified in the call

```
Class.forName("com.sun.midp.io.j2me.http.Protocol")
```

Here you will find the source code for the implementation of the HTTP protocol. As an example, on my system the full path translates to:

```
c:\j2me\midp1.0.3fcs\src\share\classes\com\sun\midp\io\
    j2me\http\protocol.java
```

Before moving on, let's have a closer look at the definitions of the classes and methods in the GCF. Hopefully this will provide some insight as you work through the examples that follow.

---

[1]Implementations of MIDP 1.0 are required to provide support for HTTP. Implementations may choose to offer other protocols.

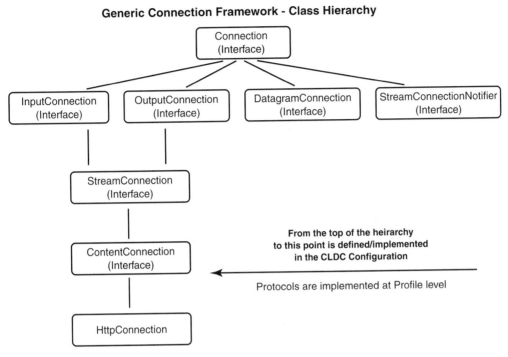

Generic Connection Framework - Class Hierarchy

Figure 14–1 Connection hierarchy

```
Connection    (public abstract interface Connection)
   public void close()

InputConnection (public abstract interface InputConnection extends Connection)
      public InputStream openInputStream()
      public DataInputStream openDataInputStream()

OutputConnection (public abstract interface OutputConnection extends Connection)
      public OutputStream openOutputStream()
      public DataOutputStream openDataOutputStream()

   StreamConnection (public abstract interface StreamConnection extends
                     InputConnection,OutputConnection)

      ContentConnection (public abstract interface ContentConnection extends Stream-
                         Connection)
         public long getLength()
```

```
        public String getEncoding()
        public String getType()

        HttpConnection (public interface HttpConnection extends ContentConnection)
            20+ methods for communicating over HTTP

Connector (public class Connector)
    public static Connection open(String name)
    public static Connection open(String name, int mode)
    public static Connection open(String name, int mode, boolean timeouts)
    public static DataInputStream openDataInputStream(String name)
    public static DataOutputStream openDataOutputStream(String name)
    public static InputStream openInputStream(String name)
    public static OutputStream openOutputStream(String name)
```

HTTP Connection

In MIDP 1.0 the only protocol that is guaranteed to be implemented is http.[2] Through the class `HttpConnection` you can communicate with a web server or any remote device that supports HTTP.

Portability

The only `Connection` interface that is required in MIDP 1.0 is `HttpConnection`. If portability is a concern, use only this interface. Implementations may support other protocols, such as datagrams or sockets, but there is no guarantee these will be available on other devices running MIDP 1.0.

HTTP is known as a request/response protocol. A client initiates a request, sends it to a server with an address specified as a Uniform Resource Locator (URL), and a response is returned from the server. This is how a web browser and web server work together. You type in the URL (e.g.,

---

[2]If a device does not directly support HTTP, there will need to be a gateway that converts the device protocol to HTTP prior to communicating with a remote server.

www.corej2me.com) and then the web browser creates a package of information (more on this in a moment), sends the request out over the network, receives information from a web server and displays the result in the browser.

Hypertext Transfer Protocol

The implementation of HTTP in MIDP 1.0 is based on version 1.1. The HTTP specification can be downloaded from:

```
http://www.ietf.org/rfc/rfc2616.txt
```

The specification for URLs can be found at:

```
http://www.ietf.org/rfc/rfc1738.txt
```

Creating a Connection

The Connector class has seven methods to create a connection with a server (see Table 14.1). There are three variations of the open() method. The first requires only the address of the server. The second method accepts a mode for reading/writing (see Table 14.2). The third option includes a boolean flag that indicates if the caller of the method can manage timeout exceptions. The remaining methods open various input and output streams.

Here is a call to create a ContentConnection. Refer back to Figure 14–1 to see the Connection hierarchy.

```
// Create a ContentConnection
String url = "http://www.corej2me.com"
ContentConnection connection =
          (ContentConnection) Connector.open(url);
```

One option to read data over this connection is through an Input-Stream:

```
InputStream iStrm = connection.openInputStream();

  // ContentConnection includes a length method!
int length = (int) connection.getLength();
if (length > 0)
{
  byte imageData[] = new byte[length];

  // Read the data into an array
  iStrm.read(imageData);
}
```

Table 14.1 CLDC Connector Methods: javax.microedition.io.Connector	
Method (each declared static)	*Description*
static Connection **open**(String name)	Create connection in READ_WRITE mode (see Table 14.2)
static Connection **open**(String name, int mode)	Create connection with specified mode
static Connection **open**(String name, int mode, boolean timeouts)	Create connection with specified mode, handling timeouts exceptions
static InputStream **openInputStream**(String name)	Create connection input stream
static OutputStream **openOutputStream**(String name)	Create connection output stream
static DataInputStream **openDataInputStream**(String name)	Create connection data input stream
static DataOutputStream **openDataOutputStream**(String name)	Create connection data output stream

Table 14.2 CLDC Connector Modes: javax.microedition.io.Connector	
Mode	*Description*
READ	Open connection for read only
WRITE	Open connection for write only
READ_WRITE	Open Connection for read and write

The code creates a connection with a server by specifying a URL, opens an InputStream and reads data from the remote server into an array. For this example, there is no need to send or receive HTTP commands.

For the sake of argument, let's create an InputStream connection and bypass ContentConnection altogether. As you'll see, the obvious loss with this approach is no method to determine the length of the data:

```
// Create an InputStream connection
String url = "http://www.corej2me.com/midpbook_v1e1/ch14/duke.png"
InputStream iStrm = (InputStream) Connector.openInputStream(url);
```

```
try
{
    byte imageData[] = new byte[2500];

    // Read the data into an array
    int length = iStrm.read(imageData);
}
```

When we get to the first example, we'll see how to use a `ByteArray-OutputStream` to take the guesswork out of determining how large an array to allocate if the length is not known.

Although you may find yourself opening many types of connections (the aforementioned are just a sample), the heart and soul of this chapter is devoted to `HttpConnection`. Here's how we may open such a connection:

```
String url =  "http://www.corej2me.com/midpbook_v1e1/ch14/duke.png"
HttpConnection http = (HttpConnection) Connector.open(url);
```

Once open, this connection offers access to various streams (`Input-Stream`, `DataInputStream`, to name a few). However, as we'll see, the advantage to using this connection lies with the HTTP commands at our disposal.

The key point to hold onto is this: Regardless of the type of connection, whether it be `ContentConnection`, `HttpConnection` or otherwise, communication with a server always begins with a call to one of the seven methods in the `Connector` class, Table 14.1.

Example: Download and View PNG Image

Example 14.1 will download and display a PNG image. There is no need for any specific HTTP functionality; therefore, we'll open a `ContentConnection`, create an `InputStream` and download the image data directly into an array.

We begin by creating a `TextBox` to enter the URL where the image is located. This is accompanied by two `Commands`, one to exit and one to view the image (see Figure 14–2).

Pressing "View" will initiate the connection to the URL. Once connected, the image data is downloaded into an array and a new `Image` object is created and appended to a `Form`. The `Form` is then set as the current `Displayable` (see Figure 14–3). Once "Back" is chosen from the `Form`, the user is returned to the `TextBox`.

Figure 14-2   TextBox to enter a URL
of PNG image

Figure 14-3   PNG image downloaded
over a network connection

Example 14.1   ViewPng.java

```
/*--------------------------------------------------
 * ViewPng.java
 *
 * Download and view a png file
 *--------------------------------------------------*/
import javax.microedition.midlet.*;
import javax.microedition.lcdui.*;
```

(continued)

Example 14.1   (Continued)

```java
import javax.microedition.io.*;
import java.io.*;

public class ViewPng extends MIDlet implements CommandListener
{
  private Display display;
  private TextBox tbMain;
  private Form fmViewPng;
  private Command cmExit;
  private Command cmView;
  private Command cmBack;

  public ViewPng()
  {
    display = Display.getDisplay(this);

    // Create the Main textbox with a maximum of 75 characters
    tbMain = new TextBox("Enter url",
        "http://www.corej2me.com/midpbook_v1e1/ch14/duke.png",75,0);

    // Create commands and add to textbox
    cmExit = new Command("Exit", Command.EXIT, 1);
    cmView = new Command("View", Command.SCREEN, 2);
    tbMain.addCommand(cmExit);
    tbMain.addCommand(cmView );

    // Set up a listener for textbox
    tbMain.setCommandListener(this);

    // Create the form that will hold the png image
    fmViewPng = new Form("");

    // Create commands and add to form
    cmBack = new Command("Back", Command.BACK, 1);
    fmViewPng.addCommand(cmBack);

    // Set up a listener for form
    fmViewPng.setCommandListener(this);
  }

  public void startApp()
  {
```

(continued)

Example 14.1 *(Continued)*

```
    display.setCurrent(tbMain);
}


public void pauseApp()
{ }


public void destroyApp(boolean unconditional)
{ }


/*--------------------------------------------------
 * Process events
 *--------------------------------------------------*/
public void commandAction(Command c, Displayable s)
{
  // If the Command button pressed was "Exit"
  if (c == cmExit)
  {
    destroyApp(false);
    notifyDestroyed();
  }
  else if (c == cmView)
  {

    // Download image and place on the form
    try
    {
      Image im;
      if ((im = getImage(tbMain.getString())) != null)
      {
        ImageItem ii = new ImageItem(null, im,
              ImageItem.LAYOUT_DEFAULT, null);

        // If there is already an image, set (replace) it
        if (fmViewPng.size() != 0)
          fmViewPng.set(0, ii);
        else  // Append the image to the empty form
          fmViewPng.append(ii);
      }
      else
        fmViewPng.append("Unsuccessful download.");

      // Display the form with the image
      display.setCurrent(fmViewPng);
    }
```

(continued)

Example 14.1 *(Continued)*

```
    catch (Exception e)
    {
      System.err.println("Msg: " + e.toString());
    }
  }
  else if (c == cmBack) {
    display.setCurrent(tbMain);
  }
}

/*---------------------------------------------------
 * Open connection and download png into a byte array.
 *--------------------------------------------------*/
private Image getImage(String url) throws IOException
{
  ContentConnection connection =
              (ContentConnection) Connector.open(url);
  InputStream iStrm = connection.openInputStream();
  Image im = null;

  try
  {
    // ContentConnection includes a length method
    byte imageData[];
    int length = (int) connection.getLength();
    if (length != -1)
    {
      imageData = new byte[length];

      // Read the png into an array
      iStrm.read(imageData);
    }
    else  // Length not available...
    {
      ByteArrayOutputStream bStrm = new ByteArrayOutputStream();

      int ch;
      while ((ch = iStrm.read()) != -1)
        bStrm.write(ch);

      imageData = bStrm.toByteArray();
      bStrm.close();
    }
```

(continued)

Example 14.1   *(Continued)*

```
      // Create the image from the byte array
      im = Image.createImage(imageData, 0, imageData.length);
    }
    finally
    {
      // Clean up
      if (iStrm != null)
        iStrm.close();
      if (connection != null)
        connection.close();
    }

    return (im == null ? null : im);

  }
}
```

Let's spend our time looking over the code to create the connection and download the image data. Here is bulk of `getImage()`:

```
private Image getImage(String url) throws IOException
{
  ContentConnection connection = (ContentConnection) Connector.open(
    url);
  InputStream iStrm = connection.openInputStream();
  Image im = null;

  try
  {
    // ContentConnection includes a length method
    byte imageData[];
    int length = (int) connection.getLength();
    if (length != -1)
    {
      imageData = new byte[length];

      // Read the png into an array
      iStrm.read(imageData);
    }
    else  // Length not available...
    {
      ByteArrayOutputStream bStrm = new ByteArrayOutputStream();
```

```
      int ch;
      while ((ch = iStrm.read()) != -1)
        bStrm.write(ch);

      imageData = bStrm.toByteArray();
      bStrm.close();
    }

    // Create the image from the byte array
    im = Image.createImage(imageData, 0, imageData.length);
  }
  finally
  {
    // Clean up
    ...
  }
  return (im == null ? null : im);
}
```

Once a `ContentConnection` and `InputStream` have been established, we attempt to reference the length of the data. If the length can be determined we read the results into the array `imageData` in one fell-swoop:

```
iStrm.read(imageData);
```

If the length is not available, we must read characters one at a time. Fortunately, Java provides a very convenient and efficient means to handle this. Using a `ByteArrayOutputStream` characters are read into an internal byte array, with Java handling any resizing of the array. Once done, we simply transfer the stream contents into our image array.

```
ByteArrayOutputStream bStrm = new ByteArrayOutputStream();

int ch;
while ((ch = iStrm.read()) != -1)
  bStrm.write(ch);

imageData = bStrm.toByteArray();
```

Regardless of how the data was transferred into our array, all that's left is to create a new Image and close the connection and stream on our way out.

In the method `commandAction()` the image is placed onto a Form and displayed.

Note

You cannot always count on knowing the length of the incoming data. Therefore, you should have a block of code that can read the data one character at a time.

Example: Download and View with InputStream

To show the flexibility of the `Connection` interface, let's change the previous example to download the same data with an `InputStream`. We need to change only a few lines of code in the method `getImage()`. Here is the updated version:[3]

```
private Image getImage(String url) throws IOException
{
  InputStream iStrm =
        (InputStream) Connector.openInputStream(url);
  Image im = null;

  try
  {
    ByteArrayOutputStream bStrm = new ByteArrayOutputStream();

    int ch;
    while ((ch = iStrm.read()) != -1)
      bStrm.write(ch);

    // Place into image array
    byte imageData[] = bStrm.toByteArray();

    // Create the image from the byte array
    im = Image.createImage(imageData, 0, imageData.length);
  }
  finally
  {
    // Clean up
    if (iStrm != null)
```

---

[3]If you have downloaded the example source code, this MIDlet can be found in the same directory as `ViewPng.java`. The filename is `ViewPng2.java`.

```
      iStrm.close();
  }

  return (im == null ? null : im);


}
```

One drawback is the absence of a method to determine the length of the incoming data. However, this is not much of a concern, simply use a `ByteArrayOutputStream` to read the data and move the results into the destination array.

Client Request

Up to this point, we have not had a need to send or receive HTTP commands. The objective was simply to create a connection and download a stream of data. It's time to shift gears and learn how to create and manage communication through the `HttpConnection` class.

HTTP is referred to as a request/response protocol: a client requests information, a server sends a response. The most common example is the interaction between a web browser (the client) and a web server. This section and the next will look at the details of the client request and the server response.

Request Method

A client request, known as the request entity, consists of three sections: request method, header and body. There are three request methods[4] available using `HttpConnection` (see Table 14.3).

Table 14.3 Request Method: javax.microedition.io.HttpConnection	
Request	*Description*
GET	Request information—data sent as part of URL
POST	Request information—data sent in separate stream
HEAD	Request only "metainformation" about a resource

[4]Don't confuse the use of the word "method" in this context with a method in a Java class. Method as it is used here comes directly from the HTTP 1.1 specification, as in "a client sends a request to the server in the form of a request method."

All three request methods inform a server that a client is requesting some type of information. For `GET` and `POST`, what differs is how data from the client is transferred to the server. Both methods, along with `HEAD`, will be explained in a moment.

You specify the request method of an `HttpConnection` through `setRequestMethod()`

```
HttpConnection http = null;
http = (HttpConnection) Connector.open(url);
http.setRequestMethod(HttpConnection.GET);
```

Table 14.4 Client Request Methods: javax.microedition.io.HttpConnection

Method	*Description*
void **setRequestMethod**(String method)	Set the request method (GET, POST or HEAD)
void **setRequestProperty**(String key, String value)	Set a request property (header information)
String **getRequestMethod**()	Get the current setting of the request method (GET, POST, HEAD)
String **getRequestProperty**(String key)	Get the current setting of a request property (header value)

Using `GET`, the body (data) of the request becomes part of the URL. This is known as URL encoding. For example, using the analogy of a web browser, assume we have a form with two fields—color and font. The names of the fields on the form, as defined in the HTML code, are `userColor` and `userFont`. When the form has been completed and is ready to be sent, the values entered onto the form will be appended onto the URL. The resulting URL may look similar to the following:

```
http://www.corej2me.com/formscript?userColor=blue&userFont=courier
```

Notice the "?" after the URL. This signifies the end of the URL and start of the form data. All information is sent through "key-value" pairs such as `userColor=blue, userFont=courier`.[5] Multiple key-value pairs are separated with "&".

---

[5]If there are spaces in the "value," replace them with "+". For example, "golf clubs" becomes "golf+clubs".

Data submitted using POST is sent separately from the call to the URL. Put another way, the request to open a connection to a URL is sent as one stream, any data is sent as a separate stream. There are two major benefits of POST over GET:

1. POST has no limit to the amount of data that can be sent. This is not the case for the request method GET. When a server processes a GET request, the data from the end of the URL is stored in an environment variable (known as a query string). When sending a large amount of data, you run the risk of over-running the environment variable.

2. POST sends data as a separate stream; therefore, the contents are not visible as part of the URL.[6]

HEAD works in the same manner as GET, with the client sending the body as part of the URL. However, the server will not return a body in its response (more on the server response in a moment). HEAD is generally used for retrieving information about a resource on a server. For example, you may want information about the last modified date of a file; however, it may not be necessary to retrieve the file contents.

Header Information

The second part of a client request is header information. The HTTP protocol defines over 40 header fields. Some of the more common are Accept, Cache-Control, Content-Type, Expires, If-Modified-Since and User-Agent. Headers are set by calling setRequestProperty().

```
HttpConnection http = null;
http = (HttpConnection) Connector.open(url);
http.setRequestMethod(HttpConnection.GET);
http.setRequestProperty("If-Modified-Since",
                    "Mon, 16 Jul 2001 22:54:26 GMT");
```

---

[6]POST in and of itself is not a secure means to send data. However, data sent as a separate stream is not as easily accessible to prying eyes as including the data as part of the URL.

Body

Data to be transferred from the client to the server is referred to as the body of the request. As mentioned, GET sends the body as part of the URL. POST sends the body in a separate stream.

Server Response

Once a client has packaged together the request method, header and body, and sent it over the network, it is now up to the server to interpret the request and generate a response known as the response entity. As with the client request, a server response consists of three sections: status line, header and body.

Creating the response on the server side is beyond the scope of this discussion. Instead, we will concern ourselves with how to pull information from the server response.

Status Line

The status line indicates the outcome of the client request. For HttpConnection, there are over 35 status codes reported. HTTP divides the codes into three broad categories based on the numeric value mapped to the code.

    1xx—information
    2xx—success
    3xx—redirection
    4xx—client errors
    5xx—server errors

For example, HTTP_OK (status code 200) indicates the client request was successfully processed.

When sending a response, a server includes the protocol version number along with the status code. Here are a few sample status lines:

```
HTTP/1.1 200 OK
HTTP/1.1 400 Bad Request
HTTP/1.1 500 Internal Server Error
```

When interpreting status codes, you have two options: retrieve the message or the code.

```
http.getResponseMessage();
http.getResponseCode();
```

The first returns only the text portion, such as OK or Bad Request. The later returns the code, such as 200 or 400.

Table 14.5 Response Methods: javax.microedition.io.HttpConnection	
Method	*Description*
int **getResponseCode**()	Get the response code (numeric)
String **getResponseMessage**()	Get the response message (text)

Header

Like the client, the server can send information through a header. These key-value pairs can be retrieved in various shapes and forms through the methods in Table14.6.

Table 14.6 Server Response Methods: javax.microedition.io.HttpConnection	
Method	*Description*
String **getHeaderField**(int n)	Get header field value looking up by index
String **getHeaderField**(String name)	Get header field value looking up by name
long **getHeaderFieldDate**(String name, long def)	Get named field as a long (representing the date)
int **getHeaderFieldInt**(String name, int def)	Get named field as an integer
String **getHeaderFieldKey**(int n)	Get header field key using index
long **getDate**()	Get header field "date"
long **getExpiration**()	Get header field "expires"
long **getLastModified**()	Get header field "last-modified"

As an example, let's assume the server sent a header key-value pair content-type=text/plain. As a further assumption, the key-value pair will be the first entry in the header, and with this assumption, it will have an index value of 0. This header informs the client that the body of the response will be returned as plain text (as compared to HTML text, etc.). The following calls all reference the same key-value pair:

```
// Header field at index 0: "content-type=text/plain"
http.getHeaderField(0);                  // "text-plain"
http.getHeaderField("content-type");     // "text-plain"
http.getHeaderFieldKey(0);               // "content-type"
```

Custom Header Fields

There are three methods for retrieving specific header fields sent from the server: `getDate()`, `getExpiration()` and `getLastModi-fied()`. However, with the remaining methods in Table 14-6, you can retrieve any header a server may send, including custom headers, which are not defined in the HTTP specification.

As an example, if a server created a custom header field `Custom-ProductCode`, the value of the header may be obtained as follows:

```
String code = http.getHeaderField("Custom-ProductCode");
```

In Example 14.4 we'll create a custom header in a Java servlet and show how to search for the header inside a MIDlet.

Body

The body is the data sent from the server to the client. There are no methods defined in `HttpConnection` for reading the body. The most common means to obtain the body is through a stream, as shown in the following example.

Example: Download a File

To get a feel for setting up a client request and pulling apart a server response, let's create a MIDlet that requests to read the contents of a file over a network connection. The URL and connection request follow:

```
url = "http://www.corej2me.com/midpbook_v1e1/ch14/getHeaderInfo.txt";
HttpConnection http = null;
...
// Create the connection
http = (HttpConnection) Connector.open(url);
```

The client request is straightforward:

```
//----------------
// Client Request
//----------------
// 1) Send request method
http.setRequestMethod(HttpConnection.GET);

// 2) Send header information (this header is optional)
http.setRequestProperty("User-Agent",
                        "Profile/MIDP-1.0 Configuration/CLDC-1.0");

// 3) Send body/data - No data for this request
```

Using a GET request method, send one header field and no data.

The server response is a little longer, showing all the header fields (accessed in several ways) and the contents of the requested file.

```
//----------------
// Server Response
//----------------
// 1) Get status Line
System.out.println("Msg: " + http.getResponseMessage());
System.out.println("Code: " + http.getResponseCode());

// 2) Get header information
if (http.getResponseCode() == HttpConnection.HTTP_OK)
{
  System.out.println("field 0: " + http.getHeaderField(0));
  ...

  System.out.println("key 0: " + http.getHeaderFieldKey(0));
  ...

  System.out.println("content: " +
                     http.getHeaderField("content-type"));
  ...

  // 3) Get data (show the file contents)
  String str;
  iStrm = http.openInputStream();
```

```
int length = (int) http.getLength();

if (length != -1)
{
  // Read data in one chunk
  byte serverData[] = new byte[length];
  iStrm.read(serverData);
  str = new String(serverData);
}
else  // Length not available...
{
  ByteArrayOutputStream bStrm = new ByteArrayOutputStream();

  // Read data one character at a time
   int ch;
   while ((ch = iStrm.read()) != -1)
     bStrm.write(ch);

   str = new String(bStrm.toByteArray());
   bStrm.close();
}

System.out.println("File Contents: " + str);
}
```

Step 3 (above) creates an `InputStream` and reads the body of the server response. The data sent from the server is the contents of the text file requested in the URL:

```
http://www.corej2me.com/midpbook_v1e1/ch14/getHeaderInfo.txt"
```

The output is shown in Figure 14–4.

Example 14.2   ViewFile.java

```
/*-------------------------------------------------
 * ViewFile.java
 *
 * Send client request (method, header, body)
 * Get server response (status, header, body)
 *-------------------------------------------------*/
import javax.microedition.midlet.*;
import javax.microedition.io.*;
import java.io.*;
```

(continued)

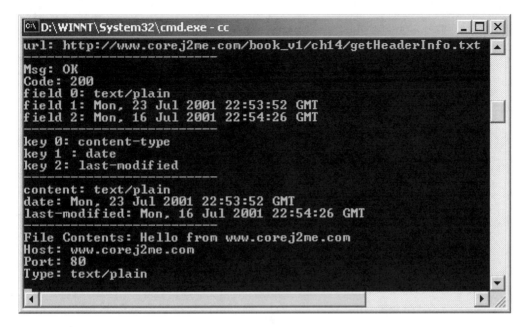

Figure 14–4 Server response from client GET request

Example 14.2   (Continued)

```java
public class ViewFile extends MIDlet
{
  private String url =
    "http://www.corej2me.com/midpbook_v1e1/ch14/getHeaderInfo.txt";

  public void startApp()
  {
    try
    {
      processRequest();
    }
    catch (Exception e)
    {
      System.err.println("Msg: " + e.toString());
    }
  }
```

(continued)

Example 14.2 *(Continued)*

```
private void processRequest() throws IOException
{
  HttpConnection http = null;
  InputStream iStrm = null;

  try
  {
    // Create the connection
    http = (HttpConnection) Connector.open(url);

    //----------------
    // Client Request
    //----------------
    // 1) Send request method
    http.setRequestMethod(HttpConnection.GET);

    // 2) Send header information (this header is optional)
    http.setRequestProperty("User-Agent",
        "Profile/MIDP-1.0 Configuration/CLDC-1.0");
    // http.setRequestProperty("If-Modified-Since",
    //     "Mon, 16 Jul 2001 22:54:26 GMT");

    // If you experience IO problems, try
    // removing the comment from the following line
    //http.setRequestProperty("Connection", "close");

    // 3) Send body/data - No data for this request

    //----------------
    // Server Response
    //----------------
    System.out.println("url: " + url);
    System.out.println("------------------------");

    // 1) Get status Line
    System.out.println("Msg: " + http.getResponseMessage());
    System.out.println("Code: " + http.getResponseCode());

    // 2) Get header information
    if (http.getResponseCode() == HttpConnection.HTTP_OK)
    {
```

(continued)

Example 14.2 *(Continued)*

```
System.out.println("field 0: " + http.getHeaderField(0));
System.out.println("field 1: " + http.getHeaderField(1));
System.out.println("field 2: " + http.getHeaderField(2));
System.out.println("-------------------------");

System.out.println("key 0: " + http.getHeaderFieldKey(0));
System.out.println("key 1 : " + http.getHeaderFieldKey(1));
System.out.println("key 2: " + http.getHeaderFieldKey(2));
System.out.println("-------------------------");

System.out.println("content: " +
   http.getHeaderField("content-type"));
System.out.println("date: " + http.getHeaderField("date"));
System.out.println("last-modified: " +
   http.getHeaderField("last-modified"));
System.out.println("-----------------------");

// 3) Get data (show the file contents)
String str;
iStrm = http.openInputStream();
int length = (int) http.getLength();
if (length != -1)
{
  // Read data in one chunk
  byte serverData[] = new byte[length];
  iStrm.read(serverData);
  str = new String(serverData);
}
else  // Length not available...
{
  ByteArrayOutputStream bStrm =
        new ByteArrayOutputStream();

  // Read data one character at a time
  int ch;
  while ((ch = iStrm.read()) != -1)
    bStrm.write(ch);

  str = new String(bStrm.toByteArray());
  bStrm.close();
}
```

(continued)

Example 14.2   (Continued)

```
        System.out.println("File Contents: " + str);

        //----------------------------
        // Show connection information
        //----------------------------
        System.out.println("Host: " + http.getHost());
        System.out.println("Port: " + http.getPort());
        System.out.println("Type: " + http.getType());
      }
    }
    finally
    {
      // Clean up
      if (iStrm != null)
        iStrm.close();
      if (http != null)
        http.close();
    }
  }

  public void pauseApp()
  { }

  public void destroyApp(boolean unconditional)
  { }
}
```

Example: if-modified-since Header

Let's make one minor change to the previous example. Update the client section to look as follows:

```
        //---------------
        // Client Request
        //---------------
        // 1) Send request method
        http.setRequestMethod(HttpConnection.GET);

        // 2) Send header information (this header is optional)
        http.setRequestProperty("User-Agent",
            "Profile/MIDP-1.0 Configuration/CLDC-1.0");
```

```
http.setRequestProperty("If-Modified-Since",
    "Mon, 16 Jul 2001 22:54:26 GMT");

// 3) Send body/data - No data for this request
```

When the server receives the header if-modified-since[7] it compares the date of the resource (on the server) with the date passed in the header. If the resource has not been modified since the requested date, no body is returned. You may find this helpful to keep the server from sending a body that has not changed since the last request.

Figure 14–5 shows the output of this MIDlet if the server does not return a body.

Connection Header

You'll notice several examples in this chapter include the following line:

```
// If you experience IO problems, try
// removing the comment from the following line
// http.setRequestProperty("Connection", "close");
```

When setting this header to "close" it tells the server to close the connection after the response is sent. The reason for this explicit option has to do with the ability of a server to maintain a persistent connection with a client. When making multiple requests to a server, you may experience a performance increase because the connection is reused over multiple requests.

However, if the Content-Length header is not used, or has an incorrect value, the client may block waiting for data that will never arrive. If you find you are having problems receiving data, remove the comment to force the server to close the connection once it has completed sending its response. If this fixes the problem, look closely at the Content-Length value that you are sending.

---

[7]Header requests are not case-sensitive. If-Modified-Since is equivalent to if-modified-since.

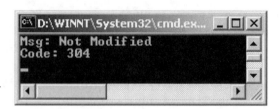

Figure 14–5   Using "if-modified-since" header

Connection Information

Once a connection has been established, there are several methods available to obtain information about the connection. Each is listed in Table 14.7.

Table 14.7   Connection Methods: javax.microedition.io.HttpConnection

Method	Description
String **getFile**()	Get filename from the URL
String **getHost**()	Get host from the URL
int **getPort**()	Get port from the URL
String **getProtocol**()	Get protocol from the URL
String **getQuery**()	Get the query string (only valid with a GET request)
String **getRef**()	Get the reference portion of URL[1]
String **getURL**()	Get the entire URL

[1]This is optional. The reference portion is defined in RFC2396.

Looking back at Example 14.2, notice the following lines near the bottom of the method processRequest().

```
System.out.println("Host: " + http.getHost());
System.out.println("Port: " + http.getPort());
System.out.println("Type: " + http.getType());
```

At the bottom of Figure 14–4 you'll see the results:

```
Host: www.corej2me.com
Post: 80
Type: plain/text
```

As an additional example, look at the code block shown next.

```
url = http://www.corej2me.com/midpbook_v1e1/ch14/getInfo.txt?color=blue
...
http = (HttpConnection) Connector.open(url);
http.setRequestMethod(HttpConnection.GET);
...
System.out.println("file: " + http.getFile();
System.out.println("protocol: " + http.getProtocol());
System.out.println("URL: " + http.getURL());
System.out.println("query: " + http.getQuery());
```

The output based on the URL specified would look as follows:

```
file:      /midpbook_v1e1/ch14/getInfo.txt
protocol:  http
URL:       http://www.corej2me.com/midpbook_v1e1/ch14/getInfo.txt?color=blue
query:     color=blue
```

Java Servlets

Examples 14.3, 14.4, and 14.5 all communicate with a Java servlet. To limit the time you need to spend fussing with a web server that supports servlets, I have found a home for all the servlet code at `www.mycgiserver.com`. As of this writing, all hosting was not only free of charge, there was no marketing or other pesky advertising placed inside responses from the server. What this means to you is that each example should work "out-of-the-box."

On the other hand, if you have access to a web server that supports Servlets, or would like to learn more about how Servlets work, the source code is included.

One note regarding how the Servlets are invoked from within the following MIDlets. The URL for each example will contain a reference to the package "corej2me":

```
String url = "http://www.mycgiserver.com/servlet/corej2me.
            cookieServlet";
String url = "http://www.mycgiserver.com/servlet/corej2me.
            getNpostServlet"
```

(continued)

```
String url = "http://www.mycgiserver.com/servlet/corej2me.url_
            rewriteServlet";
```

The package name is required by *mycgiserver* to differentiate my servlets from those of others running on the same server. If you would like more information about Servlets, here are a few helpful links:
Servlet Technology from Sun:

```
http://java.sun.com/products/servlet/index.html
```

Tomcat is a free, open-source implementation of the Java Servlet specification:

```
http://java.sun.com/products/servlet/download.html
```

Example: GET and POST to a Java Servlet

Constructing a client request using GET and POST are different enough to warrant an example using each. The next example will connect with a Java servlet to look up a bank account balance. Obviously, the account number, password and balance are all fictitious; however, this might get your wheels spinning.

Client Request

The main Form will hold two TextFields, an account number and password (see Figure 14–6).

Figure 14–6   Enter account information before GET or POST

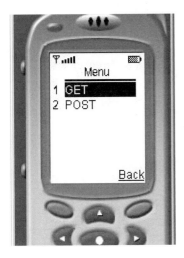

Figure 14–7 Use GET or Post request
method to send the data

Once the form has been completed and the user chooses the "Menu" option, there will be a choice as to the request method for sending the data (see Figure 14–7).

The receiving end of the client request will be a Java servlet. The account information will be stored in a database, named acctInfo, located on the same machine as the servlet. The database, `acctInfo`, will contain three columns (account, password, balance) and is populated with the following information:

account (integer)	password (varchar)	balance (integer)
225	yellow	3070
701	blue	9125
901	green	417830

When using GET as the request method, we append the data onto the end of the URL. Here is the code for creating the client request:.

```
// Data is passed at the end of url for GET
String url =
  "http://www.mycgiserver.com/servlet/corej2me.GetNpostServlet" +
  "?" +
  "account=" + tfAcct.getString() + "&" +
  "password=" + tfPwd.getString();

try
{
  http = (HttpConnection) Connector.open(url);
```

```
//----------------
// Client Request
//----------------
// 1) Send request method
http.setRequestMethod(HttpConnection.GET);
// 2) Send header information - none
// 3) Send body/data -  data is at the end of URL

//----------------
// Server Response
//----------------
iStrm = http.openInputStream();
// Three steps are processed in this method call
ret = processServerResponse(http, iStrm);
}
```

If you pick up nothing else, notice how the URL of the servlet has been modified to accommodate the data. Look carefully: the first character after the servlet address is "?", which signifies the end of the URL and the start of the data. The data is then passed as key-value pairs, separating each with "&".

```
"account=12345&password=xyz"
```

The same request, sent as a POST, looks as follows:

```
// Data is passed as a separate stream for POST (below)
String url =
    "http://www.mycgiserver.com/servlet/corej2me.GetNpostServlet";

try
{
  http = (HttpConnection) Connector.open(url);
  oStrm = http.openOutputStream();

  //----------------
  // Client Request
  //----------------
  // 1) Send request type
  http.setRequestMethod(HttpConnection.POST);

  // 2) Send header information. Required for POST to work
  http.setRequestProperty("Content-Type",
        "application/x-www-form-urlencoded");
```

```
// 3) Send data
// Write account number
byte data[] = ("account=" + tfAcct.getString()).getBytes();
oStrm.write(data);

// Write password
data = ("&password=" + tfPwd.getString()).getBytes();
oStrm.write(data);
oStrm.flush();

//----------------
// Server Response
//----------------
iStrm = http.openInputStream();
// Three steps are processed in this method call
ret = processServerResponse(http, iStrm);
}
```

The first noticeable difference is the URL; there is no reference to the data. Also, notice the header field

```
http.setRequestProperty("Content-Type",
        "application/x-www-form-urlencoded");
```

When using POST, the servlet will fail without this header. A separate OutputStream is used to send both the account number and password. Pay attention to the fact that each is sent as a name value pair by separating the key from the value with an =; for example, account=123. One last important detail, look at the line for sending the password:

```
data = ("&password=" + tfPwd.getString()).getBytes();
```

Even though we are not appending the data onto the URL, multiple key value pairs still need to be separated with &. Once all this is complete, it's now up to the servlet to interpret what we've sent and generate a response.

Server Response

Although this section won't give a lengthy tutorial on writing servlets, there will be enough information to clearly understand how a servlet interprets a client request and generates a response.

Writing Servlets

If you would like to compile the servlet code, you will need to download and install the Java Servlet Development Kit (JSDK).

```
http://java.sun.com/products/servlet/archive.html
```

A servlet will run one of two methods, depending on whether the client request method is GET or POST.

```
doGet(HttpServletRequest req, HttpServletResponse res)
doPost(HttpServletRequest req, HttpServletResponse res)
```

The parameter `HttpServletRequest` provides access to the client data that initiated the request to the servlet. `HttpServletResponse` is used to package a response for the client.

```
protected void doGet(HttpServletRequest req,
                 HttpServletResponse res)
         throws ServletException, IOException
{
  String acct = req.getParameter("account"),
         pwd = req.getParameter("password");

  String balance = accountLookup(acct, pwd);

  if (balance == null)
  {
   res.sendError(res.SC_BAD_REQUEST, "Unable to locate account.");
    return;
  }

  res.setContentType("text/plain");
  PrintWriter out = res.getWriter();
  out.print(balance);
  out.close();
}
```

The first course of action is to look for parameters that may have been sent as part of the client header. These values will be stored in the variables acct and pwd. These values correspond to the textfields on the client form (see Figure 14–6). With this information, the servlet can then search the database in an attempt to look up the account balance. If the search fails an error is returned to the client; otherwise, a response containing the balance is created.

```
res.setContentType("text/plain");
PrintWriter out = res.getWriter();
out.print(balance);
out.close();
```

The first line above creates a header field specifying the "content-type." This informs the client that the data from the server will be sent as plain text. Next, the servlet obtains a resource to write text to the client. The last steps are to output the balance and close the writer.

The code inside `doPost()` is identical. The reason for not consolidating the code is to illustrate the point that data can be sent using either `GET` or `POST` and processed in the same fashion on the server.

There is one last detail, and that is how the servlet looks up information in the account database.

```
private String accountLookup(String acct, String pwd)
{
  ...
  // These will vary depending on your server/database
  Class.forName("sun.jdbc.odbc.JdbcOdbcDriver");
  con = DriverManager.getConnection("jdbc:odbc:acctInfo");

  Statement stmt = con.createStatement();
  ResultSet rs = stmt.executeQuery("Select balance from acctInfo
    where account = " + acct + "and password = '" + pwd + "'");

  if (rs.next())
    return rs.getString(1);
  else
    return null;
  ...
}
```

Through JDBC, a connection[8] is established with the database. A simple Structured Query Language (SQL) statement will search the database. If the result set is not empty, return the account balance as a `String`.

---

[8]The JDBC driver and call to `getConnection()` will vary depending on your server and database.

Updating the Client

Now that the client has sent a request and the server has responded, the MIDlet needs to interpret the server reply and update the display with the account balance.

```
processServerResponse(HttpConnection http, InputStream iStrm)
{
  //Reset error message
  errorMsg = null;

  // 1) Get status Line
  if (http.getResponseCode() == HttpConnection.HTTP_OK)
  {
    // 2) Get header information - none

    // 3) Get body (data)
    int length = (int) http.getLength();
    if (length > 0)
    {

      byte servletData[] = new byte[length];
      iStrm.read(servletData);

      // Update the string item on the display
      siBalance.setText(new String(servletData));

      return true;
    }
    else
      errorMsg = new String("Unable to read data");
  }
  else
    // Use message from the servlet
    errorMsg = new String(http.getResponseMessage());

  return false;
}
```

We pull apart the server response in three chunks. First, we look at the status line to verify the server was able to fulfill the request. The next step is to read any header information, but there is none for this MIDlet. The body of the server response contains what we are after—the account balance. With this in hand we can update `siBalance`, the `StringItem` that shows the account balance on the form. The end result is displayed in Figure 14–8.

Figure 14–8 Account balance
obtained from a Java servlet

Example 4.3   GetNpost.java

```
/*----------------------------------------------------
 * GetNpost.java
 *
 * Use GET or POST to communicate with a Java servlet.
 * The servlet will search a database for the balance
 * of an account.
 *----------------------------------------------------*/
import javax.microedition.midlet.*;
import javax.microedition.lcdui.*;
import javax.microedition.io.*;
import java.io.*;

public class GetNpost extends MIDlet implements CommandListener
{
  private Display display;      // Reference to Display object
  private Form fmMain;          // The main form
  private Alert alError;        // Alert to error message
  private Command cmGET;        // Request method GET
  private Command cmPOST;       // Request method Post
  private Command cmExit;       // Command to exit the MIDlet
  private TextField tfAcct;     // Get account number
  private TextField tfPwd;      // Get password
  private StringItem siBalance; // Show account balance
  private String errorMsg = null;
```

(continued)

Example 4.3 *(Continued)*

```java
public GetNpost()
{
  display = Display.getDisplay(this);

  // Create commands
  cmGET = new Command("GET", Command.SCREEN, 2);
  cmPOST = new Command("POST", Command.SCREEN, 3);
  cmExit = new Command("Exit", Command.EXIT, 1);

  // Textfields
  tfAcct = new TextField("Account:", "", 5, TextField.NUMERIC);
  tfPwd = new TextField("Password:", "", 10,
                        TextField.ANY | TextField.PASSWORD);

  // Balance string item
  siBalance = new StringItem("Balance: $", "");

  // Create Form, add commands & components, listen for events
  fmMain = new Form("Account Information");
  fmMain.addCommand(cmExit);
  fmMain.addCommand(cmGET);
  fmMain.addCommand(cmPOST);

  fmMain.append(tfAcct);
  fmMain.append(tfPwd);
  fmMain.append(siBalance);

  fmMain.setCommandListener(this);
}

public void startApp()
{
  display.setCurrent(fmMain);
}

public void pauseApp()
{ }

public void destroyApp(boolean unconditional)
{ }

public void commandAction(Command c, Displayable s)
```

(continued)

Example 4.3 *(Continued)*

```
{
  if (c == cmGET || c == cmPOST)
  {
    try
    {
      if (c == cmGET)
        lookupBalance_withGET();
      else
        lookupBalance_withPOST();
    }
    catch (Exception e)
    {
      System.err.println("Msg: " + e.toString());
    }
  }
  else if (c == cmExit)
  {
    destroyApp(false);
    notifyDestroyed();
  }
}

/*-------------------------------------------------
 * Access servlet using GET
 *-----------------------------------------------*/
private void lookupBalance_withGET() throws IOException
{
  HttpConnection http = null;
  InputStream iStrm = null;
  boolean ret = false;

  // Data is passed at the end of url for GET
  String url =
   "http://www.mycgiserver.com/servlet/corej2me.GetNpostServlet"
    + "?" +
   "account=" + tfAcct.getString() + "&" +
   "password=" + tfPwd.getString();

  try
  {
    http = (HttpConnection) Connector.open(url);
```

(continued)

Example 4.3   (Continued)

```
    //---------------
    // Client Request
    //---------------
    // 1) Send request method
    http.setRequestMethod(HttpConnection.GET);
    // 2) Send header information - none
    // 3) Send body/data -  data is at the end of URL

    //---------------
    // Server Response
    //---------------
    iStrm = http.openInputStream();
    // Three steps are processed in this method call
    ret = processServerResponse(http, iStrm);
  }
  finally
  {
    // Clean up
    if (iStrm != null)
      iStrm.close();
    if (http != null)
      http.close();
  }

  // Process request failed, show alert
  if (ret == false)
    showAlert(errorMsg);
}

/*--------------------------------------------------
 * Access servlet using POST
 *--------------------------------------------------*/
private void lookupBalance_withPOST() throws IOException
{
  HttpConnection http = null;
  OutputStream oStrm = null;
  InputStream iStrm = null;
  boolean ret = false;

  // Data is passed as a separate stream for POST (below)
  String url =
    "http://www.mycgiserver.com/servlet/corej2me.GetNpostServlet";
```

(continued)

Example 4.3 *(Continued)*

```
try
{
  http = (HttpConnection) Connector.open(url);
  oStrm = http.openOutputStream();

  //----------------
  // Client Request
  //----------------
  // 1) Send request type
  http.setRequestMethod(HttpConnection.POST);

  // 2) Send header information. Required for POST to work!
  http.setRequestProperty("Content-Type",
          "application/x-www-form-urlencoded");

  // If you experience connection/IO problems, try
  // removing the comment from the following line
  //http.setRequestProperty("Connection", "close");

  // 3) Send data/body
  // Write account number
  byte data[] = ("account=" + tfAcct.getString()).getBytes();
  oStrm.write(data);
  // Write password
  data = ("&password=" + tfPwd.getString()).getBytes();
  oStrm.write(data);
  oStrm.flush();

  //----------------
  // Server Response
  //----------------
  iStrm = http.openInputStream();
  // Three steps are processed in this method call
  ret = processServerResponse(http, iStrm);
}
finally
{
  // Clean up
  if (iStrm != null)
    iStrm.close();
  if (oStrm != null)
    oStrm.close();
```

(continued)

Example 4.3   (Continued)

```
      if (http != null)
        http.close();
    }

    // Process request failed, show alert
    if (ret == false)
      showAlert(errorMsg);
}

 /*-------------------------------------------------
 * Process a response from a server
 *------------------------------------------------*/
 private boolean processServerResponse(HttpConnection http,
               InputStream iStrm) throws IOException
 {
   //Reset error message
   errorMsg = null;

   // 1) Get status Line
   if (http.getResponseCode() == HttpConnection.HTTP_OK)
   {
     // 2) Get header information - none

     // 3) Get body (data)
     int length = (int) http.getLength();
     String str;
     if (length != -1)
     {
       byte servletData[] = new byte[length];
       iStrm.read(servletData);
       str = new String(servletData);
     }
     else  // Length not available...
     {
       ByteArrayOutputStream bStrm = new ByteArrayOutputStream();

       int ch;
       while ((ch = iStrm.read()) != -1)
         bStrm.write(ch);

       str = new String(bStrm.toByteArray());
       bStrm.close();
     }
```

(continued)

Example 4.3 (Continued)

```java
        // Update the string item on the display
        siBalance.setText(str);
        return true;

    }
    else
        // Use message from the servlet
        errorMsg = new String( http.getResponseMessage());

    return false;
}

/*-------------------------------------------------
 * Show an Alert
 *-----------------------------------------------*/
private void showAlert(String msg)
{
    // Create Alert, use message returned from servlet
    alError = new Alert("Error", msg, null, AlertType.ERROR);

    // Set Alert to type Modal
    alError.setTimeout(Alert.FOREVER);

    // Display the Alert. Once dismissed, display the form
    display.setCurrent(alError, fmMain);
}
}
```

Note: You **do not** need to compile the servlet code to run this MIDlet.
The compiled code is online at the url specified in the MIDlet:

```
"http://www.mycgiserver.com/servlet/corej2me.GetNpostServlet"
```

```java
/*-------------------------------------------------
 * GetNpostServlet.java
 *
 * Show how GET and POST from client can access and
 * process the same data.
 * Account information is maintained in a database
 *   (connecting with jdbc)
 *
 * Table: acctInfo
 * Columns:
```

(continued)

Example 4.3   (Continued)

```
*    account    - integer
*    password   - varchar
*    balance    - integer
*-------------------------------------------------*/
package corej2me;

import java.util.*;
import java.io.*;
import javax.servlet.*;
import javax.servlet.http.*;
import java.sql.*;

public class GetNpostServlet extends HttpServlet
{
  protected void doGet(HttpServletRequest req,
                       HttpServletResponse res)
                       throws ServletException, IOException
  {
    // Same code appears in doPost()
    // Shown both places to emphasize that data is received thru
    // different means (environment variable vs stream),
    // yet processed the same inside the servlet
    String acct = req.getParameter("account"),
           pwd = req.getParameter("password");

    String balance = accountLookup(acct, pwd);

    if (balance == null)
    {
      res.sendError(res.SC_BAD_REQUEST,
           "Unable to locate account.");
      return;
    }

    res.setContentType("text/plain");
    PrintWriter out = res.getWriter();
    out.print(balance);
    out.close();
  }

  protected void doPost(HttpServletRequest req,
                        HttpServletResponse res)
                        throws ServletException, IOException
```

(continued)

Example 4.3 *(Continued)*

```java
{
  // Same code appears in doGet()
  // Shown both places to emphasize that data is received thru
  // different means (stream vs environment variable),
  // yet processed the same inside the servlet
  String acct = req.getParameter("account"),
         pwd = req.getParameter("password");

  String balance = accountLookup(acct, pwd);

  if (balance == null)
  {
    res.sendError(res.SC_BAD_REQUEST,
        "Unable to locate account.");
    return;
  }

  res.setContentType("text/plain");
  PrintWriter out = res.getWriter();
  out.print(balance);
  out.close();
}

/*-----------------------------------------------
 * Lookup bank account balance in database
 *-----------------------------------------------*/
private String accountLookup(String acct, String pwd)
{
  Connection con = null;
  Statement st = null;
  StringBuffer msgb = new StringBuffer("");

  try
  {
  // These will vary depending on your server/database
  Class.forName("sun.jdbc.odbc.JdbcOdbcDriver");
    con = DriverManager.getConnection("jdbc:odbc:acctInfo");

    Statement stmt = con.createStatement();
    ResultSet rs = stmt.executeQuery("Select balance from
        acctInfo where account = "
      + acct + "and password = '" + pwd + "'");
```

(continued)

Example 4.3 *(Continued)*

```
   if (rs.next())
     return rs.getString(1);
   else
     return null;
  }
  catch (Exception e)
  {
   return e.toString();
  }
}


/*-------------------------------------------------
* Information about servlet
*----------------------------------------------*/
public String getServletInfo()
{
  return "GetNpostServlet 1.0 - www.corej2me.com";
}
}
```

Session Management with Java Servlets

HTTP is a stateless protocol. A client makes a request and a server generates a response. There is no persistent connection between the two.[9] However, having a means for a server to recognize subsequent requests from a client opens the door to many possibilities.

The most familiar example is that of an online shopping cart. As you stroll through a store, selecting a few things on the way, somewhere on a remote server resides information about the products you've selected. When you are ready to make your purchase, just as in the "real-world," you take your shopping cart to the checkout counter and away you go.

Such interaction between a client and server can be accomplished only if the server can recognize requests as originating from the same client. With a Java servlet there are two common ways in which this is done: url-rewriting and cookies. The next two examples will demonstrate each concept.

---

[9]Although web servers may offer options to facilitate ongoing communication between a client and server, there is no persistent connection capability built into the HTTP protocol.

Figure 14–9 Left, the startup screen; right, total updated from servlet

Example: URL Rewriting

The gist of the next MIDlet is to keep track of golf scores on a remote server. We would like to enter the score for each hole, one by one. The server will keep a tally of the running total and report this back to the client after each score is entered. Figure 14–9 shows the initial screen on the left, before submitting the first score. The screen-shot on the right is the display after receiving a response from the servlet with the current total.

Figure 14–10 Updated total from servlet

Figure 14–11   Initial client request using GET

After submitting the score for the second hole, the servlet will update the total and report back to the client (see Figure 14–10).

The servlet can tally scores for any number of golfers. Therefore, it must have a means to correlate an incoming client score with the appropriate running total. On the server side, this concept is often referred to as session tracking.

Figure 14–11 illustrates the initial request from the MIDlet. Notice the request method is GET. We know this by looking at the data appended onto the URL. The key-value pair `score=3` is the score for the golfer's first hole.

The servlet will create a new session and a corresponding session ID to track requests from the client. The incoming URL (from the client) is modified to include the session ID. A header is sent to the client indicating this new "rewritten" URL. Also, the servlet sends the current running total for the golfer's score as the body of the response (which is score for the first hole only, at this point; see Figure 14–12).

The client will receive the response from the servlet and will check for a header indicating the URL has been rewritten. If found, all future requests will be made through this new URL.

Each subsequent request from the client, using the rewritten URL, makes it possible for the servlet to recognize who initiated the request. With the session ID in hand, the servlet maintains an ongoing dialog with the client

Figure 14–12   Servlet response

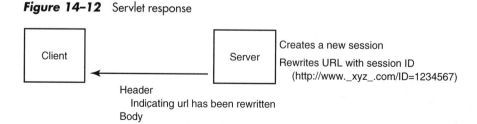

Figure 14–13 Client sends future requests using the rewritten URL

specifically, updating the running total of scores submitted. Figure 14–13 illustrates this idea. The client calls the servlet with the rewritten url (and the score for the next hole) and receives the total for all scores submitted in the body of the server response.

The client code for sending a request and processing a server response is shown here:

```
url = "http://www.mycgiserver.com/servlet/corej2me.Url_rewriteServlet";
...
private void updateTotal(String score) throws IOException
{
  HttpConnection http = null;
  InputStream iStrm = null;
  boolean ret = false;

  try
  {
    // When using GET, append data onto the url
    String completeURL = url + "?" + "score=" + score;

    http = (HttpConnection) Connector.open(completeURL);

    //-----------------
    // Client Request
    //-----------------
    // 1) Send request method
    http.setRequestMethod(HttpConnection.GET);
    // 2) Send header information - none
    // 3) Send body/data -  data is at the end of URL

    //---------------
    // Server Response
    //---------------
    iStrm = http.openInputStream();
```

```
    // 1) Get status Line - ignore for now
      System.out.println("Msg: " + http.getResponseMessage());
      System.out.println("Code: " + http.getResponseCode());

    // 2) Get header information
    // See if header includes a rewritten url
    // if yes, update url for all future servlet requests
    String URLwithID = http.getHeaderField("Custom-newURL");

    if (URLwithID != null)
      url = URLwithID;

  // 3) Get body/data - the new running total is returned
  String str;
  int length = (int) http.getLength();
  if (length != -1)
  {
    byte servletData[] = new byte[length];
    iStrm.read(servletData);
    str = new String(servletData);
  }
  else  // Length not available...
  {
    ByteArrayOutputStream bStrm = new ByteArrayOutputStream();

    int ch;
    while ((ch = iStrm.read()) != -1)
      bStrm.write(ch);

    str = new String(bStrm.toByteArray());
    bStrm.close();
  }

  // Update the stringitem that shows total
    siTotal.setText(str);
  }
  ...
}
```

The client request is short and sweet: Append the current score onto the URL and open the connection. In the response from the server, check for a header indicating a rewritten URL.

```
    String URLwithID =
          http.getHeaderField("Custom-newURL");
```

The header "Custom-newURL" is known as a custom header.[10] This header was created and sent from the servlet to indicate that the original URL has been modified. All future requests will go through this URL. The client also reads the body of the server response, which contains the current running total of all scores entered. This value is then shown on the display through the StringItem, siTotal.

Let's move to the code on the server side. There are two main concerns of the servlet: managing the session and updating the running total.

```
doGet(HttpServletRequest req, HttpServletResponse res)
{
  try
  {
    // Get session information
    HttpSession session = req.getSession(true);

    // If a new session, we need to rewrite the URL for client
    if (session.isNew())
    {
      // Get the URL that got us here
      String incomingURL = HttpUtils.getRequestURL(req).toString();

      // Encode by adding session ID onto URL
      String URLwithID = res.encodeURL(incomingURL);

      // Send back a header to client with new re-written URL
      res.setHeader("Custom-newURL", URLwithID);
    }
    ...
}
```

Fortunately, working with sessions from a developer point of view is very straightforward. Through a call to getSession() and isNew(), the servlet can determine if there is an existing session between itself and the client. If not, the incoming URL is rewritten (encoded) with the session ID and a custom header is created to notify the client.

The remainder of the code in doGet(), shown in Example 14.4, re-trieves the current running total for the session associated with the client, updates the total with the score the client sent and sends result back to the client.

---

[10]It is custom in the sense that it is not one of the defined headers in the HTTP specification.

Example 14.4   Url_rewrite.java

```java
/*--------------------------------------------------
 * Url_rewrite.java
 *
 * Use Java servlets sessions to tally golf scores.
 * Session management is done using url-rewriting.
 *--------------------------------------------------*/
import javax.microedition.midlet.*;
import javax.microedition.lcdui.*;
import javax.microedition.io.*;
import java.io.*;

public class Url_rewrite extends MIDlet implements CommandListener
{
  private Display display;      // Reference to display object
  private Form fmMain;          // The main form
  private TextField tfScore;    // Enter new score
  private int indxTextField;    // Index on of the textfield
  private StringItem siTotal;   // Running total
  private Command cmExit;       // A Command to exit the MIDlet
  private Command cmUpdate;     // Update score on servlet
  private int holeNumber = 1;   // Current hole
  private static final int MAX_HOLES = 18;
  private String url =
  "http://www.mycgiserver.com/servlet/corej2me.Url_rewriteServlet";

  public Url_rewrite()
  {
    display = Display.getDisplay(this);

    // Enter scores
    tfScore = new TextField("Enter score for Hole #1",
                            "", 2, TextField.NUMERIC);

    // Current running total
    siTotal = new StringItem("Total: ", "");

    // Commands
    cmExit = new Command("Exit", Command.EXIT, 1);
    cmUpdate = new Command("Send", Command.SCREEN,2);

    // Create Form, add components, listen for events
    fmMain = new Form("");
```

(continued)

Example 14.4   (*Continued*)

```
  // Save index of textfield, it is removed
  // after entering 18 values
  indxTextField = fmMain.append(tfScore);
  fmMain.append(siTotal);
  fmMain.addCommand(cmExit);
  fmMain.addCommand(cmUpdate);
  fmMain.setCommandListener(this);
}

public void startApp()
{
  display.setCurrent(fmMain);
}

public void pauseApp()
{ }

public void destroyApp(boolean unconditional)
{ }

/*-------------------------------------------------
 * Process events
 *-----------------------------------------------*/
public void commandAction(Command c, Displayable s)
{
  if (c == cmExit)
  {
    destroyApp(false);
    notifyDestroyed();
  }
  else if (c == cmUpdate)  // Send score for next hole
  {
    // If nothing in the text field or max scores entered
    if (tfScore.getString().equals("") ||
                holeNumber > MAX_HOLES)
      return;
    else
    {
      try
      {
        // Update the score on remote server
        updateTotal(tfScore.getString());
```

(*continued*)

Example 14.4   (Continued)

```
          // If entered the maximum, remove the
          // textfield from the form
          if (++holeNumber > MAX_HOLES)
          {
            fmMain.delete(indxTextField);
            return;
          }

          // Change the label   & reset contents
          tfScore.setLabel("Enter score for Hole #" +
                           holeNumber);
          tfScore.setString("");
        }
        catch (Exception e)
        {
          System.err.println("Msg: " + e.toString());
        }
      }
    }
}


/*----------------------------------------------------
 * Send client request. Receive server response
 *
 * Client: Send score for next hole.
 *
 * Server: Check for custom header 'Custom-newURL'
 *         If found, update the MIDlet URL for all
 *         future requests. Any data returned is
 *         current total for all scores entered.
 *----------------------------------------------------*/
private void updateTotal(String score) throws IOException
{
  HttpConnection http = null;
  InputStream iStrm = null;
  boolean ret = false;

  try
  {
    // When using GET, append data onto the url
    String completeURL = url + "?" + "score=" + score;
```

(continued)

Example 14.4   *(Continued)*

```
http = (HttpConnection) Connector.open(completeURL);

//----------------
// Client Request
//----------------
// 1) Send request method
http.setRequestMethod(HttpConnection.GET);
// 2) Send header information - none

// If you experience connection/IO problems, try
// removing the comment from the following line
//http.setRequestProperty("Connection", "close");

// 3) Send body/data -  data is at the end of URL

//----------------
// Server Response
//----------------
iStrm = http.openInputStream();

// 1) Get status Line - ignore for now
// System.out.println("Msg: " + http.getResponseMessage());
// System.out.println("Code: " + http.getResponseCode());

// 2) Get header information
// See if header includes a rewritten url
// if yes, update url for all future servlet requests
String URLwithID = http.getHeaderField("Custom-newURL");

if (URLwithID != null)
  url = URLwithID;

// 3) Get body/data - the new running total is returned
String str;
int length = (int) http.getLength();
if (length != -1)
{
  byte servletData[] = new byte[length];
  iStrm.read(servletData);
  str = new String(servletData);
}
else  // Length not available...
```

(continued)

Example 14.4   (Continued)

```
        {
          ByteArrayOutputStream bStrm = new ByteArrayOutputStream();

          int ch;
          while ((ch = iStrm.read()) != -1)
            bStrm.write(ch);

          str = new String(bStrm.toByteArray());
          bStrm.close();
         }

        // Update the stringitem that shows total
        siTotal.setText(str);
      }
      finally
      {
        // Clean up
        if (iStrm != null)
          iStrm.close();
        if (http != null)
          http.close();
      }
    }
  }
}
```

Note: You **do not** need to compile the servlet code to run this MIDlet. The compiled code is online at the url specified in the MIDlet:

```
   "http://www.mycgiserver.com/servlet/corej2me.Url_rewriteServlet"
```

```
/*--------------------------------------------------
 * Url_rewriteServlet.java
 *
 * Use url-rewriting to manage sessions.
 * Keeps a running total of golf scores for a
 * round of 18 holes (client sends score for each
 * hole, one at a time).
 *--------------------------------------------------*/

package corej2me; // Required for mycgiserver.com
```

(continued)

Example 14.4 *(Continued)*

```java
import java.util.*;
import java.io.*;
import javax.servlet.*;
import javax.servlet.http.*;

public class Url_rewriteServlet extends HttpServlet
{
  /*-------------------------------------------------
   * Initialize the servlet
   *-----------------------------------------------*/
  public void init(ServletConfig config) throws ServletException
  {
    super.init(config);
  }


  /*-------------------------------------------------
   * Handle a GET request from client
   *-----------------------------------------------*/
  protected void doGet(HttpServletRequest req,
                       HttpServletResponse res)
                       throws ServletException, IOException
  {
    try
    {
      // Get session information
      HttpSession session = req.getSession(true);

      // If a new session, we need to rewrite the URL for client
      if (session.isNew())
      {
        // Get the URL that got us here
        String incomingURL =
            HttpUtils.getRequestURL(req).toString();

        // Encode by adding session ID onto URL
        String URLwithID = res.encodeURL(incomingURL);

        // Send back a header to client with new re-written URL
        res.setHeader("Custom-newURL", URLwithID);
      }
```

(continued)

Example 14.4   *(Continued)*

```java
      // Get the next score (parameter) passed in
      int nextScore = Integer.parseInt(req.getParameter("score"));

      // Get the ongoing total saved as part of the session
      // Convert to an integer "object"
      Integer sessionTotal =
          (Integer) session.getValue("sessionTotal");

      // Running total from session and score passed in
      int runningTotal = nextScore;
      if (sessionTotal != null)
        runningTotal += sessionTotal.intValue();

      // Update the session total, must save as an "object"
      session.putValue("sessionTotal", new Integer(runningTotal));

      // Send back to client the new running total
      res.setContentType("text/plain");
      PrintWriter out = res.getWriter();
      out.write(Integer.toString(runningTotal));
      out.close();
    }
    catch (Exception e)
    {
      System.err.println("Msg: " + e.toString());
    }
  }

  /*--------------------------------------------------
   * Information about servlet
   *------------------------------------------------*/
  public String getServletInfo()
  {
    return "Url_rewriteServlet 1.0 - www.corej2me.com";
  }
}
```

Example: Cookies

I frequent one website to catch up on news, check the value of my investments and see the current weather forecast. As long as I access the site from the same computer, I never need to log on, yet the site brings up information that I have previously set as my preferences (news and weather for my hometown, stocks that I have invested in, etc.).

How is such an interaction accomplished? Typically it's done through the use of a cookie. Let's walk through a hypothetical scenario:

- You visit a website and set your preferences.
- The web server stores your preferences in a database on the server.
- A cookie is sent to your browser containing the row number in the database where your preferences are stored.
- The browser stores the cookie on your local file system.
- When returning to the same site, your browser sends the cookie with the unique row number to the web server.
- The web server queries the database using the row number, compiles information based on your preferences and sends the results to your browser.

Although this interaction is simplified, such a scenario may be one means for a website to provide a custom interface.

HTTP State Management Mechanism

You can read the specifics of state management using cookies by following this link:

HTTP State Management Mechanism
`http://www.ietf.org/rfc/rfc2109.txt`

In its broadest definition a cookie is a key-value pair, as in `ID=1234567`. There are a number of optional parameters that may by sent as part of a cookie (such as how long to store the cookie on the client), but for our needs this definition will be adequate.

Let's write an example that allows a server (more specifically, a Java servlet) to uniquely identify a MIDlet (the client) using a cookie.

Upon receiving the first request from the client, the servlet will create a unique ID. This ID, along with the current date, will be stored in a database (more on this in a moment). The servlet will send to the client a header containing the ID. To keep a reference to the ID, the client will write this value to persistent storage and this ID will act as the cookie (see Figure 14–14).

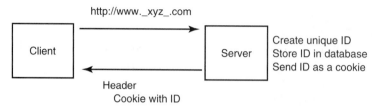

Figure 14-14   Initial request from client to server

Each subsequent request from the client to the servlet will be accompanied by a header with the cookie that uniquely identifies the client. To verify that the client has been identified by the servlet, the servlet will look up the client ID in a database, retrieve the date the client visited (last access date)

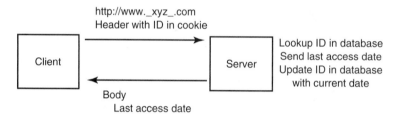

Figure 14-15   All subsequent requests from client will send cookie (ID) in the header

and return this as the body to the client. The client will in turn display the date on the device.

In Figure 14–16, the client displays the unique ID generated by the servlet upon the client's first visit. With each subsequent visit, the ID is passed to the

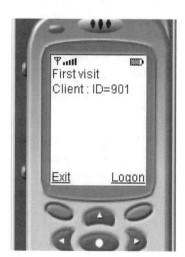

Figure 14-16   First visit to the server. Displayed is the unique client ID generated by the servlet.

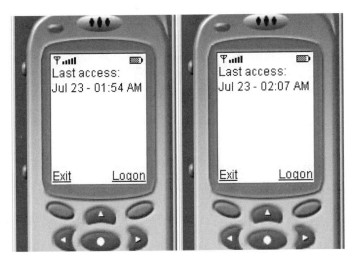

Figure 14–17 Client accessing the servlet at two different times

servlet and the last visit date is retrieved from the database and returned to the client. Figure 14–17 shows the client display for two additional visits.

Client Implementation

Whenever the MIDlet is started, the method readCookie() is called to try and locate the cookie (client ID) in persistent storage. This is analogous to your web browser looking for a cookie on the file system. If a record is found, the contents are stored in the variable cookie. If not, the variable will have a value of null (the latter is true the first time the MIDlet is run, prior to connecting with the servlet).

```
public void readCookie()
{
  ...
  if (rs.getNumRecords() > 0)
  {
    // Only one record will ever be written, safe to use '1'
    if (rs.getRecordSize(1) > recData.length)
      recData = new byte[rs.getRecordSize(1)];

    len = rs.getRecord(1, recData, 0);

    cookie = new String(recData);
  }
}
  ...
}
```

The method connect() will be called when the user selects "Logon" (see Figure 14–16). The client request is created with the request method GET.[11] If a cookie has been read from persistent storage (which won't be the case on the first call to the servlet), a header is sent with the contents of the cookie.

```
private void connect() throws IOException
{
  ...
  try
  {
    // Create the connection
    http = (HttpConnection) Connector.open(url);

    //----------------
    // Client Request
    //----------------
    // 1) Send request method
    http.setRequestMethod(HttpConnection.GET);

    // 2) Send header information
    if (cookie != null)
      http.setRequestProperty("cookie", cookie);

    // 3) Send body/data - No data for this request
  ...
}
```

Upon receiving a response from the servlet, the client will look for a header with the key set-cookie.[12] If a cookie was received, this is the first contact with the servlet, and the value of the cookie is the unique ID the servlet created for the client. The client will store this value in persistent storage and sets the variable cookie equal to that same value.

```
//----------------
// Server Response
//----------------
// 1) Get status Line
if (http.getResponseCode() == HttpConnection.HTTP_OK)
{
  // 2) Get header information
  String tmpCookie = http.getHeaderField("set-cookie");
```

---

[11]This could be done using POST as well. It sounds like a good exercise.

[12]The set-cookie header sent from a server must not exceed 256 bytes for MIDP devices.

```
// Cookie will only be sent back from server only if
// client (us) did not send a cookie in the first place.
// If a cookie is returned, we need to save it to rms
if (tmpCookie != null)
{
  writeRecord(tmpCookie);

  // Update the MIDlet cookie variable
  cookie = tmpCookie;

  fmMain.append("First visit\n");
  fmMain.append("Client : " + cookie + "\n");
}
else  // No cookie sent from server
{
  // 3) Get data, which is the last time of access
  iStrm = http.openInputStream();
  int length = (int) http.getLength();
  String str;
  if (length != -1)
  {
    byte serverData[] = new byte[length];
    iStrm.read(serverData);
    str = new String(serverData);
  }
  else  // Length not available...
  {
    bStrm = new ByteArrayOutputStream();

    int ch;
    while ((ch = iStrm.read()) != -1)
      bStrm.write(ch);

    str = new String(bStrm.toByteArray());
  }

  // Append data to the form
  fmMain.append("Last access:\n" + str + "\n");
  }
}
```

The next request from the client to the servlet will include the cookie that has the client's unique ID. Upon receiving the client request, the servlet will locate the ID in a database and return the date of the client's last visit. The client code to read and display the last visit data from the servlet is shown in the preceding code in step 3.

The reason for saving and displaying the last access date is only to verify that the client is being recognized by the servlet. You could extend this idea to save whatever would be appropriate for your application. For example, an online game may make use of cookies to associate a client (an individual playing the game) with a score stored in a database.

Server Implementation

The core functionality provided by the servlet is in doGet(). The first request from the client will not contain a cookie. In this case the servlet will create a unique ID for the client (more on this in a moment), get the current date and write both values to the database. A cookie will also be created that contains the ID and will be sent as part of the header in response to the client.

```
void doGet(HttpServletRequest req, HttpServletResponse res)
{
  // Get cookie from the header
  Cookie[] cookies = req.getCookies();

  //----------------------------------------------
  // If cookie passed in...
  // 1) Lookup the client ID in the database
  //    and save the last access date
  // 2) Update the last access date in database
  // 3) Return to the client date from step 1
  //----------------------------------------------
  if (cookies.length != 0)
  {
    // There will be only one cookie
    Cookie theCookie = cookies[0];
    String id = theCookie.getValue();

    // Lookup client ID and get last access date
    String strLastAccess =
      lookupLastAccessDate(Integer.parseInt(id));

    // Update database with current date
    updateLastAccessDate(Integer.parseInt(id));

    // Send back the last access date to the client
    res.setContentType("text/plain");
    PrintWriter out = res.getWriter();
```

```
   out.print(strLastAccess);
   out.close();
}
else   // No Cookie
{
   //-------------------------------------------
   // Generate a client ID. To keep the database
   // from growing out of control, this will not
   // generate a new ID for each client.
   // Instead, grab a random ID from the array
   // clientID's[]. The end result is the same
   // as far as the client is concerned.
   //-------------------------------------------

   // Random value between 0 and the number of
   // entries in the client list array
   int random = (int) Math.round(clientIDs.length *
                                  Math.random());

   // Get the client ID to send in the cookie
   int ID = clientIDs[random];

   // Update database with current date
   updateLastAccessDate(ID);

   // Create new cookie and send ID in the header
   Cookie cookie = new Cookie("ID", Integer.toString(ID));
   res.addCookie(cookie);
   }
}
```

Servlet methods

The method doGet() is called when a client sends a request method of GET. doPost() is called when a client sends a request method of POST.

Subsequent requests from the client will be accompanied by the cookie. Using the ID of the cookie lookupLastAccessDate() will search the database for the client ID.

```
String strLastAccess = lookupLastAccessDate(Integer.parseInt(id));
```

If a match is found, the last access date will be returned to the client.

```
res.setContentType("text/plain");
PrintWriter out = res.getWriter();
out.print(strLastAccess);
```

Here is the format of the database, clientInfo, used by the servlet.

clientID (integer)	LastAccess (varchar)
123	
456	
789	
225	
701	
901	

To keep the database from growing out of control, a row will not be inserted for each new client request. Instead, the database will have six unique IDs, and accordingly, six rows. When a new client request is received, the ID generated for the client will be pulled from a "pool" of IDs, which are stored in the array clientIDs[].

In a production environment this approach would be unacceptable. However, for our needs to test the interaction between the client and server, this implementation will suffice.

The code to search and update the database is included in Example 14.5.

Example 14.5   Cookie.java

```
/*---------------------------------------------------
* Cookie.java
*
* Pass a cookie (stored in rms) between the MIDlet
* and a Java servlet. The cookie is generated
* by the servlet on the first visit.
*---------------------------------------------------*/
import javax.microedition.midlet.*;
import javax.microedition.lcdui.*;
import javax.microedition.rms.*;
import javax.microedition.io.*;
import java.io.*;
```

(continued)

Example 14.5 *(Continued)*

```java
public class Cookie extends MIDlet implements CommandListener
{
  private Display display;
  private TextBox tbMain;
  private Form fmMain;
  private Command cmExit;
  private Command cmLogon;
  private String cookie = null;
  private RecordStore rs = null;
  static final String REC_STORE = "rms_cookie";
  private String url =
    "http://www.mycgiserver.com/servlet/corej2me.CookieServlet";

  public Cookie()
  {
    display = Display.getDisplay(this);

    // Create commands
    cmExit = new Command("Exit", Command.EXIT, 1);
    cmLogon = new Command("Logon", Command.SCREEN, 2);

    // Create the form, add commands, listen for events
    fmMain = new Form("");
    fmMain.addCommand(cmExit);
    fmMain.addCommand(cmLogon);
    fmMain.setCommandListener(this);

    // Read cookie if available
    openRecStore();
    readCookie();

    // System.out.println("Client cookie: " + cookie);
  }

  public void startApp()
  {
    display.setCurrent(fmMain);
  }

  public void pauseApp()
  { }
```

(continued)

Example 14.5 *(Continued)*

```java
public void destroyApp(boolean unconditional)
{
  closeRecStore();  // Close record store
}

public void openRecStore()
{
  try
  {
    // The second parameter indicates that the record store
    // should be created if it does not exist
    rs = RecordStore.openRecordStore(REC_STORE, true);
  }
  catch (Exception e)
  {
    db("open " + e.toString());
  }
}

public void closeRecStore()
{
  try
  {
    rs.closeRecordStore();
  }
  catch (Exception e)
  {
    db("close " + e.toString());
  }
}

/*----------------------------------------------------
 * Write cookie to rms
 *--------------------------------------------------*/
public void writeRecord(String str)
{
  byte[] rec = str.getBytes();

  try
  {
    rs.addRecord(rec, 0, rec.length);
  }
  catch (Exception e)
```

(continued)

Example 14.5 *(Continued)*

```
    {
      db("write " + e.toString());
    }
  }


  /*-------------------------------------------------
   * Read cookie from rms
   *---------------------------------------------*/
  public void readCookie()
  {
    try
    {
      byte[] recData = new byte[25];
      int len;

      if (rs.getNumRecords() > 0)
      {
        // Only one record will ever be written, safe to use '1'
        if (rs.getRecordSize(1) > recData.length)
          recData = new byte[rs.getRecordSize(1)];

        len = rs.getRecord(1, recData, 0);

        cookie = new String(recData);
      }
    }
    catch (Exception e)
    {
      db("read " + e.toString());
    }
  }


  /*-------------------------------------------------
   * Send client request and recieve server response
   *
   * Client: If cookie exists, send it to the server
   *
   * Server: If cookie is sent back, this is the
   *         clients first request to the server. In
   *         that case, save the cookie. If no cookie
   *         sent, display server body (which indicates
   *         the last time the MIDlet contacted server).
   *---------------------------------------------*/
```

(continued)

Example 14.5   (Continued)

```java
private void connect() throws IOException
{
  InputStream iStrm = null;
  ByteArrayOutputStream bStrm = null;
  HttpConnection http = null;

  try
  {
    // Create the connection
    http = (HttpConnection) Connector.open(url);

    //----------------
    // Client Request
    //----------------
    // 1) Send request method
    http.setRequestMethod(HttpConnection.GET);

    // If you experience connection/IO problems, try
    // removing the comment from the following line
    //http.setRequestProperty("Connection", "close");

    // 2) Send header information
    if (cookie != null)
      http.setRequestProperty("cookie", cookie);

      // System.out.println("Client cookie: " + cookie);

    // 3) Send body/data - No data for this request

    //----------------
    // Server Response
    //----------------
    // 1) Get status Line
    if (http.getResponseCode() == HttpConnection.HTTP_OK)
    {
      // 2) Get header information
      String tmpCookie = http.getHeaderField("set-cookie");

      // System.out.println("server cookie: " + tmpCookie);

      // Cookie will only be sent back from server only if
      // client (us) did not send a cookie in the first place.
      // If a cookie is returned, we need to save it to rms
      if (tmpCookie != null)
```

(continued)

Example 14.5 *(Continued)*

```
    {
      writeRecord(tmpCookie);

      // Update the MIDlet cookie variable
      cookie = tmpCookie;

      fmMain.append("First visit\n");
      fmMain.append("Client : " + cookie + "\n");
    }
    else  // No cookie sent from server
    {
      // 3) Get data, which is the last time of access
      iStrm = http.openInputStream();
      int length = (int) http.getLength();
      String str;
      if (length != -1)
      {
        byte serverData[] = new byte[length];
        iStrm.read(serverData);
        str = new String(serverData);
      }
      else  // Length not available...
      {
        bStrm = new ByteArrayOutputStream();

        int ch;
        while ((ch = iStrm.read()) != -1)
          bStrm.write(ch);

        str = new String(bStrm.toByteArray());
      }

      // Append data to the form
      fmMain.append("Last access:\n" + str + "\n");
    }
  }
}
finally
{
  // Clean up
  if (iStrm != null)
    iStrm.close();
```

(continued)

Example 14.5   (Continued)

```
          if (bStrm != null)
            bStrm.close();
          if (http != null)
            http.close();
      }
  }

  /*-------------------------------------------------
   * Process events
   *-----------------------------------------------*/
  public void commandAction(Command c, Displayable s)
  {
    // If the Command button pressed was "Exit"
    if (c == cmExit)
    {
      destroyApp(false);
      notifyDestroyed();
    }
    else if (c == cmLogon)
    {
      try
      {
        // Logon to the servlet
        connect();
      }
      catch (Exception e)
      {
        db("connect " + e.toString());
      }
    }
  }

  /*-------------------------------------------------
   * Simple message to console for debug/errors
   * When used with Exceptions we should handle the
   * error in a more appropriate manner.
   *-----------------------------------------------*/
  private void db(String str)
  {
    System.err.println("Msg: " + str);
  }
}
```

(continued)

Example 14.5 (Continued)

Note: You **do not** need to compile the servlet code to run this MIDlet.
The compiled code is online at the url specified in the MIDlet:

" http://www.mycgiserver.com/servlet/corej2me.CookieServlet"

```java
/*-------------------------------------------------
 * CookieServlet.java
 *
 * Use a cookie to identify clients
 *------------------------------------------------*/
package corej2me; // Required for mycgiserver.com

import java.util.*;
import java.io.*;
import javax.servlet.*;
import javax.servlet.http.*;
import java.sql.*;
import java.text.*;

public class CookieServlet extends HttpServlet
{
  // Pool of client ID's
  private static int[] clientIDs = {123, 456, 789, 901, 225, 701};

  protected void doGet(HttpServletRequest req,
                       HttpServletResponse res)
                       throws ServletException, IOException
  {
    // Get cookie from the header
    Cookie[] cookies = req.getCookies();

    //-------------------------------------------
    // If cookie passed in...
    // 1) Lookup the client ID in the database
    //    and save the last access date
    // 2) Update the last access date in database
    // 3) Return to the client date from step 1
    //-------------------------------------------
    if (cookies.length != 0)
    {
      // There will be only one cookie
      Cookie theCookie = cookies[0];
      String id = theCookie.getValue();
```

(continued)

Example 14.5   *(Continued)*

```
        // Lookup client ID and get last access date
        String strLastAccess =
            lookupLastAccessDate(Integer.parseInt(id));

        // Update database with current date
        updateLastAccessDate(Integer.parseInt(id));

        // Send back the last access date to the client
        res.setContentType("text/plain");
        PrintWriter out = res.getWriter();
        out.print(strLastAccess);
        out.close();
    }
    else  // No Cookie
    {
      //-----------------------------------------
      // Generate a client ID. To keep the database
      // from growing out of control, this will not
      // generate a new ID for each client.
      // Instead, grab a random ID from the array
      // clientID's[]. The end result is the same
      // as far as the client is concerned.
      //-----------------------------------------

      // Random value between 0 and the number of
      // entries in the client list array
      int random = (int)
            Math.round(clientIDs.length * Math.random());

      // Get the client ID to send in the cookie
      int ID = clientIDs[random];

      // Update database with current date
      updateLastAccessDate(ID);

      // Create new cookie and send ID in the header
      Cookie cookie = new Cookie("ID", Integer.toString(ID));
      res.addCookie(cookie);
    }
}
```

(continued)

Example 14.5   *(Continued)*

```java
/*--------------------------------------------------
 * Update database with last access date for client ID
 *-------------------------------------------------*/
private void updateLastAccessDate(int ID)
{
  Connection con = null;
  Statement st = null;
  StringBuffer msgb = new StringBuffer("");

  try
  {
    // These will vary depending on your server/database
    Class.forName("sun.jdbc.odbc.JdbcOdbcDriver");
    con = DriverManager.getConnection("jdbc:odbc:acctInfo");

    Statement stmt = con.createStatement();

    // Create a date format
    SimpleDateFormat format =
        new SimpleDateFormat ("MMM dd - hh:mm aa");
    String strDate = format.format(new java.util.Date());

    ResultSet rs =
      stmt.executeQuery("UPDATE clientInfo set lastAccess = '" +
        strDate + "' where clientID = " + ID);
  }
  catch (Exception e)
  { }
}

/*--------------------------------------------------
 * Lookup the client ID in database and get the
 * last access date
 *-------------------------------------------------*/
private String lookupLastAccessDate(int id)
{
  Connection con = null;
  Statement st = null;
  StringBuffer msgb = new StringBuffer("");
```

(continued)

Example 14.5 *(Continued)*

```
try
{
  // These will vary depending on your server/database
  Class.forName("sun.jdbc.odbc.JdbcOdbcDriver");
  con = DriverManager.getConnection("jdbc:odbc:acctInfo");

  Statement stmt = con.createStatement();
  ResultSet rs =
    stmt.executeQuery("Select lastAccess from
                      clientInfo where clientID = " + id);

  if (rs.next())
    return rs.getString(1);
  else
    return null;
}
catch (Exception e)
{
  return e.toString();
}
}

/*--------------------------------------------------
 * Information about servlet
 *------------------------------------------------*/
public String getServletInfo()
{
  return "CookieServlet 1.0 - www.corej2me.com";
}
}
```

Example: Download Data in the Background

Each of the examples we've encountered up to this point have been received or transmitted minimal amounts of data. When downloading a file, for instance, we only had to wait a few seconds to see the results. Obviously, this won't always be the case.

If you intend to write MIDlets that communicate over a network it will be important to make the applications as responsive as possible. Put another way, if a user is sending or receiving information, they should ideally have the option to continue to use the application while the communication is completed in the background.

The last example for this chapter is a modification of the PNG viewer that we wrote earlier. In the first version of the MIDlet, once the download of the image was initiated, the application would simply wait for the download to complete. It almost appears as if the application has "locked up." The version that we will write in this section will download the image in a separate thread, leaving the application responsive to user .

Here's how the MIDlet works. The main interface is a textbox that accepts the URL of a PNG image (see the screen-shot on the left in Figure 14–18). Once *View* has been selected, an alert is shown indicating the download has begun (see Figure 14–18 on the right). The alert is not modal; instead, it will appear on the display for approximately 3 seconds.

After the alert has been displayed, the user will be returned to the textbox. Because the download is working through a separate thread, the user can move about, as indicated in the left screen-shot in Figure 14–19. Notice that I have deleted several characters in the textbox to show that the interface is responsive.

Once the download is complete, the thread notifies the MIDlet and an alert is displayed to indicate whether or not the download was successful (see the screen-shot on the right of Figure 14–19).

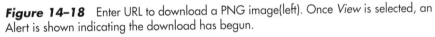

Figure 14–18 Enter URL to download a PNG image(left). Once *View* is selected, an Alert is shown indicating the download has begun.

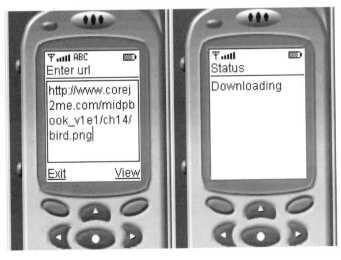

Figure 14–19 While waiting for the download, the TextBox is responsive to user input (left). Once complete, an Alert is shown.

If the download is successful, the image is displayed on a form (see Figure 14–20). Should the download fail, the user is once again returned to the textbox.

Figure 14–20 PNG image displayed on a Form

Example 14.6　ViewPngThread.java

```
/*-------------------------------------------------
* ViewPngThread.java
*
* Download and view a png file. The download is
* done in the background with a separate thread
*-------------------------------------------------*/
import javax.microedition.midlet.*;
import javax.microedition.lcdui.*;
import javax.microedition.io.*;
import java.io.*;

public class ViewPngThread extends MIDlet
                           implements CommandListener
{
  private Display display;
  private TextBox tbMain;
  private Alert alStatus;
  private Form fmViewPng;
  private Command cmExit;
  private Command cmView;
  private Command cmBack;
  private static final int ALERT_DISPLAY_TIME = 3000;
  Image im = null;

  public ViewPngThread()
  {
    display = Display.getDisplay(this);

    // Create the Main textbox with a maximum of 75 characters
    tbMain = new TextBox("Enter url",
     "http://www.corej2me.com/midpbook_v1e1/ch14/bird.png", 75, 0);

    // Create commands and add to textbox
    cmExit = new Command("Exit", Command.EXIT, 1);
    cmView = new Command("View", Command.SCREEN, 2);
    tbMain.addCommand(cmExit);
    tbMain.addCommand(cmView );

    // Set up a listener for textbox
    tbMain.setCommandListener(this);
```

(continued)

Example 14.6   (Continued)

```java
  // Create the form that will hold the png image
  fmViewPng = new Form("");

  // Create commands and add to form
  cmBack = new Command("Back", Command.BACK, 1);
  fmViewPng.addCommand(cmBack);

  // Set up a listener for form
  fmViewPng.setCommandListener(this);
}

public void startApp()
{
  display.setCurrent(tbMain);
}

public void pauseApp()
{ }

public void destroyApp(boolean unconditional)
{ }

/*----------------------------------------------------
 * Process events
 *--------------------------------------------------*/
public void commandAction(Command c, Displayable s)
{
  // If the Command button pressed was "Exit"
  if (c == cmExit)
  {
    destroyApp(false);
    notifyDestroyed();
  }
  else if (c == cmView)
  {
    // Show alert indicating we are starting a download.
    // This alert is NOT modal, it appears for
    // approximately 3 seconds (see ALERT_DISPLAY_TIME)
    showAlert("Downloading", false, tbMain);
```

(continued)

| Example 14.6 | *(Continued)* |

```
      // Create an instance of the class that will
      // download the file in a separate thread
      Download dl = new Download(tbMain.getString(), this);

      // Start the thread/download
      dl.start();
    }
    else if (c == cmBack)
    {
      display.setCurrent(tbMain);
    }
  }


  /*--------------------------------------------------
   * Called by the thread after attempting to download
   * an image. If the parameter is 'true' the download
   * was successful, and the image is shown on a form.
   * If  parameter is 'false' the download failed, and
   * the user is returned to the textbox.
   *
   * In either case, show an alert indicating the
   * the result of the download.
   *--------------------------------------------------*/
  public void showImage(boolean flag)
  {
    // Download failed...
    if (flag == false)
    {
      // Alert followed by the main textbox
      showAlert("Download Failure", true, tbMain);
    }
    else  // Successful download...
    {
      ImageItem ii = new ImageItem(null, im,
                          ImageItem.LAYOUT_DEFAULT, null);

      // If there is already an image, set (replace) it
      if (fmViewPng.size() != 0)
        fmViewPng.set(0, ii);
      else  // Append the image to the empty form
        fmViewPng.append(ii);
```

(continued)

Example 14.6   *(Continued)*

```
      // Alert followed by the form holding the image
      showAlert("Download Successful", true, fmViewPng);
    }
}

/*-------------------------------------------------
 * Show an alert with the parameters determining
 * the type (modal or not) and the displayable to
 * show after the alert is dismissed
 *-----------------------------------------------*/
public void showAlert(String msg, boolean modal,
                      Displayable displayable)
{
    // Create alert, add text, associate a sound
  alStatus = new Alert("Status", msg, null, AlertType.INFO);

    // Set the alert type
    if (modal)
      alStatus.setTimeout(Alert.FOREVER);
    else
      alStatus.setTimeout(ALERT_DISPLAY_TIME);

    // Show the alert, followed by the displayable
    display.setCurrent(alStatus, displayable);
  }
}

/*-------------------------------------------------
 * Class - Download
 *
 * Download an image file in a separate thread
 *-----------------------------------------------*/
class Download implements Runnable
{
  private String url;
  private ViewPngThread MIDlet;
  private boolean downloadSuccess = false;

  public Download(String url, ViewPngThread MIDlet)
  {
    this.url = url;
    this.MIDlet = MIDlet;
  }
```

(continued)

Example 14.6 *(Continued)*

```
/*---------------------------------------------------
* Download the image
*-------------------------------------------------*/
public void run()
{
  try
  {
    getImage(url);
  }
  catch (Exception e)
  {
    System.err.println("Msg: " + e.toString());
  }
}

/*---------------------------------------------------
* Create and start the new thread
*-------------------------------------------------*/
public void start()
{
  Thread thread = new Thread(this);
  try
  {
    thread.start();
  }
  catch (Exception e)
  {
  }
}

/*---------------------------------------------------
* Open connection and download png into a byte array.
*-------------------------------------------------*/
private void getImage(String url) throws IOException
{
  ContentConnection connection =
            (ContentConnection) Connector.open(url);
  InputStream iStrm = connection.openInputStream();
  ByteArrayOutputStream bStrm = null;
  Image im = null;
```

(continued)

Example 14.6   (Continued)

```
try
{
  // ContentConnection includes a length method
  byte imageData[];
  int length = (int) connection.getLength();
  if (length != -1)
  {
    imageData = new byte[length];

    // Read the png into an array
    iStrm.read(imageData);
  }
  else  // Length not available...
  {
    bStrm = new ByteArrayOutputStream();

    int ch;
    while ((ch = iStrm.read()) != -1)
      bStrm.write(ch);

    imageData = bStrm.toByteArray();
  }

  // Create the image from the byte array
  im = Image.createImage(imageData, 0, imageData.length);
}
finally
{
  // Clean up
  if (connection != null)
    connection.close();
  if (iStrm != null)
    iStrm.close();
  if (bStrm != null)
    bStrm.close();
}

// Return to the caller the status of the download
if (im == null)
  MIDlet.showImage(false);
else
```

(continued)

Example 14.6   *(Continued)*

```
  {
    MIDlet.im = im;
    MIDlet.showImage(true);
  }
  }
}
```

Begin by looking at the code in commandAction(). Once the user se-lects *View* we display an alert and create an instance of the class that will download the image. Before leaving, we begin the download by starting the thread.

```
...
else if (c == cmView)
{
  showAlert("Downloading", false, tbMain);

  // Create an instance of the class that will
  // download the file in a separate thread
  Download dl = new Download(tbMain.getString(), this);

  // Start the thread/download
  dl.start();
}
...
```

The code that downloads the image is basically the same code we've used before. All that's changed is that once the download has completed, we need to determine whether or not it was successful and return this status to the MIDlet. Here is a section of code from the method getImage().

```
  // Return to the caller the status of the download
  if (im == null)
    MIDlet.showImage(false);
  else
  {
    MIDlet.im = im;
    MIDlet.showImage(true);
  }
```

There are two remaining steps. First, show an alert indicating whether or not the download was successful. Second, if the download was successful display a form with the image; otherwise, return to the textbox.

These two steps are carried out over two methods: showImage() and showAlert(). The first method deciphers the result of the download and prepares a call to the second method. Notice in showImage() that if the download was successful an ImageItem is created and placed onto a form.

One more important point: the final parameter passed to showAlert() is the Displayable object to show once the alert is dismissed. In the case of a successful download the form fmViewPng, containing the image, is shown. For a failed download, the textbox tbMain is displayed.

```
public void showImage(boolean flag)
{
  if (flag == false)
  {
    // Alert followed by the main textbox
    showAlert("Download Failure", true, tbMain);
  }
  else  // Successful download...
  {
    ImageItem ii = new ImageItem(null, im,
        ImageItem.LAYOUT_DEFAULT, null);

    // If there is already an image, set (replace) it
    if (fmViewPng.size() != 0)
      fmViewPng.set(0, ii);
    else  // Append the image to the empty form
      fmViewPng.append(ii);

    // Alert followed by the form holding the image
    showAlert("Download Successful", true, fmViewPng);
  }
}
```

Inside showAlert() an alert component is constructed based on the parameters passed in. The last line of this method sets the current displayable to the alert, and once acknowledged by the user, the displayable becomes the value passed in from the method showImage().

```
public void showAlert(String msg, boolean modal,
                  Displayable displayable)
{
  // Create alert, add text, associate a sound
  alStatus = new Alert("Status", msg, null, AlertType.INFO);
```

```
  // Set the alert type
  if (modal)
    alStatus.setTimeout(Alert.FOREVER);
  else
    alStatus.setTimeout(ALERT_DISPLAY_TIME);

  // Show the alert, followed by the displayable
  display.setCurrent(alStatus, displayable);
}
```

MIDP FOR THE PALM OS

Topics in this Chapter

- Device Requirements
- Download
- Installation
- MIDlets
- Configuring Preferences
  - Advanced PRC Conversion
  - Developer (Debugging) Application
  - Palm OS Implementation

Chapter 15

Running MIDlets on a device with the Palm OS requires a few steps above and beyond what we've addressed up to this point. In a nutshell, the Java software must be installed and we need to convert a MIDlet(s) to the format understood by the Palm OS, a Pilot resource file (PRC).

A few thoughts before moving on. All information presented in this chapter pertains to "MIDP for Palm OS, Version 1.0." If you download a newer version, there may very well be changes to both the functionality, as well as the look and feel.

For the remainder of this chapter, when using the word "device" this will refer to any device running the Palm OS that has MIDP installed. If you don't have access to an actual device, see the sidebar "Palm OS Emulator." Any differences between a device and the emulator, in regard to installation or otherwise, will be noted throughout the chapter.

Palm APIs

There are no specific Palm APIs supported in MIDP for the Palm OS. Although this may seem to be an oversight, it is intentional. You must remember that MIDP is targeted to a wide range of mobile devices, from cellular phones to PDAs. If there was an API made available for any one device, such as the Palm, MIDlet(s) would not be portable across all devices that have a version of MIDP installed.

Throughout this chapter the word synchronization will refer to the process of transferring software from a computer to a device running the Palm OS and MIDP software. It is not important whether you use the Palm Desktop and HotSync or a third party application, as long as the end result is the same, that PRC files are successfully installed on the device.

Palm OS Emulator (POSE)

If you do not have a device that is running the Palm OS, but would like to write MIDlets for this platform, you can download the Palm OS Emulator (POSE):

http://www.palmos.com/dev/tech/tools/emulator/

The emulator can mimic various devices, including the Palm IIIc, which supports color. Alas, the emulator does not include a ROM image, which is the actual OS stored as a file. If you join the Palm Alliance Program, you can download various ROM images onto your computer and you are off and running:

http://www.palmos.com/alliance/join/

Because the emulator is running the actual OS that you'd find on a Palm device (or any device running the Palm OS), there are few differences that we need to concern ourselves with. Therefore, the remainder of this chapter will only differentiate between using an emulator versus a device when necessary.

Device Requirements

Before going any further, you need to verify that your device is running (emulator included) at least version 3.5 or above of the Palm OS. You can locate the version number by starting the Application Launcher, followed by tapping the Menu icon, each shown in Figure 15–1.

Once the menu appears, as shown on the left in Figure 15–2, select *Info*. From the information screen choose *Version*.

The version number will appear across the top of the display, as in Figure 15–3.

Figure 15–1 Application Launcher and Menu Icons

Figure 15–2 Select "Info" followed by "Version"

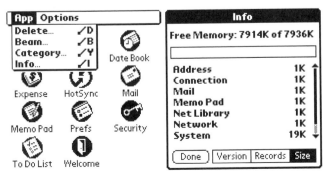

Figure 15–3 Palm OS version number

A few more stat's: The installed footprint of the Java Software is approximately 585 kilobytes, not including heap spaces requirements and memory consumed by a running MIDlet. It is recommended that your device has at least 4 megabytes of memory.

Download

You can download MIDP for the Palm OS from the following location:

`http://java.sun.com/products/midp4palm`

For Version 1.0, there were two separate downloads, one for the documentation, one for the program files.

I recommend you extract the entire contents of each file, which totals approximately 2 megabytes, onto a local drive off the root directory. From here forward, this will be referred to as the install directory.

The files consist of the MIDP implementation for the Palm OS, demo applications in both JAR/JAD and PRC formats, utilities to convert JAR/JAD files to PRC files, documentation, and of course, the obligatory license and copyright information.

Installation

The Java software for the Palm OS is referred to as Java HQ (in release 1.0). This software must be installed on the device before we can run MIDlets.

Installation of Java HQ is as simple as transferring the file `MIDP.prc` to the device. Locate this file in the install directory (`\PRCfiles`) and perform a synchronization to transfer the file.

Note for POSE

Right click on the emulator to bring up the options menu, see Figure 15–4. Select Install Application/Database, choose Other to locate `MIDP.prc`.

You can verify the installation by returning to the Applications Launcher, locating the *Java HQ* icon, and tapping it once. The About screen should appear as shown in Figure 15–5.

Figure 15–4 Right click on the emulator to bring up the options menu.

Figure 15–5 Application Launcher and Java HQ

MIDlets

This section will cover all aspects of working with MIDlets using the Palm OS. This includes converting MIDlet suites to Palm OS files, transferring MIDlets to a device, as well as running, beaming and removing MIDlets.

PRC Converter Tool

MIDlet's are typically distributed as a pair of files, a JAD and JAR, which comprise the "MIDlet suite." In order to run MIDlets on the Palm OS these files must be Converted to a Palm resource file (PRC).

The PRC Converter Tool is a Java Swing application that is started from a command prompt, by typing "converter" in the directory \Converter, lo-

---

JAVA_PATH

Before running the converter, you must have a reference to the location of a JDK or Java Runtime Environment (JRE) directory in the environment variable JAVA_PATH. For example:

```
JAVA_PATH=c:\jdk1.3.1
or
JAVA_PATH=c:\jre
```

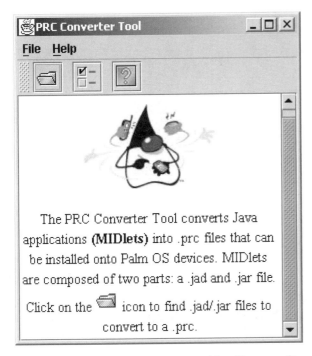

Figure 15–6 Program to convert jad/jar file to .prc file

cated off the install directory. Once up and running you'll see the screen shown in Figure 15–6.

You have the option to specify the output location of the PRC files. From the File menu choose *Preferences*, you'll see the screen shown in Figure 15–7.

Figure 15–7 Set location to store.prc files

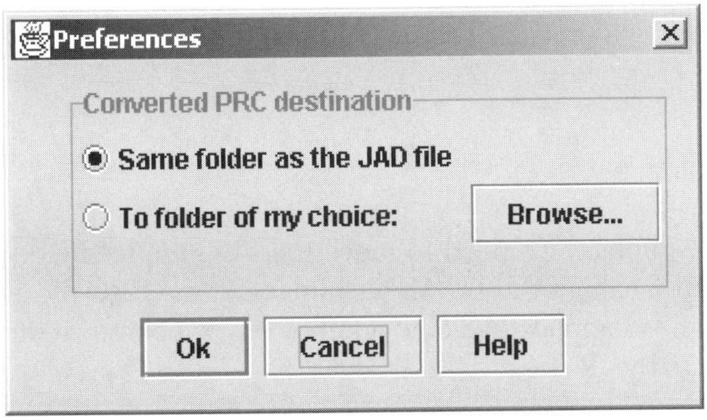

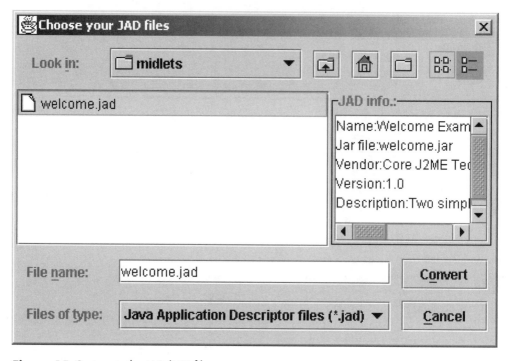

Figure 15–8 Locate the JAD/JAR file to convert

From here you can select to have PRC files written to the same location as the JAD/JAR files or specify a directory (folder) elsewhere to house the output.

To continue the conversion process, select the Folder icon or choose *Convert* from the File menu. In either case, the screen shown in Figure 15–8 will be displayed. Locate the JAD and JAR files you would like to convert (both must exist in the same directory). Select Convert to generate the PRC file. The original files will remain intact.

Install

Once the conversion is complete, we need to move the PRC file to the device. There is nothing special about this transfer: simply treat the PRC file as you would any other Palm OS application. Said another way, synchronize the file from your computer to the device.

Note for POSE

Right-click on the emulator to bring up the options menu. Select Install Application/Database *and choose* Other *to locate the PRC file to install.*

Run

A MIDlet is run on a Palm OS device in exactly the same manner as any other application. From the Application Launcher, tap the icon of the program.

Example: TodoList, Doodle and Translate

Let's install and run three examples that were created earlier in the book. The first example is from Chapter 12, the Todo List MIDlet. The original JAR and JAD files have been converted to a PRC file, which is located in the examples directory shown below:

```
\examples\ch15\TodoList\TodoList.prc
```

Creating the PRC file was as simple as pointing the PRC Converter Tool at `TodoList.jad` in the directory above. The second and third MIDlets are taken from examples in the Chapter 9, Doodle and Translate. I have combined these MIDlets into one suite. The resulting PRC file is in the following directory:

```
\examples\ch15\Graphics\Graphics.prc
```

Here are the steps to create the PRC file:

1. Create a new directory for the MIDlet files
2. Copy `bolt.png` from `\examples\ch9\Translate` to the new directory
3. Copy `Translate.class` and `TranslateCanvas.class` from `\examples\ch9\Translate` to the new directory
4. Copy `Doodle.class` and `DoodleCanvas.class` from `\examples\ch9\Doodle` to the new directory

5. Create a file `manifest.txt` with the following contents:
```
MIDlet-Name: Graphics
MIDlet-Version: 1.0.0
MIDlet-Vendor: Core J2ME Technology
MIDlet-1: Doodle, ,Doodle
MIDlet-2: Translate, ,Translate
MicroEdition-Profile: MIDP-1.0
MicroEdition-Configuration: CLDC-1.0
```

6. Create a file `Graphics.jad` with the following contents:
```
MIDlet-Name: Graphics
MIDlet-Version: 1.0.0
MIDlet-Vendor: Core J2ME Technology
MIDlet-1: Doodle, ,Doodle
MIDlet-2: Translate, ,Translate
MIDlet-Jar-URL: Graphics.jar
MIDlet-Jar-Size: 4578
```

7. Create a JAR file by running the Java archive application as follows:
```
jar cvfm Graphics.jar manifest.txt Doodle.class
        DoodleCanvas.class Translate.class
            TranslateCanvas.class bolt.png
```

8. Create the PRC file by pointing the PRC Converter Tool at the file `Graphics.jad`

Load both PRC files (`TodoList.prc` and `Graphics.prc`) onto your device by synchronizing, or for POSE, installing as we have done previously. From the Application Launcher locate the icons "Graphics" and "Todo List." You should see a display similar to the left screen-shot in Figure 15–9.

Figure 15–9 Install MIDlets, "Todo List" and "Graphics"; Application Launcher "Icon View" on left, "List View" on right

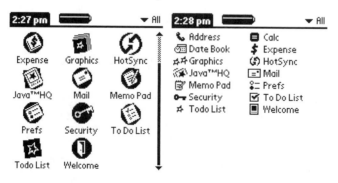

Example 15.1   Graphics.jad

```
MIDlet-Name: Graphics
MIDlet-Version: 1.0.0
MIDlet-Vendor: Core J2ME Technology
MIDlet-1: Doodle, ,Doodle
MIDlet-2: Translate, ,Translate
MIDlet-Jar-URL: Graphics.jar
MIDlet-Jar-Size: 4147
```

Example 15.2   TodoList.jad

```
MIDlet-Name: Todo List
MIDlet-Version: 1.0.0
MIDlet-Vendor: Core J2ME Technology
MIDlet-1: TodoList, ,TodoMIDlet
MIDlet-Jar-URL: TodoList.jar
MIDlet-Jar-Size: 9233
MIDlet-Data-Size: 1500
```

If you look closely at the left screen-shot in Figure 15–9 you'll see a slight difference in the icons that were created for each MIDLet: "Graphics" has what looks like several icons, one on top of the other. If we compare the application descriptor files, it should be clear why the icons appear as they do.

`Graphics.jad` contains two MIDlets within the suite, Doodle and Translate. `TodoList.jad` contains just one MIDlet. Java HQ provides one of two default application icons depending on the whether or not the suite contains one or more MIDlets. If the Application Launcher is switched to "View by List" a second set of default icons are shown for the MIDlets, see the right screen-shot in Figure 15–9. In the section "Advanced PRC Conversion" we'll introduce an additional means to convert a MIDlet to a PRC file where we can specify the icon(s) associate with the MIDlet.

Tap on the "Graphics" icon to open the MIDlet suite. Once running, you'll see a list of the MIDlets available, (see Figure 15–10). Choose the arrow next to the MIDlet you would like to run.

Because there is only one MIDlet in the `TodoList.jad` file, selecting the "Todo List" icon (from Figure 15–9) immediately launches the application (see Figure 15–11).

Figure 15-10 Multiple MIDlets within a suite; Doodle MIDlet running on the right

Figure 15-11 Todo List MIDlet

Remove

To remove a MIDlet suite, return to the Applications Launcher and tap the Menu icon. From the menu choose *Delete*, which will display a list of all the applications that you can remove (see Figure 15–12).

Figure 15-12 Removing an application

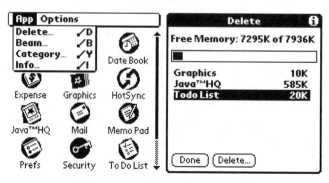

Figure 15-13 Confirmation before deleting an application

Once you choose an application there will be a screen to confirm your decision. After deletion, there is no going back (see Figure 15–13).

Beam

Devices running the Palm OS support transferring of information using an infrared port. If you are using an actual device, not the emulator, you can beam MIDlets from the Applications Launcher. Tap the Menu icon and choose *Beam.*

Note

Although you can beam MIDlet suites from one device to another, Java HQ is not "beamable."

Figure 15-14   Beaming applications

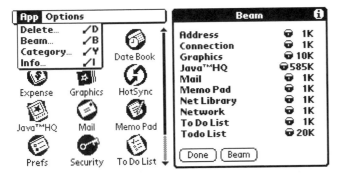

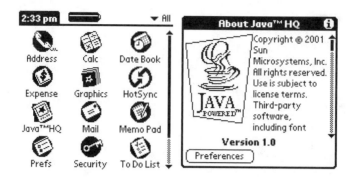

Figure 15-15   Configure preferences from "Java HQ"

Configuring Preferences

Preference settings are divided into two areas: Global and Application. There are two ways to access the dialog box for configuring preferences. First, from the Applications Launcher, select the *Java HQ* icon (see Figure 15–15).

You can also access the preferences dialog from any MIDlet that is running. Tap the Menu icon on the device, select the *Options* menu, and choose *Java Preferences* (see Figure 15–16).

There is an important distinction between the preferences you can configure based on where the dialog was invoked (see Figure 15–17).

When choosing to configure preferences from "Java HQ," you only have access to Global preferences. From within a MIDLet, you have an additional option to configure the preferences for that specific application.

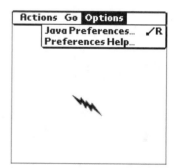

Figure 15-16   Configure preferences from within a MIDlet

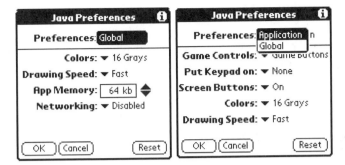

Figure 15–17 On the left, preferences from "Java HQ"; On the right, preferences from within a MIDlet

Global

There are four global configuration settings: Colors, Drawing Speed, Application Memory and Networking. Settings within this category apply to all MIDlets.

1. **Color**: The default setting will be determined based on the capability of the device. That is, if the device supports 16 grays, that will be the setting. You may opt to decrease the color setting below the default in an effort to increase application performance.

2. **Drawing Speed**: If you prefer drawing operations to be as smooth as possible, chose *Smooth*. If application speed is preferred over smoothness of drawing, choose *Fast*.

Figure 15–18 Global preferences

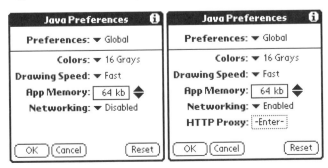

3. **App Memory:** You can tailor how much memory to set aside for applications. There is no rocket science in determining the default. It is based on the amount of memory installed on your device. If you choose to increase this value, applications may have more elbow room. However, there is a caveat: There is no guarantee the device will always be able to provide the amount you've requested.

4. **Networking:** There are two choices for networking: *disabled* and *enabled.* When choosing *enabled,* you can also specify an HTTP proxy (see the screen-shot on the right of Figure 15–18).

Confirming Preferences

When changing any preference from within a MIDlet, before leaving the dialog box, you have a choice as to when the changes will take effect.

    Restart: Shutdown and restart the application with the new preferences.

    Later: Return to the application. New preferences will be in place when restarting the application.

    Cancel: Ignore changes and return to the application.

Figure 15-19 Confirming changes

Application

There are five configuration settings that apply to applications: Game Controls, Put Keypad On, Screen Buttons, Colors and Drawing Speed (see left screen-shot in Figure 15–20).

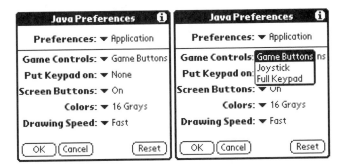

Figure 15–20 Application preferences

Game Controls

Three options are available for Game Controls, each listed on the right screen shot in Figure 15–20. It should be apparent that settings within this category are primarily intended for games. The idea is to provide a compatible means to manage the game actions (UP, DOWN, LEFT, RIGHT) defined in the Canvas class. If you need a review, head back to Chapter 9.

1. **Game Buttons:** With this option, the "traditional" keys/buttons on the device are used to generate events (see Figure 15–21).

Figure 15–21 Game controls and the "Game Buttons" setting

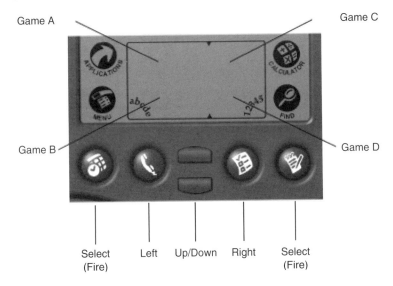

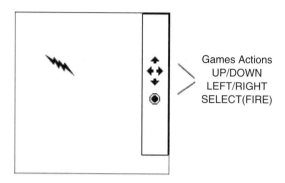

Figure 15–22   Game controls and the "Joystick" setting

2. **Joystick:** In place of using the keys defined on the device, this option displays directional arrows and "Select/Fire" button in a separate window. Figure 15–22 shows the MIDlet "Translate" (see Chapter 9, Example 9.9) running with the Joystick option.

3. **Full Keypad:** Setting the game control to "Full Keypad" will display a window that can generate all the game actions and key events that are supported for mobile devices. Figure 15–23 shows the "Translate" MIDlet with the keypad.

Put Keypad on

When the Game Control is set to either *Joystick* or *Full Keypad,* this option allows a choice between displaying the controls on the right or left.

Figure 15–23   Game controls and the "Full Keypad" setting

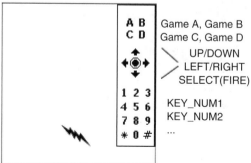

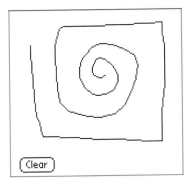

Figure 15–24 Screen buttons on

Screen Buttons

If a MIDlet is running short of screen real estate, setting this option to *Off* will remove all buttons from the display. Don't despair, all options will be available through the menu. Figure 15–24 shows the MIDlet "Doodle" (see Chapter 9, Example 9.3) with Screen Buttons set to *On*.

Figure 15–25 shows the clear command available in the menu when setting Screen Buttons to *Off*.

Colors

Choose the color preference. The default setting will be determined based on the capability of the device.

Figure 15–25 Screen buttons Off

Drawing Speed

Smooth drawing tends to be the preference for animation; however, drawing operations take more time. *Fast,* on the other hand, spends less time drawing, with the upshot that the animation is not as smooth.

Overriding Global Preferences

When setting values for *Colors* and *Drawing Speed* inside Application Preferences, these values will override the values of the same name in the Global Preferences. This allows you to tweak the settings for a specific application without affecting others.

Example: keyCodes and gameActions

In Chapter 9 we wrote two MIDlets to experiment with key codes and game actions. The MIDlets have been combined into one MIDlet suite and converted to the following Palm resource file:

`\examples\ch15\Events\Events.prc`

To get a feel for event handling with the Palm OS interface, give these MIDlets a spin.

Advanced PRC Conversion

Previously we used the PRC Converter Tool to convert a MIDlet(s) to a Palm resource file. Although the Converter Tool works fine, often times you will need more control over the contents of the generated resource file. For example, the Converter Tool does not allow you to specify a Palm creator ID, a sequence of four characters used to uniquely identify your application. As an additional example, you cannot specify the icon(s) the Palm we will use when displaying your application in the Application Launcher, instead, default application icons are created for you, see Figure 15–9.

Converting a Spotlet to a MIDlet

If you have a Spotless application that you would like to convert to a MIDlet, Chapter 3 of the Developer's Notes contains an abundance of information including event handling, user interface and database conversion. You can find the Developer's Notes document in the following directory of your MIDP for Palm OS installation:

```
\midp4palm1.0-docs\dev.pdf
```

Command-line Converter

MakeMIDPApp is a command-line PRC converter. It is a Java class file stored in Converter.jar, which is the same file that contains the classes for the PRC Converter Tool. Here is the command-line syntax to start the Command-line Converter:

```
java -cp Converter.jar com.sun.midp.palm.database.MakeMIDPApp
   [options] <jar file>
```

Here is an additional example specifying the full path to the JAR file:

```
java -cp c:\midp4palm1.0\Converter\Converter.jar
     com.sun.midp.palm.database.MakeMIDPApp [options] <jar file>
```

Following are the various command line options available:

- -help

  Display the command line syntax.

- -icon <file>

  This icon will be shown by the Application Manager when the "View by Icon" preference is chosen. The icon should be 32 × 32 pixels. For release 1.0 of MIDP of the Palm, only bitmaps that are black and white (1 bit) are supported. The available file formats are: .bmp (Windows bitmap); .pbm (Portable bitmap); .bin (Palm OS bitmap). See Example 15.4.

- -smallicon <file>

  This icon will be shown by the Application Manager when the "View by List" preference is chosen. The icon should be a

15 × 9 pixels. See −icon option for additional information. See Example 15.4.

- −name <name>

Name to display alongside the MIDlet in the Application Launcher. The maximum length should be in the range of 9 to 11 characters. If this parameter is not specified, the name created will be the MIDlet-Name attribute in the JAD file, or JAR manifest.

- −longname <name>

Full application name, displayed when deleting or beaming. The maximum length should be no more than 31 characters. If this parameter is not specified, the name created will be a combination of the MIDlet-Name and MIDlet-Vendor attributes in the JAD file, or JAR manifest.

- −creator <id>

All Palm applications have a creator ID. These four character names are used to uniquely identify an application. If you do not specify a creator ID, this conversion program (as does the PRC Converter Tool) will generate one for you, with a value in the range "VM00" to "VM99." Also, if you do not specify the creator ID, you must include the command line option −type data

Palm maintains an online database of creator ID's in which you can query/request ID's.

http://www.palmos.com/dev/tech/palmos/creatorid/

- −outfile <file> or −o <file>

The name of the PRC file to create. If you do not specify this option the resulting PRC file has the same name as the JAR file parameter on the command line, with a .prc extension. The one exception is if you specify the −jad option, as shown below.

- −jad <file>

The name of the application descriptor file to use during the conversion process. Information inside the JAD is used when creating a PRC file. If you specify this parameter, and do not specify the −outfile parameter, the resulting PRC file will have the filename passed into this parameter, with a .prc extension.

- -type <type>

   Represents the type of application being converted, valid parameters are: appl or data. The default, if this parameter is not specified, is appl.

- -verbose or -v

   Request additional information be displayed during the conversion process. Specifying the option twice (e.g. -v -v) requests all possible messages be displayed.

Let's look at several examples:

Example 15.3

```
java -cp Converter.jar com.sun.midp.palm.database.MakeMIDPApp -v
      -creator abcd TodoList.jar
```

Without specifying the -icon and -smallicon, the conversion process will create two default icons, as shown in Figure 15–9. The option -outfile was not specified, thus, the PRC file will have the same name as the JAR file, with a .prc extension, TodoList.PRC.

Example 15.4

```
java -cp Converter.jar com.sun.midp.palm.database.MakeMIDPApp -creator efgh
      -icon TodoLargeIcon.bmp -smallicon TodoSmallIcon.bmp -jad TodoList.jad
      -v -v TodoList.jar
```

We've specified the icons to display in the Application Launcher for both "View by Icon" and "View by List" see Figure 15–26. The option -outfile was not specified, thus, the PRC file will have the same name as the JAR file, with a .prc extension, TodoList.PRC. We have requested all messages be displayed during the conversion (-v -v).

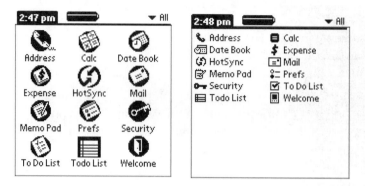

Figure 15–26   Custom icons for Todo List MIDlet

Example 15.5

```
java -cp Converter.jar com.sun.midp.palm.database.MakeMIDPApp
  -creator ijkl -name Todo -longname CoreJ2ME_Todo
  -icon TodoLargeIcon.bmp -smallicon TodoSmallIcon.bmp
  -outfile TodoMIDlet.prc -v -v TodoList.jar
```

In Figure 15–27 there are two icons for our Todo-List MIDlet. The icon (and associated MIDlet) with the name "Todo List" (bottom row) were created in Example 15.4. The name of the MIDlet was generated from the `MIDlet-Name` property in the JAD file. The name of the second icon "Todo" was specified using the –name option in this example. The PRC file created will have the name `TodoMIDlet.prc` (`-outfile` option).
The source code for Examples 15.4 and 15.5 can be found in the directory

```
\examples\ch15\Advanced_PRC_Conversion
```

Figure 15–27   Specifying the name to associate with a MIDlet icon

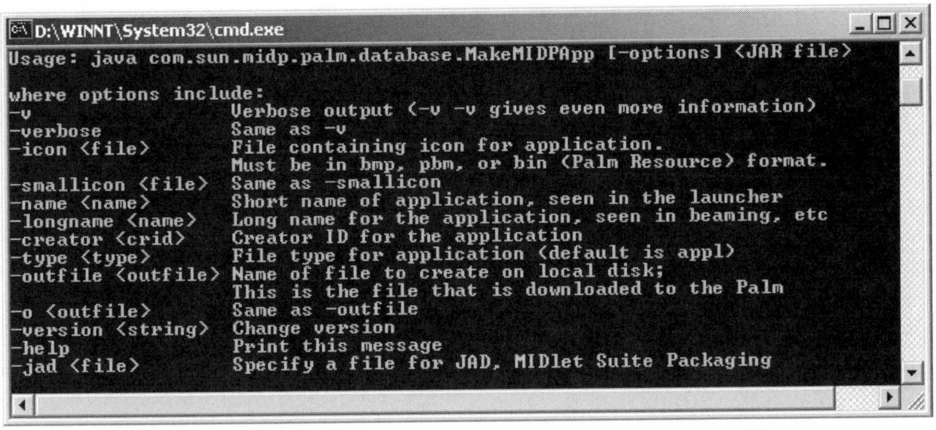

```
D:\WINNT\System32\cmd.exe                                      _ □ X
Usage: java com.sun.midp.palm.database.MakeMIDPApp [-options] <JAR file>

where options include:
-v                      Verbose output (-v -v gives even more information)
-verbose                Same as -v
-icon <file>            File containing icon for application.
                        Must be in bmp, pbm, or bin <Palm Resource> format.
-smallicon <file>       Same as -smallicon
-name <name>            Short name of application, seen in the launcher
-longname <name>        Long name for the application, seen in beaming, etc
-creator <crid>         Creator ID for the application
-type <type>            File type for application (default is appl)
-outfile <outfile>      Name of file to create on local disk;
                        This is the file that is downloaded to the Palm
-o <outfile>            Same as -outfile
-version <string>       Change version
-help                   Print this message
-jad <file>             Specify a file for JAD, MIDlet Suite Packaging
```

Figure 15–28   Command-line Converter options

Example 15.6

```
java -cp Converter.jar com.sun.midp.palm.database.MakeMIDPApp -help
```

Show help information about command line syntax, Figure 15–28.

Developer (Debugging) Application

In the process of writing, testing and debugging MIDlets there are often times when some additional insight may prove to be very helpful in tracking down problems. There is an application that accompanies MIDP for Palm OS download, `Developer.prc`, that provides access to information including memory usage and availability, messages written to `System.out` and `System.err`, and determining creator IDs for MIDlet(s) installed on a device.

Installation

Installation is as simple as transferring `Developer.prc` onto your device or emulator. The file is located in the directory `\PRCfiles`, off the install directory.

Once installed, to enable the developer application, tap on the Developer icon in the Application Launcher and choose "Show." See Figure 15–29.

Figure 15-29 Enabling the Developer Application

Features

We access the features of the Developer application through the *Preferences* dialog box. Here are the two routes to bring up the preferences screen:

1. From the Application Launcher, tap the *Java HQ* icon, select *Preferences.*
2. From within a running MIDlet, tap the *Menu* icon, select the *Options* menu and choose *Java Preferences.*

Regardless of how we access the preferences, there is an additional menu entry, *Developer.* There are three options available from within the *Developer* dialog box, *Heap Status, Save Output* and *MIDlets,* each explained below. The screen-shot on the left of Figure 15–30 shows the preferences

Figure 15-30 Preferences screen invoked from within a MIDlet; Developer preferences dialog box

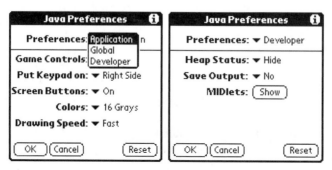

Figure 15–31 Heap space information

screen when accessed from within a running MIDlet. The right screen-shot shows the *Developer* preferences dialog.

Heap Status

There are two options, *Show* and *Hide*. Choosing *Show* informs Java HQ to display heap information upon loading a MIDlet or MIDlet suite. The total space available on the heap is shown, along with the largest chunk that can be returned in any one request, the requested size when starting the application and the actual amount returned. See Figure 15–31.

Save Output

When this option is set to *Yes*, all calls within a MIDlet to `System.out` and `System.err` are captured. Once enabled, there is an additional button ("Output") along the bottom of the *Developer* preferences dialog box, see the left screen-shot of Figure 15–32. On the right of Figure 15–32 are two application messages written to `System.out`.

Figure 15–32 Enabling "Save Output" on left; View output on right

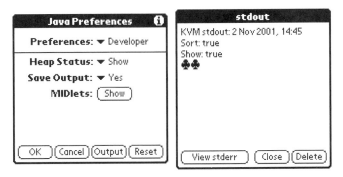

Figure 15–33 Creator ID's of
installed MIDlets

MIDlets

When you select this option, any MIDlet with a creator ID in the range VM00 to VM99 will be displayed. Any entry in this list represents a MIDlet that was automatically assigned a creator ID by either the PRC Converter Tool, or from the Command-line Converter, when not specifying the "-creator" option. See Figure 15–33

With the Developer Application installed, additional information about memory availability can be accessed when a MIDlet is active by tapping the Menu icon, selecting the *Options* menu and choosing *Memory Info*, see Figure 15–34. The following information is displayed:

rom—The size of the ROM image installed on the device.

ram—Total RAM on installed the device.

freeram—The amount of RAM that is available for use.

freeheap—Heap memory available for use.

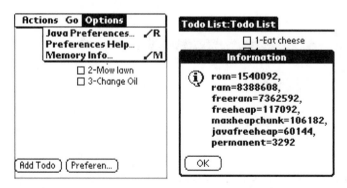

Figure 15–34 Memory information

maxheapchunk—The largest block of memory that can be allocated from *freeheap*.

javafreeheap—Java objects are allocated from this memory area. Indicates the amount available.

permanent—Memory used by the KVM.

Palm OS Implementation

There are a few details about the implementation of MIDP for the Palm OS that need clarification. Although the Palm OS implementation meets the requirements of MIDP, there is room for flexibility as far as how an implementation carries out the details set forth in the specification. This section provides a brief look at those areas that differ from the implementation of MIDP for mobile devices that we have seen previously. As you might guess, the majority of differences come down to cosmetic changes based on device display capabilities.

Command Types

The MIDP `Command` object provides a means for a MIDlet to interact with the user in a device-independent manner. As a developer, you define a `Command` and the implementation triggers an event through a soft-button or menu.

Each command that you define will have an entry in the Palm OS menu system. In addition, should there be too many commands to fit on a single menu, a dialog box will be created with a list of the remaining commands. To show how this looks on the Palm OS device, I created a MIDlet with a ridiculous number of commands as shown below:

```
cmExit = new Command("Exit", Command.EXIT, 1);
cmHelp = new Command("Help", Command.HELP, 1);
cmSave = new Command("Save", Command.SCREEN, 1);
cmX0 = new Command("X0", Command.SCREEN, 2);
...
cmX12 = new Command("X12", Command.SCREEN, 14);
```

The screen-shot on the left of Figure 15–35 shows several of the commands available along the bottom of the display. When tapping the Menu icon, the middle screen-shot in Figure 15–35 appears. Notice the option at

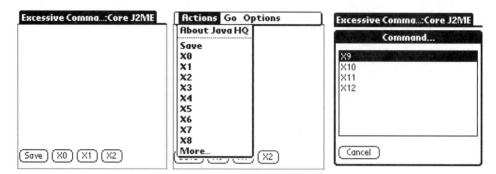

Figure 15–35 Handling more commands than the menu system will support

the bottom of the menu *"More..."* to view additional menu entries. The right screen shows a list of the commands that could not be displayed in the original menu.

The source code for MIDlet shown in Figure 15–35 can be found in the directory

```
\examples\ch15\ExcessiveCommands
```

If you refer to the middle screen-shot of Figure 15–35 you'll see that there are three options across the top of the Palm OS menu, *Actions, Go* and *Options*. MIDP places commands, based on their type into one of these three menus. The available types are listed in Table 15.1.

Table 15.1	Command Types - javax.microedition.lcdui.Command
Value	*Description*
BACK	A request to move to the previous screen
CANCEL	A request to cancel an operation.
EXIT	A request to exit the MIDlet
HELP	A request to display help information.
ITEM	A request to map the Command to an "item" on the screen.
OK	Specify positive acknowledgement from a user.
SCREEN	For Commands in which it is unlikely there will be a specific key mapping available.
STOP	A request to stop an operation.

Listed below are the Palm OS menu options and the Command types that are found within each entry.

Actions

```
ITEM
SCREEN
```

Go

```
BACK
OK
CANCEL
STOP
EXIT
```

Options

```
HELP
```

Figure 15–36 shows each of the following commands mapping into the appropriate Palm OS menu.

```
cmExit = new Command("Exit", Command.EXIT, 1);
cmHelp = new Command("Help", Command.HELP, 1);
cmSave = new Command("Save", Command.SCREEN, 1);
```

Notice that the command cmSave is also accessible on the display. All Command types, with the exception of HELP and EXIT, may be mapped to the display. If there are more commands defined than will fit on the display, commands are chosen based on their type, with the priority being: BACK, OK, CANCEL, STOP, SCREEN and ITEM.

The source code for the example shown in Figure 15–36 can be found in the directory \examples\ch15\CommandMapping

Choice Component

Although the ChoiceGroup component has a constructor and additional methods to support images alongside entries, the Palm OS does not support images in such a fashion, and accordingly, any images specified will be ignored. The right screen-shot in Figure 15–37 shows images alongside ChoiceGroup entries on a mobile device. The left screen-shot shows the same ChoiceGroup as displayed on a Palm OS device.

Figure 15-36   Command mapping

The source code for the example shown in Figure 15–37 can be found in the
directory \examples\ch15\ChoiceGroup.

Ticker Component

The Ticker component scrolls a text message along the top of the display.
If there is a title associated with the Screen component (that the Ticker
is "attached" to) the display area will be shared among the two.
Two additional features are available:

*   Tapping on the ticker will remove any title displayed, leaving
    the ticker to occupy the entire display width. Tapping a second

Figure 15-37   ChoiceGroup on Palm OS and mobile device

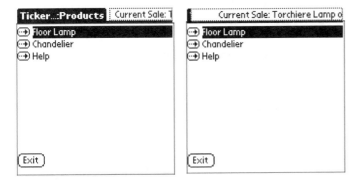

Figure 15–38 Ticker component with shared title area; Ticker (after one tap) occupying the entire screen width

time returns to the display that is shared between the title and `Ticker`. See Figure 15–38.

- The text message displayed on the `Ticker` can be dragged back and forth using the stylus.

When using a `Ticker` component with an `Alert`, the scrolling text appears as shown in Figures 15–39 and 15–40.

In Figure 15–40, notice the "count-down" timer showing how much time is remaining for the alert.

The source code for the examples shown in Figures 15–39 and 15–40 are in the directories `\examples\ch15\TickerModalAlert` and `examples\ch15\TickerNonModalAlert`.

Figure 15–39 Ticker with a modal Alert

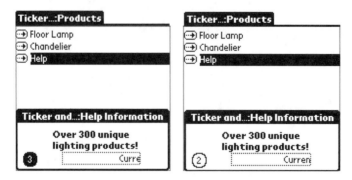

Figure 15-40   Ticker with a timed Alert

Additional Protocols

The Palm OS provides network capabilities that are not included within the MIDP specification. Following is an overview of the network options available.

inethttp / inethttps

MIDP for the Palm OS uses the Palm network library NetLib to provide the support for HTTP, as required by the MIDP specification. However, some devices (such as the Palm VII) may require use of the Palm network library INetLib to provide connection to the internet. To support devices that require the use of INetLib, MIDP for the Palm provides to support for two additional protocols, inethttp and inethttps.

Establishing a connection using either of these libraries works in an identical fashion to creating any other type of connection, the format is as follows:

```
Connector.open("protocol:address;parameters");
```

With the addition of inethttp and inethttps, MIDP for the Palm will recognize the following connection requests:

```
Connector.open("inethttp://www.some_web_address.com")
Connector.open("inethttps://www.some_web_address.com")
```

Here is a block of code that will test for the availability of the protocols and create a connection

```
boolean secureConnectionRequired = false;
HttpConnection http;
String URL = "www.some_web_address.com";

// Verify if the protocols are available
String protocol = System.getProperty("com.sun.midp.inethttp");
if ("true".equals(protocol))
{
  try
  {
    if (secureConnectionRequired)
      http = (HttpConnection) Connector.open("inethttps://" + URL);
    else
      http = (HttpConnection) Connector.open("inethttp://" + URL);
  }
  catch (Exception e)
  {
    System.out.println("Connection Error: " + e.toString());
  }
}
else
   System.out.println("inethttp and inethttps are not available");
```

The support for HTTP within the MIDP specification is quite comprehensive. Unfortunately, when using inethttp and/or inethttps there is no support for request headers (for example, Accept, Content-Type, Expires), and there is a limited set response headers available. In addition, any data sent through a request method of POST must be URL-encoded.

Sockets

There is one additional means of network communication from within a MIDlet running on MIDP for the Palm OS, a socket.

```
Connector.open("socket://www.some_web_address.com:80")
```

Reading and writing through this connection is accomplished using Input-Stream and OutputStream, respectively.

Note

inethttp, inethttps and sockets are not required protocols within MIDP 1.0. Use these classes with the caveat that MIDlets may not be portable to other MIDP devices.

Appendix A

![marble banner](marble texture)

Over the Air User Initiated Provisioning Recommended Practice

As a developer, our main interest lies with writing MIDlets. However, understanding the big picture is always a good idea. Thus an overview of the recommended procedure for transferring MIDlets from a server to a device is in order.

We'll begin with a baseline including definitions and general information. This will be followed by application discovery, MIDlet installation, upgrade and removal and reporting installation status. We'll include a brief summary of requirements for a server hosting MIDlets and will also briefly touch upon the provisioning considerations in a WAP environment.

The information will be divided into two broad sections—server and device (client)—with the great majority of information pertaining to the latter.

Before moving on, it's worth stating that the information presented in this chapter is derived from the document "Over the Air User Initiated Provisioning Recommended Practice"[1] version 1.0, which is an addendum to the MIDP.

---

[1]OTA—http://java.sun.com/products/midp/OTAProvisioning-1.0.pdf

General Information

Much of the information in this section has been covered previously. However, it bears repeating, if for no other reason then to serve as a quick refresher before using the terms as they apply to this provision.

A MIDlet suite refers to the JAD file and the JAR file that are used to package one or more MIDlets and any additional resources (such as images or application data).

The Application Management Software, also known as the Java Application Manager, is the software that implements the MIDP. It is responsible for all aspects of downloading, installing and running MIDlets on a device.

There are two attributes in the JAD file, above and beyond those in MIDP 1.0 specification (Table 3.2) that are introduced as part of this provision. *MIDlet-Install-Notify* will be presented in the section "Reporting Status to the Server" and *MIDlet-Delete-Confirm* will be discussed in the section "MIDlet Suite Removal."

Unless otherwise noted, all transfer of information between a device and server is through the HTTP protocol.[2] If a device does not directly support HTTP, there will need to be a gateway that converts the device protocol to HTTP prior to communicating with a server that hosts MIDlet suites.

Device (Client)

The majority of this provision deals with how a device interacts with a remote server to download, install and report status. Before any of these steps can be carried out, the device must first locate MIDlets suites available for download.

Application Discovery

Application discovery refers to the process of finding MIDlets to load onto a mobile device. The program that provides this service may be a custom application designed specifically for the device, or may be a more "generic" application such as a WAP browser. There are three basic concepts within application discovery:

---

[2]HTTP version 1.1 specification: http://www.ietf.org/rfc/rfc2616.txt

1. The ability to search or otherwise find information about MIDlet suites.

2. Initiate downloading of an application descriptor file (see Figure A–1).

3. Download the JAR file that contains the MIDlet(s) and any additional resources

Figure A–1 illustrates the idea of the discovery application communicating with various servers to locate and download application descriptor files. There is an important distinction here: The application descriptor and Java archive file are not necessarily on the same server. A device may browse JAD files on one server and download JAR's from another.

MIDlet Suite Installation

With an understanding of the big picture let's walk through each step in more detail. Before doing so, this is a good time to review various header

Figure A–1   Application discovery and downloading of MIDlets

fields defined in the HTTP protocol[3] that may accompany requests sent from a device to a server that hosts MIDlets.

Header Fields Sent from Device to Server

When a web server and client are communicating, the client needs a way to tell the server what it is requesting. In general, this is done through the URL. For example, a request to *http://www.corej2me.com/index.html* tells the server the client is interested in the contents of the file *index.html*.

Often times, the client would like to send additional information as part of the request; for example, the language (English, Spanish, etc.) the client prefers. Header fields are available to provide such additional information. The server response may also include header fields in its response. You can think of these fields as parameters—similar to the concept of calling a Java method, using parameters as a means to send additional information.

When sending a request for an application descriptor file, or MIDlet suite (JAR), there are several header fields that may be set by the device (client):

1. **Requesting Application Descriptor:**
   - `Accept=text/vnd.sun.j2me.app-descriptor` indicates the content type acceptable for the response is an application descriptor file sent as text
   - `Accept-Charset` can be used to specify preferred characters for the application descriptor information; for example, `Accept-Charset: UTF-8`
   - `Accept-Language` indicates the language preferred in the response; for example,
     `Accept-Language: en-US`
   - `User-Agent` contains information about the device sending the request; for example:
     `User-Agent: Profile/MIDP-1.0 Configuration/`
     `  CLDC-1.0`

2. **Requesting MIDlet (JAR):**
   - `Accept: application/java-archive` indicates a request for a Java archive file.

---

[3]Chapter 14 has an entire section devoted to explaining header fields as they apply to the client requests and server responses.

Obtain the Application Descriptor (JAD)

Before installation can begin, the device needs to download the application descriptor. This file contains attributes about the MIDlet suite, vendor and description, among others, and more importantly, requirements as they pertain to the size of the JAR and data storage required on the device. Example A.1 is a simple JAD file:

Example A.1   TodoList.jad

```
MIDlet-Name: Todo List
MIDlet-Version: 1.0.0
MIDlet-Vendor: Core J2ME Technology
MIDlet-1: Todo List, ,TodoMIDlet
MIDlet-Jar-URL: http://www.some_MIDLET_host.com/TodoList.jar
MIDlet-Jar-Size: 8288
MIDlet-Data-Size: 1500
MIDlet-Install-Notify: http://www.some_MIDLET_host.com
MIDlet-Delete-Confirm: "All todo items will be deleted."
```

If the device determines there is a discrepancy between the requirements as set forth in the application descriptor and the capabilities of the device, ideally the device would attempt to resolve the problem. For example, if the amount of persistent storage required by the MIDlet is more than the device can provide, an option would be to walk the user through various steps to remove or otherwise configure the device to free as much memory as necessary.

Important note

"If the response from the server includes a header field "set-cookie" *all subsequent requests to the server must include a header field* cookie *with the name-value pair(s) of the cookie received from the server.*

Download MIDlet Suite (JAR)

One of the required attributes in an application descriptor file is "`MIDlet-Jar-URL`." This attribute specifies the location of the JAR file that contains the MIDlet(s). Downloading of the suite is initiated by sending a request method of either GET or POST to the URL set in this attribute.

There are two special conditions that would warrant resending of a request. If the server responds with 401 (Unauthorized) or 407 (Proxy Authentication Required), the device should provide the user with the opportunity to enter additional information (such as a username and password) and resend the request.

Once again, if the server sent a "`set-cookie`" header, all subsequent requests must be accompanied by all name-value pairs in the cookie. Typically, such a cookie would be used by the server to uniquely identify the device. For general information about session management, see the section "Session Management with Java Servlets" in Chapter 14.

Reporting Status to the User

Upon successful download and installation, the device will make the MIDlet suite available through whatever means is appropriate for the implementation (e.g., through a menu, an icon on the display, etc.).

If one of the following errors occurs during download or upon validating the contents of the JAR file, the user must be notified and the system returned to the same state that existed prior to the download of the application descriptor.

- Device does not have sufficient memory to store the MIDlet suite (Code 901)
- Network error, such as a dropped connection (Code 903)
- Mismatch between the actual size of the downloaded JAR file and the size specified in the application descriptor file (JAD attribute: `MIDlet-Jar-Size`; Code 904)
- The required attributes `MIDlet-Name`, `MIDlet-Vendor`, `MIDlet-Version` in the manifest file (contained in the JAR) do not match the values in the application descriptor Code 905)

All installation status codes are listed in Table A.1.

Table A.1	Installation Status Codes

Code	Message
900	Successful
901	Insufficient memory
902	User cancelled
903	Loss of service
904	MIDlet suite size mismatch
905	Attribute mismatch
906	Invalid descriptor

Reporting Status to the Server

Once the installation is complete, which may occur as a result of a successful *or* failed/canceled installation, the host server should be notified.

There are two options for determining the destination URL to report status. If there is an attribute "MIDlet-Install-Notify" in the application descriptor file, the value of this attribute should be used as the destination URL. This attribute was added to the MIDP specification, through this provision, as a means for a provider of MIDlet suites to be notified when suites are downloaded and installed on a device. If this attribute is not available the status should be reported to the same URL from which the MIDlet JAR was downloaded—attribute MIDlet-Jar-URL in the JAD file.

If the device was sent a cookie when downloading either the application descriptor or the JAR, the cookie must be sent in the header field when reporting the status. The reason is, the cookie is most likely being used to uniquely identify the device on the server. Before sending the cookie, the device must verify that the URL specified in the attribute "MIDlet-Install-Notify" matches the combination of the domain and path set in the cookie. If the comparison fails, the cookie should not be sent.

Status information must be sent with a request method of POST. The first line in the body of the POST must include both a status code and its corresponding message. Valid responses are listed in Table A.1.

Once the status is received, the server may opt to send a response confirming receipt of the information. In the response there are only two pieces of information that are pertinent. First, there is a status code of "200 OK."

Second, if the device and server were passing a cookie back and forth as a final means to end the communication, the server should send a "set-cookie" header that includes the name-value pair "max-age=0." This will notify the device that the cookie should be immediately discarded.[4]

MIDlet Suite Upgrade

The device implementation is required to support upgrading of a MIDlet suite. There are several key concerns when performing an upgrade:

- If a user requests a suite that is already installed, the discovery application should inform the user with as much information as is relevant. For instance, installed versus upgraded version numbers, additional memory and/or persistent storage requirements, new features, and so forth. The user should be given the option to proceed or cancel.
- When appropriate, persistent data should remain intact.
- If it is detected that the original network (download) location of a currently installed suite does not match the location of a requested suite with the same name, the user should be notified. There is a chance that a MIDlet suite with the same attributes/name is available at more than one location.
- If the MIDlets are not related (i.e., one is not an upgrade to the other), but a different MIDlet altogether, instead of an upgrade being performed the original suite would be overwritten by a completely different set of code. In such a case, the user should intervene and decide if an upgrade should be performed, or if the currently installed MIDlet (and any persistent data) should be removed prior to installing the new suite.

---

[4]Specifics of state management with cookies can be found at: http://www.ietf.org/rfc/rfc2109.txt

MIDlet Suite Removal

Removing a MIDlet suite is straightforward. The device must remove the MIDlet suite, all record stores and any references to the suite (e.g., icons to start the suite, entries in a menu system, etc.). There are several important considerations:

- If there are multiple MIDlets in the suite, it should be made clear to the user that removing the suite will remove all MIDlets.
- If there are records in persistent storage, the user should be notified that all record stores will be removed.
- If the attribute "`MIDlet-Delete-Confirm`" is present in the application descriptor, the user should be prompted with a message that contains the value of this attribute. This attribute was added to the MIDP specification, through this provision, as a means to provide application-specific messages prior to deleting a suite. For instance, "Upon removing this application you will no longer have access to your online account information."

Server

The two most important features of a server that intends to distribute MIDlets is support for HTTP 1.1 and that the appropriate MIME types are configured. The former was covered in Chapter 14, so let's spend our time discussing MIME types and what is important as it relates to MIDlet suites.

MIME Types

MIME types are a platform-independent way for a server to notify a client about the content being transferred. For example, a web server can notify a browser that the content type being sent is HTML. The browser inherently knows how to parse HTML and render the output.

A web server determines the MIME type based on the extension of URL request. Looking up the extension in a mapping table, the server will notify the browser, through a header field, of the content type. A web server will typically have the following mapping, among others:

```
Extension              Content Type
.html .htm             text/html
```

If a browser were to send a request to *http://www.corej2me.com/index.html*, the server would look up the mapping for ".html" and would send the following header field to the browser:

```
"Content-Type=text/html"
```

To understand how a client determines what to do with the content type, you can look at the settings of your web browser. For example, in Netscape (4.x) choose the Edit menu, and select Preferences/Navigator/Applications. Here you'll find a list of mappings for your browser. Several of the settings for my configuration are shown here:

```
MIME Type:    application/java-archive
Handled by:   javaw

MIME Type:    text/html
Handled by:   netscape (internal)

MIME Type:    application/pdf
Handled by:   plugin
```

When a server sends the header field "Content-Type," the browser can make a determination what to do with the body of the response. For example, if I directed my browser to *http://www.corej2me.com/test.pdf* (assuming "test.pdf" is a valid file), the server response would include a header field "Content-Type=application/pdf." The browser will in turn recognize this content type (from the aforementioned list) and would start the plugin to view the pdf file.

What this boils down to for our needs is that a server that intends to host MIDlets should provide a means to return the following content types:

```
"Content Type: text/vnd.sun.j2me.app-descriptor"
"Content Type: application/java-archive"
```

This will generally be done in one of two ways:

1. Setting the following MIME types on the web server:

```
Extension    ContentType
.jad         text/vnd.sun.j2me.app-descriptor
.jar         application/java-archive
```

With this in place, when the server receives a request for a file with the extension ".jad" it will include the following header field as part of its response:

```
"Content-Type: text/vnd.sun.j2me.app-descriptor"
```

The same logic applies when requesting a ".jar" file.

2. Creating a custom application, accessed through a URL, such as a Java servlet, that recognizes the header fields:

```
"Accept: text/vnd.sun.j2me.app-descriptor"
"Accept: application/java-archive"
```

and returns the appropriate header field back to the device:

```
"Content-Type: text/vnd.sun.j2me.app-descriptor"
"Content-Type: application/java-archive"
```

Either way, with the content type information, the device knows the format of the incoming data and can process it accordingly. For example, if an application descriptor file is received, the device can then parse the file, line by line, reading the key-value pairs ("MIDlet-Name: xyz", "MIDlet-Version: 1.0.0", etc.).

WAP

A server that distributes MIDlet suites is required to support communication using the HTTP protocol, version 1.1. The interaction between a mobile device running MIDP and a server may be directly through HTTP, or if necessary, a gateway may exist between the device and the server to translate the device protocol to HTTP. Such may be the case for a device that uses a WAP browser for application discovery.

What is WAP?

The Wireless Application Protocol is a specification that provides a standard method to access content on the Internet from wireless devices. The following link is a good starting point to information about the WAP initiative:

http://www.wapforum.org

What's important is not the protocol that the device provides, but that the communication to a remote server, in the end, is through HTTP. If a translation occurs during this process, it is outside the scope of our interests as a developer. That is, the `HttpConnection` class is used for communication and any translation required is left to the device and the gateway.

For devices that provide a WAP browser, the implementation must be compatible with WAP 1.2.1 (June 2000 conformance release).[5] In addition, there are several requirements for both the device and gateway.

Device (client) requirements:

- Recognize and make the following header fields available to the discovery application and/or the Java application manager:

  ```
  Content-Type=text/vnd.sun.j2me.app-descriptor
  Content-Type=application/java-archive
  ```

- The server responses 401 (Unauthorized) and 407 (Proxy Authentication Required) must be dealt with appropriately. If you recall from the section "Download MIDlet Suite," a server that hosts a suite may respond with either of these codes. The device should provide an opportunity for the user to enter a username and password and resend the request.

- The device must be able send a request method of POST. This requirement stems from the fact that a status report sent to the server (that hosts the suite) must be through POST.

Gateway Requirements:

- It must relay the following header fields from the server to the device:

  ```
  Content-Type=text/vnd.sun.j2me.app-descriptor
  Content-Type=application/java-archive
  ```

- If user validation is necessary, responses 401 and 407 from the server must be passed to the device.

- The server header field "`set-cookie`" must be supported. This is typically used as a means for session management/tracking.

---

[5]WAP June 2000—http://www.wapforum.org/what/technical.htm

- If the device has set the header field "`Accept: */*`" the body of each server response must be passed to the device in its entirety.
- The device request method POST must be recognized and passed to the server.

Appendix B

CLDC API

ByteArrayInputStream

public class ByteArrayInputStream extends InputStream
Internal array of bytes that can be read as a stream

Fields

buf	Byte array passed in when created
count	Count of bytes in the array
mark	Current "marked" position in the array
pos	Index of the next character to be read

Constructors

ByteArrayInputStream(byte[] buf)	Create ByteArrayInputStream
ByteArrayInputStream(byte[] buf, int offset, int length)	Create ByteArrayInputStream

Methods

int **available**()	Bytes available before stream blocks
void **close**()	Closes stream and free resources
void **mark**(int readAheadLimit)	Set current position
boolean **markSupported**()	Is mark/reset supported?
int **read**()	Read next byte
int **read**(byte[] b, int off, int len)	Read bytes into an array
void **reset**()	Reset to the marked position (or beginning if no mark set)
long **skip**(long)	Skip over bytes in the stream

ByteArrayOutputStream

public class ByteArrayOutputStream extends OutputStream
Internal array of bytes (buffer) that can be written to as a stream; array grows as necessary

Fields

buf	Internal byte array to store data
count	Count of bytes in the array

(continued)

ByteArrayOutputStream   (Continued)

Constructors

ByteArrayOutputStream()	Create ByteArrayOutputStream
ByteArrayOutputStream(int size)	Create ByteArrayOutputStream, specifying initial size

Methods

void **close**()	Closes stream and free resources
void **reset**()	Toss any data in the buffer; new data is stored at beginning
int **size**()	Current size of buffer
byte[] **toByteArray**()	Convert buffer contents to an array of bytes
String **toString**()	Convert buffer contents to a string
void **write**(byte[] b, int off, int len)	Write bytes into the buffer
void **write**(int b)	Write byte into buffer

DataInput

public abstract interface DataInput
Interface for streams to read Java primitive types in platform independent manner

Methods

boolean **readBoolean**()	Read byte, nonzero value returns true, otherwise false
byte **readByte**()	Read byte
char **readChar**()	Read char
void **readFully**(byte[] b)	Read bytes into array. The number read equals the size of the array
void **readFully**(byte[] b, int off, int len)	Read bytes into array specifying offset and length
int **readInt**()	Read four bytes
long **readLong**()	Read eight bytes
short **readShort**()	Read two bytes
int **readUnsignedByte**()	Read one byte; return as an int between 0 and 255
int **readUnsignedShort**()	Read two bytes; return an int between 0 and 65535
String **readUTF**()	Read string that has been encoded as modified UTF-8
int **skipBytes**(int n)	Skip over bytes in the stream

DataInputStream

public class DataInputStream extends InputStream implements DataInput
Read Java primitive types as stream

Fields

in   Stream

Constructors

DataInputStream(InputStream in)   Create DataInputStream

Methods

int **available**()   Bytes available before stream blocks

void **close**()   Closes stream and free resources

void **mark**(int readlimit)   Set current position

boolean **markSupported**()   Is mark/reset supported?

int **read**()   Read byte, return as an integer between 0 and 255

int **read**(byte[] b)   Read into an array

int **read**(byte[] b, int off,
   int len)   Read into an array specifying offset and length

boolean **readBoolean**()   Read boolean

byte **readByte**()   Read byte

char **readChar**()   Read two bytes, return as Unicode character

void **readFully**(byte[] b)   Read bytes into array; the number read equals the size of the array

void **readFully**(byte[] b, int off,
   int len)   Read bytes into array specifying offset and length

int **readInt**()   Read four bytes

long **readLong**()   Read eight bytes

short **readShort**()   Read two bytes

int **readUnsignedByte**()   Read one byte; return as an int between 0 and 255

int **readUnsignedShort**()   Read two bytes; return an int between 0 and 65535

String **readUTF**()   Read string that has been encoded as modified UTF-8

String **readUTF**(DataInput in)   Read from the parameter "in" a string encoded as modified UTF-8

(continued)

DataInputStream   (*Continued*)

Methods (cont.)

void **reset**()	Reset stream to "marked" position
long **skip**(long n)	Skips over bytes in stream
int **skipBytes**(int n)	Skips over bytes in stream

DataOutput

public abstract interface DataOutput
Interface for streams to write Java primitive types in platform independent manner

Methods

void **write**(byte[] b)	Write array to stream
void **write**(byte[] b, int off, int len)	Write array to stream specifying the offset and length
void **write**(int b)	Write lower eight bits of integer to stream
void **writeBoolean**(boolean v)	Write boolean to the stream
void **writeByte**(int v)	Write lower eight bits of integer to stream
void **writeChar**(int v)	Write two bytes of integer parameter to stream
void **writeChars**(String s)	Write string to stream, two bytes for each character
void **writeInt**(int v)	Write integer as four bytes to the stream
void **writeLong**(long v)	Write long as four bytes to the stream
void **writeShort**(int v)	Write integer as two bytes to the stream
void **writeUTF**(String str)	Write String as UTF to the stream

DataOutputStream

public class DataOutputStream extends OutputStream implements DataOutput
Write Java primitive types to stream

Fields

out   Stream

Constructors

DataOutputStream(OutputStream out)   Create DataOutputStream

Methods

void **close**()	Closes stream and free resources
void **flush**()	Flush stream
void **write**(byte[] b, int off, int len)	Write array to stream specifiying the offset and length
void **write**(int b)	Write lower eight bits of integer to stream
void **writeBoolean**(boolean v)	Write boolean to the stream
void **writeByte**(int v)	Write lower eight bits of integer to stream
void **writeChar**(int v)	Write two bytes of integer parameter to stream
void **writeChars**(String s)	Write string to stream, two bytes for each character
void **writeInt**(int v)	Write integer as four bytes to the stream
void **writeLong**(long v)	Write long as four bytes to the stream
void **writeShort**(int v)	Write integer as two bytes to the stream
void **writeUTF**(String str)	Write String as UTF to the stream

EOFException

public class EOFException extends IOException
Indicates end of file

Constructors

EOFException()	Create EOFException
EOFException(String s)	Create EOFException with message

InputStream

public abstract class InputStream
Superclass for byte input streams

Constructors

InputStream()	Create InputStream

Methods

int **available**()	Bytes available before stream blocks
void **close**()	Closes stream and free resources
void **mark**(int readlimit)	Set current position
boolean **markSupported**()	Is mark/reset supported?
int **read**()	Read next byte
int **read**(byte[] b)	Read bytes into array
int **read**(byte[] b, int len, int off)	Read bytes into array specifying offset and length
void **reset**()	Reset stream to "marked" position
long **skip**(long n)	Skips over bytes in stream

InputStreamReader

public class InputStreamReader extends Reader
Read bytes and translate to Unicode characters (encoding is default or as specified)

Constructors

InputStreamReader(InputStream is)	Create InputStreamReader with default character encoding
InputStreamReader(InputStream is, String enc)	Create InputStreamReader with specified character encoding

Methods

void **close**()	Closes stream and free resources
void **mark**(int readAheadLimit)	Set current position

(continued)

InputStreamReader   (*Continued*)

Methods (*cont.*)

boolean **markSupported**()	Is mark/reset supported?
int **read**()	Read character
int **read**(char[] cbuf, int off, int len)	Read characters into array
boolean **ready**()	Stream available for reading
void **reset**()	Reset stream to "marked" position
long **skip**(long n)	Skip over characters in stream

InterruptedIOException

public class InterruptedIOException extends IOException
Indicates input or output was interrupted

Fields

bytesTransferred	Bytes transferred before exception

Constructors

InterruptedIOException()	Create InterruptedIOException
InterruptedIOException(String s)	Create InterruptedIOException

IOException

public class IOException extends Exception
Indicates exception occurred during input or output

Constructors

IOException()	Create IOException
IOException(String s)	Create IOException with message

OutputStream

public abstract class OutputStream
Superclass for byte output streams

Constructors

OutputStream()   Create OutputStream

Methods

void **close**()	Closes stream and free resources
void **flush**()	Flush stream
void **write**(byte[] b)	Write array to stream
void **write**(byte[] b, int off, int len)	Write array to stream specifying the offset and length
void **write**(int b)	Write byte to stream

OutputStreamWriter

public class OutputStreamWriter extends Writer
Write characters translating to bytes using encoding (default or as specified)

Constructors

OutputStreamWriter(OutputStream os)	Create OutputStreamWriter with default character encoding
OutputStreamWriter(OutputStream os, String enc)	Create OutputStreamWriter with specified character encoding

Methods

void **close**()	Closes stream and free resources
void **flush**()	Flush stream
void **write**(char[] cbuf, int off, int len)	Write array to stream
void **write**(int c)	Write character to stream
void **write**(String str, int off, int len)	Write array to stream specifying offset and length

PrintStream

public class PrintStream extends OutputStream
Add to a stream to enable printing (displaying) of Java primitive types

Constructors

PrintStream(OutputStream out)	Create PrintStream

Methods

boolean **checkError**()	Flush stream and check for error condition
void **close**()	Closes stream and free resources
void **flush**()	Flush stream
void **print**(boolean b)	Print boolean
void **print**(char c)	Print character
void **print**(char[] s)	Print array of characters
void **print**(int i)	Print integer
void **print**(long l)	Print long
void **print**(Object obj)	Print object
void **print**(String s)	Print string
void **println**()	Print line seperator
void **println**(boolean x)	Print boolean and line seperator
void **println**(char x)	Print character and line seperator
void **println**(char[] x)	Print array of characters and line seperator
void **println**(int x)	Print integer and line seperator
void **println**(long x)	Print long and line seperator
void **println**(Object x)	Print Object and line seperator
void **println**(String x)	Print String and line seperator
void **setError**()	Set error condition
void **write**(byte[] buf, int off, int len)	Write array of bytes specifying offset and length
void **write**(int b)	Write byte

Reader

public abstract class Reader
Superclass for character input streams

Fields

lock	Object that is used for synchronization

Constructors

Reader()	Create Reader where critical sections synchronize on the reader itself
Reader(Object lock)	Create Reader where critical sections synchronize on the specified object

Methods

void **close**()	Closes stream and free resources
void **mark**(int readAheadLimit)	Set current position
boolean **markSupported**()	Is mark/reset supported?
int **read**()	Read character
int **read**(char[] cbuf)	Read characters into array
int **read**(char[] cbuf, int off, int len)	Read characters into array specifying the offset and length
boolean **ready**()	Stream available for reading
void **reset**()	Reset the stream to "marked" position
long **skip**(long n)	Skip characters in stream

UnsupportedEncodingException

public class UnsupportedEncodingException extends IOException
Indicates encoding requested is not supported

Constructors

UnsupportedEncodingException()	Create UnsupportedEncodingException
UnsupportedEncodingException(String s)	Create UnsupportedEncodingException

UTFDataFormatException

public class UTFDataFormatException extends IOException

Indicates malformed UTF-8 string has been read

Constructors

UTFDataFormatException()	Create UTFDataFormatException
UTFDataFormatException(String s)	Create UTFDataFormatException with message

Writer

public abstract class Writer

Superclass for character output streams

Fields

lock	Object that is used for synchronization

Constructors

Writer()	Create Writer where critical sections synchronize on the writer
Writer(Object lock)	Create Writer where critical sections synchronize on the specified object

Methods

void **close**()	Closes stream and free resources
void **flush**()	Flush stream
void **write**(char[] cbuf)	Write array of characters
void **write**(char[] cbuf, int off, int len)	Write array of characters specifying offset and length
void **write**(int c)	Write character
void **write**(String str)	Write string
void **write**(String str, int off, int len)	Write string specifying offset and length

java.lang

ArithmeticException	Long
ArrayIndexOutOfBoundsException	Math
ArrayStoreException	NegativeArraySizeException
Boolean	NullPointerException
Byte	NumberFormatException
Character	Object
Class	OutOfMemoryError
ClassCastException	Runnable
ClassNotFoundException	Runtime
Error	RuntimeException
Exception	SecurityException
IllegalAccessException	Short
IllegalArgumentException	String
IllegalMonitorStateException	StringBuffer
IllegalThreadStateException	StringIndexOutOfBoundsException
IndexOutOfBoundsException	System
InstantiationException	Thread
Integer	Throwable
InterruptedException	VirtualMachineError

ArithmeticException

public class ArithmeticException extends RuntimeException
Arithmetic exception, such as divide by zero

Constructors

ArithmeticException()	Create ArithmeticException
ArithmeticException(String s)	Create ArithmeticException with message

ArrayIndexOutOfBoundsException

public class ArrayIndexOutOfBoundsException extends IndexOutOfBoundsException
Attempt to use an invalid array index

Constructors

ArrayIndexOutOfBoundsException()	Create ArrayIndexOutOfBoundsException
ArrayIndexOutOfBoundsException(int index)	Create ArrayIndexOutOfBoundsException
ArrayIndexOutOfBoundsException(String s)	Create ArrayIndexOutOfBoundsException

ArrayStoreException

public class ArrayStoreException extends RuntimeException
Indicates an attempt to store a type not supported by the array

Constructors

ArrayStoreException()	Create ArrayStoreException
ArrayStoreException(String s)	Create ArrayStoreException with message

Boolean

public final class Boolean
Wrap a boolean primitive type in an object

Constructors

Boolean(boolean value)	Create Boolean

Methods

boolean **booleanValue**()	Get value of object
boolean **equals**(Object obj)	Compare objects
int **hashCode**()	Get hashcode of object
String **toString**()	Get String representation of object

Byte

public final class Byte
Wrap a byte primitive type in an object

Fields

MAX_VALUE	Maximum byte value
MIN_VALUE	Minimum byte value

Constructors

Byte(byte value)	Create Byte

Methods

byte **byteValue**()	Get value of object
boolean **equals**(Object obj)	Compare objects
int **hashCode**()	Get hashcode for object
byte **parseByte**(String s)	Convert string to byte
byte **parseByte**(String s, int radix)	Convert string to byte, specifying radix (number base)
String **toString**()	Get String representation of object

Character

public final class Character
Wrap a char primitive type in an object

Fields

MAX_RADIX	Maximum radix (number base) for conversion to and from Strings
MAX_VALUE	Largest character
MIN_RADIX	Minimum radix (number base) for conversion to and from Strings
MIN_VALUE	Smallest character

Constructors

Character(char value)	Create Character

(continued)

Character   (*Continued*)

Methods

char **charValue**()	Get character value of object
int **digit**(char ch, int radix)	Get numeric value of character specifying radix (number base)
boolean **equals**(Object obj)	Compare objects
int **hashCode**()	Get hashcode for object
boolean **isDigit**(char ch)	Is character a digit?
boolean **isLowerCase**(char ch)	Is character lowercase?
boolean **isUpperCase**(char ch)	Is character uppercase?
char **toLowerCase**(char ch)	Convert character to lowercase
String **toString**()	Get String representation of object
char **toUpperCase**(char ch)	Convert character to uppercase

Class

public final class Class
Represents Java class, interface and primitive types

Methods

Class **forName**(String className)	Get Class object for the specified class
String **getName**()	Get fully qualified name of the specified object (class, interface, array class, primitive type, or void)
InputStream **getResourceAsStream**(String name)	Get resource with specified name
boolean **isArray**()	Is the object an array?
boolean **isAssignableFrom**(Class cls)	Is object the same, or a superclass or superinterface of the parameter?
boolean **isInstance**(Object obj)	Is the parameter an instance of the object?
boolean **isInterface**()	Is the object an interface?
Object **newInstance**()	Create instance of object
String **toString**()	Get String representation of object

ClassCastException

public class ClassCastException extends RuntimeException
Attempt to cast an object to a class that it is not an instance of

Constructors

ClassCastException()	Create ClassCastException
ClassCastException(String s)	Create ClassCastException with message

ClassNotFoundException

public class ClassNotFoundException extends Exception
Attempt to load a class that cannot be found

Constructors

ClassNotFoundException()	Create ClassNotFoundException
ClassNotFoundException(String s)	Create ClassNotFoundException with message

Error

public class Error extends Throwable
Abnormal error condition, usually resulting in ending of the application; typically
not caught

Constructors

Error()	Create Error
Error(String s)	Create Error with message

Exception

public class Exception extends Throwable
Indicates error condition; typically caught through a subclass

Constructors

Exception()	Create Exception
Exception(String s)	Create Exception with messsage

IllegalAccessException

public class IllegalAccessException extends Exception
Class cannot be loaded due to access restrictions

Constructors

IllegalAccessException()   Create IllegalAccessException

IllegalAccessException(String s)   Create IllegalAccessException with message

IllegalArgumentException

public class IllegalArgumentException extends RuntimeException
Indicates a method was passed an illegal argument (parameter)

Constructors

IllegalArgumentException()   Create IllegalArgumentException

IllegalArgumentException(String s)   Create IllegalArgumentException with message

IllegalMonitorStateException

public class IllegalMonitorStateException extends RuntimeException
Indicates thread trying to access a monitor it does not own

Constructors

IllegalMonitorStateException()   Create IllegalMonitorStateException

IllegalMonitorStateException(String s)   Create IllegalMonitorStateException with message

IllegalThreadStateException

public class IllegalThreadStateException extends IllegalArgumentException
Indicates thread attempt to perform illegal operation based on its current state

Constructors

IllegalThreadStateException()   Create IllegalThreadStateException

IllegalThreadStateException(String s)   Create IllegalThreadStateException with message

IndexOutOfBoundsException

public class IndexOutOfBoundsException extends RuntimeException
An index (such as array, vector or string) is out of its valid range

Constructors

IndexOutOfBoundsException()	Create an IndexOutOfBoundsException
IndexOutOfBoundsException(String s)	Create an IndexOutOfBoundsException with message

InstantiationException

public class InstantiationException extends Exception
Indicates attempt to instantiate (create instance of) a class that is either an interface or abstract

Constructors

InstantiationException()	Create an InstantiationException
InstantiationException(String s)	Create an InstantiationException with message

Integer

public final class Integer
Wrap an int primitive type in an object

Fields

MAX_VALUE	Maximum integer
MIN_VALUE	Minimum integer

Constructors

Integer(int value)	Create Integer

Methods

byte **byteValue**()	Get value of object as a byte
boolean **equals**(Object obj)	Compare objects
int **hashCode**()	Get hashcode for object
int **intValue**()	Get value of object as integer

(continued)

Integer (Continued)

Methods (cont.)

long **longValue**()	Get value of object as a long
int **parseInt**(String s)	Convert string to int
int **parseInt**(String s, int radix)	Convert string to int, specifying radix (number base)
short **shortValue**()	Get value of object as short
String **toBinaryString**(int i)	Get string value of parameter in base 2
String **toHexString**(int i)	Get string value of parameter in base 16
String **toOctalString**(int i)	Get string value of parameter in base 8
String **toString**()	Get String representation of object
String **toString**(int i)	Get String representation of specified int
String **toString**(int i, int radix)	Get String representation of specified int and radix (number base)
Integer **valueOf**(String s)	Convert string to Integer object
Integer **valueOf**(String s, int radix)	Convert string to Integer object, specifying radix (number base)

InterruptedException

public class InterruptedException extends Exception
Indicates a thread has been interrupted by a call to interrupt() method

Constructors

InterruptedException()	Create an InterruptedException
InterruptedException(String s)	Create an InterruptedException with message

Long

public final class Long
Wrap a long primitive type in an object

Fields

MAX_VALUE	Maximum long
MIN_VALUE	Minumum long

(continued)

Long *(Continued)*

Constructors

Long(long value)   Create Long

Methods

boolean **equals**(Object obj)   Compare objects

int **hashCode**()   Get hashcode for object

long **longValue**()   Get value of object as long

long **parseLong**(String s)   Convert string to long

long **parseLong**(String s, int radix)   Convert string to long, specifying radix (number base)

String **toString**()   Get String representation of object

String **toString**(long i)   Get String representation of specified long

String **toString**(long i, int radix)   Get String representation of specified long and radix (number base)

Math

public final class Math
Methods for math operations

Methods

int **abs**(int a)   Get absolute value of int

int **abs**(long a)   Get absolute value of long

int **max**(int a, int b)   Get maximum of two int values

long **max**(long a, long b)   Get maximum of two long values

int **min**(int a, int b)   Get minimum two int values

long **min**(long a, long b)   Get minimum two long values

NegativeArraySizeException

public class NegativeArraySizeException extends RuntimeException
Indicates attempt to allocate an array with a negative size

Constructors

NegativeArraySizeException()   Create a NegativeArraySizeException

NegativeArraySizeException(String s)   Create a NegativeArraySizeException with message

NullPointerException

public class NullPointerException extends RuntimeException
Indicates access to a null object

Constructors

NullPointerException()   Create a NullPointerException

NullPointerException(String s)   Create a NullPointerException with message

NumberFormatException

public class NumberFormatException extends IllegalArgumentException
Indicates attempt to convert a string to numeric type that is not supported

Constructors

NumberFormatException()   Create a NumberFormatException

NumberFormatException(String s)   Create a NumberFormatException with message

Object

public class Object
Root class of all objects

Constructors

Object()   Create Object

Methods

boolean **equals**(Object obj)   Compare objects

Class **getClass**()   Get runtime class of object

int **hashCode**()   Get hashcode for object

void **notify**()   Wakes up thread waiting on this object's monitor

void **notifyAll**()   Wakes up all threads waiting on this object's monitor

String **toString**()   Get String representation of object

void **wait**()   Wait until another thread invokes the notify() or notifyAll()

void **wait**(long timeout)   Wait until another thread invokes the notify() or notifyAll(), with a timeout

void **wait**(long timeout, int nanos)   Wait until another thread invokes the notify() or notifyAll(), with a timeout

OutOfMemoryError

public class OutOfMemoryError extends VirtualMachineError
Indicates Java virtual machine has exhausted memory (even after garbage collection)

Constructors

OutOfMemoryError()   Create OutOfMemoryError

OutOfMemoryError(String s)   Create OutOfMemoryError with message

Runnable

public abstract interface Runnable
Interface for classes that intend to be run by a thread

Methods

void **run**()   Called when an object that is implementing the Runnable interface starts the thread

Runtime

public class Runtime

Class that provides a means for interaction (minimal) with the runtime environment

Methods

void **exit**(int status)	Exit the Java application
long **freeMemory**()	Free memory available
void **gc**()	Run garbage collector
Runtime **getRuntime**()	Get runtime object associated with current Java application
long **totalMemory**()	Get total amount of memory used by the Java Virtual Machine

RuntimeException

public class RuntimeException extends Exception

Superclass of exceptions thrown during normal operation of the Java virtual machine

Constructors

RuntimeException()	Create RuntimeException
RuntimeException(String s)	Create RuntimeException with message

SecurityException

public class SecurityException extends RuntimeException

Indicates a security violation

Constructors

SecurityException()	Create SecurityException
SecurityException(String s)	Create SecurityException with message

Short

public final class Short
Wrap a short primitive type in an object

Fields

MAX_VALUE	Maximum short
MIN_VALUE	Minimum short

Constructors

Short(short value)	Create Short

Methods

boolean **equals**(Object obj)	Compare objects
int **hashCode**()	Get hashcode for object
short **parseShort**(String s)	Convert string to short
short **parseShort**(String s, int radix)	Convert string to short, specifying radix (number base)
short **shortValue**()	Get value of object
String **toString**()	Get String representation of object

String

public final class String
Methods for operating on a string of characters; once allocated, a string *cannot* be modified

Constructors

String()	Create String
String(byte[] bytes)	Create String from array of bytes using platform default character encoding
String(byte[] bytes, String enc)	Create String from array of bytes using specified character encoding
String(byte[] bytes, int off, int len)	Create String from array of bytes, specifying offset and length, using platform default character encoding
String(byte[] bytes, int off, int len, String enc)	Create String from array of bytes, specifying offset and length, using specified character encoding

(continued)

String   (Continued)

Constructors (cont.)

String(char[] value)	Create String from array of characters
String(char[] value, int offset, int count)	Create String from array of characters, specifying offset and count
String(String value)	Create String from an existing string
String(StringBuffer buffer)	Create String from a string buffer

Methods

char **charAt**(int index)	Get character at index
int **compareTo**(String anotherString)	Compare two strings
String **concat**(String str)	Concatenate parameter onto string
boolean **endsWith**(String suffix)	Determine if string ends with specified string
boolean **equals**(Object anObject)	Compare objects
byte[] **getBytes**()	Convert string into an array of bytes using the platform's default character encoding
byte[] **getBytes**(String enc)	Convert string into an array of bytes using the specified character encoding
void **getChars**(int srcBegin, int srcEnd, char[] dst, int dstBegin)	Copies characters from string into an array, specifying source and destination
int **hashCode**()	Get hashcode for object
int **indexOf**(int ch)	Get index of first occurrence of specified character
int **indexOf**(int ch, int fromIndex)	Get index of specified character, starting the search at the specified index
int **indexOf**(String str)	Get index of the substring
int **indexOf**(String str, int fromIndex)	Get index of the substring, starting the search at the specified index
int **lastIndexOf**(int ch)	Get index of last occurrence of specified character
int **lastIndexOf**(int ch, int fromIndex)	Get index of specified character, searching from the end of the string towards the beginning, starting at the specified index
int **length**()	Get length of string
boolean **regionMatches**(boolean ignoreCase, int toffset, String other, int ooffset, int len)	Compare two substrings

(continued)

String (Continued)

String **replace**(char oldChar, char newChar)	Replace all occurrences of a character
boolean **startsWith**(String prefix)	Determine if string starts with specified string
boolean **startsWith**(String prefix, int toffset)	Determine if string starts with specified string starting at index
String **substring**(int beginIndex)	Get substring from specified index to end of string
String **substring**(int beginIndex, int endIndex)	Get substring from specified begin index to specified end index
char[] **toCharArray**()	Convert string to an array of characters
String **toLowerCase**()	Convert to lowercase
String **toString**()	Return this object
String **toUpperCase**()	Convert to uppercase
String **trim**()	Remove white space from beginning and end
String **valueOf**(boolean b)	Convert boolean to string object
String **valueOf**(char c)	Convert character to string object
String **valueOf**(char[] data)	Convert character array to string object
String **valueOf**(char[] data, int offset, int count)	Convert character array to string object, specifying offset and count
String **valueOf**(int i)	Convert int to string object
String **valueOf**(long l)	Convert long to string object
String **valueOf**(Object obj)	Convert object to string object

StringBuffer

public final class StringBuffer
Methods for operating on a string of characters; unlike strings, a string buffer can be modified once allocated.

Constructors

StringBuffer()	Create empty string buffer that will hold 16 characters
StringBuffer(int length)	Create empty string buffer that will hold the specified number of characters
StringBuffer(String str)	Create string buffer from a string

(continued)

StringBuffer (Continued)

Methods

StringBuffer **append**(boolean b)	Append boolean
StringBuffer **append**(char c)	Append character
StringBuffer **append**(char[] str)	Append an array of characters
StringBuffer **append**(char[] str, int offset, int length)	Append array of characters specifying offset and length
StringBuffer **append**(int i)	Append integer
StringBuffer **append**(long l)	Append long
StringBuffer **append**(Object obj)	Append object
StringBuffer **append**(String str)	Append string
int **capacity**()	Get number of characters that may be stored, without allocating more space
char **charAt**(int index)	Get character at specified index
StringBuffer **delete**(int start, int end)	Delete character(s)
StringBuffer **deleteCharAt**(int index)	Delete character
void **ensureCapacity**(int **minimum** Capacity)	Ensures the capacity is at least equal to the specified parameter
void **getChars**(int srcBegin, int srcEnd, char[] dst, int dstBegin)	Copy from string buffer into array
StringBuffer **insert**(int offset, boolean b)	Insert boolean
StringBuffer **insert**(int offset, char c)	Insert character
StringBuffer **insert**(int offset, char[] str)	Insert character array
StringBuffer **insert**(int offset, int i)	Insert integer
StringBuffer **insert**(int offset, long l)	Insert long
StringBuffer **insert**(int offset, Object obj)	Insert object
StringBuffer **insert**(int offset, String str)	Insert string
int **length**()	Get count of characters in the string buffer
StringBuffer **reverse**()	Reverse contents of string buffer
void **setCharAt**(int index, char ch)	Set character at the specified index to another character
void **setLength**(int newLength)	Set the length of string buffer
String **toString**()	Get String representation of object

StringIndexOutOfBoundsException

public class StringIndexOutOfBoundsException extends IndexOutOfBoundsException

Indicates access outside the valid range of a string

Constructors

StringIndexOutOfBoundsException()	Create StringIndexOutOfBoundsException
StringIndexOutOfBoundsException(int index)	Create StringIndexOutOfBoundsException
StringIndexOutOfBoundsException(String str)	Create StringIndexOutOfBoundsException

System

public final class System

Class that provides access (minimal) to system methods and fields

Fields

err	Standard error output stream
out	Standard output stream

Methods

void **arraycopy**(Object src, int srcPosition, Object dst, int dst_position, int length)	Copy one array to another
long **currentTimeMillis**()	Returns the current time in milliseconds
void **exit**(int status)	Terminates the currently running Java application
void **gc**()	Runs garbage collector
String **getProperty**(String key)	Gets system property indicated by the specified key
int **identityHashCode**(Object x)	Get hashcode for object

Thread

public class Thread implements Runnable

A class to provide multiple threads of execution within the Java virtual machine

Fields

MAX_PRIORITY	Maximum priority for a thread
MIN_PRIORITY	Minimum priority for a thread
NORM_PRIORITY	Default priority assigned to thread

Constructors

Thread()	Create Thread
Thread(Runnable target)	Create Thread and invoke run() method of target

Methods

int **activeCount**()	Active threads in the virtual machine
Thread **currentThread**()	Get reference to currently executing thread
int **getPriority**()	Get threads priority
boolean **isAlive**()	Is thread alive?
void **join**()	Wait for thread to die
void **run**()	If thread was constructed using Runnable object, call that object's run() method
void **setPriority**(int newPriority)	Set priority of thread
void **sleep**(long millis)	Put thread to sleep for specified number of milliseconds
void **start**()	Begin execution of thread by calling the run() method of the thread
String **toString**()	Get String representation of object
void **yield**()	Allow other threads to execute by temporarily pausing

Throwable

public class Throwable
Root class of all errors and exceptions

Constructors

Throwable()   Create Throwable

Throwable(String message)   Create Throwable with message

Methods

String **getMessage**()   Get error message

void **printStackTrace**()   Output stack trace to standard error stream

String **toString**()   Get String representation of object

VirtualMachineError

public abstract class VirtualMachineError extends Error
Indicates Java virtual machine error (such as insufficient resources)

Constructors

VirtualMachineError()   Create a VirtualMachineError

VirtualMachineError(String s)   Create a VirtualMachineError with message

java.util

Calendar	NoSuchElementException
Date	Random
EmptyStackException	Stack
Enumeration	TimeZone
Hashtble	Vector

Calendar

public abstract class Calendar
Methods for date and time conversion, arithmetic and formatting

Fields

JANUARY

FEBRUARY

MARCH

APRIL

MAY

JUNE

JULY

AUGUST

SEPTEMBER

OCTOBER

NOVEMBER

DECEMBER

MONDAY

TUESDAY

WEDNESDAY

THURSDAY

FRIDAY

SATURDAY

SUNDAY

AM

PM

AM_PM

DATE

MONTH

YEAR

MILLISECOND

SECOND

MINUTE

HOUR

(continued)

Calendar (Continued)

DAY_OF_MONTH

DAY_OF_WEEK

HOUR_OF_DAY

Constructors

Calendar()	Create calendar using default time zone and locale

Methods

boolean **after**(Object when)	Compare time
boolean **before**(Object when)	Compare time
boolean **equals**(Object obj)	Compare objects
int **get**(int field)	Get field value
Calendar **getInstance**()	Return calendar using default time zone and locale
Calendar **getInstance**(TimeZone zone)	Return calendar using the specified time zone and default locale
Date **getTime**()	Get calendar current time as date
long **getTimeInMillis**()	Get calendar current time as long
TimeZone **getTimeZone**()	Get timezone
void **set**(int field, int value)	Set field to specified value
void **setTime**(Date date)	Set calendar time using specified date
void **setTimeInMillis**(long millis)	Set calendar time using long
void **setTimeZone**(TimeZone value)	Set calendar timezone using specified timezone

Date

public class Date
Represent a specific time

Constructors

Date()	Create Date using current time
Date(long date)	Create Date from long value specifying seconds since January 1, 1970, 00:00:00 GMT

(continued)

Date   *(Continued)*

Methods

boolean **equals**(Object obj)	Compare objects
long **getTime**()	Get milliseconds since January 1, 1970, 00:00:00 GMT
int **hashCode**()	Get hashcode
void **setTime**(long time)	Set time based on the number of milliseconds since January 1, 1970 00:00:00 GMT

EmptyStackException

public class EmptyStackException extends RuntimeException
Indicates the stack is empty

Constructors

EmptyStackException()	Create EmptyStackException

Enumeration

public abstract interface Enumeration
Interface that defines methods to iterate through set of values

Methods

boolean **hasMoreElements**()	More elements available in enumeration
Object **nextElement**()	Get next element in enumeration

Hashtable

public class Hashtable
Hashtable (associative array) mapping keys and values

Constructors

Hashtable()	Create empty Hashtable with default capacity
Hashtable(int initialCapacity)	Create empty Hashtable, specifying initial capacity

(continued)

Hashtable   (*Continued*)

Methods

void **clear**()	Clear all keys from hashtable
boolean **contains**(Object value)	Is there a key for the specified object?
boolean **containsKey**(Object key)	Is there an object for the specified key?
Enumeration **elements**()	Get an enumeration to iterate through the values in hashtable
Object **get**(Object key)	Get value at specified key
boolean **isEmpty**()	Is hashtable empty
Enumeration **keys**()	Get an enumeration to iterate through the keys in hashtable
Object **put**(Object key, Object value)	Map specified key to value (insert into hashtable)
void **rehash**()	Rehash contents into a hashtable with a greater capacity
Object **remove**(Object key)	Remove key and value from hashtable
int **size**()	Get the number of keys
String **toString**()	Get string representation of hashtable contents

NoSuchElementException

public class NoSuchElementException extends RuntimeException
Indicates there are no more elements in an enumeration

Constructors

NoSuchElementException()	Create NoSuchElementException
NoSuchElementException(String s)	Create NoSuchElementException with message

Random

public class Random
Generate pseudo-random numbers

Constructors

Random()	Create random number generator
Random(long seed)	Create random number generator, specifying the seed value

(*continued*)

Random   *(Continued)*

Methods

int **next**(int bits)	Get next random number
int **nextInt**()	Get next random number as uniformly distributed integer
long **nextLong**()	Get next random number as uniformly distributed long
void **setSeed**(long seed)	Set seed

Stack

public class Stack extends Vector
Last in, first out (LIFO) data structure

Constructors

Stack()	Create empty Stack

Methods

boolean **empty**()	Is stack empty?
Object **peek**()	Peek at top object without popping from stack
Object **pop**()	Remove object at the top of stack
Object **push**(Object item)	Push an object onto the stack
int **search**(Object o)	Locate an object on the stack; returns distance from the top

TimeZone

public abstract class TimeZone

A timezone.

Constructors

TimeZone()	Create Timezone

Methods

String **getAvailableIDs**()	Get supported timezones
TimeZone **getDefault**()	Get default timezone on host
String **getID**()	Get ID (name) of timezone

int **getOffset**(int era,
    int year, int month,
    int day, int dayOfWeek,
    int millis)
	Get milliseconds to add to GMT to convert specified date to timezone

int **getRawOffset**()	Get GMT offset (milliseconds to GMT) for this timezone
TimeZone **getTimeZone**(String ID)	Get timezone for the specified ID (name)
boolean **useDaylightTime**()	Does timezone observe "daylight savings"

Vector

public class Vector

Array of objects that will automatically increase in size as necesssary

Fields

capacityIncrement	How much the vector grows by when capacity is reached
elementCount	Count of elements in vector
elementData	Array that holds vector contents

Constructors

Vector()	Create empty Vector
Vector(int initialCapacity)	Create empty Vector specifying initial capacity
Vector(int initialCapacity, int capacityIncrement)	Create empty Vector specifying intial capacity and increment

(continued)

Vector   (Continued)

Methods

`void addElement(Object obj)`	Add object to vector
`int capacity()`	Get number of objects that may be stored, without allocating more space
`boolean contains(Object elem)`	Is the specified object in the vector?
`void copyInto(Object[] anArray)`	Copy vector contents into an array
`Object elementAt(int index)`	Get object at specified index
`Enumeration elements()`	Get an enumeration
`void ensureCapacity(` `   int minCapacity)`	Ensure vector will hold at a minimum the specified number of elements
`Object firstElement()`	Get first element in vector
`int indexOf(Object elem)`	Search for first occurence of object
`int indexOf(Object elem,` `   int index)`	Search for first occurence of object beginning at specified index
`void insertElementAt(` `   Object obj, int index)`	Insert object at specified index
`boolean isEmpty()`	Is vector empty?
`Object lastElement()`	Get last object in vector
`int lastIndexOf(Object elem)`	Find last occurrence of specified object
`int lastIndexOf(Object elem,` `   int index)`	Search backwards for an object beginning at the specifed index
`void removeAllElements()`	Empty the vector
`boolean removeElement(` `   Object obj)`	Remove first occurrence of specified object
`void removeElementAt(int index)`	Delete object at specified index
`void setElementAt(Object obj,` `   int index)`	Set (replace) object at specified index
`void setSize(int newSize)`	Set new size for the vector
`int size()`	Get number of objects currently in vector
`String toString()`	Get string representation of vector contents
`void trimToSize()`	Change size of vector (array) to the actual number of objects stored

javax.microedition.io

Connection	DatagramConnection
ConnectionNotFoundException	InputConnection
Connector	OutputConnection
ContentConnection	StreamConnection
Datagram	StreamConnectionNotifier

Connection
public abstract interface Connection

A "generic" connection

Methods

void **close**()   Close connection

ConnectionNotFoundException
public class ConnectionNotFoundException extends IOException

Indicates requested connection "target" could not be found

Constructors

ConnectionNotFoundException()   Create ConnectionNotFoundException

ConnectionNotFoundException(String s)   Create ConnectionNotFoundException

Connector
public class Connector

Static methods to create and open a connection

Fields

READ	Open for read only
READ_WRITE	Open for read and write
WRITE	Open for write only

Methods

Connection **open**(String name)	Create/open connection for read/write
Connection **open**(String name, int mode)	Create/open connection specifying mode
Connection **open**(String name, int mode, boolean timeouts)	Create/open connection with mode and timeout
DataInputStream **openDataInputStream**(String name)	Create/open data input stream
DataOutputStream **openDataOutputStream**(String name)	Create/open data output stream
InputStream **openInputStream**() String name	Create/open input stream
OutputStream **openOutputStream**(String name)	Create/open output stream

ContentConnection
public abstract interface ContentConnection extends StreamConnection

Interface extending a stream connection which accomodates data

Methods

String **getEncoding**()	Get encoding information of data (e.g. http "Content-Encoding" header field)
long **getLength**()	Get total length of data
String **getType**()	Get information about the type of data (e.g. http "Content-Type" header field)

Datagram
public abstract interface Datagram extends DataInput, DataOutput

Interface for datagram communicatio

Methods

String **getAddress**()	Datagram address
byte[] **getData**()	Get byte array containing the data
int **getLength**()	Get length of data
int **getOffset**()	Get current offset into the data
void **reset**()	Reset length and offset and start read/write from beginning
void **setAddress**(Datagram)	Set datagram address based on address of specified datagram
void **setAddress**(String)	Set datagram address to the specified string

void **setData**(
    byte[] buffer,
    int offset, int len)
	Set datagram data from byte array

void **setLength**(int len)	Set datagram length

DatagramConnection
public abstract interface DatagramConnection extends Connection

Interface to describe the capabilities of a datagram connection

Methods

int **getMaximumLength**()	Get maximum datagram length
int **getNominalLength**()	Get nominal datagram length
Datagram **newDatagram**(byte[] buf, int size)	Create datagram from specified information

Datagram **newDatagram**(
    byte[] buf, int size,
    String addr)
	Create datagram from specified information

Datagram **newDatagram**(int size)	Create datagram from specified information
Datagram **newDatagram**(int size, String addr)	Create datagram from specified information
void **receive**(Datagram dgram)	Receive datagram
void **send**(Datagram dgram)	Send datagram

InputConnection
public abstract interface InputConnection extends Connection

Interface to describe the capabilities of an input stream connection

Methods

DataInputStream **openDataInputStream**()	Open data input stream
InputStream **openInputStream**()	Open input stream

OutputConnection
public abstract interface OutputConnection extends Connection

Interface to describe the capabilities of an output stream connection

Methods

DataOutputStream **openDataOutputStream**()	Open data output stream
OutputStream **openOutputStream**()	Open output stream

StreamConnection
public abstract interface StreamConnection extends InputConnection, OutputConnection

Interface to describe the capabilities of a stream connection

StreamConnectionNotifier
public abstract interface StreamConnectionNotifier extends Connection

Interface to describe the capabilities of a stream connection notifier

Methods

StreamConnection **acceptAndOpen**()	Create server-side socket connection

Appendix C

Alert: javax.microedition.lcdui.Alert
public class Alert extends Screen

Field/Method	Description
Field	
FOREVER	Specifies the Alert is visible until acknowledged by the user (also known as modal); see setTimeout()
Constructor	
Alert(String title)	Create a new Alert
Alert(String title, String alertText, Image alertImage, AlertType, alertType)	Create a new Alert with an Image and an associated sound (AlertType)
Method	
int **getDefaultTimeout**()	Get default time Alert is displayed
Image **getImage**()	Get Image associated with Alert
String **getString**()	Get text associated with Alert
int **getTimeout**()	Get actual time Alert will be displayed
AlertType **getType**()	Get the AlertType
void **setImage**(Image img)	Associate an Image with Alert
void **setString**(String str)	Set text for Alert
void **setTimeout**(int time)	Set amount of time to display Alert
void **setType**(AlertType type)	Set the AlertType

AlertType: javax.microedition.lcdui.AlertType
public class AlertType

Field/Method	Description
Field	
ALARM	Indicates arrival of a previous request to be notified
CONFIRMATION	Indicates completion of an event or action
ERROR	Indicates an error has occurred
INFO	Indicates general, non-critical information
WARNING	Indicates potential problem or situation
Method	
boolean **playSound**(Display display)	Play a sound on the device

Canvas: javax.microedition.lcdui.Canvas
public abstract class Canvas extends Displayable

Field/Method	Description	Value
Field		
Game Actions		
UP	Move up	1
DOWN	Move down	6
LEFT	Move left	2
RIGHT	Move right	5
FIRE	Fire	8
GAME_A	Custom	9
GAME_B	Custom	10
GAME_C	Custom	11
GAME_D	Custom	12
Key Codes[1]		
KEY_NUM0	ITU-T key 0	48
KEY_NUM1	ITU-T key 1	49

(continued)

Canvas: javax.microedition.lcdui.Canvas (Continued)

KEY_NUM2	ITU-T key 2	50
KEY_NUM3	ITU-T key 3	51
KEY_NUM4	ITU-T key 4	52
KEY_NUM5	ITU-T key 5	53
KEY_NUM6	ITU-T key 6	54
KEY_NUM7	ITU-T key 7	55
KEY_NUM8	ITU-T key 8	56
KEY_NUM9	ITU-T key 9	57
KEY_STAR	ITU-T key *	42
KEY_POUND	ITU-T key #	35

Method

int **getGameAction**(int keyCode)	Get the game action, if any, for the key code
int **getHeight**()	Get the canvas height
int **getKeyCode**(int gameAction)	Determine key code for a game action
String **getKeyName**(int keyCode)	Get name for a key code[2]
int **getWidth**()	Get the canvas width
boolean **hasPointerEvents**()	Does the platform support a pointer?
boolean **hasPointerMotionEvents**()	Does the platform detect pointer motion ("click/point and drag")?
boolean **hasRepeatsEvents**()	Does the implementation support repeated keys?
void **hideNotify**()	Application manager has removed the canvas from the display
boolean **isDoubleBuffered**()	Does implementation provide double buffering?
void **keyPressed**(int keyCode)	Invoked when a key is pressed
void **keyReleased**(int keyCode)	Invoked when a key is released
void **keyRepeated**(int keyCode)	Invoked when a key is held down (repeated)[3]
abstract void **paint**(Graphics g)	Draw onto the canvas using the Graphics object specified
void **pointerDragged**(int x, int y)	Invoked when pointer dragged
void **pointerPressed**(int x, int y)	Invoked when pointer pressed
void **pointerReleased**(int x, int y)	Invoked when pointer released
final void **repaint**()	Request the canvas to be painted

(continued)

Canvas: javax.microedition.lcdui.Canvas   *(Continued)*

`final void repaint(int x, int y,` `  int width, int height)`	Request a specified region of canvas be painted
`final void serviceRepaints()`	Immediately process any pending paint requests
`void showNotify()`	Application manager is about to show the canvas on the display

[1]ITU-T is the standard telephone keypad.
[2]Can display text associated with a game action if converted to a key code.
[3]May not be supported on all devices.

Choice: javax.microedition.lcdui.Choice
public interface Choice

This class defines fields and methods for components that allow a user to select from predefined elements. The fields and methods defined in this class are shown in ChoiceGroup and List, which implement this interface.

ChoiceGroup: javax.microedition.lcdui.ChoiceGroup
public class ChoiceGroup extends Item implements Choice

Field/Method	*Description*
Field[1]	
`EXCLUSIVE`	Only one selection available at any time
`MULTIPLE`	Zero or more selections available at any time
`IMPLICIT`	Not available for ChoiceGroup; see List
Constructor	
`ChoiceGroup(String label, int choiceType)`	Create a ChoiceGroup with no elements

`ChoiceGroup(String label, int choiceType,`
`  String[] stringElements,`
`  Image[] imageElements)`
	Create a ChoiceGroup and populate with data from the arrays

Method	
`int append(String stringPart, Image imagePart)`	Add element to end
`void delete(int elementNum)`	Delete element
`Image getImage(int elementNum)`	Get Image associated with element

(continued)

ChoiceGroup: javax.microedition.lcdui.ChoiceGroup   *(Continued)*

`int getSelectedFlags(` `boolean[] selectedArray_return)`	Store selection status in an array
`int getSelectedIndex()`	Get the index of the selected element
`String getString(int elementNum)`	Get text (String) associated with element
`void insert(int elementNum,` `String stringPart, Image imageElement)`	Insert element
`boolean isSelected(int elementNum)`	Is the element currently selected?
`void set(int elementNum, String stringPart,` `Image imagePart)`	Set (replace) element
`void setSelectedFlags(boolean[] selectedArray)`	Set selection status from an array
`void setSelectedIndex(int elementNum,` `boolean selected)`	For MULTIPLE ChoiceGroup, set element to specified boolean value
	For EXLCUSIVE ChoiceGroup, set element to true
	IMPLICIT not available for ChoiceGroup
`int size()`	Number of elements

[1]From Choice interface, also used with List.

Command: javax.microedition.lcdui.Command
public class Command

Field/Method	Description
Field	
BACK	Request to move to the previous screen
CANCEL	Request to cancel an operation
EXIT	Request to exit the MIDlet
HELP	Request to display help information
ITEM	Request to map the Command to an "item" on screen
OK	Specify positive acknowledgement from a user
SCREEN	For Commands in which it is unlikely there will be a specific key mapping available
STOP	Request to stop an operation

(continued)

Command: javax.microedition.lcdui.Command   (*Continued*)

Constructor

Command(String label, int commandType, int priority)	Create a new Command

Method

int **getCommandType**()	Get type assigned to Command
String **getLabel**()	Get label assigned to Command
int **getPriority**()	Get priority assigned to Command

CommandListener: javax.microedition.lcdui.CommandListener
public interface CommandListener

Method	*Description*
void **commandAction**(Command c, Displayable d)	Called when the Command "c" on the Displayable "d" initiates an event

DateField: javax.microedition.lcdui.DateField
public class DateField extends Item

Field/Method	*Description*
Field	
DATE	Allows the user to edit only the date
TIME	Allows the user to edit only the time
DATE_TIME	Allows the user to edit both the date and time
Constructor	
DateField(String label, int mode)	Create DateField
DateField(String label, int mode, TimeZone timeZone)	Create DateField with specified TimeZone information

(continued)

DateField: javax.microedition.lcdui.DateField   (Continued)

Method	
Date **getDate**()	Get current value
int **getInputMode**()	Get the current input mode
void **setDate**(Date date)	Set new date/time value
void **setInputMode**(int mode)	Set new input mode

Display: javax.microedition.lcdui.Display
public class Display

Method	Description
void **callSerially**(Runnable r)	Request a runnable object be called after repainting
Displayable **getCurrent**()	Get current Displayable object
static Display **getDisplay**(MIDlet m)	Get Display object for this MIDlet
boolean **isColor**()	Does the device support color?
int **numColors**()	How many colors (or shades of gray) are available?
void **setCurrent**(Alert alert, Displayable nextDisplayable)	Show an Alert followed by the specified Displayable object Show a new Displayable object
void **setCurrent**(Displayable nextDisplayable)	

Displayable: javax.microedition.lcdui.Displayable
abstract public class Displayable

Method	Description
void **addCommand**(Command cmd)	Add Command to Displayable object
boolean **isShown**()	Is the Displayable object visible on the screen?
void **removeCommand**(Command cmd)	Remove Command from Displayable object
void **setCommandListener**(CommandListener l)	Add CommandListener to Displayable object

Font: javax.microedition.lcdui.Font
public final class Font

Field/Method	Description
Field	
FACE_MONOSPACE	Monospace characters
FACE_PROPORTIONAL	Proportional characters
FACE_SYSTEM	System characters
STYLE_BOLD	Bold characters
STYLE_ITALIC	Italicized characters
STYLE_PLAIN	Plain characters
STYLE_UNDERLINED	Underlined characters
SIZE_LARGE	Large characters
SIZE_MEDIUM	Medium characters
SIZE_SMALL	Small characters
Method	
int **charsWidth**(char[] ch, int offset, int length)	Get the advance for a series of characters
int **charWidth**(char ch)	Get the advance for specific character
int **getBaselinePosition**()	Get font ascent (baseline to top of character)
static Font **getDefaultFont**()	Request the system Font
int **getFace**()	Get the current face
static Font **getFont**(int face, int style, int size)	Request a new Font
int **getHeight**()	Get font height (distance between baselines)
int **getSize**()	Get the current size
int **getStyle**()	Get the combination of style attributes as one integer (logically or'ed)
boolean **isBold**()	Is the bold (style) attribute set?
boolean **isItalic**()	Is the italic (style) attribute set?
boolean **isPlain**()	Is the plain (style) attribute set?
boolean **isUnderlined**()	Is the underlined (style) attribute set?
int **stringWidth**(String str)	Get the advance for a String
int **substringWidth**(String str, int offset, int length)	Get the advance for a sub-string of a String

Form: javax.microedition.lcdui.Form
public class Form extends Screen

Method	Description
Constructor	
Form (String title)	Create a form
Form (String title, Item[] items)	Create a form and add Item(s) in the array
Method	
int **append**(Image img)	Append an Image
int **append**(Item item)	Append an Item
int **append**(String str)	Append a String
void **delete**(int itemNum)	Delete an Item
Item **get**(int itemNum)	Get an Item
void **insert**(int itemNum, Item item)	Insert an Item prior to the item specified
void **set**(int itemNum, Item item)	Set (replace) an Item
void **setItemStateListener**(ItemStateListener iListener)	Add a listener
int **size**()	Get the number of Items on a form

Gauge: javax.microedition.lcdui.Gauge
public class Gauge extends Item

Method	Description
Constructor	
Gauge(String label, boolean interactive, int maxValue, int initialValue)	Create a new gauge
Method	
int **getMaxValue**()	Get maximum allowed gauge value
int **getValue**()	Get current value of gauge
boolean **isInteractive**()	Is this an interactive gauge?
void **setMaxValue**(int maxValue)	Set maximum allowed gauge value
void **setValue**(int value)	Set new value for gauge

Graphics: javax.microedition.lcdui.Graphics
public class Graphics

Field/Method	Description

Field

Stroke Style

SOLID	Draw solid lines
DOTTED	Draw dotted lines

Anchor Points

BASELINE	Baseline of text
BOTTOM	Bottom of text/image
HCENTER	Center of text/image
LEFT	Left of text/image
RIGHT	Right of text/image
TOP	Top of text/image
VCENTER	Center of image

Method

void **clipRect**(int x, int y, int width, int height)	Intersect this rectangle with the current clipping rectangle to create a new clipping region
void **drawArc**(int x, int y, int width, int height, int startAngle, int arcAngle)	Draw an arc inside bounding box specified by x,y and width, height
void **drawChar**(char character, int x, int y, int anchor)	Draw one character
void **drawChars**(char[] data, int offset, int length, int x, int y, int anchor)	Draw an array (or subset) of characters
void **drawImage**(Image img, int x, int y, int anchor)	Draw an image
void **drawLine**(int x1, int y1, int x2, int y2)	Draw line specifying starting and end points
void **drawRect**(int x, int y, int width, int height)	Draw a rectangle
void **drawRoundRect**(int x, int y, int width, int height, int arcWidth, int arcHeight)	Draw a rounded rectangle

(continued)

Graphics: javax.microedition.lcdui.Graphics   *(Continued)*

void **drawString**(String str, int x, int y, int anchor)	Draw a String
void **drawSubstring**(String str, int offset, int len, int x, int y, int anchor)	Draw a sub-string of a String

void **fillArc**(int x, int y, int width,
  int height, int startAngle, int arcAngle)
	Fill an arc inside bounding box specified by x,y and
	  width,height

void **fillRect**(int x, int y, int width, int height)	Fill a rectangle
void **fillRoundRect**(int x, int y, int width, int height, int arcWidth, int arcHeight)	Fill a rounded rectangle
int **getBlueComponent**()	Get the blue component of the current color
int **getClipHeight**()	Get height of the current clipping region
int **getClipWidth**()	Get width of the current clipping region
int **getClipX**()	Get x coordinate of the current clipping region
int **getClipY**()	Get y coordinate of the current clipping region
int **getColor**()	Get current color as one integer value
Font **getFont**()	Get the current Font
int **getGrayScale**()	Get current grayscale
int **getGreenComponent**()	Get the green component of the current color
int **getRedComponent**()	Get the red component of the current color
int **getStrokeStyle**()	Get the current stroke style
int **getTranslateX**()	Get the current translated x coordinate
int **getTranslateY**()	Get the current translated y coordinate
void **setClip**(int x, int y, int width, int height)	Set the clipping rectangle
void **setColor**(int RGB)	Set color by combining each color component (Red, Green, Blue) into one integer value
void **setColor**(int red, int green, int blue)	Set color specifying each color component (Red, Green, Blue) separately
void **setFont**(Font font)	Set the current Font
void **setGrayScale**(int value)	Set the grayscale
void **setStrokeStyle**(int style)	Set the stroke style
void **translate**(int x, int y)	Translate the origin (0, 0) for a Graphics object

---

HttpConnection: javax.microedition.io.HttpConnection
public interface HttpConnection extends ContentConnection

Field/Method	Description
Field[1]	
GET	GET request method
HEAD	HEAD request method
HTTP_ACCEPTED	Status Code: 202 Message: The request has been accepted for processing, but the processing has not been completed
HTTP_BAD_GATEWAY	Status Code: 502 Message: The server, while acting as a gateway or proxy, received an invalid response from the upstream server it accessed in attempting to fulfill the request
HTTP_BAD_METHOD	Status Code: 405 Message: The method specified in the Request-Line is not allowed for the resource identified by the Request-URL
HTTP_BAD_REQUEST	Status Code: 400 Message: The request could not be understood by the server due to malformed syntax
HTTP_CLIENT_TIMEOUT	Status Code: 408 Message: The client did not produce a request within the time that the server was prepared to wait. The client MAY repeat the request without modifications at any later time
HTTP_CONFLICT	Status Code: 409 Message: The request could not be completed due to a conflict with the current state of the resource
HTTP_CREATED	Status Code: 201 Message: The request has been fulfilled and resulted in a new resource being created
HTTP_ENTITY_TOO_LARGE	Status Code: 413 Message: The server is refusing to process a request because the request entity is larger than the server is willing or able to process
HTTP_EXPECT_FAILED	Status Code: 417 Message: The expectation given in an Expect request-header field could not be met by this server, or, if the server is a proxy, the server has unambiguous evidence that the request could not be met by the next-hop server

(continued)

HttpConnection: javax.microedition.io.HttpConnection   *(Continued)*

HTTP_FORBIDDEN	Status Code: 403 Message: The server understood the request, but is refusing to fulfill it. Authorization will not help and the request SHOULD NOT be repeated
HTTP_GATEWAY_TIMEOUT	Status Code: 504 Message: The server, while acting as a gateway or proxy, did not receive a timely response from the upstream server specified by the URL (e.g., HTTP, FTP) or some other auxiliary server (e.g., DNS) it needed to access in attempting to complete the request
HTTP_GONE	Status Code: 410 Message: The requested resource is no longer available at the server and no forwarding address is known
HTTP_INTERNAL_ERROR	Status Code: 500 Message: The server encountered an unexpected condition that prevented it from fulfilling the request
HTTP_LENGTH_REQUIRED	Status Code: 411 Message: The server refuses to accept the request without a defined Content-Length
HTTP_MOVED_PERM	Status Code: 301 Message: The requested resource has been assigned a new permanent URL and any future references to this resource SHOULD use one of the returned URLs
HTTP_MOVED_TEMP	Status Code: 302 Message: The requested resource resides temporarily under a different URL
HTTP_MULT_CHOICE	Status Code: 300 Message: The requested resource corresponds to any one of a set of representations, each with its own specific location, and agent-driven negotiation information is being provided so that the user (or user agent) can select a preferred representation and redirect its request to that location
HTTP_NO_CONTENT	Status Code: 204 Message: The server has fulfilled the request but does not need to return an entity-body, and might want to return updated meta information
HTTP_NOT_ACCEPTABLE	Status Code: 406 Message: The resource identified by the request is only capable of generating response entities that have content characteristics not acceptable according to the accept headers sent in the request

(continued)

HttpConnection: javax.microedition.io.HttpConnection *(Continued)*

`HTTP_NOT_AUTHORITATIVE`	Status Code: 203 Message: The returned metainformation in the entity-header is not the definitive set as available from the origin server, but is gathered from a local or a third-party copy
`HTTP_NOT_FOUND`	Status Code: 404 Message: The server has not found anything matching the Request-URL. No indication is given of whether the condition is temporary or permanent
`HTTP_NOT_IMPLEMENTED`	Status Code: 501 Message: The server does not support the functionality required to fulfill the request
`HTTP_NOT_MODIFIED`	Status Code: 304 Message: If the client has performed a conditional GET request and access is allowed, but the document has not been modified, the server SHOULD respond with this status code
`HTTP_OK`	Status Code: 200 Message: The request has succeeded
`HTTP_PARTIAL`	Status Code: 206 Message: The server has fulfilled the partial GET request for the resource
`HTTP_PAYMENT_REQUIRED`	Status Code: 402 Message: This code is reserved for future use
`HTTP_PRECON_FAILED`	Status Code: 412 Message: The precondition given in one or more of the request-header fields evaluated to false when it was tested on the server
`HTTP_PROXY_AUTH`	Status Code: 407 Message: This code is similar to 401 (Unauthorized), but indicates that the client must first authenticate itself with the proxy
`HTTP_REQ_TOO_LONG`	Status Code: 414 Message: The server is refusing to service the request because the Request-URL is longer than the server is willing to interpret
`HTTP_RESET`	Status Code: 205 Message: The server has fulfilled the request and the user agent SHOULD reset the document view that caused the request to be sent
`HTTP_SEE_OTHER`	Status Code: 303 Message: The response to the request can be found under a different URL and SHOULD be retrieved using a GET method on that resource

(continued)

HttpConnection: javax.microedition.io.HttpConnection   (*Continued*)

HTTP_TEMP_REDIRECT	Status Code: 307 Message: The requested resource resides temporarily under a different URL
HTTP_UNAUTHORIZED	Status Code: 401 Message: The request requires user authentication
HTTP_UNAVAILABLE	Status Code: 503 Message: The server is currently unable to handle the request due to a temporary overloading or maintenance of the server
HTTP_UNSUPPORTED_RANGE	Status Code: 416 Message: A server SHOULD return a response with this status code if a request included a Range request-header field
HTTP_UNSUPPORTED_TYPE	Status Code: 415 Message: The server is refusing to service the request because the entity of the request is in a format not supported by the requested resource for the requested method
HTTP_USE_PROXY	Status Code: 305 Message: The requested resource MUST be accessed through the proxy given by the Location field
HTTP_VERSION	Status Code: 505 Message: The server does not support, or refuses to support, the HTTP protocol version that was used in the request message
POST	POST request method

Method

long **getDate**()	Get header field "date"
long **getExpiration**()	Get header field "expires"
String **getFile**()	Get filename from the URL
String **getHeaderField**(int n)	Get header field value looking up by index
String **getHeaderField**(String name)	Get header field value looking up by name
long **getHeaderFieldDate**(String name, long def)	Get named field as a long (representing the date)
int **getHeaderFieldInt**(String name, int def)	Get named field as an integer
String **getHeaderFieldKey**(int n)	Get header field key using index
String **getHost**()	Get host from the URL

(*continued*)

HttpConnection: javax.microedition.io.HttpConnection   (*Continued*)

long **getLastModified**()	Get header field "last-modified"
int **getPort**()	Get port from the URL
String **getProtocol**()	Get protocol from the URL
String **getQuery**()	Get the query string (only valid with a GET request)
String **getRef**()	Get the reference portion of URL[1]
String **getRequestMethod**()	Get the current setting of the request method (GET, POST, HEAD)
String **getRequestProperty**(String key)	Get the current setting of a request property (header value)
int **getResponseCode**()	Get the response code (numeric)
String **getResponseMessage**()	Get the response message (text)
String **getURL**()	Get the entire URL
void **setRequestMethod**(String method)	Set the request method (GET, POST or HEAD)
void **setRequestProperty**(String key, String value)	Set a request property (header information)

[1]All HTTP status code information is taken directly from HTTP Protocol 1.1 http://www.ietf.org/rfc/rfc2616.txt

Image: javax.microedition.lcdui.Image
public class Image

Method	*Description*
Create an Image[1]	
static Image **createImage**(String name)	Create immutable image from resource
static Image **createImage**(Image source)	Create immutable image from existing Image
static Image **createImage**(byte[] imageData, int imageOffset, int imageLength)	Create immutable image from array data
static Image **createImage**(int width, int height)	Create mutable image
Method	
Graphics **getGraphics**()	Get reference to Graphics object for *mutable* image
int **getHeight**()	Get the height of Image
int **getWidth**()	Get the width of Image
boolean **isMutable**()	Determine if image is mutable

[1]Note: Constructor is not used to create an Image.

ImageItem: javax.microedition.lcdui.ImageItem
public class ImageItem extends Item

Field/Method	Description
Field	
LAYOUT_CENTER	Center the image horizontally
LAYOUT_DEFAULT	Use the default layout of device implementation
LAYOUT_NEWLINE_AFTER	Insert a newline after the image is drawn
LAYOUT_NEWLINE_BEFORE	Insert a newline before the image is drawn
LAYOUT_LEFT	The image should appear on the left
LAYOUT_RIGHT	The image should appear on the right
Constructor	
ImageItem(String label, Image img, int layout, String altText)	Create an ImageItem
Method	
String **getAltText**()	Get alternate text to display if image cannot be shown on the device
Image **getImage**()	Get Image associated with ImageItem
int **getLayout**()	Get the current layout directives
void **setAltText**(String text)	Set alternate text to display if image cannot be shown on the device
void **setImage**(Image img)	Set Image to be associated with ImageItem
void **setLayout**(int layout)	Set new layout directive

Item: javax.microedition.lcdui.Item
abstract public class Item

Method	Description
String **getLabel**()	Get the label assigned to the Item
void **setLabel**(String label)	Set label for the Item

ItemStateListener: javax.microedition.lcdui.ItemStateListener
public interface ItemStateListener

Method	Description
void **itemStateChanged**(Item item)	Called when "item" has been changed

List: javax.microedition.lcdui.List
public class List extends Screen implements Choice

Field/Method	Description
Field[1]	
EXCLUSIVE	Only one selection available at any time
IMPLICIT	Selection of an element generates an event
MULTIPLE	Zero or more selections available at any time
Constructor	
List(String title, int listType)	Create a new List with no elements
List(String title, int listType, String stringElements[], Image imageElements[])	Create a new List and populate with data from the arrays
Method	
int **append**(String stringPart, Image imagePart)	Add element to end
void **delete**(int elementNum)	Delete an element at specified index
Image **getImage**(int elementNum)	Get Image of element at specified index
int **getSelectedFlags**(boolean[] selectedArray_return)	Store selection status in an array
int **getSelectedIndex**()	Get index of selected element
String **getString**(int elementNum)	Get text of element at specified index
void **insert**(int elementNum, String stringPart, Image imagePart)	Insert element at specified index
boolean **isSelected**(int elementNum)	Is the element currently selected
void **set**(int elementNum, String stringPart, Image imagePart)	Set (replace) element at specified index
void **setSelectedFlags**(boolean[] selectedArray)	Set selection status from an array

(continued)

List: javax.microedition.lcdui.List   *(Continued)*

`void setSelectedIndex(int elementNum, boolean selected)`	For MULTIPLE List: set element to specified boolean value; For EXLCUSIVE List: set element to true For IMPLICIT List: set element to true
`int size()`	Number of elements in List

[1]From Choice interface, also used with ChoiceGroup.

MIDlet: javax.microedition.midlet.MIDlet
public abstract class MIDlet

Method	Description
Communication from Application Manager to MIDlet	
`abstract void destroyApp(boolean unconditional)`	MIDlet is about to be shut down
`abstract void startApp()`	MIDlet has been placed into active state
`abstract void pauseApp()`	MIDlet is about to be placed into paused state
Communication from MIDlet to Application Manager	
`final void notifyDestroyed()`	MIDlet is requesting to be shut down
`final void notifyPaused()`	MIDlet is requesting to be paused
`final void resumeRequest()`	MIDlet is requesting to become active (after being paused)
Attribute Request from MIDlet to Application Manager	
`final String getAppProperty(String key)`	Get attributes from jar and/or jad files

MIDletStateChangeException: javax.microedition.midlet.MIDletStateChangeException
public class MIDletStateChangeException extends Exception

Method	Description
`MIDletStateChangeException()`	Create exception object with no text
`MIDletStateChangeException(String s)`	Create exception object with text

RecordComparator: javax.microedition.rms.RecordComparator
public interface RecordComparator

Fields/Method	Description
Field	
EQUIVALENT	The records passed to compare() method are equivalent
FOLLOWS	Based on the sort algorithm in the compare() method, the first parameter follows the second
PRECEDES	Based on the sort algorithm in the compare() method, the first parameter precedes the second
Method	
int **compare**(byte[] rec1, byte[] rec2)	Compare records to determine sort order.

RecordEnumeration: javax.microedition.rms.RecordEnumeration
public interface RecordEnumeration

Method	Description
Method	
void **destroy**()	Free all resources held by the enumeration
boolean **hasNextElement**()	Does enumeration have more records going forward?
boolean **hasPreviousElement**()	Does enumeration have more records going backward?
boolean **isKeptUpdated**()	Will enumeration re-index as record store changes?
void **keepUpdated**(boolean keepUpdated)	Set whether enumeration will re-index as record store changes
byte[] **nextRecord**()	Get the next record number in result set
int **nextRecordId**()	Get ID of the next record in result set
int **numRecords**()	Number of records in the enumeration (result set)
byte[] **previousRecord**()	Get previous record in result set
int **previousRecordId**()	Get ID of the previous record in result set
void **rebuild**()	Rebuild enumeration index
void **reset**()	Reset enumeration to beginning

RecordFilter: javax.microedition.rms.RecordFilter
public interface RecordFilter

Method	Description
boolean **matches**(byte[] candidate)	Search a record for a specific value

RecordListener: javax.microedition.rms.RecordListener
public interface RecordListener

Method	Description
void **recordAdded**(RecordStore recordStore, int recordId)	Called when record is added
void **recordChanged**(RecordStore recordStore, int recordId)	Called when record is changed
void **recordDeleted**(RecordStore recordStore, int recordId)	Called when record is deleted

RecordStore: javax.microedition.rms.RecordStore
public class RecordStore

Method	Description

Constructor

No constructor. See openRecordStore()

Method

Method	Description
int **addRecord**(byte[] data, int offset, int numBytes)	Add a record
void **addRecordListener**(RecordListener listener)	Add a listener to detect record store changes
void **closeRecordStore**()	Close record store
void **deleteRecord**(int recordId)	Delete a record
static **void deleteRecordStore**(String recordStoreName)	Delete record store
RecordEnumeration **enumerateRecords**(RecordFilter filter, RecordComparator comparator, boolean keepUpdated)	Build an enumeration for traversing records in the record store
long **getLastModified**()	Last modified date of the record store
String **getName**()	Name of the record store

(continued)

RecordStore: javax.microedition.rms.RecordStore   *(Continued)*

`int getNextRecordID()`	Number of the next record when adding a new record to the store
`int getNumRecords()`	Number of records in the record store
`byte[] getRecord(int recordId)`	Return a byte array containing record data
`int getRecord(int recordId, byte[] buffer, int offset)`	Return record data in array parameter, copying data beginning at the specified offset
`int getRecordSize(int recordId)`	Size in bytes of a record
`int getSize()`	Total bytes occupied by record store
`int getSizeAvailable()`	Current space (bytes) available for records; This will change as records are added/deleted
`int getVersion()`	Record store version number
`static String[] listRecordStores()`	List record stores in MIDlet suite
`static RecordStore openRecordStore(String recordStoreName, boolean createIfNecessary)`	Open record store. Optionally, create the store if it does not already exist.
`void removeRecordListener(RecordListener listener)`	Remove listener
`void setRecord(int recordId, byte[] newData, int offset, int numBytes)`	Set (replace) data in a record

The following table lists all record store exception classes.

Record Store Exceptions

Constructors	*Description*
javax.microedition.rms.InvalidRecordIDException	
InvalidRecordIDException()	Create InvalidRecordIDException
InvalidRecordIDException(String message)	Create InvalidRecordIDException with message
javax.microedition.rms.RecordStoreException	
RecordStoreException()	Create RecordStoreException
RecordStoreException(String message)	Create RecordStoreException
javax.microedition.rms.RecordStoreFullException	
RecordStoreFullException()	Create RecordStoreFullException
RecordStoreFullException(String message)	Create RecordStoreFullException with message

(continued)

Record Store Exceptions

`javax.microedition.rms.RecordStoreNotFoundException`

`RecordStoreNotFoundException()`	Create RecordStoreNotFoundlException
`RecordStoreNotFoundException(String message)`	Create RecordStoreNotFoundException with message

`javax.microedition.rms.RecordStoreNotOpenException`

`RecordStoreNotOpenException()`	Create RecordStoreNotOpenException
`RecordStoreNotOpenException(String message)`	Create RecordStoreNotOpenException with message

Screen: javax.microedition.lcdui.Screen
public abstract class Screen extends Displayable

Method	Description
Ticker **getTicker**()	Get Ticker associated with the Screen
String **getTitle**()	Get title associated with the Screen
void **setTicker**(Ticker ticker)	Set Ticker for the Screen
void **setTitle**(String s)	Set title for the Screen

StringItem: javax.microedition.lcdui.StringItem
public class StringItem extends Item

Method	Description
Constructor	
StringItem(String label, String text)	Create a new StringItem
Method	
String **getText**()	Get current value of the text
void **setText**(String text)	Set new value of the text

TextBox: javax.microedition.lcdui.TextBox
public class TextBox extends Screen

Method	Description
Field[1]	
CONSTRAINT_MASK	Used to determine the current value of constraint
ANY	Allow any character input
EMAILADDR	Allow only characters that are valid within email address
NUMERIC	Allow only numbers (both positive and negative)
PASSWORD	Masks all character input to provide privacy
PHONENUMBER	Allow only characters that are valid as a phone number
URL	Allow only characters that are valid within a URL
Constructor	
TextBox(String title, String text, int maxSize, int constraints)	Create a new TextField
Method	
void **delete**(int offset, int length)	Delete characters
int **getCaretPosition**()	Get current input position
int **getChars**(char[] data)	Place TextBox contents into an array
int **getConstraints**()	Get the constraints defined
int **getMaxSize**()	Get total characters that can be stored
String **getString**()	Place TextBox contents into a String
void **insert**(String src, int position)	Insert characters from a String
void **insert**(char[] data, int offset, int length, int position)	Insert characters from an array into specified "position"
void **setChars**(char[] data, int offset, int length)	Replace TextBox contents with data from an array
void **setConstraints**(int constraints)	Set the constraints
int **setMaxSize**(int maxSize)	Set total characters that can be stored
void **setString**(String text)	Set (replace) TextBox contents from a String
int **size**()	Number of characters currently in TextBox

[1]From TextField class.

TextField: javax.microedition.lcdui.TextField
public class TextField extends Item

Field/Method	Description
Field[1]	
CONSTRAINT_MASK	Used to determine the current value of constraint
ANY	Allow any character input
EMAILADDR	Allow only characters that are valid within email address
NUMERIC	Allow only numbers (both positive and negative)
PASSWORD	Masks all character input to provide privacy
PHONENUMBER	Allow only characters that are valid as a phone number
URL	Allow only characters that are valid within a URL
Constructor	
TextField(String label, String text, int maxSize, int constraints)	Create a new TextField
Method	
void **delete**(int offset, int length)	Delete characters at a specified offset
int **getCaretPosition**()	Get current caret (cursor) position
int **getChars**(char[] data)	Get contents of TextField into an array
int **getConstraints**()	Get constraints defined for TextField
int **getMaxSize**()	Get max number of characters in TextField
String **getString**()	Get contents of TextField into a String
void **insert**(String src, int position)	Insert String at a specified offset
void **insert**(char[] data, int offset, int length, int position)	Insert specified characters from array into TextField at a specified offset
void **setChars**(char[] data, int offset, int length)	Set (replace) characters with data from array
void **setConstraints**(int constraints)	Set constraints for TextField
int **setMaxSize**(int maxSize)	Set max number of characters in TextField
void **setString**(String text)	Set (replace) Text Field contents from String
int **size**()	Number of characters currently in TextField

[1]Also used in TextBox

Ticker: javax.microedition.lcdui.Ticker
public class Ticker

Method	Description
Constructor	
Ticker(String str)	Create a new Ticker with the specified ticker text
Method	
String **getString**()	Get the text associated with the Ticker
void **setString**(String str)	Set the text to associate with the Ticker

Timer: java.util.Timer
public class Timer

Method	Description
Constructor	
Timer()	Create timer
Method	
void **cancel**()	Ends the timer and any scheduled tasks
void **schedule**(TimerTask task, long delay)	Schedule a task to occur after a delay
void **schedule**(TimerTask task, long delay, long period)	Schedule a fixed-delay repeating task that starts after a delay
void **schedule**(TimerTask task, Date time)	Schedule a task to occur on specific date
void **schedule**(TimerTask task, Date firstTime, long period)	Schedule a fixed-delay repeating task that starts on specific date
void **scheduleAtFixedRate**(TimerTask task, long delay, long period)	Schedule a fixed-rate repeating task that starts after a delay
void **scheduleAtFixedRate**(TimerTask task, Date firstTime, long period)	Schedule fixed-rate repeating task that starts on specific date

TimerTask: java.util.TimerTask
public abstract class TimerTask implements java.lang.Runnable

Method	Description
Constructor	
TimerTask()	Create timer task
Method	
boolean **cancel**()	End the task
abstract void **run**()	Place code in this method to carry out the action of the task
long **scheduledExecutionTime**()	Time when the last run task was scheduled to occur

Index

B

C

U

W

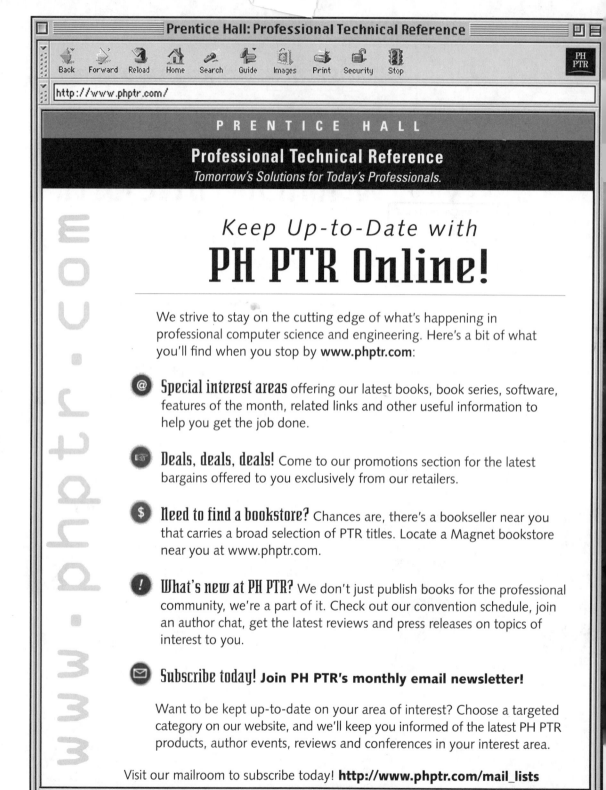